DIARY
OF A
DYSTOPIAN
ERA

*A history teacher struggles to navigate a
pandemic and the politics of 2020–2021*

LOIS LARKEY

ARCHWAY
PUBLISHING

Archway Publishing books may be ordered through booksellers or by contacting:

Archway Publishing
1663 Liberty Drive
Bloomington, IN 47403
www.archwaypublishing.com
844-669-3957

Scripture taken from The Torah: A Women's Commentary, copyright 2008 Women of Reform Journalism.

ISBN: 978-1-6657-1052-7 (sc)
ISBN: 978-1-6657-1053-4 (e)

Library of Congress Control Number: 2021915488

Print information available on the last page.

Archway Publishing rev. date: 09/08/2021

Dedication

For connecting with us, nurturing us, for your care and concern, for your love and support, for the gracious gift of your time, for lifting us up when we faltered, we are deeply grateful to each of you:

Rabbi Daniel Cohen
Rabbi Alexandra Klein
Cantor Rebecca Moses
Cantor Joan Finn

Because of you, our wonderful Sharey Tefilo community became a loving family. There are no words to adequately express how deeply thankful we are for everything you did for us this past year.

Grateful thanks to Suzanne Hamstra, our cantor intern, who arrived just in time for Lockdown, hit the ground running, and became an immediate member of the temple family with beautiful music and so much more.

Endorsements

Every word Larkey writes, every thought she expresses, is intensely felt, revealing the great love she has for her country and her deep concerns about where it is heading. Trump supporters will not like it, but everyone else will find her insights fascinating and, yes, even helpful in making sense of today's news.

—Don and Petie Kladstrup, authors of ***Wine & War: the French, the Nazis and the Battle for France's Greatest Treasure*** and ***Champagne Charlie: the Frenchman Who Taught America to Love Champagne*** (to be published by Potomac Books November 1, 2021

Lois Larkey is one of those rare souls whose insight, empathy and intelligence make her the very best of educators. Her vivid perceptions about these troubling and compelling times are not only thought provoking and illuminating, they are the whole and honest truth.

—Elizabeth Brundage, author of The Vanishing Point and All Things Cease to Appear

"Lois Larkey is an educator through and through, as I know from deeply formative personal experience. In these incisive pages she teaches all of us – with intelligence, passion, wit, and a keen eye on history – exactly why this current moment in the life of our nation is so pivotal and so perilous. Larkey has given us both an indispensable chronicle of our troubled times and reasons to hope for a better future."

—Ben Reiter, *New York Times* bestselling author of *Astroball*

Preface

Suddenly, we were in an historic moment. A virus we knew nothing about arrived on both coasts, and it was deadly. Indeed, the last time there was a devastating pandemic was in 1918, one hundred years ago. On March 11th, the order came from my New Jersey Governor Murphy to "shelter in place." We couldn't go outside, and we needed to wear a mask and socially distance from our friends and family. Many of us were going to live alone, because our families lived somewhere else.

How long would it last? We didn't know. Citizens were dying. Would I catch the coronavirus and die alone in a hospital without my family? I was afraid, and felt very disconnected,

Armed with books, Netflix, Zoom and food, the solitary days began. Music was calming, but twenty-four hours are very challenging with no structure or schedule. I started to make a list of how I would spend the days. It was at that point that I decided to document such an historic time in my life, and in all of our lives. Writing is very nourishing for me, and being able to look back at how we behaved and how we survived would answer a lot of questions when my memory wasn't quite so sharp. Writing my observations and feelings on a daily basis forced me to focus, gave me a purpose and a project. I began tentatively, but then the momentum grew with the pandemic, and the politics left us in the lurch. The president would do nothing to save Americans' lives. The reality was stunning, and my anger motivated me to write.

The pandemic was spreading. I saw pictures of hospitals overflowing, and that filled me with dread. Refrigerator trucks were brought in to serve as morgues for the dead, because there were no places to bury or keep them in a funeral home.

With each passing day, the possibility of anonymity, of dying with no funeral, family or friends, became overwhelming. More and more, my purpose, and this project, became important as a legacy for my grandchildren- something to leave behind, if we never got to know one another or see one another again.

Gratefully, my synagogue's Adult Education Committee filled the days with classes, speakers, art classes, meditation, and activities that were diverse and wonderfully engaging. Our clergy kept us connected offering "coffee with the clergy" three mornings a week. The question, "How is everybody doing" allowed each of us to share our fears, our grief and our loneliness. We were bolstered by words of solace, hope and wisdom.

A number of things became clear. Time, while it may seem endless, is not limitless. Survival is its own creative act. Despite quarantining, it was clear that immersing myself in the news was important. I started writing about the day's events. While writing was very satisfying, it was also terrifying. Watching the news and talking to friends, it was apparent that we were all of the same mind. None of us had any idea how this would end.

Writing a few days each week was affirming. Since the election would be November 3rd, that would be my final day to write, in the hope that this pandemic would be over by then and we would have a new president.

I was wrong. Both the pandemic and the politics fooled me. Yes, Joe Biden won the presidency by seven million votes, but there was no concession from the loser. The tradition of "peaceful transfer of power" was broken, and it was shocking. Every president, since George Washington, honored the election of the next winner. The world saw America as a beacon of honesty and fairness in our elections, with the Constitution setting the process. But now, there was disbelief and nervousness in the middle of a chaotic pandemic. The loser was foiling Joe Biden at every turn. The expected timely transition was purposely delayed by the enraged poor loser. The world was watching. What had happened to America? It was unsettling.

The Covid-19 deaths kept rising. I began in my own personal war with an ignorant, selfish and unconcerned president. Masks were politicized. Never leaving my apartment except to get the mail and take a brief walk to the park, daily writing continued. That routine created a structure and set an important goal. Having a purpose saved my emotional life, and my physical life as well.

As devastating as the situation was with Covid-19, millions of jobs were lost, and there were long lines of citizens in line for food, often for the first time. That realization, seen on television, was overwhelming.

In the midst of so much tragedy, Donald Trump began his reelection campaign, ignoring the death and destruction of his own citizens. There were two different universes; the president divided us into "blue states" and "red states."-, masks and no masks. The leader of the free world ignored half of the country, and made it plain that only the half that voted for him mattered. I kept writing.

Joe Biden won the presidency by seven million votes, but there was no concession from the loser. The tradition of "peaceful transfer of power" was broken, and it was shocking.! Every president, since George Washington, honored the election of the next winner. For two centuries, the world saw American elections as beacons of honesty and fairness, with the Constitution setting the process. And now, there was disbelief and nervousness in the middle of a pandemic. The loser was foiling Joe Biden at every turn with vengeful actions. The expected timely transition was purposely delayed by the president and no ascertainment. The world was watching. What had happened to America? When will the Biden government take the helm?

I decided to move my blog writing to Inauguration Day, January 20, 2021. Surely by then things will have calmed down, and the new government would be in place.

There is an old Yiddish saying, "Man plans and God laughs." Was that ever true in 2020-21! Beyond our wildest dreams, we are in uncharted territory. This is truly one for the history books. It became clear that our democracy is in jeopardy, I kept writing, totally unaware of the horror that was to come.

Lois Larkey
January 13, 2021
South Orange, New Jersey

March 11, 2020 LOCKDOWN!

Thoughts for a Difficult Time from the Larkey Lowdown

> And the people stayed home. And read books, and listened, and rested, and exercised, and made art, and played games, and learned new ways of being, and were still. And listened more deeply. Some meditated, some prayed, some danced. Some met their shadows. And the people began to think differently.
>
> —Kitty O'Meara

March 30, 2020

Words Matter

Words matter like they've never mattered before, for good and for ill. The president's words—"hoax" for instance—convinced many people that the coronavirus was not a big deal. Nothing to worry about. They socialized, ignored the wise words of Dr. Anthony Fauci, and the crisis grew to epic proportions. It is still growing.

Words matter. As Charlie Sykes, of The Bulwark wisely observed this morning on MSNBC, "Donald Trump is the arsonist who wants to be a fireman." How are we going to survive?

Words matter. Lessons learned from 9/11: Tell your loved ones how much they matter—daily. Kiss your loved ones as they leave in the morning, because you never know if you will see them again.

Words matter. Because this virus is so infectious, we cannot kiss our loved ones or even touch them. We have to do the exact opposite, and that is why words matter more than ever.

How will we use our words? We will *make dates to talk on ZOOM*—really talk.

Connect with friends and family. We have more time than we know and less time than we know.

Let loved ones hear how much you care—say those words!

Don't be afraid to say that you are scared. It's a very scary time. I am scared.

Words matter.

April 6, 2020

Random Acts of Kindness Matter as We approach Our Pearl Harbor Moment

Yes, it's been a terrible month filled with death, destruction, disinformation and demagoguery …

But we have seen our friends, neighbors, and total strangers come forward to add sunshine and goodness for kids and adults alike. Their actions brought smiles. We are Americans, and we are generous and strong.

Let's name those times and keep track of them so that they will nourish us in the next weeks, which will be brutal. A few of these gracious acts come immediately to mind.

The South Orange / Maplewood Fire and Police Departments are putting on birthday parades for children whose birthdays are in April but cannot celebrate out of their homes.

Then there is the generous guy who set up a pizza tent in Central Park and is donating over five hundred pizzas daily to the health care workers in the nearby hospitals.

The members of Temple Sharey-Tefilo Israel in South Orange, NJ, donated their iPads to the patients in the ICU unit at St. Barnabas Hospital in Livingston

Grateful citizens are coming out on their balconies every evening in Manhattan at 7:00 p.m. to clap and thank the healthcare workers for their superhuman efforts to keep us alive

Wherever you live, you must know many more examples. Will you share them in reply to this blog? It will warm our hearts to read many more instances.

Stay home and be safe!

April 9, 2020

Quarantine in the Time of the Holidays

Being quarantined is a new experience for Americans. We have always been so free to move around and to worship as we pleased. Peter Golden, the author who lived in South Orange, posted the following insight on Facebook yesterday that I want to share. He reminded me how lucky I am to be free, even free to quarantine for my own well-being, and not have to hide.

Peter posted a marvelous picture of Aunt Eva's Passover sponge cake, and he wrote:

> My great-grandfather lost his wife at a young age and remarried a woman from Poland. I called her, "Aunt Eva," and she made a wonderful Passover sponge cake. Lately, I've been thinking about Aunt Eva's family. They hid from the Nazis in the Warsaw ghetto, until some were able to escape by navigating through the sewers. When I feel ragged from being shut in against the pandemic, I remind myself that people have been through worse. Generally speaking, I've discovered that keeping your standards high for victimhood is quite helpful.

To all my friends and relatives, whether you celebrate Easter or Passover, I wish you good health, much joy connecting with your families on Zoom, and peace.

April 12, 2020

At Passover and Easter: Finding Blessings in the Midst of Tragedy

There's no doubt that celebrating Passover and Easter in the midst of a pandemic is beyond challenging. So far, the pandemic has killed thousands. Amazingly, when things are at their worst, opportunities that we never imagine, emerge.

When so many people are dying, one might think that we shouldn't be celebrating anything. But wait! Look around at your family members and friends who are healthy, and there is reason to be grateful. Even if they are not nearby, Zoom has enabled us to connect, have conversations, and tell one another we love them.

Similarly, we can reach out to friends or reconnect with people we haven't talked with in way too long—childhood friends, college friends, and people we may have neglected in our rushed and busy lives. Reach out to someone who has been on your mind for years. Make a list, and call each one.

Stories abound. Keep a small journal and record your experiences. So many people have performed acts of kindness, stepped up and shown amazing leadership on the local level.

There are stories of Passover "seders," with family members online, who normally were too far away to travel. Joyfully, Zoom has brought us together, albeit in small portrait boxes, but we can talk to each other. Something good has come out of a seemingly horrible situation. We are more flexible than we knew! Pictures of relatives on each chair made it real and brought memories of past seders.

Similarly, Easter dinner, one that I was privileged to enjoy with friends through the years, has separated us, but I can still smell the crown roast of lamb with all the fixings. Again, their pictures on each chair made it real. Try it!

While we won't be marching in the Easter parades, Easter bonnets are being made and posted online for all to see! Creative and gorgeous, they bring smiles…

How to manage the day? A few suggestions:

It's a beautiful day in South Orange, New Jersey. Wherever you are (it snowed in Vermont!), take a walk and let the incredibly clean air course through your lungs.

You might want to watch the marvelous Fred Rogers movie that was made with Tom Hanks, who is a coronavirus survivor. It will nourish you, make you stronger, and put a smile on your face.

Console someone who you know has suffered a loss. Kindness rewards the giver as much as the recipient. Kindness nourishes each of us.

Take a virtual tour of a museum you've always wanted to visit, perhaps the Louvre in Paris or the Metropolitan Museum in New York (one of my faves, but I'm unable to see it in person right now). There are virtual tours of everything you ever wanted to see. Go onto a website and enjoy the trip!

Read a book that will nourish you, whether it be a biography (*Becoming* by Michelle Obama), humorous poetry by Ogden Nash, or whatever interests you that you've always wanted to discover, but never had the time. Now, there is more time than we ever knew. Use it wisely and enjoy!

Music! Put your favorite on, whether it be popular (Taylor Swift or the Beatles?) or classical (Brahms or Beethoven?). Music nourishes the brain and the soul. If you live alone, keep music on all day, for company and to sing along and perhaps to dance!

Find a way to make a difference. Many people are donating online to send dinners to hospitals and rescue squads. You will find your own niche. There are hundreds of opportunities. Again, kindness and generosity nourishes the giver.

Keep the faith. Sheltering in place seems to be working. Wear your mask at all times! Wash hands, keep socially distant if you must go outside.

April 14, 2020

Elections Have Consequences—You *Must* Vote Donald Trump out of Office

My absentee ballot came in the mail yesterday! That piece of paper reminded me that I want to speak with everyone who is reading this blog.

We are experiencing the most horrific health crisis in a century. The election put a callous, ignorant, narcissistic moron in charge of the greatest country on earth, America. Approximately 327 million citizens are in danger, because the president ignored the warnings. He knew the virus came in January, but he chose to ignore it. Moreover, Donald Trump doesn't read the President's Daily Brief (PDB), because he doesn't read. Further, if he hears something that is not in his own perceived self-interest, his re-election, Trump ignores it. As for disdaining the obvious, he blames others when the consequences of doing nothing result in twenty-three thousands of our friends and neighbors dying.

For me, watching television is often very upsetting. Pictures of people in hospital hallways are chilling. We are running out of beds.

Donald Trump is a very dangerous man. If you voted for him, or if you decided not to vote at all (if Hillary Clinton was not your cup of tea), America is in trouble. Voting decisions have serious consequences. The first three years of Trump destroying the norms, and our democracy, were just a lead up to this present tragic nightmare.

Our country, and our lives as we have known them, will never be the same. It is crucial that each of us take whatever skills we have and put them to good use, to make sure that this man never has another four years.

I hope to comment on various aspects of the problem facing us for the rest of the week. Please weigh in with your own thoughts, comments, and ideas. I love reading your responses.

April 15, 2020

An American King with Absolute Power? Nonsense! That's Why We Fought the Revolution

One thing is clear: Donald Trump has *never* read the Constitution.

When a president declares a national emergency, he is now in charge of putting all the resources of the United States government behind the states that need the help. Donald Trump has not mobilized a massive effort to initiate nationwide testing. He has not invoked the Defense Production Act, which can make ventilators and other necessities. He needs to appoint a tsar, as George Bush appointed Army Commander Russel Honore to handle the Hurricane Katrina disaster. The U.S.Army is perfectly suited to move men and materiel in a "war." Make no mistake, we are in a *war*.

The "tsar" would implement the following:

1-TESTING, TESTING, TESTING. Three months ago, Trump should have instituted a nationwide testing program, including antibody testing. We can do nothing without it. In addition, millions of masks were scheduled to be sent to every American household, but Donald Trump cancelled that plan. He doesn't like the way masks look. Vanity, thy name is Donald Trump, even if masks would save lives.

2- CONTACT TRACING- Part and parcel of a concentrated WAR on the virus. We need to know who had contact with one another, who is contagious, and who is effectively immune.

3. The Army "tsar" would take control of the SUPPLY CHAIN, making sure that hospitals and healthcare workers receive the masks, PPE protective clothing and ventilators that are so desperately needed.

Without a centralized war on the virus, and an emphasis on the safety and health of three hundred million citizens, there is no way we can open any part of our country.

Centralization eliminates states bidding against one another for necessary materials. The American citizens paid for our national stockpile, and it needs to be available to the states, without favoritism or politics.

In World War 2, President Franklin Roosevelt utilized the entire resources of the country to fight the war. Manufacturing was adapted to turn out airplanes on a daily basis. The entire country pulled together for the war effort. Donald Trump said the virus posed a war threat, and then did nothing. That is malfeasance, possibly treason, since he did say we are in a war.

April 21, 2020

Trump Whiplash! Yes, but citizens' empathy and kindness come to the fore …

For the last six days, Donald Trump led us through a litany of his misguided disinformation, as he tried to navigate around the TRUTH. In his own self-interest, he totally FAILED to act in order to protect all the people who live here. Because of his callous desire to hide the truth, 43,000 people have now died. They didn't need to die, especially without family to speak last words and hold their hands. Painfully, we are all forbidden to visit.

I won't go through the dizzying list of his ever-changing messages during the so-called "briefings," that were really campaigns for his re-election.

Rather, I'd like to pay tribute to the spirit, commitment and dedication of the thousands of healthcare workers across the country. They go to work every day, often without proper protection, leaving their families, watching people die, despite their best efforts to save them. It is breathtaking to hear these doctors, nurses and aids speak about their experiences, their frustrations, and their sadness at not being able to do more. Yet, they have not given up. These wonderful healthcare professionals were often holding the hand of a dying patient, and filling in for the relative who was not allowed to be there. What empathy and kindness! What compassion and love!

In that vein, we have seen no empathy or remorse from the President of the United States, and that is stunning. He is unable to show any emotion whatsoever. Forty-three thousand people died up to this date, partly because of Donald Trump's ineptitude and lack of caring. Frank Bruni wrote a marvelous opinion piece in the NYT, about the fact that Donald Trump lacked a soul. I recommend it to you.

On the positive side, the journalists, who Trump bashed every day since the beginning of his campaign, have taken to talking about the people we have lost. In beautiful tributes at the end of each of their news programs, Nicolle Wallace and David Muir, to name just a few, highlight citizens' lives and honor them. The tributes are wonderful biographies, and we realize the depth of the losses for our country.

Similarly, The American people are incredibly appreciative, and they show it in thousands of ways: making masks, clapping from their balconies at 7PM in New York, providing food, donating online and so much more. This tragedy has brought us to our knees, but we are not beaten. The governors of many states have stepped up to fill the gaping void left by the president. The leadership of the governors of New York, New Jersey and Connecticut, who formed a consortium, is bold and courageous. Similarly, Governor Hogan of Delaware, and Governor Charlie Baker of Massachusetts, both Republicans, have told the truth and worked to protect their citizens.

Empathy and kindness are alive and well in the American psyche. Thank goodness.

This writing from Lao Tzu, the Chinese philosopher, expresses so much to keep close to our hearts.

"Kindness in words creates confidence.

Kindness in thinking creates profoundness.

Kindness in giving creates love."

April 22, 2020

Earth Day 2020:

On the **50th anniversary of Earth Day,** let's do everything possible to make sure that our planet-and the people on it-survive.

What has the Global Lockdown done to impact our planet?

What of the environmental changes? There are many.

One such change …

There is a lowering of carbon emissions, and the result is CLEAN AIR.

The WATER in Venice, Italy is CLEAR for the first time in decades, and there is so much more …

Because of the restrictions on working together, much of the activities that we would normally do on Earth Day are not possible.

BUT … a few simple suggestions.

Take a wonderful walk in your neighborhood and breathe in the beautifully clean air. Take deep breaths and let your lungs relish in the newness of it.

Do the outdoor work for which your yard has been crying out for attention.

Send away for some seeds and start planting your backyard and the pots on your patio.

BE **HOPEFUL** that we will be able to enjoy our yards and live on the planet- if we take care of the earth and ourselves …

HAPPY EARTH DAY TO ALL!

April 25, 2020

Mitch McConnell is shameless

Yes, really bad. His suggestion that New York should declare bankruptcy, rather than have the federal government give money to cover the huge debt from the coronavirus, is scandalous. WHY?

New York Sends More Federal Tax Dollars to Washington than it Gets in Return

New York paid $26.6 billion more in taxes to the federal government (in 2018) than it got back in federal spending.

In fact, New York was one of just seven states that paid more tax dollars than it received back, with a per capita deficit of $1,363. (Per capita balance of payments is the difference between taxes paid to Washington and federal spending received.) Only the neighboring states of New Jersey (-$2,792) and Massachusetts (-$1,419) fared worse.

New York Governor Andrew Cuomo indicated that **New York puts in 116 billion more to the federal pot than it takes out.**

In contrast, **Kentucky, Mitch McConnell's state, takes $148 billion FROM the federal fund than it puts in.** McConnell, getting down in the gutter, said he didn't want a "Blue State bail-out," clearly putting politics into the conversation, when 15,000 human beings have already died.

Moreover, McConnell's comments and point of view are frankly outrageous. The people who died are not red or blue, Democrat or Republican. They are Americans, and that is why I am talking about this today. America needs to remember that we are red, white and blue, **one country,** trying to survive a major pandemic, a once in a lifetime tragedy. Let's get ourselves together and take a page from the courage of the healthcare workers.

E PLURIBUS UNUM (from many, ONE)

* If you would like to see a comparison chart of all 50 states, go onto google.

April 26, 2020

More Good News

It's hard to imagine that, with 50,000 Americans dead, there could be any good news.

But there is good news worth celebrating! We have seen seriously ill people survive the virus, and leave the hospital to the cheers of the healthcare workers who brought them back from near death. Every person who survives is crucial to our sense that we can fight this brutal virus and sometimes win the war.

Hope is the key for each of us, and it is the strongest feeling that helps everyone get through each day. Watching a victory serves to fuel our hopes for the future. There are small and large victories everywhere.

John Krasinski has a program happily entitled "Some Good News." Recently, a little girl appeared online, and her dream of seeing *Hamilton had been* quashed when we all had to shelter in place. The youngster showed her ticket and- like magic- Lin Manuel Miranda appeared in another window=- to the shock and amazement of the child. Then, with the click of a mouse, all of the original cast appeared, each in his own living room, and they sang the opening song of *Hamilton*. *Th*e youngster's face glowed, as did the faces of the cast, and all of us who were lucky enough to be watching. What a marvelous moment!

Generosity like this has been happening all over the country, and throughout the world. Our better angels are appearing in nooks and crannies, and in large spaces as well.

An especially happy team was Will Smith, the actor, and Dr.Anthony Fauci, answering children's questions online. One adorable little girl asked Dr. Fauci if there was any danger that the Tooth Fairy could get the virus. Tony Fauci, very delightfully and seriously, assured her that the Tooth Fairy was not in danger.

Another inspiring event happened, this time in the UK. Captain Tom Moore. 100 years old, walked 100 laps of his garden, raising the equivalent of 35 million American dollars for the National Health Service in the United Kingdom. In addition to Captain Tom, an incredibly beautiful result happened. A six-year old boy, who has spina bifida, emulated Captain Moore, and walked on his own crutches, raising 300,000 for the British NHS. Captain Tom's role model, as he struggled to complete his goal, inspired the little boy, the UK, and people everywhere. The Queen was well aware of both worthy events, and ultimately Tom Moore became Sir Tom Moore.

Our better angels are hard at work and succeeding in small ways and large. Humanity is showing itself everywhere, as we each struggle to make a difference, to survive and to help others.

May 1, 2020

"There are lies, damn lies, and statistics ..." (Mark Twain)

Donald Trump has never had even a fleeting relationship with the Truth. Unfortunately, Twain is not here to give Trump the piece of his mind that is deserved. Watching the supposed "briefings," as thousands of our citizens die daily, is breathtakingly frustrating and aggravating.

Then there are the statistics. What must Dr. Fauci be thinking? He keeps his own counsel, and a straight face. Trump lies. Trump lies all the time, and the American people are reacting. Unfortunately, people who listen to FOX News believe what Trump says. However, the statistics don't lie. We are woefully behind in testing per capita than all the other countries, and we should not open any part of the country, despite Donald Trump's urging.

The polls taken in the last week show Donald Trump losing to Joe Biden in the key states by as much as 8 to 10%. In a countrywide matchup, Trump loses to former Vice- President Biden by 10 percentage points.

The lies have finally caught up to the liar-in-chief. But have his followers realized? We don't know. Mixed messages are dangerous to a democracy.

May 5, 2020

It's Teacher Appreciation Day!

In years past, I never thought much about Teacher Appreciation Day, even though I was a teacher for decades. The day, like other days of its kind, seemed somehow forced. Don't we always appreciate our mothers, those we love, and our fathers? Our teachers? Apparently not. Moreover, parents just assumed that we were doing our jobs, which of course, we were. But what a job it is!

Capturing a child's imagination, reaching everyone on her own level, stopping bullying, reading body language to see if someone is sad, bored, upset or fascinated, requires a psychologist, in addition to a purveyor of information. In an age when a teacher can't give a physical hug without having a lawsuit, giving verbal hugs and understanding become the key to connecting and creating a bond. Letting students know that they can be their best, even if they are not sure, is what teachers often succeed in doing. I'm always warmed by the famous people who are interviewed when they say that one particular teacher made the difference.

Covid-19 has changed all that. With millions of children home, parents have become their children's teachers, and parents are having an epiphany. Teaching is not as easy as it seems.

The tragedy of the pandemic, has actually brought good things to light. Many of our better angels have emerged. The bravery and dedication of the healthcare workers have awed us. In addition, we have come to realize the importance of the bus drivers, workers who man the grocery stores and fill the shelves, so many people who might have been taken for granted and were sometimes invisible, until now. We are seeing with a different awareness, a sharper lens, and appreciating all individuals.

The same is true for the teachers in our country. Parents, tasked with suddenly teaching their own children, are realizing what teachers do all day, how challenging it is and how hard. There is a new respect. I have heard hundreds of comments on television, and in person, about the realization of teaching as a difficult profession, and a low-paying profession. Perhaps that will change now?

A grateful nation is celebrating its teachers with a new passion today. With that appreciation comes a deep desire for school to start next year. Parents and their children need to be returning to their normal lives, but it is not clear that will be possible. We need a federal response, and there has been none from the White House.

May 8, 2020

Justice for All?

Every day in the world of Donald Trump, there are too many disturbing things to discuss. Should I talk about the nurse who was rudely contradicted in the Oval office, because we actually don't have enough protective coverings? Or the shooting of an unarmed black teenager by two white men in Georgia, who were not immediately arrested? Or the callous lies surrounding the numbers of deaths – (75,000 human beings to date called a "success?"), that will result in opening the country? The list of choices is unfortunately long, and today my head hurts.

On a very positive note, today is the 75th anniversary of VE day, Victory in Europe day, when the Germans surrendered, bringing an end to nearly six years of war. Unfortunately, I have to leave that historic moment for another time.

Today, **one event annoyingly overrides all others-the Justice Department's filing to drop the prosecution of Michael Flynn**. Yes, the same Michael Flynn who twice lied to the FBI and pleaded "guilty" in open court. The same Michael Flynn who Judge Sullivan angrily said, "you sold out your country," and Sullivan was "not hiding my disgust or my disdain for this criminal offense," by Flynn's behavior.

Even earlier, this is the same Michael Flynn who Barack Obama fired, and then told Donald Trump not to bring him back into the White House. Trump, like a child who has been told "don't touch the hot coals," brought Flynn back as his National Security Advisor, a post that did not need Senate confirmation. You can't make this up! Simultaneously, Flynn was on the payroll of Turkey, and trying to get sanctions on Russia removed. He was already making money from his important connections, as a picture of Flynn on his cell phone at the Trump Inauguration later proved.

All of this is outrageous and deeply concerning, as we watch the dismantling of our legal system, which is the basis of our democracy. We are at a serious inflection point for the Constitution, and for our country.

Worse still, Bill Barr, the Attorney General, who is supposed to uphold the rule of law in the United States, is doing Donald Trump's bidding. He has given Flynn what amounts to a "get out of jail free card" as he goes about dismantling the Department of Justice, insulting the lawyers, the Mueller report and the intelligence agencies. Our country is in jeopardy when citizens can't trust the Justice Department, and all the other agencies tasked with protecting the Constitution.

Justice for all? Clearly not. Only Donald Trump's friends, criminals and liars get to walk away free.

May 12, 2020

Witness to History

Again, there are so many events happening: Mothers' Day, White House mask mess, forty million losing jobs, danger of opening too soon, Trump lying, and thousands dying, ad infinitum. My head is spinning!

While each of these is important to discuss in its own right, there are two historic events that I believe override the others on this day.

The Supreme Court is hearing the cases involving Donald Trump's taxes, and whether the bankers and accountants must turn over the records. Hearings begin at 10am, and they will be teleconferenced, since the Court is hearing remotely! We can all hear the proceedings, and that in itself is historic. For marvelously detailed explanations of the cases, I commend you to the extraordinary Adam Liptak of *the New York Times.*

Is the president above the law? There are serious Constitutional issues at stake here. The U.S. House of Representatives brought two cases, and the Manhattan District Attorney brought another case.

However, the last case of its type was when Richard Nixon refused to give over the tapes that bore witness to the Watergate crimes. The Supreme Court, if memory serves, decided 9 to 0 (that hasn't happened in a long time) that Nixon had no legal right to withhold them. Days later, Nixon resigned.

Dr. Anthony Fauci is also testifying at 10am on Capitol Hill today, without Donald Trump lurking threateningly behind him. Dr. Fauci has self-quarantined, having been exposed to the virus in a virtually "maskless" White House. He has signaled that he plans to testify the cold, hard truth about the government's lack of effective response and the tragic result for the nation.

We will return to each of these historic events in the next days.

Enjoy the day. **We are all witness to history.**

May 13, 2020

"Maskgate"

How is it that a simple direction-"wear a mask"-has become a red state/ blue state political issue? Donald Trump, through his own vanity, doesn't think it would "look good" for him to wear a mask, and he said as much when he announced that important safety precaution to the country.

"To mask or not to mask, that is the question."

All of a sudden, wearing a mask, or not, became an issue-not of science and protection, but of politics. If you wear a mask you are often maligned as a blue state liberal. If you decline to wear a mask, you are doing what Donald Trump is doing- eschewing the science and clearly showing a lack of respect for the concept of Americans uniting and protecting one another.

Frankly, it is appalling that Donald Trump's ignorance of science, and disrespect for healthcare, influences so many people. Trump and Pence walk around the White House with no masks, force everyone else who is currying favor, to go without a mask. Trump's disrespect carried to the Mayo Clinic, when he toured with no mask, despite the fact that masks were required and everyone else complied.

Are people such blind sheep that they follow a moron down the road of being infected with Covid-19, and possibly dying? Who are these people that the word of Dr. Anthony Fauci has not penetrated their brains? Donald Trump should be ashamed of dividing the country. His followers will be open to disease, infecting others and adding to the chaos of our worst healthcare crisis in one hundred years.

May 17, 2020

Quarantine: We are physically apart, but somehow more connected

During the last eight weeks, our lives have been effectively put on ZOOM, and the consequences are rather fascinating. Churches and synagogues have put their entire programs online, and added more, in order to connect congregants to the clergy and to one another. The range of opportunities runs from toddler and family time, to Adult Education-interesting speakers and challenging classes. Public libraries have done the same, putting book conversations online and keeping people connected to reading and discussing ideas. The Newark Public Library had a marvelous panel of scholars analyzing Philip Roth's book, *The Plot Against America* (now a PBS series) with over one hundred people on the call.

In addition, we have had weddings, funerals, college reunions, musical concerts and graduations, to name but a few, bringing people together online. While they didn't necessarily know one another prior to lockdown, friendships have developed online. At first, Zoom may have seemed impersonal, but the experience of talking with others has actually proved quite the opposite. For one thing, more people are attending programs than ever before, keeping their brains occupied and their souls nourished. (It's easy when you don't have to get dressed or drive somewhere, right?) One example, this spring was a Zoom Passover *seder*, enjoyed by over one hundred families at my Temple-Sharey Tefilo-Israel. In fact, people reported that relatives who live far from the east coast were now present and able to participate, where they might not normally have been able to make the trip. Yes, we are physically separate, but connected in more ways than we ever knew.

After eight weeks "sheltered at home," and conversations with over seventy people of all ages and religions, I perceive a remarkable change in our humanity. We are immensely grateful to, and keenly aware of, the healthcare workers who risk their lives every day to save us. Moreover, we are looking for ways to thank them-sending food to hospitals, donating, making masks and so much more. Americans are generous by nature, and this is a serious time of need.

Since it is getting warmer, people are choosing to sit outside-often on their front lawns, talking to their neighbors, and meeting neighbors who they may not have known before. There is a sense that "we are all in this together." Small and large acts of kindness, especially concerning groceries and aiding older citizens, are happening every day. We have united to battle this insidious virus, and have learned a great deal about one another, and I would venture to say, about ourselves.

What is it about life that is so valuable? Our relationships, new and old, are the key. Understanding that life is fragile and can be snatched from any of us at a moment's notice, makes us keenly aware of time, which is fleeting. Minutes lost can never be regained. So, we are grateful for these new experiences, deeper understandings and an awareness of our surroundings and the people who enrich our lives.

There will be more to come as the pandemic continues-new challenges, many disappointments, worries, fears, and even nightmares. We will have to invent creative ways to manage our lives and connect with our loved ones. As the weeks unfold, I hope to comment on the virus and ways to survive it, and conquer our fears, both physically and emotionally.

Disappointingly, we still do not have a national plan to fight the virus, and deaths continue to rise. The president falsely claims that the virus will "go away magically," which is nonsense.

May 22, 2020

Leadership in a Crisis

What makes a good leader? That question has been the center of conversation in the last two months, because, shockingly, America has lost nearly 100,000 souls. How did that happen? Why did it happen? Did it have to happen?

For the last four weeks, I surveyed more than thirty people from all walks of life, and a similar pattern emerged. What are the qualities required in an effective leader, and specifically, the President of the United States?

intelligence- Not able to know everything, a good leader processes information from all sources, listens to the experts in a variety of fields, reads reports and relies on his seventeen intelligence agencies and department heads, in order to ultimately set policy.

Communication- a leader must communicate honestly and clearly with the American people. **Truth** is essential-no mixed messages

Integrity – The President takes an oath to "preserve, protect and defend the *Constitution* of the United States." Because the *Bill of Rights* contains the first ten amendments, implicit in that oath is safeguarding the safety of the three hundred thirty million citizens, rather than putting one's own political and personal interests first.

Humility -freedom from pride or arrogance. This would include speaking honestly about mistakes, admitting things might have been done differently or better. Being able to assess one's shortcomings and failures is difficult, but essential in a great leader.

Empathy – one of the most important qualities of a leader in a crisis. The ability of the president to show emotion, to put himself in the shoes of those who are grieving, to offer solace and share the sadness of the country, is essential. All the leaders we have had, until now, have been faced with horrific crises, and they have shown their humanity. Some extraordinary examples were George W. Bush after 9/11 and Barack Obama after the Newtown school shooting of first graders.

Unfortunately, there have been many more crises in the last few years-synagogue and church shootings, mass shootings and now a health crisis of untold magnitude, a once in one hundred years' pandemic.

When Donald Trump was surprisingly elected President, we watched as he dismantled the norms of the country- the State Department, Defense, and Justice, removed America from its leadership in NATO, the Paris Accord, and so much more over the last three years.

One recurring question was, "what would he do if there was a **real** crisis?" Now we know-absolutely nothing positive. In his own interest, he downplayed the threat, and people began dying. He rejects science, and refuses to tell the American people the truth about the dangers of the virus. He will not talk about the importance of wearing a mask. Moreover, he has spent exactly four minutes showing any sorrow that almost 100,000 citizens have died. The tragedy for our country is too big to put into words.

Leaders have to take responsibility for solving a problem in a crisis, especially a pandemic that happens once in a hundred years. Trump has taken no responsibility, putting the onus on the Governors, when the federal government could have solved the problem much sooner and more effectively. As a result of denial and inactivity, thousands more people have died. Columbia University recently calculated that if Trump had put sheltering in place one week earlier, 36,000 people would not have died. Imagine what would have happened if he read the reports and listened to the science and acted in January, when he knew there was a threat. For one thing, we would not have 35 million people unemployed and thousands continuing to die.

As we ponder leadership and the importance of picking someone to lead our country, let's keep these personal characteristics in mind. **Intelligence, communication**, **integrity, honesty, humility**, and **empathy** are a good roadmap when evaluating people for whom to **VOTE,** and we must vote, always.

May 25, 2020

Bravery- above and beyond what any of us can imagine

White headstones stand row upon row of graves at Arlington National Cemetery and in Normandy, France. Sacred ground. The respectful, hushed quiet, broken only by a light breeze whistling through the trees. The beauty of these places is indescribable. Here lie the brave men who stormed the beaches in "Operation Overlord," the codename for the Battle of Normandy, and the beginning of the Allied victory.

This Memorial Day weekend, as we watch the real time footage from June 6ᵗʰ, 1944, the contrast to the sacred resting place is stark. The Germans were entrenched high above the beaches where the landing would have to take place. Omaha Beach, Gold Beach, Juno Beach, Sword Beach and Utah, added at the last moment. Five thousand amphibious ships, with young men, 85% of whom had never seen combat, the clanking noise of bullets hitting the landing ships, men dying and falling in the water, now turned red with their blood. Chaos and terror, yet they still moved ineluctably toward the beaches. Many climbed the daunting heights and scaled the bluffs, which were practically straight up, a seemingly impossible feat. As we watch the footage, the horror and the bravery of the day is breathtaking.

Today is the day that we remember these men, and all men and women of the military, who laid down their lives so that we can live in freedom.

Walking in each of these exquisite monuments to bravery, we must stop to remember, pay tribute and ponder the bravery that put freedom and democracy above all else, including life itself.

Thomas Jefferson's "All men are created equal," that he wrote into the *Declaration,* is the basis of our democracy, still aspirational and not yet achieved for all. With our freedom comes a serious responsibility, and in 2020 we have to defend legislation that followed World War Two-The Civil Rights Act of 1964 and the Voting Rights Act of 1965. These laws are under attack in 2020. Therefore, we must work to ensure that no soldiers died in vain-that the idea bigger than themselves will be carried on by the next generations, honored and preserved by hard work and dedication. It's up to us and those who will follow us.

Take a moment at 3PM as TAPS is played, to be grateful for the sacrifices of so many others, so that we can live free.

May 27, 2020

Once in a Lifetime

In a lifetime of teaching, there was only one really stubborn boy in my classes, an obstinate and recalcitrant sixth grader. He was the youngster who, no matter what I said, would do the exact opposite. One word from any teacher, and he would dig in his heels, mock another student, and take pleasure in the attention he was getting from his classmates. A clumsy oaf, overweight, a nasty bully and a big mouth, he was the star of his own show every day. He relished in it. After two months, we brought in psychologists to discuss his infantile and obstreperous behavior. Stubborn, hateful and angry, he continued, despite many efforts to tame him, while trying to keep the other students from being victimized.

Not smart, and failing in school, he played Nintendo and had lots of other toys that his classmates wanted. They let him get away with his constant show, so they could play. This kid was not a good athlete, but he always got the ball, because the other boys were afraid of him. His "potty mouth" was the scourge of our classroom. Needless to say, he spent a lot of time in the principal's office. When he was caught stealing, he lied and blamed it on a weaker boy. Parents were called to school numerous times, but it was clear that they didn't know what to do with him either, and they planned on military academy after sixth grade.

It was a very long grind that year, and finally June arrived. I breathed a sigh of relief, secure in the knowledge that this sociopath would be in some other place, not our school and not in my life. That was decades ago, and in many years of teaching no other kid has ever emerged to create the havoc that we endured that year.

I wondered what kind of adult he became, but I never heard about him in the years that followed. Perhaps he is in jail, arrested after stealing money from a company where he worked? This was possible, based on the serious personality disorder that he had.

My particular nightmare is that this kid, so long gone, has emerged as the President of the United States. Not the same person, certainly, but the same frightening personality: an inveterate liar, a brutal bully, incredibly dumb, and putting on a show every day to call attention to himself. The "stable genius" knows nothing, reads nothing, and bloviates to hide his lack of knowledge. He brags about how smart he is, and then shows his stupidity once he opens his mouth. The tragedy for the nation, and for the global world, is that a total moron is in charge of what used to be the greatest country on earth.

You already know many of the problems, too many to recount. The health of every citizen is at stake when this vain, infantile, oppositional president refuses to wear a mask, which clearly is the key to flattening the curve and getting the country back to work. The narcissist who said, "I alone can fix it," has left everything to the states. The nightmare continues, as we become aware that there is no plan, no oversight, no intelligent involvement by the federal government, because the president takes "no responsibility" for the deaths, the chaos, the confusion which requires a solution. Our country is essentially rudderless, in the most serious crisis of this century.

In my wildest dreams I never thought that the dangerous sixth grader in my classroom would ever return, but he has, and in spades. We are in for a long, painful ride, since it is only the second inning of a nine-inning game. We need to wear our masks, wash our hands, and VOTE this nightmare out of office in November.

May 30, 2020

Is Our Democracy as strong as we thought it was?

The Constitutional Convention took place from May 14 to September 17, 1787, in Philadelphia, Pennsylvania. While it was originally called to revise the Articles of Confederation, which were weak, many delegates had much bigger plans for the convention. Some of the best minds among the founding fathers were in attendance: Alexander Hamilton, Ben Franklin, James Madison and William Samuel Johnson, who headed up the committee. There were major disagreements.

Ben Franklin, at age 81, was the elder statesman of the convention. He gave his final speech to the assembled group.

"When you assemble a number of men, to have the advantage of their joint wisdom, you inevitably assemble with these men all their prejudices, their passions, their errors of opinion, their local interests and their selfish views." Franklin thought it impossible to expect a "perfect production" from such a gathering, but he believed that the Constitution they had just drafted, "with all its faults," was better than any alternative that was likely to emerge.

Nearly all the delegates harbored objections, but they put them aside and signed. Few of them believed that the new federal Constitution alone would be enough to create a unified nation out of a collection of independent republics. However, in 1787, there were more similarities than there are in 2020, and our democracy is now in danger of being torn apart.

There is a story that when Franklin was leaving the Convention, a group of citizens approached him, and asked what sort of government the delegates had created. His answer was, "a republic, if you can keep it."

And therein lies the rub. We are far more diverse than those who committed to the doctrine of "popular sovereignty,"-democracy-as the rationale for their successful rebellion. In 1787, there was a solid belief in the principles of English common law and constitutionalism,

As we have seen in Minneapolis this week, there is much that needs to be done to even begin to achieve the goals of the founding fathers. However, they knew that our Constitution is neither a self-actuating nor a self-correcting document. It requires the constant attention and devotion of all citizens. Only then will the phrase, "all men are created equal" be a common-held belief in the "pursuit of happiness."

June 2, 2020

Two viruses converge and the nation is on fire

June 2, 2020

Our country is in danger of losing its democracy. Actually, this is nothing new. I was worried about my country when, as a college student in the sixties, the National Guard was called out to escort black students, like James Meredith and Ruby Bridges, to school without being harmed. In the south, there were angry insults, dangerous hoses and vicious dogs, yet the federal government protected the students. It was the law.

The founding fathers knew that The Constitution was not a perfect document. Compromises between the small and large states created serious flaws. How can you say that "all men are created equal," and not count them equally, not give them the vote or recognize the single biggest problem-slavery.? How were the slaves to be treated and counted? We fought a Civil War that was supposed to resolve that question. Following the Emancipation Proclamation, the passage of the 13th, 14th and 15th Amendments was met with the rise of the Ku Klux Klan and the poll tax, designed to prevent black citizens from voting. We are still plagued by voter suppression, led by President Trump, which is stunning. We have a president who doesn't want everyone to be able to vote. It is counter-intuitive to all of our values.

Our very first virus is RACISM, in our country from its birth, and present all these years. White citizens could not stand the promise of "all men are created equal' being fulfilled. One answer was that police departments in the country were filled with white men, many of whom came with their bigotries from birth.

The years after the Civil War continued to make the African-American community second-class citizens. The slaves, who were freed in the south, couldn't read or write, so there were only menial jobs, if any. In the north, while things seemed as if they might be better, in fact, the discrimination was subtler and often unspoken- mediocre to terrible schools, job discrimination, the lowest salaries for menial jobs, housing discrimination, inadequate healthcare, if there was any at all. The list is long and painful. The conditions of severe poverty put the African-American communities at a disadvantage that was almost impossible to overcome, but not impossible.

Fast forward to 2020, and the arrival of a SECOND VIRUS-COVID-19. It is a killer for sure, and in order to stay safe, citizens were required to stay home. The result has been catastrophic – businesses immediately collapsed, 40 million people lost their jobs, people cannot pay their rent or buy food or anything. We are rightly scared and worried about the future.

Combined with the virtually overnight realization that we are in the midst of a pandemic, such as the one in 1918, the terrible truth is that the virus affects African-Americans in outsize numbers. The result is a perfect storm of a healthcare crisis, instant job loss, anxiety over food and housing, and now the knowledge that even in this nightmare, African-Americans have an unequal chance of surviving.

Two viruses: RACISM and COVID-19. The murder of a black man, George Floyd, in broad daylight by four Minneapolis policemen was too much to bear. It was gasoline poured on the flames of frustration, resentment and hatred over many decades. Black and white citizens took to the streets, and for the last many days, they have been protesting. The First Amendment in the Bill of Rights allows "redress of grievances" and "peaceful assembly." However, anger spilled over and some bad actors and disruptors, inserted themselves into mostly peaceful protests. Those actions muddied the waters. Unfortunately, looting at night from many outside actors and youngsters seeing an opportunity, has created a terrible situation. Looting will not be helpful to the cause of the peaceful protestors.

I would be remiss if I did not mention our THIRD VIRUS-Donald J. Trump, who unfortunately was elected President of the United States three and a half years ago. A racist, founder of the "birther" movement that challenged Barack Obama's citizenship, Trump is a negative actor in the healthcare crisis as well. His words are incendiary. He challenges the healthcare experts and refuses to wear a mask or encourage people to stay home. The list of his lies and disinformation is well-known by all of us. He is fighting the guidelines of his own government. President Trump is a disruptor, and dangerous to the health of our country, both literally and figuratively.

What is the danger here? The crowded protests are going to create a spike in the virus. More people will die, and the country will be mired in another social and healthcare crisis. With the flu season coming in the fall, our country needs a leader, one who unites us, and there is no one to be found. Many governors have been setting an example and explaining why sacrifice is for the greater good, so we can all live healthy and free. Governor Cuomo of New York has been especially outstanding on a daily basis, since he talks to the American people at 11am on television.

Three viruses converging at the same time is frightening, for even the strongest of us. We need to look for ways to lead in our own communities. Search for opportunities to help our friends and loved ones, to love our neighbor and take care of ourselves. As we realize the problems, we will come together to find good solutions and change our communities, so they work for everyone. Out of the pain will come unity and progress forward.

June 4, 2020

June 1, 2020-Inflection point!

In every crisis there is always a moment -an inflection point, if you will-when events will either turn around in an inspiring way, or go south.

In a weekend that was a seesaw of violence, peaceful protesting, looting, mixed messages, police presence, National Guard, Trump tweeting, and chaos, it was hard to know which way would prevail.

In much the same way that Nancy Pelosi said that, "Donald Trump will impeach himself," Trump actually provided his own inflection point. Frustrated, wanting to show how he would "dominate" the streets, he ordered the military to clear Lafayette Square of the **peaceful** marchers. They had a constitutional right to protest, and yet they were roughly forced out of the square by mounted police, prison guards recruited for the event, rubber bullets, tear gas, a helicopter overhead hitting the branches of trees -all by the order of the President. It was unexpected and sudden.

Shockingly, Donald Trump ordered our American military to move against our own citizens. This is never supposed to happen. There has always been the understanding that there is a separation between the political and the military. It was an outrageous abuse of presidential power. For what purpose? Donald Trump, holding a borrowed Bible, wanted to have a photo-op in front of St. John's Church, often referred to as "the President's church," since so many presidents, going back to Madison, had worshipped there. It did not appear that Donald Trump came to worship.

The event was a propaganda stunt-obviously transparent, as Trump nervously held the Bible-upside down. Episcopal Bishop Mariann Budde, was outraged, and said so. She had not been told that Trump was coming. She said that he "just used a Bible as a prop, and a church of my diocese as a backdrop for a message antithetical to the teachings of Jesus and everything our church stands for."

The abuse was too much for the United States Generals, who were formerly in the military. They had largely stayed quiet. There was an understanding that the military leaders would not criticize a sitting president, but this was a bridge too far. Former chairman of the Joint Chiefs General Mullen, issued a statement, saying that Trump's orders cannot be trusted, that he will "politicize" the troops and he said, "Citizens are not the enemy."

Former Secretary James Mattis denounced Trump in *The Atlantic magazine,* in a very powerful message worth reading. With the military and all the clergy coming out against Donald Trump's revolting, disrespectful and unconstitutional actions, the tide turned. Secretary of Defense Mark Milley, who had been taken along on the stunt, realized his error and publicly announced his apology, and said that the military should never be used against our citizens. Donald Trump was furious at Milley.

Three former presidents (Carter, Clinton and Bush), issued beautiful statements, and former President, Barack Obama, was on television openly criticizing the actions of the last two days. He reached out to the next generation, promising support and suggesting that there is much to do. "We should move forward in order to achieve justice for all."

There will be more to come, more people gaining the courage to speak and to push for justice. We should all stay alert to the opportunities in our communities to be a force for change. We have lived through the beginning of a new awakening, and we need to take advantage of it.

June 5, 2020

JUST MERCY

"Justice, justice shall you pursue (Deuteronomy 16:20). <u>The Torah</u>, <u>A Women's Commentary</u> <u>Reform Judaism Publishing; New York; 2008</u>

The events of the last many days have trained all of our eyes and hearts on justice: social justice, legal justice and economic justice.

In the name of justice, I want to recommend to you one of the most powerful books ever written on this subject-*Just Mercy: A Story of Justice and Redemption, by Bryan Stevenson.* It is the true story, written by Stevenson, describing his experience when he came to Alabama after Harvard Law School. Working for a nonprofit, he represented a man on death row. I won't say more, except that it is a riveting look into the challenges of racial hatred and the white legal system in the south.

In addition to the book, there is an equally extraordinary movie-"Just Mercy," which is free this month.

Reading the book and seeing the movie will give you an inside look at the poverty, the culture and the brutality facing the African-American community, since the beginning of our country.

With the events of the last eight days, we have begun a journey toward understanding the difficulties, and the start of a dialogue among citizens, which should lead to a more just and kind world.

June 6, 2020

June 6, 1944 Operation Overlord in France-a time of American grit and bravery

Today, I have the honor of writing about the liberating of France by the American, Canadian and British forces. That historic effort was a proud time in our history. Despite the tragic loss of life, it was one of America's most extraordinary moments, since it stands in stark contrast to our political disgrace at home, and on the world stage at present. We need to pay attention to the differences.

What was so extraordinary about the success of Operation Overlord? All three countries had a common purpose-to defeat the Germans and free France. That purpose, and the cooperation that was required to achieve the greatest war effort ever undertaken, succeeded because of the bravery and courage of more than 150,000 soldiers and sailors. They landed on five beaches, scaled impossibly steep, straight up hills, and were attacked by the heavily entrenched Germans, who had a perfect view of the landing.

Studying WW2 can be fascinating for a lifetime, partly because of the individuals who made the success. Others are often unknown, because they are not named in history books. One of the most crucial roles was actually played by a little-known organization-the OSS-Office of Strategic Services, which later became the American CIA. It was a wartime intelligence agency of the United States. Many of the men involved were behind the lines-taking out bridges and other crucial, physical sites. Their actions served to delay the ability of the Germans to move through France. Navy Admiral William McCraven has written a fascinating book about these activities-*Operation Overlord: the OSS and the Battle* for France.

Honoring this day is important for many reasons. On the one hand, it recalls the men and women who are referred to as "the greatest generation," because of their bravery, sacrifice and single-minded purpose. It is also a day when many families visit the cemeteries in Normandy and in Arlington, Virginia, as well as throughout our country, to pay respects and thank the family members who fought so we can be free.

I want to suggest that we should think carefully about the years of war and sacrifice that it took to defeat the enemy. We have been "sheltering in place" for a mere three months, in order to defeat another enemy: Covid-19, in order to flatten the curve.

However, after three months, many people lost their resolve and insisted that we "reopen" the country, spurred on by President Trump for his own political reasons, and no sense of keeping Americans safe. When we see the spike in the virus three weeks from now, that should be a wakeup-call that we need to be more disciplined, sacrifice going to the Jersey shore and wear our masks in order to keep one another safe. We have not won this war yet. There are people dying across our country every day.

Of course, the murder of George Floyd, and the important protesting that ensued, has seriously complicated matters. While the response in our country and across the world is positive, there is a healthcare danger. Marching so close to one another, often without masks, indicates that many of the marchers might become infected with the virus. Whether or not to march, is clearly a serious decision that each individual must make.

Whatever the answer, we can be proud on this day of those heroes of WW2, the thousands of healthcare heroes fighting the Covid-19 virus, and everyone now fighting for social justice to make our country a much better place.

Character matters: Good leaders take Responsibility for their actions

June 15, 2020

The last time I wrote was June 6th-D-Day. The week of June 8th to the 13th was one of the craziest news weeks of my lifetime. Every time I began to write, five other things happened. It was impossible to know where to focus, what to make of events and how to evaluate what was being done, especially when the president tweeted obvious disinformation. I took a breather, except that it was a dizzying week, and no calm breaths were to be had.

Let me begin where I ended, on June 6th. Character matters. After Eisenhower rallied the troops, he went to his headquarters and wrote another letter.

"Our landings in the Cherbourg-Havre area have failed to gain a satisfactory foothold and I have withdrawn the troops. My decision to attack at this time and place based upon the best information available. The troops, the air and the Navy did all that bravery and devotion to duty could do. If any blame or fault attaches to the attempt it is mine alone."

Eisenhower took complete responsibility for the program, and that is what outstanding leaders do when citizens' lives are at stake.

Among all the bizarre things that happened last week, Trump signed an executive order waiving environmental laws, spoke about turning the country "back to business," in the midst of a pandemic, while the unemployment rate was at 16.3%. We already know that he sent in the military to clear Lafayette Square, so he could take a photo-op with a borrowed Bible.

Meanwhile, protestors were marching in support of justice for George Floyd, and African-Americans who have been victimized for four hundred years. The tide was turning. Because of the video of George Floyd's murder made public by an astute seventeen-year-old with a phone, white America was realizing that there have been systemic violations in police forces for hundreds of years. Change has to happen. What followed were days of mostly peaceful black, brown and white marchers walking together. However, Donald Trump chose to describe the citizens as "thugs" and "domestic terrorists." The First Amendment guarantees that Congress shall grant the right to "peacefully gather" and also have "redress of grievances."

And there is more, the mostly do-nothing Republican Senate opened hearings into the origins of the Russia investigation. Really.

In response to sending in the military to fight our citizens, eighty-nine former Department of Defense officers sent a letter indicating they "were alarmed." General Milley and Secretary of Defense Esper issued statements, basically apologizing for their roles in Lafayette Square. The Pentagon sent the National Guard and the military back to their bases.

The polls showed that more than 70% of America approved of the peaceful protestors. Trump was still fighting with Muriel Bowser, the Mayor of Washington, DC., who asked him to get federal troops out of her city. Trump dug in. She responded by having a huge "black lives matter" painted in black on yellow across the street in front of the White House, and visible to Donald

Trump. She then renamed Pennsylvania Avenue "Black Lives Matter Plaza," so Trump now lives at 1600 Black Lives Matter Plaza. The Mayor won the day.

And the week continued. The Stock Market plunged 1862 points. The Republican convention had to be moved, because the governor of North Carolina said that he would not have thousands of people crammed into an indoor space, citing health concerns, which are of little concern to Donald Trump. The convention has partially been moved to Jacksonville, Florida, where there are not enough hotel rooms. Five large cruise ships will be used.

Can you think of a bigger opportunity to contract the Coronavirus? Totally confused by all this change, the Republican party decided not to have a platform, which is the reason conventions have meetings in the first place. Are you dizzy yet? I was.

Moving on, as a result of serious pressure, politically obtuse Donald Trump moved the date of "Juneteenth" to the next day, the 20th, and people attending the rally were asked to sign a "disclaimer." Perhaps the administration has finally admitted that the virus is dangerous?

There is more. John Bolton decided to publish his book without the OK from the White House. Moreover, furious at the CNN poll putting Joe Biden well ahead of Trump, the president filed a "cease and desist" order against CNN. Simultaneously, the seemingly oblivious president was encouraging the country to reopen, as coronavirus numbers were spiking upward. The president's desire to open was clearly political, and showed a callous disregard of citizens' lives.

You see a lot of anger in this week, don't you? The president was calling people names, fighting with the military, engaging negatively with the Mayor of DC, with CNN, and so much more. I had to stop writing, because my head was beginning to spin when I looked at the list. Only half of my list had been covered.

Here is the most important question. **What is missing from this narrative?**

You guessed it. In forty-seven days, there were **no** briefings on the Covid-19 from the White House. It is as if the virus, which has killed 117,000 people to date, is not important. Dr. Fauci is nowhere to be found, having been side-lined, except by invitation to talk shows, saying this is his "worst nightmare." Donald Trump finds the virus inconvenient for his re-election campaign, cares not one whit for the death and destruction that his inaction has caused, and has spent only four and a half minutes talking about those citizens we have lost.

Of course, Donald Trump would like to forget the virus altogether. He hoped that it would disappear, "magically,", and ignored it until it could not be swept under the rug entirely. In the meantime, the president refused to take a leadership role, putting the burden on state governors, instead. Precious time was lost in January and February, and thousands of people died who didn't have to contract the virus. There was no move made to use the federal government in a concerted effort to fight the war on the virus-to buy the supplies that were needed and distribute them to hospitals. Trump did not activate the Defense Production Act as Franklin Roosevelt did in the Second World War.

In fact, when asked, Donald Trump said he took "no responsibility" for what happened. His lack of leadership is shameful. We needed to have something like a Marshall Plan: testing, swabs, PPE hospital gowns, the works. The President of the United States, did NOTHING. This is malfeasance, and he should resign, or be physically removed from office. He has ignored the CDC guidelines, refuses to wear a mask and has influenced many others not to wear masks. We have a president who doesn't believe in science and rejects it. I recall the cartoon-Pogo-"We have met the enemy, and he is us."

June 19, 2020

The Supreme Court: A beacon of light in a dark time

The hard truth is that only one branch of our three branches of government is actually working for the people, despite the efforts of the democratic House. The Supreme Court of the United States, handed down two historic decisions. On Monday, SCOTUS, voting 6 to 3, ruled that a landmark civil rights law protects gay and transgender workers from workplace discrimination. The decision was surprising, because two conservative judges, Chief Justice John Roberts (appointed by George W. Bush) and Justice Neil Gorsuch (appointed by Donald Trump) agreed with the 4 more liberal justices.

Justice Neil Gorsuch wrote for the majority. "An employer who fires an individual merely for being gay or transgender defies the law."

That historic decision extended workplace protection to millions of people in the country, even after Donald Trump thought he had transformed the court with his two appointments. The most important concept here is that the Justices of the Supreme Court are not supposed to be partisan, no matter who appointed them. Rather, they are jurists, often brilliant legal scholars, reading the law as it is written, and interpreting it to the best of their ability. In this case, Title VII of the Civil Rights Act of 1964 was in question. Most important, because they are appointed for life, Supreme Court Justices are independent, and owe no one president their allegiance. This is a lesson that Donald Trump learned in spades this week.

A major contribution to the case is that Rutgers Law School, often a hotbed of Constitutional brilliance. played a role in making history. Professor Katie Eyer's *amicus brief*, and her other work on LGBTQ rights, informed legal strategy in the case, which is Bostock v. Clayton. Her writings influenced Justice Gorsuch's majority opinion in the ruling.

Rutgers has long been in the forefront of recognizing legal talent. You may remember that Ruth Bader Ginsberg was hired by Rutgers when other law schools had turned her down. She was one of only eight women in her Harvard Law class, when hiring women was not universally accepted, to say the least. In fact, the Dean of Harvard Law School indicated that the eight women in RBG's class, were taking up a seat that a man could have held.

The historic work of the Supreme Court continued. On Thursday, in a 5 to 4 court ruling, (Chief Justice Roberts joined the liberal Justices), SCOTUS blocked the Trump administration from ending the Deferred Action for Childhood Arrivals program, known as "Dreamers."

The Trump administration had been building a wall against immigrants for three years- there was a wall of paperwork, fees, arbitrary administrative obstacles and blocking access to legal advice and due process. Trump's war also included nearly 650,000 unauthorized immigrants who were brought here as children, and were shielded from deportation and granted work permits through the Obama-era DACA program.

While Trump made immigration his signature program, all of his efforts have been stunningly unpopular. A recent Pew poll found that 72%, including a majority of Republicans, felt that the country is strengthened by immigrants. In fact, of the 27,000 "dreamers," brought here as children, many are healthcare workers-doctors, nurses and all manner of helpers, who have been fighting the pandemic to keep Americans safe.

Thursday's SCOTUS ruling found that the Trump administration, while having the authority to terminate DACA, had done so in a "wrong" way. The brief violated the Administrative Procedure Act. The Court called the case "arbitrary and capricious," clearly aggravated by the sloppy work of the Trump administration's lawyers. There is much more to be said about the efforts of the Trump administration to block immigrants, but I will save that for another day.

Oh yes, John Bolton's book is now in the hands of the media across the land, and it is the tell-all that it was touted to be months ago. However, John Bolton will only be a footnote in history, when he could have changed history. Had he testified during the impeachment hearings, his words could have mattered greatly. Unfortunately, the potential millions made by his book deal were too seductive. Character counts, as we have been saying this week, and throughout this blog.

I sleep better at night knowing that John Roberts and Neil Gorsuch put the country first, at least in this particular case.

Friday night massacre?

Late Friday night, everyone was experiencing the noisy chaos in Tulsa, Oklahoma of social justice protests, the Covid-19 surging numbers and the prospect of Donald Trump's rally, a serious threat to our legal system was put in motion by Donald Trump's administration. Friday night is often when most of the country is either asleep or not paying attention. It has become the "go to" time for Donald Trump to fire people without warning, and catch everyone off guard.

June 21, 2020

The first salvo came when Attorney General Barr announced the resignation of the top federal prosecutor in Manhattan, Geoffrey Berman. He is the United States Attorney for the Southern District of New York. That particular office has been at the forefront of inquiries into the corruption of Donald Trump's inner circle, and brought many more momentous cases throughout the decades.

Mr. Berman said "I have not resigned, and have no intention of resigning my position." He said that he learned he was "stepping down" from a Justice Department news release. This has been the rude and disrespectful way that the Trump administration has fired all of the many people, who ultimately Donald Trump felt were in the way of his personal goals to protect his friends and himself.

The firing created an unusual problem, because Mr. Berman was appointed by the judges of the United States District Court, and not by the Senate. Technically, Mr. Barr could not fire him. To break the standoff, Donald Trump fired Geoffrey Berman Friday night, shortly after Mr. Berman said he was "not resigning."

Why is this important? The United States Attorney's office in Manhattan is the most famous federal prosecutor's office in the country. The Southern District, as it is called, is prized by law school graduates as a plum job. As such, it has prosecuted famous cases through Democratic and Republican administrations. Most important, there is a tradition of independence away from the Justice Department and from political Washington. Normally, a president would not insert himself into a situation like this, but Donald Trump does not respect the concept of agency independence, and he injects himself everywhere.

That brings me to why this is such a dangerous firing. The independence of the "Sovereign District of New York," has been inviolate until now. U.S attorneys are usually replaced by the first assistant. However, Donald Trump chose to replace Mr. Berman with an outsider who is not a litigator or a former prosecutor, and never worked in the office of the Southern District. Trump has named Jeff Clayton, chairman of the Securities and Exchange Commission, a friend who basically said he would like the job. Naming one's friends and relatives, especially if they are not qualified, has a distinctly negative effect on the morale of the agency or department. This is not normal, because the process matters.

Notably, Mr. Berman's office is conducting investigations into the finances of the Trump inaugural committee, and looking into contributions from foreigners, which are illegal. The Southern District is also involved in investigating friends of Rudy Giuliani, as well as Mr. Giuliani himself. Some of the other high-profile cases involve Roger Stone and Michael Flynn, friends of the President, where the Justice Department under AG Barr has intervened. As a result, there have been serious objections from current and prior law enforcement officials that Barr has politicized the Justice Department. He seems to be serving as personal lawyer for Donald Trump, rather than serving the *Constitution* and the law of the land, for which he took an oath.

In addition, there are a number of other high-profile cases, such as the prosecution and guilty plea from Trump's longtime "fixer," Michael Cohen, who is now serving time in prison. That case led to a much bigger investigation, which focused on Mr. Trump's private company, and many others close to him.

Clearly, putting a friend of Donald Trump into the leadership of the Southern District could seriously compromise the heretofore independence that was the signature strength and reputation of the lawyers who work there.

Moreover, Mr. Trump has been purging many valuable public servants since the impeachment hearings, when he was acquitted by the Republican led Senate. Only Mitt Romney voted to find him guilty. Trump has fired numerous patriots and Inspectors-General, who had independent oversight on agencies, as well as other high-level people who testified at the hearings. Trump publicly embarrassed Colonel Vindman, who now needs security protection. The people who came forward at the impeachment hearings, came out of love of country, and risked their reputations and their safety in order to tell the true story. One by one, they were vilified by the president, and they subsequently lost their jobs. Losing these lifelong and committed patriots is a serious loss for our country, and a terrible lesson for all Americans.

As I noted, putting Jeff Clayton into the job of United States Attorney, for which he lacks experience and is ill-prepared, puts the work of the Southern District in jeopardy. Notably, he does have to be confirmed by the Senate first. Interestingly, Lindsay Graham, who is chairman of the Senate Judiciary Committee, may not be in favor of this appointment. Graham has indicated that he would allow New York's two Democratic Senators (Schumer and Gillibrand) to object to the nomination by a purely procedural maneuver. It is "Senatorial courtesy," and it may work well in this case.

It's important to know that the opportunity for William Barr and Donald Trump to insert themselves into any case that might hurt the President, is now an open question. Stay alert and listen carefully.

June 22, 2020

Why Leadership Matters

For the last 111 days, I and 59 million other people tuned in to Governor Andrew Cuomo's daily briefings. Listening to the briefings was like being thrown a life raft in a terrible storm.

If there are 19 million citizens in New York state, what motivated 59 million people from all over the country to watch these briefings? As a New Jerseyan who never missed a briefing, I was awed by the leadership that Governor Cuomo displayed on a daily basis.

First, the physical presentation showed an organized, dignified and considerate seating. Governor Cuomo was seated, appropriately distant with his team, who each had a name placard identifying who they were. It was clear that each team member had an area of expertise, that Governor Cuomo knew them well, and had worked with them for a long time.

Second, Andrew Cuomo spoke the truth, no matter how difficult the news. In that vein, he began with a reading of the numbers: cases, hospitalizations and deaths. There was a split screen showing charts to corroborate the numbers, which for many days were awful. When he read about the number of deaths, he showed a palpable emotion that we had lost citizens, and an acknowledgement that we needed to beat this virus. Those numbers were breathtaking, and they were climbing up the mountain. The Governor indicated that we needed to flatten the curve, and it was up to us to win this war.

How were we going to do that? Stay home, shelter in place, stay separate from elderly relatives who are vulnerable, wash our hands many times a day (try not to touch our faces), don't go outside, unless absolutely necessary, and wear a mask at all times. On its face those directions seemed simple enough, but they were challenging for New Yorkers, who like to be out and about.

Everyone listened to the Governor's voice of reason and calm, even while people were dying every day. Things were so bad that refrigerator trucks had to be brought in next to hospitals, to act as morgues. There were no places to put so many bodies, because funeral homes had run out of space. That was very scary. My children all live in Brooklyn, and those trucks were parked on the side streets near the hospitals. Night and day, police cars and ambulance sirens were blaring, with no respite. This went on for many months in April and May, and must have really frightened my grandchildren, because the noise was unrelenting,

Watching pictures from hospitals overrun with patients in the halls, and healthcare workers exhausted and sometimes dying, was very frightening. Millions of us were afraid.

However, every day, Andrew Cuomo held his briefing, was honest with the numbers, and told us that if we did certain things, we would win this war. His demeanor was assured, calm, not alarmist, informed, intelligent and reasonable. He explained that he was using science and the scientists to arrive at these conclusions. Sometime in April, the numbers started to go down, and the charts reflected that success. What joy! It was clear to all of us that what the Governor told us to do would work. We had to keep on it, and not get too cocky, or sloppy or lazy. Keep to the rules.

Meanwhile, everything in New York and New Jersey was shutdown. Businesses closed. There were no restaurants. The stock market tanked, and 42 million people lost their jobs. Schools closed, and parents became their children's teachers. There were no Broadway shows. All of that was devastating, but we were still listening.

No one was on the streets. Times Square was a ghost town. When we saw the surreal pictures of Manhattan, with no people and no cars, we all understood that this was serious business, and we needed to do what we were told. Governor Cuomo spoke the truth. He combined it with the science of Dr. Fauci, and we all obeyed, no matter where we lived, because we wanted to survive.

For 111 days, Andrew Cuomo was our cheerleader and our teacher, admonishing us on the one hand and encouraging us on the other, to stay the course. Realizing that the federal government was not going to institute widespread testing, New York ramped up the state testing program, in order to see where the hotspots were and what needed to be done. On the last day that Governor Cuomo reported, there were 68,000 tests (on June 10th with .9 less than 1% positive), an amazingly low number.

Every day, Andrew Cuomo said, "We are New York tough, we are strong, we are united, we are disciplined, we are smart and we are loving." Even someone from another state could relate to those qualities of character that the Governor named and reiterated. It became our mantra, and we were inspired to behave in a disciplined way, in order to stay alive and help our neighbors stay healthy.

I cannot imagine how Andrew Cuomo did those briefings every day, when the numbers kept climbing and the death toll was staggering. While we were aware that he was affected by the deaths, he never showed weakness, only resolve, and continued to appear every day like clockwork, to give the report. As a result, the citizens of New York did what he said. Notably, despite the danger, the healthcare workers continued to work and often die, while trying to save us. It was overwhelming to experience what humanity really means, what a community can do together.

There is much more that Governor Cuomo did to bring us to the point of being able to open Phase 2 today, and I hope to talk about much of it as we progress on this journey. When we look back at where we were and where we are today, it seems clear that it is leadership that makes all the difference for a country in a crisis. Governor Cuomo's leadership, honesty, information and support made the difference between success and failure. As we move into an election season, it would be important to evaluate candidates in terms of their character, their ability and yes, their leadership.

June 23, 2020

A Most dangerous situation for America and our voice/ the second Friday night massacre

Friday night, in addition to firing Geoffrey Berman, the Trump Administration dealt another serious blow to freedom. The newly appointed Trump CEO of the Voice of America, Michael Pack, fired the four top officials who oversee the US Agency for Global Media. He then fired the advisory boards of Middle East Broadcasting, Radio Free Asia, Radio Free Europe/Radio Liberty and the Open Technology Fund, all of which are under the aegis of the US Agency for Global Media. These boards consisted of journalists and men and women of distinction in their fields, who oversee a budget of close to a billion dollars. They are dedicated to providing unbiased news to the millions of people who don't have a free and independent press in their countries around the world.

Over 280 million people a week depend on the Voice of America. Founded in 1942, it offered unbiased news and a true picture of American life and values. During World War II, millions of people relied on VOA as the voice of freedom and hope. Its independence was in the Voice of America's "firewall," which "prohibits interference by any US government official in the objective, independent reporting of news."

The people who listen to the news service around the world-in 40 languages and on every media platform- are those who don't believe the propaganda of their rulers. Instead, they rely on the world's premier democracy for the truth- the United States.

Now, independence and unbiased reporting is in serious jeopardy. Up until this moment, those listeners relied on the fact that politicians were not allowed to influence the information that goes to the public. The Advisory Boards were tasked with the oversight that guaranteed unbiased stories. It should be noted that when Michael Pack was confirmed, two top Voice of America executives, two women who were both experienced, respected and independent journalists, resigned. They saw the handwriting on the wall and the danger of putting a propagandist in the role of CEO.

The Republicans, and Donald Trump in particular, have longed to gain control of one of the largest media networks in the world. By finally succeeding in putting Michael Pack at the head, they are in a position to influence everything that goes out from the Voice of America and all the other agencies that broadcast to Asia, the Middle East, Europe and monitor Russia and Al Jazeera.

Before the 2016 election, there was speculation that Donald Trump, who didn't expect to wi planned to start his own media outlet-TRUMP NEWS. He has certainly succeeded in taking over one of the most far-reaching and influential networks, and that will endanger America and especially, our credibility. If it becomes apparent to millions that the Voice of America is the voice of the Republican Party and Donald Trump, people around the world will stop listening and change the channel. That will greatly affect our image and our ability to deliver the unbiased news to people desperate for information from a free democracy.

Sadly, this change will also affect the people worldwide who have relied on the Voice of America and the other agencies. The value of a free and independent journalism is one of our watchwords. Freedom of the press is a key freedom in the First Amendment of the Bill of Rights. This is one more reason why elections matter. We need to reinstate the independent advisory boards and an unbiased leader at the Voice of America, so that the voice of the United States is trusted and inviolate.

June 27, 2020

There's a Fox in the Hen House

Today, after a two- month hiatus, the White House group tasked with overseeing the path of the coronavirus, finally held a press conference. Notably, it was not held at the White House. The President did not attend, since he has removed himself from the problem. He is only interested in his reelection. The meeting was held at the headquarters of the Health and Human Services Agency.

Vice President Pence, who Trump chose to head this group, spoke without a mask, and gave a rosy picture of the government's progress, while new cases registered a staggering single day high- 44,702. In fact, six states-Utah, Florida, South Carolina, Georgia, Tennessee and Idaho, also had their highest numbers. Hardly a success story. No wonder Donald Trump put his lackey, Mike Pence, in charge of the recovery and the meeting.

A very savvy journalist asked a question. She wanted to know how the administration could claim to be doing everything possible to defeat the virus, when there was an indoor rally in Oklahoma. In addition, there was a meeting of 3,000 students in a church venue in Wisconsin, all without masks and no social distancing. Pence, a smooth operator if there ever was one, answered by reminding all of us that "it is a free country where we have freedom of speech and assembly." A stunned silence followed that bizarre response.

There seemed to be two meetings happening in the same room. Dr. Birx went through various charts of states at warp speed, all of which showed increases in cases, and she quickly ended her portion. When Dr. Fauci spoke, wearing a mask, he reminded everyone that it is our individual behavior that will defeat the virus-washing hands, wearing masks, social distancing and staying home, if possible. He added that, in addition to our individual responsibility, we have a "societal responsibility" to everyone else in the country. The spikes occurred because many young people went out on the town, infected others, and then increased the spread, exponentially.

There is a clear disconnect within the White House Task Force. The scientists were seriously concerned about the consequences of the re-openings on one side, and the administration was on the other side. Donald Trump encouraged the re-openings, even taunted certain states, because he wants to show that the economy is on the upswing, which it isn't. Trump thinks that the Stock Market is the economy, but it is not for the majority of Americans, who don't own stocks. Forty million people lost their jobs, many businesses failed, and citizens are in lines for food. That is not normal for the United States. Congress generally comes to the fore to alleviate financial strain in times of crisis. Not this time.

Pressuring the states to open, despite the fact that the CDC guidelines had not been met, was a callous and selfish move, designed only to benefit Donald Trump, while endangering millions of citizens. The "fox in the hen house" is working against the health of the nation. Now the states are paying the price, and so is the country. Texas and Florida have actually reversed course, and closed bars.

Meanwhile, New York, New Jersey and Connecticut, states that successfully flattened the curve and are reopening very cautiously, have indicated that someone coming from another state would have to quarantine for two weeks. This included President Trump, who planned to play golf in Bedminster, New Jersey, and now he is suddenly not coming. You can't make this up, can you?

There is another disturbing fact. The White House declared that all the meetings of the group must be classified. This is startling, since it goes against the transparency of the meetings that Governor Andrew Cuomo had for 111 days, sharing all the numbers, good and bad, and encouraging the citizens to follow the CDC guidelines. The administration failed miserably in its response to the virus, and continues to fail, so it's not surprising that it wants to hide the numbers and keep the meetings secret. We are well on the way to a half million deaths at this rate.

And yet, that is not the most disturbing and serious news. On Friday night, Rachel Maddow reported that the New York Times and the Wall Street Journal each broke stories of information that was uncovered by our intelligence services. Apparently, a Russian military intelligence group offered bounties to Taliban-linked fighters if they killed American fighters. This happened during the peace talks to end the war in Afghanistan. The G.R.U (the former KGB) is behind this brutal activity against America, and it includes disinformation, killings, cyberattacks and other destabilizing operations. The New York Times said, "it's hard to overstate what a major escalation this is from Russia. Election meddling and the occasional poisoning may be one thing. Paying the Taliban to kill American troops, that's something entirely new."

This stunning news was discussed in the National Security Council, as far back as late March. The Council came up with a range of possible responses, but Donald Trump did not act on any of them. Rather, Trump strengthened the United States' ties to Russia, which were unsteady after Russia invaded Ukraine in 2014. President Obama put economic sanctions on Russia, when Russia annexed Ukraine's Crimean Peninsula.

In 2016, when it was proven that Russia meddled in our elections, President Obama increased the sanctions. That explains Vladimir Putin's desire to get Donald Trump elected. Putin figured that Trump was manageable and would remove the sanctions, once elected. Trump never spoke out against the Russian interference or anything that Russia did. In April and May, Trump continued to cement his relationship with Putin. Phone calls went back and forth between the two men, and we do not have access to what was said, which is highly irregular. Those conversations are supposed to be monitored for transparency and national security, but they were not under President Trump.

However, we do know that in June, Trump repeated something he floated in an earlier time. The president wants Russia to be included in the G7, the organization with the largest economies in the world. Russia is actually a much smaller economy, but was part of the group from 1998, until it was expelled in 2014, after Russia invaded Ukraine. Inclusion is clearly something that Putin wants, and he is using Trump to gain that end. There is, indeed, a fox in the hen house, and the fox is the President of the United States. Very disturbing.

And the fox is busy in other matters as well. On June 15th, we discovered that Trump ordered 9,500 troops to be removed from Germany. Those troops are stationed there for very strategic reasons-they support NATO against Russian aggression. If those troops do come home, America will still have 25,000 troops in Germany, but the drawdown was very disturbing to the Germans and our military leadership, that was not consulted.

This news, combined with the extraordinary fact of Russia paying the Taliban to murder our soldiers, became public this week. Unfortunately, Donald Trump did not respond to the news in public, or speak about it. Congress was not told. Ultimately, since months passed with no action, the intelligence officials leaked this information to the *New York Times* and the *Wall Street Journal*. The fox in the hen house was working with Putin to help Russia, but not America.

"Dereliction of Duty"

July 1, 2020

For the second time this month the news came at such a dizzying pace that I could not choose which of the absolutely stunning items on which to focus. Two subjects stand above the rest-the out of control spread of the Coronavirus and the outrageous scandal that the Russians paid the Taliban to murder our soldiers.

Both of these disasters can be placed directly at the feet of Donald Trump. Let's begin by examining the Coronavirus. I watched the hearings yesterday as some members of the White House Task force testified in front of a Senate Committee. The news was straightforward and frightening. Dr. Anthony Fauci, director of the National Institute of Clergy and Infectious Diseases, minced no words when he said the country is "going in the wrong direction." Earlier that day, the representative from the Centers for Disease Control, was equally blunt. She said that the virus is spreading too fast for the United States to bring it under control.

The numbers are staggering. We have more than 40,000 new cases a day. Despite the fact that the virus came from Europe, the EU has flattened its curve, and it has less than 6,000 cases a day. Dr. Fauci opined that we might have as many as 100,000 cases a day at this rate, especially if we don't follow strict guidelines. The new cases are coming from Texas, California, Florida and Arizona, many states that opened too early.

To understand the gravity of the problem, we can focus on Houston, the site of the single largest hospital center in the world, with thousands of doctors and some of the finest medical schools. The other day, the Chief of Houston Healthcare, came before the cameras and indicated that the situation was dire, that they had only five more ICU beds, and that citizens needed to be following the guidance to stay safe. Her message was chilling. When the most sophisticated hospital center in the country is in trouble, one can only imagine the fate of the people in the poorer states that don't have the resources to deal with a crisis.

Numbers don't lie. Our national confirmed deaths are 130,000, and that number is probably low. The cases in Arizona increased by 145 percent, Florida's by 277 percent, and Texas by 184 percent. The situation is so dire that healthcare workers are forced to decide which patients to treat (triage) and how to allocate the resources they have. Interviews of these workers are breathtakingly sad, as they tell what it is like to be the only "relative" during a patient's last moments. One of the saddest results of the virus is that no one is allowed to visit a family member. The virus is too contagious.

The fact that the virus has spun out of control is a direct result of Donald Trump choosing to hide its reality during January and February. Eight weeks were lost, when they could have been spent in preparation, in our federal government marshaling the resources of the country, and sending one consistent message to 319 million people. Those actions would have saved tens of thousands of lives. Donald Trump was more concerned about his re-election, and the virus was an inconvenient intrusion that he wanted to ignore. His response was a dereliction of duty to the people of our country and his duty to uphold the Constitution.

In addition, Trump rejected science, still refuses to wear a mask, and ignores the value of social distancing. In short, his behavior has sent mixed messages to the country, rather than exhorting everyone to follow the science guidance, and being a positive role model for uniting the country. He is a stubborn ignoramus.

Recently, a number of Republicans have come out in public, saying that masks are essential and easy enough to wear. Mitch McConnell announced it in the Senate the other day, and numerous other politicians are now saying that we should all follow the guidance. It seems that Donald Trump is alone on his own little island of rebellion, because others are realizing what a tragic mess and loss of lives his lack of regard for science has caused. There is so much more to be said on this subject, but the second reality- the Russian bounty scandal, must be discussed, even as it is unfolding.

On Friday night, when the news of the Russian payments first broke, it was hard to fathom. Did that really happen? Did the Russians pay the Taliban to murder our soldiers? *The New York Times* broke the story, and there was so much detail in the article, that it was hard to deny. More information came out on the weekend, and then the major question-"What did the President know and when did he know it?" Those of you who remember the Nixon era will recall that question. It is worth doing some research of Watergate and John Dean, etc., because there are analogies between the Nixon and Trump administrations.

Apparently, the intelligence agencies were onto this nightmare, as far back as 2019. It was put into the President's Daily Briefing numerous times. Of course, it is well known that the President doesn't read and doesn't care about the PDB's. That alone opens the doors for "dereliction of duty." Similar to the virus news, Donald Trump chose to ignore what the intelligence agencies found. American officials even warned England that this was happening. In addition, money was found, and most recently the *New York Times* tracked the numbers of the bank accounts from which the money was paid.

As I write, Donald Trump has made no statement concerning the outrage that any other President would have made. Many different excuses have been made, not the least of which is that Trump was "not briefed," which is a boldfaced lie. The White house is scrambling to come up with some credible answer, but truthfully, there is none. The President of the United States knew that the Russians paid the Taliban to kill our soldiers, and he did nothing about it-no warning call to Putin and no message to the country that there would be consequences.

Trump's disregard of Russian aggression is another dereliction of duty, and possibly one that is impeachable, as well as personally reprehensible. Amazingly, Trump spoke to Vladimir Putin several times after the scandal was in his PBD, and Trump even suggested that Russia be readmitted to the G7. You can't make this up. Putin is well aware that there will be no consequences for his actions against the United States.

Susan Rice, President Obama's National Security Advisor and someone on the shortlist for Biden's VP, wrote a cogent Op-Ed, indicating that Trump's response is dangerous. Reverting to his usual playbook, Trump dismissed the story as just another "hoax" in an effort to "make Republicans look bad." The disturbing truth is that Donald Trump doesn't read, and may well have ignored the briefings which occurred over many months. However, "ignorance is no defense" in the law, especially if the ignorance belongs to the President of the United States. His disregard of his duty is our terrible cross to bear, and it has resulted in a runaway virus and the deaths of soldiers serving to protect us, as they serve our country.

Many of his former advisors have said in public and in writing, Donald Trump must be removed from the Oval Office, because he is a danger to our country.

July 4, 2020- Our National Tragedy

July 3rd, 2020

July 4th weekend has always been a time of celebration. In years' past, the country came together with families under the skies filled with glorious, exploding fireworks and patriotic music. We celebrated our freedom writ large in the Declaration of Independence, our American exceptionalism, our country's achievements in every area: in science, in sports, in education and yes, our place in the global world as the greatest and wealthiest country on earth.

Nothing of the sort is happening this weekend. We are in the midst of a pandemic that has taken 130,000 lives, with no end in sight. In order to fight the raging virus, we locked down and sheltered in place. As a result of that necessity, businesses closed and are shuttered, 42 million people lost their jobs, the stock market tanked, and chaos ensued.

Why did this happen? In the Second World War and other crises, our country's leaders rallied the citizens to come together, unite, and sacrifice whatever was necessary to succeed. Franklin Roosevelt assured Americans that we were fighting for the freedom of millions of people, to keep the faith, stay disciplined and actively help the cause. Women took jobs in factories that were formerly manned by men, who were now fighting overseas. Other women drove Red Cross trucks and citizens pitched in, according to their ability. The country was unified as we fought the Nazis and the Japanese. In England, Winston Churchill exhorted the British to stay the course, even as London was being bombed nightly. Families sent their children to the country to save their lives, and in many cases to never see them again. The bravery and the astounding sacrifice of "the greatest generation," has been documented in books well worth reading.

For the first time in our lives we have a leader who neither unites us or seems to care about the horrendous loss of life that the Coronavirus is wreaking. Where the instructions were simple and clear-wear a mask, shelter at home, wash our hands and socially distance, especially inside and even among family, Donald Trump, a vain and selfish man, did not care to wear a mask, and therefore, the very act became politicized. Only Trump could manage to spread mixed-messages on FOX News and in his so-called "briefings," and thoroughly confuse the country. We are leaderless.

The results have been disastrous. Millions of people think that the virus is a "hoax," Trump's go-to description when he thinks that the reality will hurt his re-election. He did not rally the country. Rather, he ignored the virus for the first two months, indicating falsely that it would just "magically go away." In a crisis, the President of the United States has almost unlimited power to marshal resources, to use the government to obtain supplies and distribute them throughout the country.

Donald Trump did none of those things. Rather, he told each state that the Governors were on their own, leaving them to compete with one another to obtain the masks, PPE and everything else that was needed. Essentially, the President of the United States took "no responsibility" for managing this pandemic. His ignorance about science, about the meaningful statistics and the necessity of testing, was on display for all to see. Yet, the damage was done. Conventional knowledge is that people look to their President for guidance and wisdom. Sadly, indeed tragically, Trump was sending misinformation, refusing to wear a mask, and the country was split about what to do. Masks became a red and a blue issue, which is dangerous nonsense.

Thus, our tragedy continued. Those two months were wasted by the government. Trump did not utilize the power and wealth of the United States to secure and provide the resources needed, and tens of thousands of people died, needlessly. We lost valuable and beloved citizens, because there was no unified message, no leadership. Basically, in this difficult crisis, Trump abdicated responsibility, because he had no good idea of how to solve the problems and didn't appreciate what it was to actually work hard.

In addition, he doesn't like to own a decision. That is not a good quality for a president or anyone charged with problems to solve. Harry Truman had a sign on his desk-"the buck stops here," and indeed it did. Imagine the monumental decision Truman had to make when he was deciding whether to bomb Hiroshima and Nagasaki, in order to end the war and save thousands of Americans. In contrast, Trump always blames others when situations present the possibility of a problem. The man who bragged, "I alone can fix it," has fixed nothing and put the country into a major tragic mess. This is why elections matter. Imagine for a moment how different life would be under President Hillary Clinton, whether you liked her or not. As a former First Lady, Secretary of State, and a Senator, she would have mobilized the country and its resources months ago.

The President takes an oath to "preserve, protect and defend the Constitution." Implicit in that oath is the promise to protect the people in this country. Donald Trump has no sense of protecting anyone but himself and his re-election.

Because he has no feelings about the 130,000 who have already died, and more to come, Donald Trump has scheduled rallies, gatherings where people will not be wearing masks and will not be socially distant. Thinking that the only thing he needs is to have the economy back, Trump cynically played on the peoples' emotions when he taunted states like Michigan to be "liberated." The guidelines of the White House Task Force, specifically Dr. Fauci, were very clear. The curve had to be flattened before any state could consider reopening. None of that mattered to Trump, and he pressured the Republican Governors to open up their states, which they did against all the advice of the CDC and Dr. Fauci.

The results of that fiasco are now obvious, even to the Governors who have to deal with the spikes in their own states-notably, Florida, Texas, and Arizona. Thousands of Covid-19 cases are flooding hospital systems. Only now are the Governors realizing that they need to get control of this runaway train, because we are still in the first inning of a nine- inning game. Only three states had the discipline to flatten the curve-New York, New Jersey and Connecticut, and that was because the leadership was strong, told the truth, gave clear directions and indicated that we needed to be disciplined and sacrifice some freedoms for the greater good. In a worldwide crisis, that is an important concept, which I hope to talk about in a future blog.

So, here we are. Many states are shut down once again, due to the fact that 50,000 cases a day set a record this week. Beaches are closed. Except for New York, there will be no fireworks. Of course, Macy's and New York will display the "works" separately over each borough, with no gathering. The majority of states have shown a serious increase in the virus. Dr. Fauci has predicted that at this rate, we could see 100,000 cases a day. Some people, like Mitch McConnell, have now commented that we should all be wearing our masks to protect one another. The Governors, who succumbed to Donald Trump's Republican pressure, have realized that they have a mess on their hands, and they need to institute strict guidelines. Of course, guidelines and one unified message should have happened from the beginning, but our President was so self-absorbed that he subverted the good of the people to his own political interests.

It will take months to begin to flatten the curves of many states, assuming the populace follows the rules. We may be separate states, but we are one people, and we need to work together. Meanwhile, millions of businesses are still closed, millions of jobs are still lost, the economy will take years to recover, and many more people will die. The world has been watching, and the other countries are dumbfounded that the greatest country on earth is failing its citizens so miserably. Our tragedy has global consequences as well. Americans are now forbidden from traveling to many other countries that have recovered from the Covid-19. That is the ultimate humiliation. The country that, under Donald Trump, has spent so much time and money keeping others out, has now been told to stay away until it cleans up its act. We need to come together, to vote, and to look forward to July 4th weekend 2021, when we have a clear sense of what it means to be Americans once again.

July 4, 2020

E Pluribus Unum

When the country was founded, "E Pluribus Unum" was the motto proposed for the first Great Seal of the United states by John Adams, Benjamin Franklin and Thomas Jefferson in 1776. A Latin phrase meaning "From Many, One." the phrase offered a strong statement of the American determination to form a single nation from a collection of states and many people.

Of course, there was great promise for the new country to offer freedom to all men when the document was written. "We hold these truths to be self-evident, that all men are created equal, that they are endowed by their Creator with certain unalienable rights, that among these are Life, Liberty, and the Pursuit of Happiness." One problem was that the founding fathers assumed that privileged men would be free, and only white men, generally ones owning property. Apparently, they never actually considered the concept that women should also have rights, and so should black men (and women).

Even with those exclusions, the Declaration of Independence was radical for its time. Remember that a very small group of rich white men (Englishmen) were the dominant class of people for centuries, and there was no sense that wouldn't be true going forward. Their birthright gave them status, and they assumed it would be forever thus.

Imagine the shock when this group of revolutionaries, now founding fathers, on the other side of the world declared that "all men are created equal." A concept that we take for granted was certainly a shock to the system of elite men everywhere, especially Englishmen.

History shows us that the new country under George Washington, was willing to offer freedom to Jewish settlers. In a response to a letter from Moses Seixas and the Hebrew Congregation of Newport, Rhode Island, Washington's response promised not only tolerance, but full liberty of conscience to all, regardless of background and religious beliefs. The letter read, "the government of the United States, which gives to bigotry no sanction, to persecution no assistance, requires only that they who live under its protection should demean themselves as good citizens, in giving it on all occasions their effectual support."

Of course, the freedom of which the founding fathers spoke, was hardly "self-evident" when southern white men went to war against the North to guarantee the lower status of the slaves, Indians and other minorities. The South lost the Civil War, something that still sits uncomfortably on its psyche.

Lincoln signed the Emancipation Proclamation in 1863, and the 13th, 14th and 15th Amendments to the Constitution gave black men the vote, and more after the Civil War.

One of Lincoln's most extraordinary speeches is also one of the shortest. He was dedicating the hallowed ground of Gettysburg, where men fought and died for the Union. A portion of it reads, "Four score and seven years ago, our fathers brought forth on this continent, a new nation, conceived in Liberty, and dedicated to the proposition that all men are created equal." In his Gettysburg address, Lincoln said that the Civil War was "testing whether that nation, or any other nation so conceived and so dedicated can long endure."

America is still "testing" that proposition, and we are at an inflection point once again. We are recalling Ben Franklin's response to a question asking what kind of government the founders crafted, when he said, "a Republic, if you can keep it." We are in dangerous territory, with a destructor as President, and we need to come together to move our country forward, not backward. "E Pluribus Unum" requires sacrifice, patriotism, unity and pushback against white nationalism and a small group of wealthy elitists who seek to own this country while denying freedom to all others. In that regard, we have a lot of work to do.

As he was sanctifying the ground of Gettysburg, Lincoln exhorted those in attendance, "that we here highly resolve that these dead shall not have died in vain-that this nation, under God, shall have a new birth of freedom-and that government of the people, by the people, and for the people, shall not perish from the earth."

Those are words for every age.

Let's hope that July 4th, 2021 sees the fruits of our labors against racism, antisemitism and white nationalism.

Independence Day should mean something for everyone, not just some. Happy July 4th!

July 6, 2020

July 4th hijacked!

Traditionally, July 4th weekend has been an opportunity for unabashed patriotism, to remind ourselves of the vision of our founders, to listen to the words of the President and process what it means to be an American.

As I looked back to the July 4th speeches of prior presidents of both parties, their words reminded me of what makes America great.

Although it was a tumultuous time in American history – (the Challenger space shuttle exploded on live television and the US and Russia were still trying to hammer out an arms control deal), in 1986 Ronald Reagan's speech focused on unity.

"All through our history our Presidents and leaders have spoken of national unity and warned us that the real obstacle to moving forward the boundaries of freedom, the only permanent danger to the hope that is America, comes from within."

John F. Kennedy said, "For 186 years this doctrine of national independence has shaken the globe-and it remains the most powerful force anywhere in the world today. There are those struggling to eke out a bare existence in a barren land who have never heard of free enterprise, but who cherish the idea of independence."

Bill Clinton envisioned, "And together, we can make the years ahead the best years our Nation has ever had if we can rise above cynicism and doubt … Our people have always known that government could not solve all the problems and that all citizens had to be responsible to build this Nation together."

In 2014, Barack Obama said, "Our success is only possible because we have never treated those self-evident truths as self-executing. Generations of Americans have marched, organized, petitioned, fought and even died to extend those rights to others, to widen the circle of opportunity for others, and to perfect this Union we love so much."

For the first time in our history, a sitting President has abandoned all desire to unify the country. Rather, Donald Trump hijacked our National Independence Day, and turned it into a campaign rally meant to divide and rage against those who don't support him. July 4th is supposed to be a day for the country to remind itself of our aspirations and shared values, no matter what political party.

However, Donald Trump conflated the holiday with "enemies," by calling out "the radical left, the Marxists, the anarchists, the agitators, the looters," riffing off his inaugural speech that spoke of "carnage." His nasty and reckless language was meant to stoke fear into the people who came to Mt. Rushmore, which is actually owned by the Lakota Indians. He also mentioned, "fascism, communism, Nazis," all of whom he said we had "defeated." It was a veritable "salad" of hot button words meant to inflame, but it was actually meaningless. Donald Trump, who doesn't read, knows nothing of the history of the Revolution, the Civil War and anything else about which he speaks. Someone else wrote that speech, and put in ideas to make Trump sound like a powerful protector of our "heritage", about which he also knows nothing.

Most important, on July 4th, there are the really important things he did not mention: the coronavirus that has claimed 131,000 lives, the economy which is declining as a result of the unsolved healthcare crisis, social justice issues and the "black lives matter" movement that has engaged the entire country, and the military scandal of Russia paying the Taliban to kill our soldiers. All of these things are on the minds of the people in the country, and Trump decided to ignore them and paint himself as the defender of Confederate statues.

There are so many agendas that we will be discussing this week. First and foremost, there is a huge surge in the coronavirus, despite the fact that Trump falsely told Americans it was "being handled" and it would "magically go away." That is nonsense! Hospitals in Texas, Arizona, Florida and California are at capacity, a result of opening too soon. The reopening concept was pushed by Donald Trump, so that the economy would look as if it was recovering. The gross selfishness of that suggestion should impress his followers that Trump is only concerned about his own re-election and not the health of the citizens. I wonder how many people are coming to the realization that he cares not one whit about them.

Testing, testing, testing! Donald Trump resisted the importance of testing, and no national program was initiated. Instead, he left testing to each state. News programs show miles of cars lined up, so people can be tested. However, testing is so limited in each of these states, that when they get to the head of the line, in some cases only 400 tests are available. Dodger Stadium, the largest testing site in the country, was shut down today, and people standing in line were told there would be no testing. Cases and hospitalizations have surged in Los Angeles county, home to millions.

Nonetheless, in his speeches, Trump has misinformed the public and spoken outright lies. He claimed that the 99% of infectious cases were harmless. Make no mistake, a person who contracts the virus can struggle mightily with the after- effects, if they survive. There can be permanent kidney damage, lung damage, stroke, and in some cases inability to walk. These people are called "long-haulers."

There is a desperate need for the government to take the reins of this disaster, and set in place a federal program. We are six months into the year when the messages could have been delivered, but they were not. There is a total vacuum coming from the White House, and the President has been forcing the CDC and Dr. Fauci to say nothing. Directions were clear: stay home, wear a mask when out, social distancing, wash hands. If fifty states had received that message from the Commander-in-Chief (and if he had worn a mask himself) tens of thousands of people would not have died, children would be able to return to school safely, businesses would reopen, and we could get to work on solving the serious problems in the country together.

Meanwhile, Trump continues to speak to divide the country, to create a distraction from his monumental failure to protect the citizens in a healthcare crisis. Instead, he is stoking a culture war with his language on July 4th weekend, equally inappropriate and dishonest.

As we watch the country slide into a major humanitarian crisis, we should consider how important it is to choose leaders with intelligence, the courage to lead, and the strength of character to responsibly own a problem.

My thoughts are with you and your families, who I hope are staying safe and keeping healthy.

July 8, 2020

One of the greatest speeches in American history was delivered by a black man on July 4th, 1852

Frederick Douglass escaped slavery in 1832 and fled north, where he became a leader in the fight to abolish slavery entirely. On July 4th, 1852, in Rochester, New York, he gave a speech that has long been considered one of the greatest in American history. It was bold, forthright and painfully honest.

The speech began with Douglass being very congenial and chatting with the crowd. Then Douglass levied a searing critique of the United States.

"You boast of your love of liberty … while the whole political power of the nation is solemnly pledged to support and perpetuate the enslavement of three million of your countrymen."

Douglass does say that the Constitution is, *"a glorious liberty document,"*

Douglass then said, *"The Fourth of July is yours, not mine. You may rejoice. I must mourn."*

If Independence Day was a time to throw a parade, Douglass would be the rain on that parade.

"What to the American slave is your 4th of July? I answer-a day that reveals to him -more than any other days in the year-the gross injustice and cruelty to which he is the constant victim. To him, your celebration is a sham."

Douglass went on, *"It is the birthday of your national independence, and of your political freedom,"* he continued, *"The distance between this platform and the slave plantation from which I escaped is considerable.*

Toward the end, Douglass gave a sense of hopefulness, of America achieving what it could become.

"Notwithstanding the dark picture I have to this day presented of the state of the nation, I do not despair of this country. There are forces in operation which must inevitably work the downfall of slavery."

The Civil War was nearly a decade away, and slavery remained firmly in place. Douglass wanted to make it clear; this was an emergency.

Frederick Douglass (1818-1895) learned to read and write while living in a slaveholder's home, despite a ban on educating slaves. He became an eminent human rights' leader, and he was the first African-American citizen to hold a high US government rank. He became one of the most famous intellectuals of his time, advising Presidents and lecturing on human rights.

Douglass wrote many books about his life. The book, *Narrative of the Life of Frederick Douglass, an American Slave,* is a classic, often required reading in high school and college, and I recommend it to everyone. His life was a human drama, from the escape from slavery dressed as a sailor, to marrying, having five children, and becoming an eloquent, admired and honored African-American.

Douglass' speech sounded the alarm, in 1852. Now in 2020, with the death of George Floyd and the response of so many Americans, we have an opportunity to make the difference about which Frederick Douglass spoke. "Black Lives Matter" resonates for many Americans, and will be the clarion call for justice and equality, after four hundred years of injustice and victimization. We need to join in the hard work that is required of all Americans, not just some.

Addendum: There is an excellent recent book, *Frederick Douglass: Prophet of Freedom*, by David Blight, Yale University, that I also recommend.

July 11, 2020

Donald Trump-Callous Man without a Plan

Once again, this week was filled with so many breaking news stories, that it was difficult to choose a topic.

Why?

We are in the middle of five crises:

1-First, there is a **worldwide pandemic** with 135,000 Americans dying to date, and more to come. Most important, we have **a leadership crisis**. No one is in charge. Donald Trump has abdicated leadership in order to focus on his own reelection, leaving each state to its own devices and Americans receiving mixed and confusing messages.

2-As a result of the pandemic, more than 40 million people lost their jobs, creating a serious **economic crisis.** The stock market was in free fall.

3- A **social justice inflection point, and crisis** in history, brought on by the murder of George Floyd, filmed on a phone, and resulting in millions of blacks and Caucasians marching together and protesting police brutality, accepting the phrase, "black lives matter." The country may have come together when faced with the reality of police brutality and four hundred years of inequality.21

4- A crisis for our **democracy**. The **rule of law** has been challenged by the Trump administration and by Attorney General Barr, in the Mueller report and cases investigating Trump and people around him. Many Inspectors General have been fired, eliminating important oversight of the government.

5-We have a **climate crisis**, ongoing deterioration, despite the fact that little attention has been paid to the state of our planet in light of the first four crises.

Looking back before the pandemic, Donald Trump approved the most shameful, cruel and outrageous program. The United States of America, normally welcoming to asylum seekers, stopped families at the southern border and separated the children, put them in cages, and had no plan to reunite them with their parents. Some parents were deported, some children were sent to other cities in the country, and some were given to foster homes. In all cases, there was no database and no plan.

Words cannot adequately describe the callousness of this program. Families who came for asylum were denied that right, even though US law allows them to appear in court. On August 16, 2018, the Trump administration put in a "zero tolerance" immigration policy. The Department of Justice began to criminally prosecute all border crossers for illegal entry, even those who crossed for the first- time seeking asylum.

Prior to 2018, the DHS (Department of Homeland Security) border crossers were dealt with through civil proceedings in immigration courts, where many could explain that they came for asylum from violent and dangerous countries. According to several defense lawyers, Border Patrol agents lied to parents and tricked them into letting go of their children.

This disaster for families coming to this country for freedom indicated that the Trump administration was dispassionate, chaotic, disorganized and ineffective. There was no sense of planning and empathy for how dangerous it was to the mental health of youngsters to be separated from their parents, and for the parents, who were frantically trying to find their children.

I will return to this nightmare at a later date in much more detail, because it deserves serious attention. Meanwhile, a wonderful investigative journalist, Jacob Soboroff, NBC News and MSNBC correspondent, spent years at the border chronicling this terrible situation. His account of what he saw and heard was published this week in a book-*Separated: Inside an American Tragedy*. It is well worth the read.

Thinking that the immigration situation was the absolute worst that the Trump administration would put into place, that changed when the pandemic came to this country. Many of us have been following the coronavirus for the last four months, when we were ordered to "shelter in place" in New York, New Jersey and Connecticut, and told to stay home, wear a mask, wash hands, social distance if we had to go somewhere.

Not only did Donald Trump have no plan to protect the country from the coronavirus, he tried to ignore its very existence. He indicated that the fifteen cases here in January would be down to zero, that it would "magically disappear." The virus was an intrusion for Trump, something that would interfere with his reelection plans, and ruin the economy, making him look incredibly bad. There was no personal empathy for the forty million people who lost their jobs and the tens of thousands who died.

Meanwhile, as he was sending these messages to the country, NOTHING was done to make sure that we had masks, PPE equipment for healthcare workers, ventilators and everything needed to fight the virus. Trump refused to take on the role of the President, did not invoke the Defense Production Act and left everything to the Governors of the individual states to fend for themselves.

Worse, Donald Trump refused to wear a mask, so he politicized wearing a mask. People who supported him also refused, most likely catching and spreading the virus. In addition, Donald

Trump sent a message that he thought the virus was a hoax, possibly a flu, but not deserving of the serious guidelines set out by the CDC and the White House Task Force scientists. In all the polls, the trust of the citizens in the scientists is 75% to 26% in Trump.

Donald Trump continued to leave the success of fighting the virus to others. Governors Cuomo, Murphy and Lamont of New York, New Jersey and Connecticut combined to give daily instructions and reports to the citizens, and they were successful in encouraging people to be disciplined, "stay home, wear a mask, wash hands and socially distance." Those three states flattened the curve, but Trump managed to influence many other states to ignore the discipline required to get the cases down.

Because the pandemic affected our economy, with 40 million people losing jobs, and businesses closed, Donald Trump was not satisfied with that result. He encouraged Republican governors to "liberate" their states, to open them, so that the economy would seem to be recovering. Meanwhile, he was insulting the Governors who held the line for their citizens and kept to the guidelines. Tens of thousands of citizens have died, and there is no end in sight. To date, 135,000 people have died, because Trump did not act to get the supplies needed by healthcare workers, did not send one consistent message to the entire country. In his own best interest, he held rallies, he was a virus denier, just as he is a science-denier and a climate-denier. Trump seems unmoved by the loss of life in a country that he heads. He is only concerned with his image and reelection.

It is important to note that it is now July, and NOTHING has been done to restock the supplies that are needed for a major spike in all the other states that Trump egged on to open-Florida, Arizona, Texas, Alabama and more. They are at capacity. The healthcare workers are exhausted and they are forced to use PPE and masks over again. Sadly, many dedicated and brave healthcare workers have died.

Shockingly, Vice President Pence, who is supposed to be in charge of leading the fight, announced at a press conference the other day that healthcare workers have been told to "preserve and reuse" gowns, masks and everything else. That is outrageous! The richest country on earth did not learn the lesson from April, and has repeated the same thing, Indeed, the situation in July is far worse than it was in April, and tens of thousands more people will die. Texas had to get refrigerator trucks, because there is no room in the morgues for the dead.

Donald Trump dropped the ball purposely on fighting the virus. He did not want to "own" this problem. He made no plan, because he didn't want to talk about the virus and the numbers of dead. It would make things look bad for his reelection. His behavior is more than malfeasance in office; it is nonfeasance. He has the blood of tens of thousands of citizens who died needlessly on his hands.

And his callousness continues. Donald Trump just announced that he wants all school children to return to classrooms in the fall. Of course, he has no plan, and this is basically none of his business. Trump most likely is unaware that he cannot "mandate" for the public schools. Citizens pay taxes and organize their schools, hire administrators, elect school boards, hire teachers and run their schools. Because he thinks that everything is his business, Trump has intruded into an area where he has no standing and knows nothing.

Whether, when and if children will return to school is an extremely complicated and delicate issue. Local citizens, school boards, teachers and parents have been working on this for months. A few things seem clear.

Donald Trump does not care about the people involved and has NO PLAN to even suggest. He just wants everyone back to school for the optics of it. He also threatened school systems that decide it is not safe at this time, and they will keep children online for a long time. Rather than being helpful, Trump has threatened to withhold money from those districts, when there is more money needed to properly implement the physical changes and the personnel changes that would be required.

Solving this problem will require the wisdom of Solomon, and there are no easy answers. Each local town and school will have to evaluate the age group and the needs of the families, as well as the age of the teachers, many of whom are in the vulnerable range.

The main concern is the health and safety of children, teachers, bus drivers, janitors and all the ancillary workers required. Just contemplating that-even in New York where the curve was flattened, is a monumental job. Mayor deBlasio and ultimately Governor Cuomo will make the decisions.

Donald Trump has no concept of how monumental the problem is. He went to private school, and his children and grandchildren attend private school. That said, the private schools are facing the same problems, but they have the resources in many cases to provide for the solutions. I do want to point out that all it takes is one child infected with the virus who can spread it among everyone else, and game over. Preventive measures must be put into place on a daily basis to monitor children and adults alike.

That brings us back to Donald Trump and how he ignored testing in March. It is universally accepted that the country needs widespread testing, contact tracing, etc. in order to have the data necessary to make decisions. Now it is July, and long lines of citizens are waiting hours in their cars to be tested. Even though Trump has bragged about 40 million tests-we have three hundred million people in this country, so he still doesn't understand what is needed.

More disturbing, he and VP Pence are still telling the country that things are "going well." That is a bold-faced lie. All the numbers indicate the exact opposite. We are in a much more serious virus tsunami than in April. Trump has tried to muzzle Dr. Fauci, who has not been allowed at a White House briefing in two months.

Again, Donald Trump's plan is to obfuscate, to lie and to spread misinformation, when the American people need one consistent message in order to stay healthy and defeat the pandemic. Until then, more people will die and the curve will continue upward. To borrow a phrase from Jacob Soboroff's book, this is our "American tragedy."

July 14, 2020

The Year of Magical Thinking

July 14, 2020

The coronavirus pandemic has highlighted the need for rigorous science, demonstrating-in real time-what the consequences can be when world leaders pay inadequate attention to what the science says. In his response to Covid-19, President Trump made statements that ignore, question or distort mainstream science. Long before the virus arrived-even before he became president-Trump was using similar techniques to deny climate change.

Then the Coronavirus arrived, from Europe.

Trump said, "It's nothing. It will go away."

"The coronavirus. We only have fifteen cases. Soon, they will be down to zero."

"The Coronavirus is going to disappear. One day-it's like a miracle-it will disappear." (February 28, 2020)

Robert Redfield, director of the Centers for Disease Control and Prevention, said in an interview on CNN that the virus was likely here to stay, probably for many months.

"Now the virus that we're talking about-you know, a lot of people think that goes away in April with the heat-as the heat comes in. Typically, that will go away in April. We're in great shape though." (February 10, 2020)

Some coronaviruses are seasonal. Scientists still don't know whether the virus that causes COVID-19 will be seasonal. Findings of a recent study suggest that the virus is spreading most readily in cooler temperature zones. The *Washington Post* reports, however, that the study does not conclude that the virus will be significantly reduced in the summer.

Trump proceeded to blame the Democrats, since he had no one to blame but himself.

"Now the Democrats are politicizing the coronavirus. You know that, right? Coronavirus. They're politicizing it … And this is their new hoax." (February 28, 2020)

By this time, the U.S. had confirmed 60 cases of coronavirus. The CDC had already warned the public to prepare for the virus to spread, assuring them that it was not a hoax. Important guidelines -stay home, wear a mask, socially distance, wash hands, were announced to the country, but Trump refused to wear a mask, thereby politicizing it, and all the other guidelines, leaving the country confused. Who to believe?

Trump continued the lying and mixed messages.

"Anybody that needs a test can have a test. They are all set. They have them out there. In addition to that they are making millions more as we speak but as of right now and yesterday anybody that needs a test, that is the important thing." (March 6, 2020)

Contrary to Trump's assertion, patients and healthcare workers were complaining that they could not get access to coronavirus tests. A few days later, testifying to a House committee, Dr. Anthony Fauci, director of the National Institute of Allergy and Infectious Diseases, acknowledged tests were not yet widely available. 'The idea of anybody getting it easily the way people in other countries are doing it-we're not set up for that."

Donald Trump, eager to ignore the death toll and wanting the country to get back to work, bullied some of the states, many with Democratic governors, who were trying to keep the citizens healthy. "Liberate Michigan" became a call, as he tried to push Gretchen Whitmer to reopen.

Some of the states that he bullied to open-Florida, Arizona and Texas, for instance, are now inundated with viruses that are spiking. The governors are learning a massive lesson, and beginning to understand the consequences of listening to Trump's unfounded ideas, served up on tweets. There were no substantive reasons for these states to reopen, because they had not flattened the curve. Now they are out of control, and Donald Trump is still ignoring reality and spreading his "magical thinking." However, people are dying.

And Trump continued to tell his stories.

"I always treated the Chinese virus very seriously, and have done a good job from the beginning, including my very early decision to close the 'borders' from China-against the wishes of almost all." Many lives were saved. The Fake News new narrative is disgraceful and false!" (March 18, 2020)

Trump was urged to stop calling COVID-19 the "Chinese Virus," a term he used repeatedly, and that people have called racist and dangerous. Asian citizens have been very insulted by the term, and they have also been victims of hate speech and violent crimes, often against older Asian citizens. It is horrible.

Many public health experts have criticized the administration's lack of preparation and failure to act quickly when the virus was first recognized in January. Joe Biden wrote an OP-ED in January, saying that America is unprepared for a virus or pandemic. He knew the situation from being Vice President in the Obama administration, when they fought the ebola outbreak.

The deaths-of the numbers that were supposed to be going away, according to Donald Trump-have reached 135,000 as of this date, and are continuing to rise.

There are entirely too many of these lies and distortions to report. Recently, Trump has begun to criticize Dr. Fauci, demeaning him, even though he is a highly respected scientist who has served many presidents of both parties.

Polls show that Americans trust Dr. Fauci (76%) more than Donald Trump's handling of the coronavirus (26%). Trump. The ultimate narcissist is jealous of Dr. Fauci, and has side-lined him. Trump and Fauci have not met for a briefing in two months.

Magical thinking does not make a virus disappear. Hard work and uniting the country will do the job. That takes leadership. Do your job, Mr. President. The virus knows no political parties, no boundaries and no favorites. It kills all Americans, indiscriminately, and we are losing a lot of very special citizens. Give up your "magical thinking," and tune into science.

July 18, 2020

The Ultimate Selfish, Dangerous Idea-send all children back to school in the fall … with no federal plan or support

July 15, 2020

Donald Trump, in a desperate last- ditch effort to show that the country is recovering, announced that "all school children should go back to school in the fall." Really? We are in the midst of the most serious health crisis in American history, with no national plan, 140,000 dead, and rising numbers in a majority of states.

Trump's "mandate" is so transparent. If everything opened and children were back in school, it would seem as if the country is on a good path. Donald Trump, in his own self-interest, wants businesses and schools to open, despite the danger of contracting the virus, spreading it and having thousands more die. He is, after all, running for reelection, his numbers are way down and he only cares about himself.

Fortunately, Trump has no standing to make this decision. When we send our children into harm's way, it can never be a unilateral "one size fits all." Whether children return to school will be decided by state and local people. The decision relies on the data, and where each locality is able to plan for the health and safety of the children and all others involved. These decisions are incredibly difficult, and they require the wisdom of Solomon.

Fortunately, we do have some role models. Other countries, such as South Korea, Australia, New Zealand, Norway, Finland, Singapore, Denmark and Austria have been able to reopen schools. How were they successful? The governments immediately locked down each country, and then put in mitigations that required every citizen to wear a mask and to socially distance. Each country instituted countrywide testing for every citizen, followed by contact tracing. Orders for individuals were to wash hands many times a day and be alert not to touch their faces, eyes, etc., if possible.

Tragically, the United States response was to do nothing. In fact, Donald Trump politicized wearing masks. As a result, we wasted four months, between March and June, with no consistent message to wear masks, no countrywide testing program and no stockpiling of PPE for healthcare workers. Now it is July. Donald Trump's non-leadership left the states to fend for themselves, and to compete for supplies. In many cases, states were forced to spend more money than if the federal government had assumed control and taken responsibility. As we've discussed before, Donald Trump tried to tell the country that the virus was like a flu, was nothing much, and it would go away, "magically."

Some governors rose to the occasion brilliantly. Larry Hogan, President of the Governors' Conference and a Republican, used his ability to get millions of masks from South Korea, where his wife was born. He wrote a scathing Op-Ed of Trump in the *Washington Post* on July 16, titled "*Fighting Alone.*" It is well worth reading.

Massachusetts' Governor, Charlie Baker, also a Republican, sent a consistent message to his citizens to wear masks and socially distance. Then he held meetings sharing the numbers, which got low enough that the state can consider a phased reopening. Massachusetts is presently in the process of planning a "roadmap" for schools, with guidelines.

In New York, Mayor de Blasio, announced his plan for schools to reopen for at least some in-person instruction in the fall. Proposing three models of staggered in-person instruction, de Blasio's blended learning plan would allow for in-person attendance to range from one to three days a week. However, Governor Cuomo said for in-person classes to be allowed, a region must be in Phase 4 of reopening, which New York City is not. School districts must also be in regions where the daily infection rate remains at 5% or lower, over a fourteen day average. Cuomo said that final decisions on reopening will be made during the first week of August. Even though the state did remarkably well, flattening the curve, Governor Cuomo is being cautious.

States that followed Trump-Arizona, Texas, Florida, Alabama and Georgia, are now in serious trouble, with Covid-19 raging and hospitals overwhelmed. There are lessons to be learned here. Some leaders are seeing that a simple direction that can save lives needs to be accepted as good for America, not politics. Governor Kay Ivey, Republican of Alabama, has just changed her mind and mandated masks.

To be clear, if Donald Trump had acted responsibly in March and marshaled the powerful forces of the federal government, we would not be in this situation. If there was an immediate lockdown, a countrywide testing process and an order for citizens to wear masks, the curve would have flattened and schools would be able to open this fall. Parents would not be faced with terrible choices about child care and whether or not they could go back to work. This is a nightmare of Donald Trump's making. He sowed the seeds of doubt in his followers, and now the country is in chaos. In July, we are in a worse place than we were in April, and that reality is staggering.

Trump, in his cruel and dismissive comments, indicated that there is an acceptable risk of some children dying as long as everyone is back in school. That is callous, self-serving, outrageous, and absolutely unacceptable.

Facts matter. Science matters. Numbers don't lie. The coronavirus is infecting citizens, and numbers in thirty-nine states out of fifty are rising. Common sense should tell the leaders that this is not the environment where you decide to send children and their teachers to school. The states that have good leaders have positive results. In addition to Cuomo, Murphy and Lamont of NY, NJ and Connecticut, Charlie Baker in Massachusetts, Hogan of Delaware, as well as Vermont and New Hampshire, states have flattened the curve sufficiently to consider opening the schools in various configurations. Health and safety are the priority.

Yes, children need to go back to school. One estimate was that 71% of students suffered when distance learning was initiated. Many students were never able to take advantage of learning on the internet. Twenty million students rely on meals when they are in school. In addition, being in school protects numerous students from child abuse. There is also a large population of disabled students who are served in school, so missing school is damaging. These are sad facts, but they need to be taken into consideration when making decisions.

One disturbing reality is that Donald Trump has been criticizing Dr. Anthony Fauci, and discrediting him. Moreover, this week there was an announcement that the hospital numbers which are normally sent to the CDC to be evaluated, would now go directly to HHS, Health and Human Services. That is very suspect.

For example, it was found that Florida was actually hiding its numbers when Governor Ron de Santis refused to adhere to simple guidelines. Now, Florida is a hotspot with raging numbers, and is slated to host the Republican convention in a few weeks. The concept that Trump has mandated the numbers to bypass the CDC, which is the preeminent science organization in our country and the world, going instead to HHS, indicates that Trump wants control of the numbers. Control means that those numbers can be manipulated and used for personal political purposes. There is so much lack of courage in these leaders. I want to leave this story and turn to a man of culture and courage, who died last night.

I don't want to let this moment pass without mentioning that we lost one of the finest American journalists last night in Paris. Christopher Dickey died of a heart attack at age 68. It is a tragic loss much too early, of an erudite gentleman, a brilliant writer, and fascinating war correspondent. Chris Dickey reported from Paris, always live, no matter how early he had to get up to make the news show. He was a marvelous storyteller, and he managed to meet all the people he needed to know in order to get a good story. I am so sorry that he is gone. I always wanted to be a foreign correspondent, and he was one of my idols.

You might also go onto YouTube to pull up the latest words from Chris about how horrified he was at what is happening to America. It was the day that protestors stormed the Michigan state house with guns in opposition to Governor Whitmer. Chris Dickey was a true patriot and an example of a proud American, who recognized and reported on our failings as well as our victories. He loved this country, and he saw the best and the worst of America from the vantage point of Paris.

July 20, 2020

John Lewis, "the conscience of the Congress," died at the age of 80 on Friday night

July 18, 2020

We've lost a great American hero. Born in Alabama, John Lewis was the son of a sharecropper, and had only seen two white people for the first few years of his life. As a youngster, he went to the public library to borrow a book, and was told that black children were not allowed to take out books. As a result of being denied a book, John Lewis decided that he was going to be an educated man. He graduated from Fisk University and went on to higher education.

There are so many wonderful stories about John Lewis. I first became aware of him when he was one of the original thirteen "Freedom Riders", black and white activists, who rode down south to sit in at lunch counters. Because it was a nonviolent movement, I wondered how they were going to protect themselves. In truth, they got bloodied, often arrested, yet their resolve never faltered. I was in college and the stories of the risks and bravery were stunning. More people joined the "Freedom Rides" on buses. We had a classmate who rode on a "freedom" bus, was arrested and put in jail. I remember the entire school raising money to free her.

John Lewis was just seventeen when he wrote a letter to Martin Luther King expressing his desire to be part of the movement. King wrote back and invited him to join his inner circle. John Lewis was the youngest, and he was impatient and also a firebrand. The older activists had seen so much disappointment and, as a result, had a much longer arc of expectations.

John Lewis was in the forefront of the efforts to end the Jim Crow laws. He was arrested more than forty times, and often bloodied. On the march across the Edmund Pettus Bridge from Selma to Montgomery, he was in the front, and his skull was fractured. Expecting to spend the night in jail, he brought a backpack, two books and a toothbrush. Having been seriously injured, he wound up in the hospital instead.

From then on, the march was known as "Bloody Sunday." The activists were marching for voting rights. Shortly afterwards, President Lyndon Johnson saw the newsreel of the violence, and he was horrified. He pledged to protect the black population, and in 1965 he signed the Voting Rights Act into law.

In 1963, at age twenty-three, John Lewis was the youngest speaker at the March on Washington. In his fiery speech, Lewis showed his impatience when he said, "How long can we be patient? We want our freedom and we want it now!" He was brash, and inspirational. Martin Luther King mentored him, and was incredibly impressed with Lewis' toughness, dedication, passion and bravery.

John Lewis married and lived in Atlanta with his wife and five children. He was elected to Congress, and represented the 5th Congressional district for seventeen terms, since 1987. He was the dean of the Georgia Congressional delegation, and was often referred to as the "moral voice of the Congress." Having been denied a book as a black child, he wrote and published a number of books.

Barack Obama presented John Lewis with the Medal of Freedom, acknowledging the amazing courage and persistence with which he continued the fight. Since the medal could be presented by the first black President, it was a very meaningful moment in the White House.

After the murder of George Floyd, John Lewis, standing among the black and white protestors in Lafayette square, said he was very hopeful that things had changed and would continue to be different. He saw that moment as an inflection point.

John Lewis was passionate, and his passion inspired students in the next generation. He mentored many young people, encouraged them to become fighters for civil rights and to run for office.

While he was a fighter, John Lewis was diagnosed with pancreatic cancer last December, and said that it was, "the fight of his life." Unfortunately, he lost that fight last Friday, and we lost a great American.

July 20, 2020

Two extraordinary interviews, bookends to a disturbing weekend in Portland, Oregon

The weekend began with Mary Trump, having written a scathing book about her uncle Donald, giving her reasons that he is "unfit for office." Rachael Maddow was the masterful interviewer, and we heard a litany of dreadful realities, in addition to the 20,000 lies tabulated by *The Washington Post,* and other stories we know from the last three years. It was during the evening, that we learned of the sad death of Congressman Lewis. The juxtaposition of a truly fine man, now gone, with a callous unfeeling man, ever-present, was strangely chilling. Donald Trump is the antithesis of the late John Lewis.

On Sunday evening, another disturbing interview was a wild and woolly ride. Chris Wallace, a truly fine reporter from FOX News, interviewed Donald Trump. When he asked Trump how he would assess his presidency, Trump complained about all the unfair treatment he got. Wallace tried valiantly to get Trump back to his question, to no avail.

Wallace: "What about the good parts, sir?"

Trump: No, no. I want to do this. I have done more than any other president in history in the first three and a half years, and I've done it through suffering through investigations by a bunch of thieves, crooks," etc.

Wallace could not get him away from rehashing his grievances, and he ended the interview.

It was disturbing to hear Trump's version of the Covid-19 cases that were caught by young people. "some of those cases are those of young people who heal in a day. They have the sniffles and we put it down as a test. Many of them—don't forget, I guess it's like 99.7 percent, people are going to get better, and in many cases, they're going to get better very quickly." This is absolute nonsense. Trump is unaware of the trajectory of the virus, or the residual ailments that remain after people of all ages recover.

These two interviews were bookends to a bizarre weekend. The most important and truly disturbing event is that the federal government sent in troops, unmarked, with tear gas and weapons, to stop what they described as "violent anarchists." This was the second time that Trump set troops on private citizens, and it is dangerous. It looks like we are living in a third world country. The local Portland police indicated that they could handle the fireworks, graffiti and other things done in the city, but Trump wanted to call the troops.

The mayor, both Senators, and the Governor of Oregon have requested the troops to be withdrawn, but Trump refuses. Ted Wheeler, the Mayor of Portland, noted that the protests were winding down before the federal troops came and escalated the situation.

Trump and AG William Barr indicated they are working with the Acting Head of the Department of Homeland Security to "go in" to make communities safe. That indicates more federal troops will be coming to our cities, and that is outrageous. Rather than protecting the country from the coronavirus, Trump is putting himself out as the protector of the people from "violent anarchists."

We are not a third world country, but under Donald Trump we are becoming one. He is threatening to send troops to our other cities. The leadership of the cities need to respond strongly and legally.

The Oregon US Attorney recognized that the administration had gone too far. He said, "Based on news accounts circulating that allege federal law enforcement detained two protestors without probable cause, I have requested the Department of Homeland Security Office of the Inspector General to open a separate investigation directed specifically at the actions of DHS personnel."

The Oregon Attorney General reacted instantly. Ellen Rosenblum sued the Department of Homeland Security and the Marshals Service in federal court, to try to get court order to stop federal agents for "the current escalation of fear and violence in downtown Portland."

It is clear that Trump is using the federal troops to violate the rights of citizens. Although there is little to do with public safety and more to do with politics, it is a very disturbing turn of events. As citizens, we need to be watching carefully, and responding.

More on this in my next blogs.

Meanwhile, pay close attention. Donald Trump is desperate due to his tanking poll numbers, and he is using desperate measures that damage our democracy.

July 21, 2020

What are federal law enforcement officers doing in Portland?

There have been protestors on the streets of Portland since shortly after the death of George Floyd. Mostly, the protests have been peaceful, although there have been incidents of violence, property damage and vandalism from outside groups. These demonstrations have gone on for fifty-four days.

As I mentioned yesterday, there is a strange cohort of what appears to be about 100 federal law enforcement officers on the streets of Portland. Why is it strange? For one thing, they are not wearing identifiable uniforms or any other insignia. For another, they are not driving marked law enforcement vehicles, and they are not identifying themselves either publicly or to those whom they have detained and arrested. Apparently, they are there due to an Executive Order from Donald Trump to protect monuments and federal property. However, they have clashed violently with peaceful protestors, assaulting them and sometimes grabbing them off the streets and shoving them into unmarked vans.

One troubling example, of which there is a video, shows a Navy veteran who was troubled by what he saw on his television. Never having been in a protest, he came down and tried to engage these forces in conversation. A graduate of Annapolis, he asked them if they were aware of their oath to the Constitution, whereupon they responded by beating him, pepper spraying him and breaking his hand. Another man's skull was fractured and he is in the hospital.

Considering that the complaints from the Department of Homeland Security against what it calls "violent anarchists," are primarily graffiti and minor vandalism, the local police have indicated that they are well able to handle the situation.

This hearkens back to Lafayette Square, a few weeks ago, when Donald Trump and AG Barr sent similar forces to clear the way, so that Trump could take a photo-op with a Bible, which he was holding upside down.

Similar to that event, when DC Mayor Bowser strongly opposed federal troops moving peaceful protestors, the Portland governor, mayor and the sheriff, have insisted that they don't want what looks like a para-military force on their streets. We have never seen the likes of this in our country until Donald Trump took office. He has abused the presidency to a fare thee well. The presence of a paramilitary force has actually inflamed the situation in Portland. More citizens have taken to the streets to defend the protestors against the feds. Notably, the "Wall of Moms," dressed in yellow shirts, waved their hands above the heads and sang: "Hands up, please don't shoot me."

Equally disturbing is that Chad Wolf, the Acting Homeland Security Secretary, has repeatedly claimed that he doesn't need local authorities' permission to come into Portland. It's important to note that Wolf is just the "Acting" Director. He is not a confirmed member of the Cabinet. He has not received Senate confirmation for the job, and that is the way that Trump operates. He only appoints "acting" people, so he can control them and they don't have to be qualified to undergo Senate approval. Wolf dismissed objections to the federal intervention by saying, "I don't need an invitation by the state, state mayors or state governors to do our job. We're going to do that, whether they like us there or not." That statement sets up an immediate adversarial relationship that can only further inflame the citizens against the feds, who are already physically dangerous.

Worse still, Donald Trump has announced that it will be sending similar federal officers to Chicago, and perhaps New York, Baltimore, etc., all cities that he described as being run by "liberal Democrats." This is purely political, and it seems to be a shift away from the pandemic numbers, which he would like to ignore, to the idea that he is the law and order president. Things are not going well in his re-election campaign, and Trump is desperately seeking a new line.

Of the Portland stunt, he said, "We're going to have more federal enforcement, that I can tell you. In Portland, they've done a fantastic job. They've been there three days and they really have done a fantastic job in a very short period of time, no problem." It appears that the federal government believes it has the power to deploy federal law enforcement authorities across the country, even over the objections of the relevant local and state officials. This is hardly the case, but Donald Trump continues to live in his own world of "magical thinking."

This is all about our democracy, and we need to keep an eye on the events as they unfold.

July 22, 2020

The Trump Virus

July 21, 2020

Donald Trump returned to the podium tonight to give what was billed as a "briefing" on the coronavirus. He came with no science experts-Dr. Fauci and Dr. Birx were nowhere in sight. Right out of the gate, Trump referred to the virus as the "**China** virus," repeating a dangerous racist accusation that insults Chinese citizens and promulgated violence when it was first used. He pointedly repeated the term, "Chinese virus," in his short speech. The blame game has become a part of the Trump commentary throughout the last six months. Trump "takes no responsibility" for the spread of this virus.

It was six months to the day that the first virus was diagnosed in America, on January 20th, 2020. Ironic. Worried that a pandemic would make the economy look bad, which would endanger his re-election, Donald Trump chose to ignore the reality of a major healthcare crisis. He came up with no national strategy. As president, he had the power to institute a testing, tracing, the Defense Production Act, and a consistent message on masks and social distancing, but he punted, and left it to the governors.

Six months later, with 142,000 Americans dead, Donald Trump still has no national plan. He referenced that he was "working on a strategy," but we've heard that before, and he put nothing forward. If he did have a plan, he would have to admit that he was wrong in the beginning. He will never admit that he was wrong.

In fact, with his numbers tanking, Donald Trump, forced by his advisors, realized that he needed a course correction and that the country's number one concern was the healthcare crisis. His initial non- response and the rambling briefings accounted for a steep slide in his numbers, and he was on track to lose the election.

The healthcare crisis has to be solved before the economy can recover. Only then can the country reopen. In reality, the speech was for political purposes, rather than a true belief in the science of Dr. Fauci, who is esteemed by the majority of the country. Notably, Trump did not invite Dr. Fauci to appear with him at the briefing.

Trump read from a prepared text in a monotone voice, showing no empathy for our dead citizens. After months of pushback, the president finally said that people should wear a mask, the first time ever, although it was not a full-throated endorsement. He also said that if people cannot do social distancing, they should wear a mask. Trump sounded very unenthusiastic about this speech, which thankfully stuck to the script, and lasted just twenty minutes. He took a few questions, although nothing about Russia paying the Taliban to kill our soldiers or the streets of Portland.

I have no idea if that speech will make a difference in the perception that the president did nothing to protect us. If this speech had been given in the first week in April, it would have made a difference and saved 40,000 citizens. Reading it now leaves Donald Trump a day late and a dollar short. Having four months to learn about the situation, Trump seems to know nothing about the virus, the numbers, or how to fix the problem.

That said, Donald Trump continued to spread misinformation. With 80,000 dead since his last briefing, he said that the virus will "just disappear." In the most serious public health crisis in the history of our country, the president doesn't seem to understand that nationwide testing is crucial. Rather, he indicated that testing produces more cases, instead of finding out who has the virus. He did say that "things will get worse before they get better," but I don't think he knows how bad.

The CDC has reported that the true number of cases is much larger than reported. Painting a rosier picture would be dangerous. Donald Trump reported that fatalities fell 75%, which he said was "a great number." The truth is that fatalities are up 54%. These are real **people** who died, not just percentages. Trump went on to extol our testing, but we have labs empty, because there are no supplies for scientists with which to test. We have only tested a small percentage of the population, and it takes days to get the results, which makes them useless.

Further, Trump said that he has been supporting the governors 100%, which we know is not true. He said that "no governor needs anything right now." In fact, our governors have been begging the government for more supplies and help, as they battle rising cases, shortages of PPE and filled hospital beds. Trump also said that hospitals are open for elective surgery. That claim can't be true in Texas, Florida, Arizona, Alabama, and California, because the hospitals are filled with rising

Covid-19 cases. In those states, refrigerator trucks had to be brought in to act as morgues, and a call went out to funeral directors to help with the overflow of deaths.

Trump showed a chart comparing where we are compared to the rest of the world, and bragged that our testing is the best in the world." The president said he has "learned a great deal about the virus," and the government has been "relentless from the beginning." In fact, the danger was denied, the virus was called a "democratic hoax," confusing and politicizing millions of people in the country. Now we are in a chaotic mess that is worse than the April briefing.

I would like to suggest that, from now on, this disaster be called the TRUMP VIRUS. After all, he owns it. The lives of 140,000 are on his hands, and there will be more. Denying responsibility is shameless, and unpatriotic. He took an oath, after all.

Donald Trump: You Could have been a contender

July 23, 2020

Four months ago, Dr. David Ho, an eminent virologist and researcher, appeared on the Rachael Maddow show and said that Americans have two choices. Simultaneously, we could shut the entire country and shelter in place, wear masks, wash hands, practice social distancing even at home, and we could defeat the virus within a number of weeks.

Or, we could ignore that advice and the country would be opening sequentially. In that case, the virus would claim hundreds of thousands of lives and would go on for years. Unfortunately, we are in the latter group, because Donald Trump chose to ignore the virus for months. He has just acknowledged the value of masks (he keeps it in his pocket), and social distancing (but not at his hotel the other night).

This epiphany came when Trump realized that his poll numbers have tanked, and that the virus is the number one concern of citizens of both parties.

Dr. Ho brought these comparative charts.

For the last few times, Donald Trump has put himself out in front of the cameras to give what he terms, a "briefing" on the coronavirus, which he insultingly continues to name the "China" virus. I would caution Trump against continuing that insult, because some of our most eminent Chinese-Americans are scientists who have been solving problems in this country for decades.

Dr. Ho was a resident at Cedars-Sinai in 1981, when he came in contact with some of the first reported cases of what was later identified as AIDS. He has been at the forefront in research of the AIDS pandemic. That research formed the foundation for the pioneering effort to treat HIV "early and hard," and in demonstrating the control of patients receiving combination antiretroviral therapy. This was the turning point in the epidemic when an automatic death sentence was transformed into a manageable disease.

Dr. Ho returned to the Maddow Show the other night and reiterated that, while it would not be impossible, we have to make a bold decision to shut down, otherwise our country will be mired in this disaster for a long time.

Donald Trump should not be appearing and giving a rosy picture about how things are improving in many states. He should have Dr. Fauci appear with him, use charts and actual numbers, present choices, no matter how difficult.

It's time to make a consistent national plan. It takes discipline, will and leadership. The governors of New York, NJ and Connecticut saw the choice and led their states to flatten the curve. Donald could have done it four months ago. He could have been a leader, a contender, and he chose to do nothing. Thousands more people will die, needlessly, and their blood is on his hands.

I highly recommend reading Dr. David Ho's biography and complete CV. It is inspiring.

John Lewis: love and forgiveness were his guiding principles

July 23, 2020

Days ago, I wanted to write about love and forgiveness, the two guiding principles of John Lewis' life, but disturbing news stories kept interfering. Today, without further adieu, I want to pay tribute to Congressman Lewis' humanity.

By now, we have become aware of John Lewis' history- how he overcame the poverty of a sharecropper's son, went to college, married and represented Georgia's 5th district since 1987. The biography alone is inspiring. However, what came through in his own words was that, despite being beaten, jailed more than 40 times, and physically hurt on numerous occasions, John Lewis described himself as a forgiving person. As an example, he told the story of the Ku Klux Klan member who told him that, years earlier, he had beaten John Lewis, who answered, "'I forgive you." As videos of his life played during the week, similar stories emerged, again and again.

In addition, when he talked about the feelings that he thought were the most important, he answered that love was the single most important thing that human beings must have for one another. In this difficult time that is so hate-filled, the concept of love being the key to humanity is powerful and bears contemplating.

Perhaps, while he was fighting for justice, Lewis also loved his fellowman, even though they were flawed and hated him. The ability to forgive those who have hurt us shows a personal strength of character that few people have, but it is worth cultivating.

As I am writing this, I want to tell you about my mother. July 23rd, today, is actually her birthday, (she would be 113 were she alive), and she was all about love and forgiving. My mom loved my dad and me unequivocally, as well as her closest family. She sip, and always looked for the best in people. In fact, she was optimistic about life, and shared that idea with me often.

The forgiving part was more difficult to impart to a youngster, but she would encourage me to forgive a playmate, or someone else who might have done something that was difficult to accept. My mother always looked on the bright side of things, and no matter how nasty or insulting a situation became, she would encourage me to forgive it. Retaliation was never an option, because it was debilitating

July 25, 2020

Millions face eviction and Republican Senators leave town for the weekend/Trump cancels Florida and shifts to "law and order" in the wake of his tanking poll numbers

July 24, 2020

Senate Majority Leader, Mitch McConnell is usually able to get his Republicans in line for a major vote. He failed this week, and that failure will have disastrous repercussions for millions of Americans. Enhanced unemployment benefits ($600 additional weekly check) end now, and the Senate Republicans left town, with McConnell saying that he won't have a plan for "weeks." In addition, a four-month federal moratorium on rent collection and eviction is expiring. This is an outrageous dereliction of duty on the part of the Republicans in the Senate, especially in the midst of a pandemic.

What will be the result? Millions of Americans will not be able to pay their rent or mortgages. Many will become homeless. Furthermore, our citizens will not have money for food, or anything that the additional check was helping to fund. There are no words to describe how horrible this is for everyone, especially those with children. Americans are anxious enough about the virus, and now they may be forced to live in very close quarters just to have a roof over their heads. The Senate Republicans left Americans high and dry in the midst of the chaos that Donald Trump has caused. It was a callous and uncaring response.

What chaos you ask? He caused confusion by giving false and misleading information about the existence of the virus to the American public, as early as February/March. Then he politicized something as important (and simple) as wearing a mask. Trump would not be wearing one, he announced. He refused to initiate a nationwide testing program, which the CDC indicated would be necessary to fight the pandemic. De. Fauci also touted the importance of masks and testing, and Trump did not support either.

For weeks, Donald Trump, virus denier ("it's a hoax") came before the American people on television and basically used the time for a campaign speech- to criticize Democrats, insult Joe Biden and everyone else he considered to be his enemy. Without a script, he rambled on for an hour or more, while thousands of people were dying in front of our eyes. It is our American scandal, the worst in the history of the country.

In contrast, the House Democrats passed a stimulus Bill and sent it to the Senate in May. It reinstated a $600 help and other means to support peoples' small businesses. That bill sat on Mitch McConnell's desk and nothing got done. It is still sitting there. With no empathy for American citizens, Republican Senators left town. Interestingly, the Republicans are not fighting the Democrats. They are fighting amongst themselves, and disagreeing about what fiscal solution is proper. Many Senators have the idea that the enhanced unemployment money was actually a disincentive to get back to work. That seems to be a cynical interpretation of helping citizens pay their bills.

Fast forward to this past week when Donald Trump decided to resume his "briefings." The truth is that his advisors showed him a map of the states where the virus is spiking. They very strongly showed Trump that his poll numbers were directly related to his failure to lead on the coronavirus. The country needed a leader and a strong plan and got nothing, so people have switched their votes to Joe Biden, who is leading by double digits in many battleground states. According to the narrative, Trump finally realized the virus actually matters most to citizens (it took six months!), and he decided to change his message. Of course, he is a day late and a dollar short. However, he came out to speak with the people, reading a prepared script, filled with phony ideas of how much he cares about the safety and security of Americans. Then, he announced a bombshell. Based on his sudden concern, he is cancelling the Republican Convention that was to be held in Jacksonville, Florida.

In truth, many people were not planning to attend anyway. At least six Republican Senators (including Mitt Romney) announced they would not be there. The RNC was having trouble raising money for the event, and reservations were trickling in. It looked like it could be another Tulsa, with scant attendance and even less enthusiasm. Moreover, all of the room reservations needed to be cancelled by Monday. Otherwise, the RNC would be responsible for all the money. Changing plans from North Carolina to Florida had already cost a small fortune.

Most important, Trump's key advisors showed him on a map that the virus was spiking and spreading in red states, his voters, and would most likely continue on that trajectory. He finally started to understand that this was a major crisis for the country and for himself. Only then, did Donald Trump cancel Florida, and he actually half-heartedly told the American people they should probably wear a mask.

Of course, the irony of Trump's situation is that it's hard to cancel an event to keep people safe, while you are telling the entire country that school children must go in person. That leaves his credibility somewhere between a rock and a hard place. But never fear, it is not his decision anyway. The states and local schools and colleges will make their own decisions, based only on the number one priority of the safety of children and adults involved.

Trump's "briefings" had a shallow feel to them. For one thing, he did not invite Dr. Fauci or anyone else to share the meeting. Trump was jealous of Dr. Fauci, because polls showed that citizens believed Fauci. It was only the "Trump show," and it fell flat.

Donald Trump is in a corner. The economy is in bad shape, with more than 40 million people having lost their jobs. Another1.4 million filled for unemployment last week. In addition, the "Back Lives Matter" protests have motivated black and white citizens to march together for justice.

The virus, the economy, and "black lives matter" are the three issues that matter to Americans right now. Donald Trump is feeling boxed in by the possibility that he may lose the election. He is desperate, and so he has switched to the all too familiar theme of "law and order." Nixon used it, as did Reagan, but this is different. Trump characterized "democratic, liberal" cities as being hotbeds of crime that needed him to go in and fix the problems. That is very dangerous.

Even though there were mostly peaceful protests in Portland, Oregon, Donald Trump sent in what amounts to be a para-military force to the city. Unfortunately, the people were not there to solve problems. In fact, the protests were winding down, and the arrival of the police force inflamed the citizens. More citizens arrived, and a "Wall of Moms" formed to protect the protestors from the federal troops. The "Moms" were tear-gassed. Veterans arrived to protect the entire situation against the feds.

One of the bulwarks of our country is the right to protest. That right is in the First Amendment of the Constitution. Sending in troops to attack peaceful protestors is unconstitutional. We will discuss how dangerous this is to our democracy in my next blog.

Meanwhile, keep your eyes open, watch the news and look for conversations around "fascism," by thought leaders who see Trump's actions as threatening our democracy.

There *are wonderful resources to read. Madeleine Albright wrote a book called "Fascism," a few years ago. There is a marvelous article in the Atlantic by Anne Applebaum*. I highly recommend an Op-Ed in the New York Times today, sent to me by my friends in Paris. *American Catastrophe Through*

German Eyes. The Germans are worried about what they see on our streets. Make a folder and collect some of these writings, because our democracy will be a major issue in the next 100 days.

Meanwhile, please stay safe and keep healthy, wear your mask, wash your hands and practice social distancing. Enjoy the weekend to the best of your ability …

It's time for the "F" word: fascism

July 26, 2020

In the middle of a tragic pandemic, the resulting economy, where tens of millions have lost their jobs, and protestors peacefully marching in solidarity for justice, Donald Trump sent paramilitary forces into Portland, Oregon to supposedly "keep the peace." The result was the exact opposite. The men were uninvited and provoked anger and violence. These forces, many from Homeland Security, are Border Patrol and other groups untrained in maintaining calm during reasonable protests.

The picture of mostly unmarked troops in riot gear, picking up peaceful citizens and shoving them into unmarked vehicles on American streets, is chilling. For older Americans, who lived through the Holocaust in Germany, the tactics are particularly frightening, and reminiscent of fascism and the Nazis. This is Donald Trump's brand of showing his own power, especially since his personal situation is actually quite weak. Americans are angry, sick and afraid of dying, frightened, out of work and resentful of a president who could have provided leadership. but did nothing. Being basically tone-deaf, Trump amazingly managed to ignore these realities until this week, when he was shown a map of the spreading virus into the "red" states, and his poll numbers. He came face to face with the prospect of crushing defeat.

Rather than trying to alleviate the terrible coronavirus situation, Donald Trump reverted to type and started to create chaos in another area. The new problem was now "law and order" in America's mostly "democrat liberal" cities, and he was sending in troops to save the situation.

Looking back in history, In 1933, after the Reichstag burned, Hitler issued the "Decree of the Reich President for the Protection of People and State," as his means to seize power. Now, he is threatening to send troops into more cities, although the mayors and governors have indicated they do not want them coming. The unwanted police have only provoked trouble, rather than actually solving problems.

Michael Steinberg, history professor at Brown, wrote to Op-Ed columnist, Roger Cohen, this week:

"The American catastrophe seems to get worse every day, but the events in Portland have particularly alarmed me as a kind of strategic experiment in fascism."

Steinberg continued, "The basic comparison involves racism as a political strategy … with cities demonized as places of decadence."

Trump has been tearing down our institutions piece by piece, decimating the systems by which the military and the Department of Justice, among others, operate. Wanting to eliminate oversight of his own corrupt activities, the president fired numerous Inspectors-General, who were tasked with making sure that our laws are followed. Loyal and extraordinary civil servants have been vilified and fired unceremoniously. If Trump perceived them as trying to carry out their jobs, rather than doing what he wanted, he insulted them in tweets and ended their careers. Colonel Vindman, who was on the call when Trump tried to have a "quid pro quo" with the President of Ukraine, was escorted out of the White House after he testified and lost his job, his promotion, everything. He now needs Secret Service protection. We have had four years of retaliatory politics, resulting in the fact that many people are afraid to speak even when they see something is wrong. That is very dangerous.

We seem to have gone from "American carnage," which Trump referenced in his inaugural, back to real carnage, Trump style and full circle. In four years, we have not heard a nice word about anything or anyone from Donald Trump. Americans are exhausted from the insults, the arguments, his firings-all played out on Twitter, of all inappropriate places. The country is tired, and now we are afraid that unidentified troops may be showing up in our cities, a typical fascist maneuver.

The Germans, who learned the cruel lessons of the 20th century, ultimately looked up to the Americans as the liberal democratic model. Now, the Germans are horrified at what they are seeing.

Roger Cohen, in his New York Times editorial, described what the Germans think of Trump. They see him "as the fear mongering showman wielding nationalism, racism and violence as if the 20th century held no lessons. He's the would-be destroyer of the multilateral institutions that brought European peace and made it possible for Germans to raise their bowed heads again. He is a fascist in the making."

Remember that Trump and Angela Merkel have a particularly frosty relationship. She got it right on the virus when she said, "We are not condemned to accept the spread of this virus as an inevitable fact of life." She went on to say, "We thrive not because we are forced to do something, but because we share knowledge and encourage active participation." Angela Merkel said that success largely depends on "each and every one of us." It's true that each and every one of us can fight for freedom, our good health and our values, by speaking out and speaking up. Democracy is NOT a spectator sport, and it can die in darkness unless we participate. Let's hope that the "F" word stands for freedom and not fascism.

July 31, 2020

Split Screen- the bad news and the good

July 30, 2020

Having spent the last six days watching the incredible tributes to Congressman John Lewis, I hoped to devote this blog to a discussion of that extraordinary man. But the news, much of it disturbing, forced a split screen. Americans saw the best and the worst in real time. While challenging, I will try to sort out the events of the last few days for all of us.

As John Lewis was being honored for his passion and perseverance to gain voting rights for all Americans, Donald Trump tweeted, "with Universal Mail-in Voting" (not absentee Voting, which is good), "2020 will be the most INACCURATE & FRAUDULENT Election in history. It will be a great embarrassment to the USA. Delay the Election until people can properly, securely and safely vote???" (his punctuation)

It is just one more example of Trump's ignorance. Mail-in voting and absentee ballots are the same thing. Moreover, in a study of many years of voting, there was minimal evidence of voter fraud. ABC News interviewed Tom Ridge, the first Secretary of Homeland Security, and a Republican appointed by George W. Bush after 9/11. Ridge confirmed, "there is no factual basis for Trump's claim of massive fraud in mail-in voting.". In fact, five states, including Utah, have been voting 100% by mail for a number of years.

Trump's suggestion that voting be delayed, was an outrageous distraction from all of his troubles, including the beauty of Lewis' funeral where three former Presidents were paying tribute. Mitch McConnell and other Republicans immediately shut down Trump's crass suggestion. The United states NEVER delayed an election- not even during the Civil War, World War One, the Great Depression or World War Two.

Of course, Donald Trump would love to delay the election, where the polls put him significantly behind. Perhaps he would be saved by the sudden appearance of a vaccine? Not likely. Donald Trump's tweets have always served to sow doubt-whether it's about the election, or mask wearing, or anything about which he wants to influence his base. He traffics in creating doubt and conspiracy theories. As a result, the country suffers from mixed- messages, which is why we don't have an organized plan to fight the pandemic.

Most important, one of the co-founders of the very conservative Federalist Society, wrote that he is "appalled by the president's recent tweet seeking to postpone the November election. Until recently, I had taken, as political hyperbole, the Democrats' assertion that President Trump is a fascist. But this latest tweet is fascistic and in itself grounds for the president's immediate impeachment, by the House of Representatives and his removal from office by the Senate."

None of this is actually in the purview of the President. Article II of the Constitution explicitly gives the states total power over the selection of the presidential electors.

In the middle of the week, Herman Cain, a prominent Trump supporter and former candidate for the 2012 Republican presidential nomination, died of Covid-19 at age 74. His death is quite ironic. Cain was co-chair of "Black Voices for Trump," which always amazed me, considering how bigoted Trump is. Cain attended the indoor rally on June 20, in Tulsa, Oklahoma, without a mask, and was hospitalized in early July, having caught Covid-19.

Another Republican, Congressman Louie Gohmert, who was strongly resistant to wearing a mask and never did, was diagnosed positive with Covid-19. He was on the floor of the House for weeks before he was tested. As a result, Nancy Pelosi, Speaker of the House, mandated that everyone on the floor of the House must wear a mask, except when rising to speak. The concept that Gohmert may have infected hundreds of people in his callous disregard of others, is chilling.

More bad news. Thursday began with the announcement that the second quarter's economic news was dreadful, worse than expected. Gross domestic product (GDP), fell 9.5%. This is equal to a 32.9% annual rate of decline. The last three months- April, May and June, eliminated the economic growth of the last five years. Considering that Donald Trump was planning to run on the economy, it is no wonder that he wanted to postpone the election. The present situation exists, despite the fact that trillions have been spent to shore up the economy.

That bad news is combined with the fact that the federal unemployment benefits that added $600 weekly to state unemployment benefits, expired today. The House of Representatives passed a comprehensive bill two months ago, which has been languishing on Mitch McConnell's desk all this time. Republicans are divided on what to do, and so they have done nothing, leaving 20 million people in limbo, wondering how they are going to pay their bills. Some of the Republicans don't want to extend the $600, cynically indicating that they don't want to pay people to stay home. It is a major crisis, with bitter words passing between both sides. Reportedly, they will not even sit in the same room, leaving Steve Mnuchin to go back and forth in an effort to make a deal. Totally flummoxed by the impasse, the Senate adjourned until 3PM on Monday, and went home, leaving millions of citizens in very dire straits. There are no words…

Meanwhile, the death count of the Covid-19 is 153,000 and rising, with no national plan in sight. Dr. Fauci and the Task Force testified today, and he was cautiously optimistic about having a vaccine sometime in the winter, but no real idea whether the vaccine would be effective. Dr. Redfield, head of the CDC, also testified, as did Dr. Giroir, the head of testing for the government.

There is some good news on the judicial front. In the ongoing saga of Mike Flynn, Judge Sullivan requested an "en banc" hearing, and it will go forward on August 11th. Remember that Flynn pleaded guilty twice, and Judge Sullivan told him that he had "sold out his country." When AG

Barr and Donald Trump inserted themselves to the case and wanted charges dropped against Flynn, Judge Sullivan was furious. Hence, the new hearing.

Another very important agreement was reached. The DOJ and the Governor of Oregon came to an agreement that all those paramilitary troops are going to leave the city of Portland. It's not entirely clear when, but the Governor seems to have prevailed.

Also, realizing that he is losing, Donald Trump has paused all his advertising to reconsider the message. In the face of a tanking economy and rising numbers of dead citizens, Trump can hardly escape the poll numbers. He has continued to come before the cameras and he insists that things are much rosier than they actually are. The American people are not so dumb that we think things are going well-with millions out of work, others dying and people losing their homes. It is clearly the Trump mess.

Similarly, Trump has met serious pushback from teachers and the unions. Just saying that children should go to school in person is obviously serving only Donald Trump. There is more serious evidence that young children can die, be spreaders and are not immune to the virus. Again, the suggestion comes from a callous disregard of children's lives. Trump is focused on reopening the country, so that things look better than they actually are.. Those are damn lies, and parents are well aware of the dangers. Children will not be going to school, unless it is clear that there is safety. Period.

Jonathan Swan, from Axios, had a revealing interview with Donald Trump. In response to Swan's question, the president admitted that he didn't mention the Russian bounties on our troops to Putin. It was a stunning moment. If you can see the interview, it is worth watching.

On the wonderful side of the split screen, the tributes to John Lewis were magnificent. Jamila Thompson, Lewis' deputy Chief of Staff, brought us inside the office of a Congressman who viewed everyone as family. Her speech revealed the marvelous passion and persistence of John Lewis, and the loyalty and love of everyone on his team. Barack Obama spoke after Miss Thompson, and he laid out a plan going forward. In many ways it was a political plan rather than a eulogy. Obama did what he thought John Lewis would want, and he laid it out brilliantly, especially as an action plan for voter protection and much more.

Before he died, Lewis submitted a wonderful message that was published in the *New York Times* on the day of his funeral. I hope to spend more time on John Lewis' message and his life this weekend. The news has been coming at an unbelievable pace!

Meanwhile, stay safe and be careful. Your health is important to your loved ones and friends.

August 4th, 2020

Confusion amidst the cacophony of chaos

August 2nd, 202

Once again, there are too many things happening in a short space of a weekend. As always, good news and bad news.

The good news is that the federal troops are gone from Portland, Oregon, and the demonstrations are peaceful under the watchful eye of the state police. The president overplayed his hand, and came out the loser. It's not clear whether Donald Trump will try sending troops into other cities in the face of such a smashing failure. That said, this summer has actually seen an uptick in violence in cities, but the troops that were sent to Portland actually ginned up the violence as a public relations ploy for election ads, etc., rather than solve problems and keep the peace.

Once again, Americans are in space! After 64 days, the Space -X capsule landed safely in the Gulf of Mexico with the two astronauts being safely brought to shore. America is once again sending people into space with extraordinary technology. In addition, NASA'S **Perseverance** rover launched on July 30th, and is on its way to Mars to gather information in an effort to see if there is life on Mars. Amazing!

On the other side of the coin. Donald Trump ordered 12,000 American troops out of Germany for no apparent reason, except perhaps in response to a goal of Vladimir Putin. Our troops have provided a buffer for Germany against Russia and a strong statement by NATO in Europe. Removing those troops will be unnecessarily costly, especially in a tanking economy, and dangerous in a pandemic. It also seems to be a swipe at Angela Merkel by Trump. So much negativity weakens NATO and the United States.

Dr. Deborah Birx, on the White House Task Force, spoke truth to power and indicated that we are in a very dangerous phase: rising numbers, extraordinary "spread" and mixed messages. She warned against large group meetings and told everyone-even those in rural areas, that the virus knows no borders and is everywhere in the country. Donald Trump took umbrage at her truthfulness, and tweeted a very insulting message against Dr. Birx.

Most interesting, Jonathan Swan, as mentioned before, had a stunning interview with Donald Trump, where it was clear that Trump still doesn't understand the virus-testing, tracing, morbidity, and percentages per population. Try to access Swan's brilliant interview, where he manages, in his elegant Australian demeanor, to keep a straight face as Trump is answering his serious questions with nonsense.

Similarly, and most important, there has been NO progress on the stimulus bill. The two sides remain far apart. People are losing their homes, there is food insecurity, and families are dangerously homeless in the middle of a pandemic. The small businesses who were relying on this bill, are most likely going to fail. Donald Trump has taken no role in trying to alleviate these problems. On Saturday and Sunday, he played golf. The coronavirus is an American catastrophe of major proportions, and it could put us into a Depression that will be worse than in the 1930s.

Add to this the confusion about school reopening. Parents and children are in a state of not knowing whether it is safe to return, and what the schools have been planning for the fall. It is very upsetting for parents, who cannot plan for their own future-whether they will have to stay home and teach their children, or whether they can return to their jobs. All of this could have been avoided. If the virus had been attacked in March with a single country plan, as South Korea did. We would be largely able to move forward.

This bad news has intersected with our upcoming election. Citizens are evaluating the President's non-response and moving to support Joe Biden for President on November 3rd. Biden leads in many polls that Trump took for granted. We have the contrast of a healer versus a destructor. Citizens are exhausted, and would like some peace, calm and stability, even though solving these problems will be very challenging for the next administration.

Hold your hats for another hectic week. There is much to discuss, including the threat to the Post Office and voting by mail. There is so much noise and very little progress on each of these fronts.

August 5, 2020

"It is What It is"

August 3, 2020

As I mentioned yesterday, Donald Trump had a stunning interview with Jonathon Swan of AXIOS. It was disturbingly revelatory. When confronted with the fact that 1,000 people were dying daily, the president responded, "it is what it is," a shocking dismissal of the deaths in five months. The president clearly cannot embrace the reality of the pandemic, which is that we have 157,000 citizens who have died, no national plan to fight the virus and many more deaths to come.

The interview was wide-ranging (try to watch it in its entirety), and it showed how little Donald Trump understands about any of the issues: mail-in voting, coronavirus relief, the pain of those 30 million people who just lost the $600 checks, and the effect Trump's own disinformation has had on the 38% of the people who follow him.

Trump continues his "briefings," intended to show that he is an engaged president. As he was announcing the passage of the Great American Outdoors Act, he could not pronounce Yosemite, a very common word in America, yet he was unfamiliar with it. Perhaps he should visit our national parks and see the beauty of our country! Never one to ignore an opportunity, Trump boasted that the Act was on a par with Theodore Roosevelt, who is known as the "conservation president." The law provides up to $9.5 billion for long overdue maintenance of our national parks. Ironically, Representative John Lewis (D-Ga) introduced the bill, and it passed on a bipartisan vote. Trump got on board when two Republican Senators indicated it would help their re-election campaigns, but Trump took credit for the bill and no Democrats were invited to the signing. This kind of partisan childishness has maintained throughout Trump's presidency.

Speaking of childish behavior, Trump was asked by Jonathan Swan what his assessment was of John Lewis. The president's first response was that Lewis didn't attend his inauguration. When pressed by Swan, Trump could not bring himself to say a nice word about Lewis, and said he wasn't sure that he had ever met him. Notably, John Lewis did not attend George W. Bush's inaugural either, but Bush eulogized Lewis, along with Bill Clinton and Barack Obama, as an icon and man who fought for equality.

As for the coronavirus relief bill, the Democrats passed a bill last May, which has been sitting on Mitch McConnell's desk, languishing. Republicans tried to construct their own bill, but they started late, cannot agree among themselves, and so nothing has been done. Negotiations continue between the Democrats and the White House- Mnuchin and Mark Meadows. Trump is on the sidelines and so is McConnell.

Another shallow response to an important issue is Donald Trump's lack of understanding of mail-in voting (same was absentee ballot). Historically, mail-in voting has always helped the Republicans, who were quite good at it. The fact that Trump has insisted that it causes fraud and will yield the "most corrupt election" in American history has caused a reverse reaction. Many Republicans have decided not to apply for mail-in voting, panicking Republican leaders. Trump did an immediate about-face, when it was explained to him, and tweeted that in Florida, mail-in voting was desired, a partisan response ignoring the rest of the country. At least five states have been doing mail-in voting for years, and it is organized, with no fraud.

Similarly, Donald Trump has continued his assault on the US Post Office, and this could have serious ramifications for our elections. A large donor to Trump's campaign, Louis DeJoy, was named Postmaster General recently. As a result, there have been serious delays in mail delivery. A House Committee has requested a hearing with Dejoy, in order to address these mail delays. He will be appearing at a Congressional hearing to answer questions. The concern is that a Trump appointee could corrupt a key institution ahead of Election Day.

In addition, Trump has decided to close the CENSUS 2020 one month early. The truth is that those close to the Census, in the middle of a pandemic, feel strongly that more time is needed, not less. The Census is key to deciding allocations for districts, and much more for the next ten years. Shutting down the Census early means that many people will not be counted, and that will have serious consequences for the services provided to each location. Remember that Trump wanted to eliminate counting undocumented immigrants, but that was overruled. Nonetheless, if you haven't filled out your Census 2020 (it takes 5 minutes), please do so.

All of these issues deserve close attention. Donald Trump is trying to manipulate our institutions to his own benefit in an election year.

Indeed, eternal vigilance is the price of liberty. We need to be active in preserving our democracy.

August 6, 2020

Dangerous Misinformation and illegal behavior: foreign and domestic

August 4, 2020

Too much news. Donald Trump gave an interview on Fox News, during which he said that schools should reopen, because children are "almost immune from COVID-19." That assertion is totally false. Children have contracted the virus and some have died. Most recently, children are in danger of contracting the **Multi– System Inflammatory syndrome** (MIS-C), which is associated with COVID-19. This is a condition where different body parts can become inflamed, including the heart, lungs, kidneys, brain, skin, eyes or gastrointestinal organs.

Facebook, to its credit, took down the Trump video that falsely claimed "children are "immune to COVID-19". This is the first time that Facebook has taken down a Trump message. Perhaps it's because Mark Zuckerberg has two children, and Facebook is now watching Trump much more carefully and critically for misinformation in general.

As of this writing, 5 million Americans have contracted the virus, and 159,000 citizens have died. We still have no national plan, and flu season is arriving in the fall.

Despite the politically motivated order from Trump that "children must go back to school in person," many school systems have decided otherwise. Fortunately, this is a local and state decision. Many school districts do not have the resources to make their schools safe for children or adults. These are painful decisions, because if young children are home parents cannot go to work, unless they can work from home. These complicated decisions put parents (and teachers) somewhere between a rock and a hard place. Beyond space, many schools do not have good air filtration systems, air conditioning and much else. Especially in the poorer districts, children do not have access to the internet, computers or other resources. Many urban school buildings are very old and dilapidated.

The raging virus is a mind-boggling situation that didn't have to happen, if the president had taken a leadership role from the onset. Advisors explained to Trump that the healthcare situation had to be priority number #1. Only when the virus was under control could the country begin to open in phases, and ultimately children could go back to school in the fall. He refused that reality, never mentioned the numbers of people who have died, and offered no empathy for their families.

Elections have consequences.

There is other negative news. Thirty-two million Americans are in dire need of having a boost to their unemployment checks. In May, the House passed a coronavirus stimulus bill, reinstating the $600 weekly addition that helped people pay their rent and bills. Additionally, the Moratorium on Evictions in New York is expiring. In New Jersey, the Supreme Court controls proceedings on eviction, and it has suspended alleviation proceedings for now. The Eviction Moratorium will last until Governor Murphy declares an end to the COVID-19 health crisis, so that gives some people breathing room.

The White House leaders are unable to reach an agreement on the coronavirus bill. Trump said he would issue an Executive Order to cover the issues. Of course, the president doesn't know that the Constitution establishes that all money bills must originate in the House of Representatives. There is a logical reason for this, since the House is far more representative and should be appropriating the peoples' money.

There is more. Not surprisingly, the Republican Convention is seriously disorganized. Trump has opined that he might accept the nomination from the White House. That would be problematic because of the Hatch Act, which prohibits the use of public places for partisan purposes. It excludes the president and VP, but none of the staff who work in the White House would be able to participate. Moreover, the White House is the peoples' house, and making a campaign speech from there would be a major breaking with norms, traditions and the law.

Moreover, the "acting" Inspector General for the State Department is resigning. In fact, Trump has managed to get rid of most of the Inspector General Corps. Stephen Akard has only been in the office for three months, after Trump fired his predecessor, Steve Linick, who was investigating Secretary of State Pompeo's activities. They included an emergency declaration to permit an $8.1 billion arms deal with Saudi Arabia, despite the fact that lawmakers from both parties objected to it. Pompeo was also giving a series of elegant parties that had no government business reason, although the taxpayers were paying for them. Indeed, it seemed that Pompeo was readying a run for office when he exited the administration.

There is also the scandal of Donald Trump asking the Ambassador to Great Britain, Woody Johnson, to pressure the UK's Secretary of State for Scotland, to bring the British Open to Trump's Turnberry Golf Resort in Scotland in 2018. That event brings huge amounts of money to the host town. In 2019, it brought in more than 130 million dollars. This is another example of Donald Trump using the power of his office to line his personal pocket. The Inspector General was investigating this story when he was fired. The Deputy Chief of Mission told Ambassador Johnson that it was unethical, probably illegal, and he was also pushed out.

There will be more to report, including some good news, but I am quite tired, so I need to sign off now. Until tomorrow ...

I do want to acknowledge the brutal storm that we had the other night. Friends are without power, most likely for many days. I feel lucky to have mine. Trees are down on streets, having hit other peoples' homes. There is debris everywhere. Our towns look like war zones. When I had my former home, and we didn't have a pandemic, friends came for food, showers and a warm fire. All this has changed, sadly. I was very lucky not to lose power, but my thoughts and prayers are with everyone who did.!

Donald Trump continues to claim that "this thing will go away, like things go away." More magical thinking! Moreover, testing has gone down 3.6% in the last week, largely because Americans have become discouraged waiting in long lines for many hours, in order to be tested.

Downplaying the importance of testing created a split in the country, regarding how to respond to the virus. Trump's "Magical thinking" has continued throughout, despite the fact that today Dr. Fauci said unequivocally that the virus will "not go away." Very disturbingly, Dr. Fauci revealed that his family has been a target of dangerous threats, based on the scientific guidance he has given the country, which disagrees with Donald Trump. As a result of these threats, a security detail has now been assigned to Dr. Fauci. When Dr. Fauci spoke about the threats, he expressed amazement that people would be so anti-science, when he was giving information to help save peoples' lives. Unfortunately, when you politicize science, the result is that you get politics.

August 7, 2020

"How are you doing today?"

August 7, 2020

The answer to that question is very personal for each of us, but not entirely unknown. Millions of citizens are suffering from anxiety, isolation, confusion that comes from mixed-messages, and a concern for the future of our country, to name but a few of the most prevalent feelings.

As of this date, the American death toll from the coronavirus exceeds 160,553 and there are nearly 4.9 million Covid-19 cases. We have 5% of the population in the world, but 25% of the cases. The virus is running rampant because we have no national plan, no leadership. For the living who are struggling, there is no coronavirus relief bill. Millions of citizens are standing in long lines at food banks, and sleeping in their cars, since the Moratorium on eviction has disappeared. This is an unacceptable and shameful situation for the wealthiest nation on earth. The burden of unemployment has affected women (10%), and people of color (14%), in the greatest proportion. The virus and resulting unemployment have intersected in an historic moment. The newest model projects nearly 300,000 Covid-19 deaths by December. Staggering numbers, unless we change our behavior.

Meanwhile, the Senate has abandoned the unemployed. The president never took responsibility in the first place, and the country seems to be in a never-ending syndrome. This pandemic is killing hundreds of thousands of Americans.

Most recently, the scientists have indicated that if 95% of the population wore masks and practiced social distancing, then approximately 60,000 American lives would be saved. It's unclear that this would happen in our divided country, and it is very frustrating to know that a change would save lives. It is never too late to improve our behavior.

The Senate is home this weekend, when it should be in Washington DC, working to solve the problems for the American people. We have millions of whom lost their jobs, when the country had to shelter at home, because of the virus. Similarly, Donald Trump is in Bedminster, NJ, at his golf resort. He will play golf while thousands are dying and others are desperate for food. This callous reality boggles the mind. In addition, the restaurant industry has been decimated, and so have many other industries, including the airplane industry. Any recovery will take years, possibly decades.

Added to this are serious concerns about our national security from foreign actors. Russia, China and Iran are busy trying to undermine our elections and our national security. How do we know?

Two days ago Senator Richard Blumenthal (D-CT), tweeted that he was "shocked and appalled," having just left a classified briefing on foreign efforts to disrupt our elections. Blumenthal felt strongly that this information should be made public to the American people, although that might uncover important sources. Blumenthal objected to the fact of the secrecy, and he wants the foreign subterfuge made public. Senator Blumenthal sits on the Committee on Armed Services, and also on the Subcommittee on Cybersecurity.

As the story unfolded, the four Democrats on the Gang of Eight-which comprises the leaders in both houses of Congress met together. They demanded that the Office of the Director of National Intelligence specifically and forthrightly warn Americans of the foreign threat to our elections. The leadership included House Speaker, Nancy Pelosi (D-CA), Senate Majority Leader, Chuck Schumer (D-NY), House Intelligence Committee Chair, Adam Schiff (D-CA), and ranking Member of the Senate Select Committee on Intelligence, Mark Warner (D-VA) understood that foreign actors are attacking us. "Almost exactly four years ago, we first observed the Russians engaged in covert actions designed to influence the presidential race in favor of Donald Trump, and to sow discord in the United States. Now, the Russians are once again trying to influence the election and divide Americans, and these efforts must be deterred, disrupted and exposed."

The Director of the United States National Counter-Intelligence and Security Center is William Evanina. He tried to suggest that China, Russia and Iran were equally involved in these efforts.

The four top Democrats were alarmed at Evanina's attempt to make this look like it was just a general attack on the US election. The facts are that evidence indicates Russia is at the center once again trying to influence the election.

Pelosi, Schiff (D-CA), Schümer (D-NY) and Warner issued a joint statement. "A far more concrete and specific statement needs to be made to the American people, consistent with the need to protect sources and methods. We can trust the American people with knowing what to do with the information they receive and making those decisions for themselves. But they cannot do so if they are kept in the dark about what our adversaries are doing, and how they are doing it."

Meanwhile, some progress has been made on the domestic front. Yesterday, the Attorney General of New York, Letitia James, announced a lawsuit accusing the top leadership of the NRA (National Rifle Association) of using the nonprofit for their own personal gain. The Attorney General filed a lawsuit against Wayne Lapierre and three others. They are accused of using $3,5 million in personal travel, and up to $64 million for a yacht and other perks. New York has sued the nonprofit for self-dealing, wide-ranging fraud, and using the NRA "as a personal piggy bank." There are whistleblowers within the organization, and even the PR firm that the NRA uses, has come out against the top officers. The Attorney General is suggesting that the organization be dissolved. The NRA filed a countersuit, insisting that AG James was denying the NRA its First Amendment rights. The NRA has millions of members, and has been frustratingly successful in combating bills in Congress that would have limited assault rifles and increased background checks, to name a few issues, but those are not the reasons for the lawsuit. The rationale is illegal use of the nonprofit's funds for personal gain.

So, how are you feeling today? Hopefully, the sun will come out, you will take a good walk or drive and enjoy the fact that you are healthy. Stay safe, wear your mask and protect your neighbor and yourself.

"We have met the enemy and he is us" (Pogo)

August 8, 2020

I am watching the most bizarre scene in Bedminster, New Jersey. The President of the United States is having a press conference at his golf resort, with many of the members (in their golf shirts and shorts) who pay $350,000 for a membership, looking on. When the golfers hear Trump denigrate the press and the Democrats, they clap, and he is loving it.

> In my lifetime, I never thought I would see such a crass display of egomania and power, when other people are unemployed, hungry and dying. It is a reality show of epic proportions, put on by a callous and insecure showoff.

The supposed reason for the "press conference?" With talks between the White House (Mnuchin and Mark Meadows, not Trump) and the House collapsing, Donald Trump decided to take matters into his own hands. He signed four executive actions to provide relief from economic damage sustained during the pandemic, basically doing an end run around Congress.

The Constitution gives Congress the power to appropriate federal spending. Trump has limited authority to act unilaterally, and the Democrats could challenge him in court, based on their opinion that he overstepped, and these orders fall short of actually helping the unemployed.

Let's unpack what the four orders did:

1- One order defers payroll taxes for Americans earning less than $100,00 a year.

My analysis: This is very dangerous on many levels. Firstly, it only helps those who are employed, not the 30 million people who lost their jobs, and who need help immediately.

Moreover, payroll taxes pay for Social Security and Medicare. We put that money in so we can be assured of a social safety net later. Donald Trump and many Republicans have called these "entitlements," and they have been trying to get rid of them for years. Moreover, Trump floated the idea of eliminating the payroll tax for Americans earning $100,000 a year if he is reelected in November.

2- Rather than extend the $600 added to unemployment initially, Trump only added an extra $400 in benefits through 2020. Moreover, the federal government would pay $300 and is requiring the states to pay the remaining $100, 25% of the additional benefits.

My analysis: this is punishing for the unemployed and also for the states, each of which has huge debt as a result of Covid-19 expenses. Donald Trump has referred to the states as "red states" and "blue states," and has no desire to help states such as New York, New Jersey, Connecticut and Massachusetts, because they didn't "vote for me." The concept that we are the United States of America has never been accepted by him, and that point of view is responsible for the lack of a unified federal plan to fight the virus and many other important programs. Pitting one side against another has been Trump's modus operandi, and has resulted in a fractured and divided country.

Answering a question from the press, Trump said the additional unemployment benefits are "not a hardship," but an "incentive" to encourage people to return to work. Many Republicans had a feeling that the $600 was too much, and was a reason not to return to work, when five surveys indicated this was not true.

3- A third order would implement a moratorium on evictions, and give financial assistance to renters. However, more than 40 million renters could ultimately be forced from their homes. I honestly don't know the details of this particular order, and will have a lot of reading to do before I can comment. Sometimes, there are hidden agendas in seemingly helpful orders.

4- The fourth order would postpone student loan interest and payment through the end of 2020.

My analysis: As I understand it, the students will still owe this money back at a certain point in time.

THE BIG PICTURE: It is not known whether these orders are an adequate response to the immediate needs of the country. The Democrats -Nancy Pelosi and Chuck Schumer, issued a statement that these orders fall short, in addition to being improper.

Some serious realities and consequences:

29 million adults reported that their households didn't get enough to eat for the week ending July 7th.

States face budget shortfalls of 555 billion through 2022, according to the Center on Budget and Policy Priorities.

Again, this is where the federal government needs to step in and make sure that the states can pay their police, fire, and all the costs of administering business and protecting their citizens. The president has shown no appetite for helping the states, especially the so-called "blue states."

Equally important, states and towns need the money required to make all the changes that would allow schools to open safely. This is a major concern, and if the local towns are unable to insure the safety of its teachers, children and other essential workers, then they will have to stay online for another year. Online has serious ramifications for parents, who need to return to work, and children who need to see their friends.

Donald Trump is, indeed, the enemy within the Oval office, offering little useful help to those in the direst ofcircumstances. There will be serious ongoing discussions on all of these issues.

Returning to the story of Donald Trump's effort to get the British Open for his golf resort at Turnberry in Scotland in 2018, Rachel Maddow had the perfect guest the other night- Lewis Lukens. The Acting Inspector General, Stephen Akard, for the State Department, resigned as of last Friday. He had been on the job less than three months, and it is not clear why he wanted to leave. Trump fired his predecessor, Steve Linick, most probably under pressure from Secretary of State, Mike Pompeo. Linick was investigating Pompeo for two different issues, personal misuse of resources, and a second issue- a huge deal with Saudi Arabia, over the objections of bipartisan lawmakers.

Linick was also investigating Robert "Woody" Johnson for making the "ask" of the UK's Secretary of State for Scotland, David Mundell. The attempt to use the power of the government to line Donald Trump's pockets was illegal, and Linick was investigating when this story was about to become public.

The second-in-command at the UK Embassy was Lewis Lukens, Deputy Chief of Mission. When he became aware of the request from the president, he told Johnson he shouldn't make the request. However, Ambassador Johnson ignored that advice, went ahead and made the ask. As a result, Johnson pushed Lewis Lukens out of his job.

Lukens was the guest on Rachael Maddow's show, and he recounted the story in detail. There were reports filed on this matter, but they have been deep-sixed as "confidential," which is "highly irregular," according to Lukens. He will serve as a whistleblower, and testify to these events. Sharing a chilling evaluation of the situation in the State Department, Lewis Lukens said that the leadership is unwilling to try to block self-dealing amongst Trump's acolytes, because they know they will lose.

By firing patriotic civil servants and replacing them with his own loyal people, Donald Trump has managed to subvert the State Department, the Justice Department and the Defense Department. We are in a very dangerous period for our country, and it's important to be vigilant and alert.

Smoke and Mirrors

August 10, 2020

What President Trump did on Saturday was a mirage-basically a headline that he was going to help by providing economic relief with "executive actions." To a degree it worked in his favor, because even the BBC had a major headline indicating that he was acting when Congress could not. However, the three executive actions and one memorandum do not begin to help those in need. They do provide Trump with ammunition to make it hard for the House Democrats to go to court, which is a very clever ploy on the part of the president and his advisors.

Let's not forget that in May the House of Representatives passed a 3 trillion coronavirus relief bill, which thoughtfully responded to each of the problems that needed immediate attention before the end of July. It is known as the HEROES ACT, an acronym for Health and Economic Recovery Omnibus Emergency Solutions Act.

This act was incredibly thorough-it protected renters, extended the $600 for unemployed workers, gave money to depleted state budgets, supported hospitals and schools and tried to protect our upcoming elections, which are endangered by Russia and also President Trump, who has sowed the seeds of doubt in the outcome. The HEROES ACT was presented to the Senate on May 15th, and it languished on Mitch McConnell's (R-KY) desk.He showed no enthusiasm for taking it up with the Senate. It wasn't until the end of July that he began to consider it. By then, unemployment benefits ran out and the moratorium on evictions had ended, leaving millions of citizens in the lurch.

When the Senate began deliberating, it was clear that the Senators did not agree on which way to proceed. Senators who were up for reelection wanted measures that would clearly help their constituents. Others, like Mark Meadows, White House Chief of Staff, did not want to spend another federal dollar. They proposed 1 trillion, leaving a 2 trillion-dollar gap. In the 1 trillion, the Senate left out funding for the states, which is absolutely crucial. They also left out election funding, equally crucial.

The Democrats offered a compromise. They came down 1 trillion and suggested to the Republicans they would have a deal if they came up 1 trillion, so the bill would be 2 trillion. The White House rejected it, period, which is why everything was left in limbo. That situation made an opening for Donald Trump to look like a hero. He signed three memorandums and one executive order that basically bypassed Congress, which has the power of the purse. Trump indicated that these four measures would provide the relief for struggling Americans, but it does not appear that it does.

As I indicated yesterday, the Constitution establishes that the House of Representatives can initiate a revenue bill. There are good reasons for that, since the House is the single most representative body in Congress. The truth is that Trump cannot come up with new money. He would have to declare an emergency and borrow from FEMA, in order to use about $70 billion from Homeland Security's Disaster Relief Fund, a very dangerous idea, since a hurricane would necessitate using those funds. There are many more financial and legal machinations Trump would have to use in order to get to the number needed, and it still may fall short. Worse, much of the burden would fall on the states, because the law requires them to use 25% matching funds from the DRF (Disaster Relief fund).

Again, the Senate has abrogated its duty, because federal funds could be used if they had taken up the bill in the appropriate amount of time and decided to help the people. After all, the federal money is the taxes we pay to DC, and when it's needed, especially in a disaster, the federal government should come across with the money.

I mentioned this in an earlier blog, and it is important to remember that New York, New Jersey, Connecticut and California send more money to Washington than they ever get back. Lots of states-especially Kentucky, McConnell's state, are the "takers." They receive much more than they send.

So, this is where things stand at the moment. We have no idea what will transpire on Monday. I am going to leave the story here, because it would be impossible to speculate on how events will unfold. Meanwhile, people are dying, going hungry and losing their homes. The virus is winning.

On that worrisome note, I want to go on to a happier news break. This week, Joe Biden will announce his choice for the Democratic Vice-President running mate. The women who are on the list are talented, intelligent and impressive. It is a very deep bench of extraordinary choices.

You may have your own favorite in mind, but the wealth of talent will insure that whoever SHE is, will be outstanding!

Stay tuned.

August 10, 2020

"VEEPstakes"

August 10, 2020

For once this week, it is a pleasure to write about an upcoming historic event.

Joe Biden, presumptive Democratic Presidential candidate, is expected to name his running mate. There has been so much speculation about who that will be, and excitement over the fact that we know it will be a woman! Joe Biden announced that he would pick a woman early in the game. There was a large, deep bench of thirteen incredibly talented and experienced women he considered: Governors, Senators, Congressmen, former National Security Advisors and more.

Women have distinguished themselves with their brilliance, leadership, experience and hard work. Moreover, they are often the ones who can affect a good compromise when two sides cannot reach a deal.

Because of the pandemic, Joe Biden has been interviewing the women remotely, as far as we know. The process has been shrouded in secrecy and discretion, which is impressive.

After weeks of conversation and winnowing to a final few, Mr. Biden's search committee has carefully vetted the group. Some of the best-known candidates, like Elizabeth Warren and Kamala Harris, remain strong contenders. A number of others have risen to be high on the list and in contention.

Susan Rice, the former National Security Advisor to President Obama and Ambassador to the United Nations, is reported to be in the top tier.

In addition, Senator Tammy Duckworth of Illinois, an Iraq war combat veteran is under serious consideration, as is Karen Bass, Congresswoman, and chair of the Congressional Black Caucus. It's entirely possible that Biden's choice will be a woman of color. Black women have long been the mainstay of his political life, and it is never more important than right now. It will be very interesting to see who Joe Biden chooses.

His relationship with Barack Obama was seamless. They were the yin and yang for one another. Obama was the cerebral, brilliant President, who dug deep into bills and legislation. He was essentially an introvert, not enjoying the social life that was available to him. Biden was the warm and voluble Vice-President, always reaching out to people with a smile and empathy. The key to Biden's decision is chemistry, how well they would be good partners, as Obama and Biden were. Trust is important, since the president will be asking his VP for her honest opinion on serious problems.

We may know the answer to this question as soon as this afternoon. As I have said many times, stay tuned …

August 10, 2020

Writing at 3am in the morning, is dangerous

April 10, 2020

One of my readers (who was up at 3am), alerted me that there were errors in the "Veepstakes" blog. With apologies, I am awake at night because of a torn meniscus that is complicated by nearsightedness and the cascade of news. You deserve better.

I was, indeed, rushing to write, and excited by the concept that we are going to have a woman Vice President running-mate for Joe Biden. The news comes so fast and so hard, and it is often unbelievable. So many events interfere with my desire to process, to take my time and to analyze. However, the news will not wait for me! It is the other way around. I am on a news cycle merry-go-round, and I have to keep up with the times.

Things are not going to get better in the next few months. I will try to get more sleep, and let the blog rest before I publish. Thank you for your wonderful comments and your patience. We are in for a wild ride, I'm afraid.

The Special Needs of a "special needs" child

August 11, 2020

There has been a lot of conversation about whether children should return to school. The administration has unilaterally said that they should, which is foolhardy at best. Children do contract the virus, are "spreaders," and can infect their older grandparents, who are vulnerable. One of the scandals behind the "back to school" push, is that Betsy DeVos and Donald Trump politicized our children's health and the welfare of their families.

It's entirely possible that the majority of children should stay home and learn online for at least the next six months, perhaps longer. New York, one of the only states that actually did a good job in flattening the curve, has now declared that schools will open for children under very stringent safety measures. Governor Cuomo has indicated that his team will be watching the numbers very carefully, and they are prepared to be flexible when trouble rears its head.

One group about which there hasn't been a lot of conversation is "special needs" children. Oh, there have been whispers, and a sentence here and there, but not a huge conversation about what happens when special needs children can't go to school. The truth is that they suffer the greatest deficit. Progress that has been made, is often lost. Parents and teachers alike, who watched the small incremental steps and cheered, are now witness to reversal.

This morning, I watched one of the most moving examples of a child who is now home with his parents, presently his caregivers. You will be familiar with the father of five-year-old Henry, who is autistic since birth.

Richard Engel, journalist and author, NBC News Chief foreign correspondent, lives in London with his wife, Mary and their five -year old seriously autistic son, Henry. Since Henry cannot walk on his own, Richard and Mary carry him everywhere. His motor skills are not such that he can focus on a computer for online learning.

Henry was in a school that offered important services, and he was improving, step by step. The socialization was very important, and so was the attention from trained teachers who were working with him.

Then, COVID-19 had to shut down his school. By Mary and Richard's own analysis, Henry lost a good deal of the progress that he had made. They are now his teachers, 24/7. The documentary Richard and Mary made to acquaint people with the challenges of having a seriously autistic child, is very moving, beautiful and important. For the half hour that I watched this loving set of intelligent and dedicated parents interacting with their child, I could only imagine the physical and emotional toll on a family.

I have no first- hand knowledge of special needs children, except when I was teaching in public school, and we had a wonderful program for deaf children. But those were children who could operate in a classroom and were taken out by the program teacher, who worked with the children on a daily basis.

Richard Engel's son needs much more specialized, individualized help, and he receives it in schools that are made for that kind of care. Most children don't have the kind of resources that Richard and Mary Engel are able to provide for Henry. We need to be aware of the needs of these families and prioritize those children when the government is allocating aid in the next few months. "Special needs" children are special in ways that require our empathy, our love, our support and our attention, to the best of our ability.

At the end of the program, I was happy to see that there is a brand -new baby in Richard and Mary Engel's home. A beautiful baby boy, named Theo, was crawling around on the floor. He had just turned one.

BIDEN/HARRIS in 2020!

August 11, 2020

Joe Biden announced his choice to be his running mate. Kamala Harris will be the first woman to be Vice President of the United States!

So many historic firsts! Kamala Harris is part black, part Asian and the first Howard University alumna to run on a presidential ticket. Now California's junior Senator, she was California's Attorney General, the first woman. A formidable debater and questioner, Harris drew blood when she questioned Bill Barr and Jeff Sessions, and her talent came to the attention of everyone. She also drew Joe Biden's blood when she ran for president, but he forgave it enough to put her on the ticket.

Kamala Devi Harris was born in 1964, in Oakland, California. Her mother, Shyamala Gopalan, was a breast cancer scientist who had emigrated from Tamil Nadu, India, in 1960 to pursue a doctorate in endocrinology at UC Berkeley. Kamala Harris' father is a British, Jamaican-born American economist and professor emeritus at Stanford University. Kamala Harris has a sister, Maya.

Harris is the second African-American woman and the first Indian-American to serve in the United States Senate. She graduated from Howard University and the University of California, Hastings College of the Law.

She began her career in the Alameda County District Attorney's office, before being recruited to the San Francisco District Attorney's office, and later was the City Attorney of San Francisco's office. In 2003, she was elected the 27th district attorney of San Francisco, serving until 2011. Among her achievements as District Attorney, Harris started a program that gives first-time drug offenders the chance to earn a high school diploma and find employment.

Having completed two terms as the District Attorney of San Francisco, Kamala was elected as the first African-American and first woman to serve as California's Attorney General. In this role, she worked tirelessly to hold corporations accountable and protect the state's most vulnerable people.

Over the course of her nearly two terms in office, Kamala won a $25-billion settlement for California homeowners hit by the foreclosure crisis, defended California's landmark climate change law, and protected the Affordable Care Act. In addition, she helped win marriage equality for all Californians, and prosecuted transitional gangs that trafficked in guns, drugs, and human beings.

Kamala was elected to the United States Senate, and is now in her first term. Since taking office, she has introduced and co-sponsored legislation to raise wages for working people, reform our broken criminal justice system, make healthcare a right for all Americans, address the epidemic of substance abuse, support veterans and military families and expand access to childcare for working parents.

Interestingly, when she was a prosecutor, Kamala Harris went to court against the Public Defender, Nikki Solis. Ms. Solis wrote a wonderful Op- Ed this week (USA Today) and appeared on Rachel Maddow to say that Kamala Harris was the most progressive prosecutor in her experience. Why did she say this? Because Kamala Harris was not interested in putting people in jail. Instead, there were drug courts and programs for rehabilitation, ending in misdemeanors, not jail. Nikki Solis is an admirer of Kamala Harris for her humanity and her desire to help people, rather than put them behind bars.

In 2014, Senator Harris married Douglas Emhoff, a Jewish entertainment lawyer, and she has two Jewish stepchildren and Jewish in-laws.

We have a marvelous opportunity to turn this country around. It will be incredibly difficult, because we are faced with a pandemic, a catastrophic economic result, and a newly exciting push for equality for black and brown citizens. We all have the chance to become better versions of ourselves with a new President and Vice President-Biden/Harris in 2020. There is a new day dawning.

The Post Office and Voter Suppression-Red Warning Lights are Flashing!

August 14, 2020

First, a bit of history. In 1775, the Continental Congress agreed to make Benjamin Franklin the first Postmaster of the United States. Franklin developed much of the infrastructure that led to the creation of the first officially sanctioned postal system in our country.

In 1789, Article 1, Section 8, Clause 7 of the United States Constitution, known as the Postal Power, empowers Congress, "To establish Post Offices and Post Roads." The Postal Clause was added to the Constitution to facilitate interstate communication, as well as to create a source of revenue for the early United States, which were thirteen separate colonies. It would effectively be the glue that would connect people in the country with one another.

Not only did Congress have the power to create a postal system. It had the ability to acquire and control the land for the "post roads," to carry the mail and the buildings needed to maintain the delivery of the mail. Clearly, the establishment of post offices and delivery of the mail was crucial to the operation of the new country.

In addition, the Postal Service Act of 1792, signed by George Washington, included many provisions aimed at providing more civil rights and helping the country expand. Under the legislation, newspapers could be sent via the mail for a discounted rate, in order to develop a freedom of the press.

Now 2020, and the Post Office is under threat from Donald Trump, the postal service employs 630,000 men and women across the country, delivering the mail to citizens in a timely manner, often within a day or two. Veterans rely on mail delivery, citizens receive important checks in the mail, and medicines arrive for people who desperately need them. In the middle of a pandemic, when we are so far from our relatives and friends, the delivery of a card or letter is extremely important for everyone's mental and emotional health. Most important, the Post Office is the only entity that is required to deliver to every address in the United States, no matter how remote.

We are in a very serious situation with the election on November 3rd. The postal system needs emergency money. Twenty-five billion dollars was requested by the Board of Governors. Donald Trump has refused to fund the Post Office, primarily on political grounds. Democrats often vote by mail, and Trump is afraid that he will lose if universal mail-in voting is approved and funded. The pandemic has also clearly affected the ability of the post office to operate, because many workers have become ill with Covid-19, thereby putting a further burden on the post office.

In order to manipulate the mail, Donald Trump removed the experienced Postmaster and replaced him with a big donor, Louis DeJoy, who has no experience with the postal system. DeJoy began immediately slowing down the mail throughout the country. Equally troubling, there are reports of sorting machines being removed from post offices in Pennsylvania, Michigan and Maryland. These are the same machines that would be used to sort the thousands of ballots that we are sending to be counted. Donald Trump clearly has a plan to undermine our election. Last Friday, DeJoy fired all the top-level Post Office employees who have decades of experience, once again putting the fast delivery of the mail at risk.

Moreover, Trump's claim that mail-in voting is fraudulent and leads to cheating, has been widely debunked over the last many years. A minuscule number of ballots were found to be fraudulent (26), but Trump has floated the message that the election will be rigged. That message goes against all of our experiences with voting in 244 years. Trump is dealing in conspiracy theories, which are dangerous to our democracy, and the idea of free and fair elections.

Donald Trump has indicated that he would challenge the vote if it did not go his way, and this is very troubling, and arrogant, considering that he is behind in the polls. In addition, it is not clear that he would willingly leave the White House were Joe Biden to be the newly elected president. All of this produces distrust and anxiety, especially in the middle of a pandemic, with a cratering economy. Trump creates chaos, and we must be alert and active to make sure that our votes and those of our friends and neighbors are accessed and counted.

The red flashing lights are blinking furiously! Danger ahead … we must act!

America is in a battle for its democracy

August 15, 2020

In a press conference, the president said that he opposed funding for the cash-strapped US Postal Service, because he wanted to stop mail-in voting. He admitted aloud that he wanted to make it impossible for many votes to be counted. In addition, in the middle of a pandemic, many people will have to choose between voting and putting their health at risk, while they are standing in line at polling places. That choice is unconscionable, but the president seems not to care. In fact, his goal is to suppress the vote.

Interestingly, Donald Trump assumes that if lots of people are able to vote, he would lose. However, in the past many Republicans came out to vote in person, while the Democrats tended to vote by mail. It's not clear which party would prevail.

Nonetheless, Trump continued his assault on the Postal system. sowing distrust in the outcome, and saying this will be the "most fraudulent and dishonest election in history." None of that is even remotely true. If memory serves, in 2016, Trump was assuming Hillary Clinton was going to win, and he said the election would be rigged. Of course, the surprise was that, while 3 million votes behind Hillary, Trump won the Electoral College and the presidency. Since this happened in 2000, there is something terribly wrong with our electoral system. In 2016, Trump was obviously hedging his bets, no matter who won, and he is doing that once again.

This time, he has the power of the presidency behind him, and it allows him to manipulate the agencies and the players. Trump fired the former Postmaster General and appointed a loyal follower, Louis DeJoy, as the new leader of the postal system. Last week it was learned that DeJoy met with the president in the Oval office, an unusual meeting at best. Afterwards, DeJoy fired all the top leadership of the Postal Department, and started putting in new rules, which resulted in slowing down the mail. He eliminated overtime, and letters were sent to 46 states telling citizens that the Post Office could not guarantee that ballots would all be counted. It should have been clear to DeJoy that USPS needed to ramp up, not slow down.

Stopping the mail and slowing down all delivery will result in chaos throughout the country. Beyond ballots, veterans and thousands of people rely on the mail for medicines and checks, to name two lifelines. Moreover, USPS officials told union leaders that management was eliminating

671 sorting machines, which represent about 10% of the sorters in the country that would have handled ballots, letters and postcards.

Removing the sorters is a clear effort to influence the election, especially since the machines that were taken came from battleground states. Florida lost 11, Wisconsin lost 9, Ohio lost 35 sorters, Philadelphia lost 8 and Arizona, 5. The Secretary of State for Ohio came on television the other night and indicated that Ohio will be well able to handle the overflow, and they have three days after election day to count all the ballots. Other states are applying for similar leeway.

In an unsurprising revelation, it turns out that Louis DeJoy was named to the finance team of the Republican National Committee in 2017. His lack of any experience and this intimate connection with Trump, certainly suggests that he is a partisan who now is in charge of what is supposed to be a nonpartisan office. There is a pattern here, and Donald Trump is working his power to give himself the best chance of winning re-election. Suppressing the vote is subverting our democracy.

Yesterday, the USPS started removing those wonderful iconic blue letter boxes. The post office said it was a routine reassignment. However, there was such an outcry and pressure on DeJoy and others, that they backtracked and said they wouldn't remove any more until after the election. Why are they removing them at all?

There is a good lesson to be learned. Hundreds of people picketed and protested in front of DeJoy's house in Washington, DC. A similar thing happened in Montana. People pressure works! We need to ask questions and get active. The sorters, the loss of overtime, the delays in mail delivery are all part of a plan to weaken the post office response to the election. Beyond the election, citizens are suffering when their medicines and checks are not arriving on time. This has to stop!

The Democrats have requested an investigation into these activities. Inspector General Tammy Whitcomb of the USPS announced that she is launching an investigation into "all recent staffing and policy changes put in place" by DeJoy. She also said that she is looking into DeJoy and his compliance with ethics rules, which are related to his huge financial stakes in private companies that are actually competitors of the USPS. It seems that he has an interest in electing Donald Trump and n overseeing the demise of the USPS. This is incredibly worrisome.

There is another big story that hit the airwaves. The Government Accountability Office, which is the main audit agency in the federal government, concluded that the two top officials at the Department of Homeland Security, are not in those positions legally. The "acting" Secretary of the Department of Homeland Security, Chad Wolf, and his deputy, Ken Cuccinelli, were never confirmed for their positions by the Senate. There seems to be no Senate oversight.

The story gets better, or worse, depending on how you look at it. Wolf and Cuccinelli were moved into their jobs through the lines of succession in the department. However, those lines were altered by the previous DHS Secretary, Kevin McAleenan, who was not placed into his position properly. According to the GAO, McAleenan did not have authority to move Wolf, who had Senate confirmation for a different position, into the directorship.

Cuccinelli, who presently holds the title "Senior Official Performing the Duties of Deputy Secretary," has never been confirmed for anything. The inmates are running the asylum over in the Senate.

The Democrats immediately called for Wolf and Cuccinelli to be removed, but a DHS spokesman said that they disagree with the findings of the GAO and will "issue a formal response to this shortly." One would think this is open and shut, but apparently not.

Donald Trump's handling of the DHS raises serious questions about all of his agency appointments. DHS was established after 9/11, and now it is staffed with mostly political appointees who report to the president. Most often, Trump refuses to go through normal nomination processes, because he knows that many of his choices would not be approved even by a Republican Senate, if it was doing due diligence. He likes to have his appointees in limbo-because it gives him control over them. "I like acting," he tells reporters, because "it gives you great, great flexibility." More to the point, it gives him control over the people in those jobs. They have to do what he says, or they will lose their positions.

In reality, Trump has made practically no effort to fill positions at DHS with qualified people. In the agencies that oversee immigration, Customs and Border Protection, US Citizenship and Immigration Services, none of them has a leader that has been confirmed by the Senate. I believe there is a timeframe beyond which an "acting" has to either be confirmed or be replaced. Clearly, the Senate has done no oversight on an agency that has separated families and treated children like animals.

Tom Ridge was the first Secretary of DHS. He said that the power Trump has over that agency makes it like "the president's personal militia." That is a very scary concept. You will remember that it was Chad Wolf who oversaw the deployment of federal officers to Portland, Oregon, which ultimately ended badly for Trump.

It seems that for all the time and attention Donald Trump spends controlling agencies and moving people around, he could have mounted a massive attack on the coronavirus-lockdown, universal mask-wearing, social distancing throughout the country, and we would be able to enjoy the summer, eat in restaurants, open businesses and the kids and teachers would be going back to school safely.

After 170,000 citizens have died, Donald Trump is a no-show, when he could have been a leader. Our blood is on his hands

Democratic Convention begins, and the 100th anniversary of the 19th Amendment intersects

August 18, 2020

George Washington and Michelle Obama have one important thing in common; they both hated politics.

Precisely because he didn't want the job, the Founders insisted that Washington become the President. He was a great leader, served for two terms (April 30, 1789-March 4, 1797), and then decided that two terms were enough. After all, he led the Patriot forces to victory in the nation's War for Independence, and presided at the Constitutional Convention of 1787, which established the Constitution and the government. In his "farewell," Washington advised American citizens to view themselves as a cohesive unit and avoid political parties.

Michelle Obama was a reluctant political wife when her husband was elected President. She was the first African-American First Lady of the United States, and she brilliantly found her own way. Through four main initiatives, she became a role model for women and an advocate for healthy families, for service members and their families, supported higher education, and advocated for international adolescent girls' education. While initially hesitant, she became an extraordinary speaker on behalf of her husband, Barack Obama, and the democratic values of the country, delivering three outstanding speeches at three Democratic conventions.

The third speech was last night, as the Democratic National Convention began by holding a most unconventional celebration-online. Michelle Obama was the keynote speaker, and she brought the message home, making a moral and practical case against Donald Trump and in favor of Joe Biden. She was brilliant, only mentioned Trump's name once, and indicated that we need to make a change now, because "he is not up to the job."

She answered the question-Do you still believe that we should go high when others go low? She answered, "yes, but let's be clear, going high does not mean putting on a smile and saying nice things when confronted by viciousness and cruelty. Going high means taking the harder path. Going high means standing fierce against hatred while remembering that we are one nation under God, and if we want to survive, we've got to find a way to live together and work together across our differences."

If you did not hear her speech, it is well worth watching in its entirety.

The other speech that was brilliantly delivered last night, was that of Bernie Sanders, who I think gave the speech of his lifetime. He endorsed Joe Biden wholeheartedly, even though they don't necessarily agree on the path to certain ends. Bernie graciously indicated to his progressives that they need to vote for Biden. Sanders is a proud American, and last night he was a true patriot, warning against the surging COVID and creeping authoritarianism. Bernie Sanders warned that we have to "save our democracy from Trump." It was an inspiring and passionate speech.

There were many other striking speakers. One young woman who deeply affected me said, "My father had only one pre-existing condition. He trusted Donald Trump, went to a karaoke bar, contracted the virus, and died at age 65." I suspect that many other people, who listened to Trump say that the virus was a "hoax," have learned the same lesson.

There is much more from last night to discuss, and more to come tonight, when Dr. Jill Biden speaks, along with Alexandria Ocasio Cortez.

Happily, today is an historic day that deserves very special attention. One hundred years ago, with the Nineteenth Amendment to the Constitution, women got the vote. It was passed by Congress on June 4, 1919, and ratified on August 18th, 1920.

"The right of citizens of the United States to vote shall not be denied or abridged by the United States or any State on account of sex."

"Congress shall have the power to enforce this article by appropriate legislation."

It is ironic that we are in the middle of an historic election where the administration is interfering with the Post Office, and subverting the right to vote. For one thing, the USPS is a service, embedded in the Constitution from the beginning. In polls taken recently, 91% of citizens trust the USPS, more than any other American agency. It handles more than 5 million pieces of mail daily. In addition to postcards, letters and small packages, vital medicines for veterans and others are delivered via the Post Office. Important government checks are delivered in the U.S. mail. It doesn't matter how far away an address is, a postman will deliver to that place.

Subverting the mail is a most serious challenge to our election, and to the health of American citizens and our democracy. In an extremely rare move, Nancy Pelosi recalled the House of Representatives to meet and deal with the postal problem. The House has subpoenaed the new Postmaster General to appear before the House, and apparently, he is scheduled for next week.

The changes in the USPS present serious legal problems. For one thing, it is illegal to tamper with the mail, and most serious to tamper with elections, punishable with jail time. It's also entirely possible that this is a RICO-criminal event, depending on what the House hears from Mr. DeJoy. There is the question of whether Donald Trump gave DeJoy instructions, but they might have come through Steve Mnuchin, Secretary of the Treasury.

There is much more to discuss, and I hope to shine a light on it tomorrow

Public Pressure Works!

August 18, 2020

In the last few hours Louis DeJoy, the Postmaster General, announced that he is pulling back on the changes that he made to the USPS, until after the election. All of his changes seriously affected veterans, medicine delivery and mail delivery of checks and other personal and critical business items. The turnaround happened after pressure came from all sides: citizens countrywide who rely on the Post Office service. In fact, it is meant to be a service, not a business. From the very beginning when it was written into the Constitution, the USPS provided delivery service to all citizens, no matter where they lived. There are 630,000 postal workers, many black Americans, who are proud postmen and women workers in the post offices.

Speaker Pelosi has called the House back to DC, and it will vote on Saturday, normally a sacred day for legislators. Louis DeJoy is set to testify on Friday and next week as well.

A few crucial questions remain, primarily because the service of the USPS to its citizens is not just an election issue.

1-Will the 671 sorters be returned to their original locations? If so, will they remain?

2- Has overtime been restored? Will it remain after the election?

3- Will the blue boxes be returned, since they are the iconic means by which citizens know they can post a letter?

4- Will the high level, experienced postal people, who were fired in a Friday night massacre, be returned to their original jobs?

5- Will there be an investigation into who was put on the Board of Trustees? Are they knowledgeable and experienced in the workings of the USPS? Or not?

6- Will the appointed Postmaster General resign? He has conflicts of interest with millions of dollars invested in companies that are in opposition to the USPS. Those companies have a stake in privatizing the USPS.

It's clear that pressure works, and that is why active citizens make all the difference in our democracy. My Senator, Cory Booker (D-NJ), often says, "Democracy is not a spectator sport."

While the Post Office crisis was sorting itself out, the second night of the Democratic National Convention was held, with the actress Tracy Ellis Ross as emcee. Normally, this would be the single most important news, but there is so much else happening, the convention is one of many emerging and serious stories.

While still online, the DNC created a most clever and illuminating presentation to conduct the business of the nomination process. Beginning with Alabama, and then a tribute to John Lewis, delegates from each state stood in front of iconic scenes of their states, and gave the numbers-for Bernie Sanders and Joe Biden. These videos were a virtual travelogue of our magnificent country, were informative and much faster than the cumbersome in-person convention roll calls.

I hope that they keep that piece of the convention in years to come. In fact, there are many reasons to hold this convention virtually. One reason is financial. The money spent on conventions in prior years could now be used to help out of work and hungry citizens in each state. The theme of the convention is, "We the People," and the focus on each state allowed the delegates to describe each place in an inspiring short narrative.

When the state of Delaware was called, Delaware passed, wanting the pleasure of putting its favorite son, Joe Biden, over the top for President of the United States. At that moment, the celebratory joy was captured in many online squares of people happily clapping and cheering.

The theme of the second night was "leadership." The first item on the list was healthcare, for which Elizabeth Warren and Bernie Sanders fought, and they recorded an excellent spot for Joe Biden. Then former acting Attorney General Sally Yates, followed. You will remember that she went to the White House in person to warn the president that Michael Flynn was jeopardizing national security. (Barack Obama had already told Donald Trump not to let him back into the White House, since Obama had fired him). Like a child, one word from Obama, and Trump did the exact opposite. Now, Sally Yates had concrete evidence against Flynn, and was worried because Trump had named him his National Security Advisor. Trump ignored the evidence and fired Sally Yates. This should have been a red-flashing light, but it was ignored by the now majority Republican Senate that was so happy to be in power. That response was going to play out time and again in the ensuing years, right up until today.

Sally Yates was followed by former President Bill Clinton, who gave one of the shortest but most powerful, speeches of his career. It was a brilliant explanation of where we are, and he made a cogent argument against Trump's handling of the coronavirus. John Kerry spoke, then former Chairman of the Joint Chiefs of Staff and former Secretary of State, Colin Powell, who gave a powerful speech about the values of a democratic America and why it was important to keep them.

A poignant vignette of the evening was when Cindy McCain, John McCain's widow, narrated a video that described the special friendship between Joe Biden and John McCain (R-AZ) that went across the political aisle. The video seemed to imply that it was that friendship for Biden that influenced McCain to go against Trump and vote in favor of the Affordable Care Act.

The keynote speaker of the evening was Jill Biden, who told the story of her life with Joe, in individual stories that were warm and inspiring. She is a teacher, and spoke from her classroom. When Joe Biden was elected Vice President, Jill Biden continued to teach, and her sense of dedication to her students was palpable. If Biden/Harris wins, it is entirely possible that we will have a First Lady who is a role model for many young girls and teachers in general.

Day Number three is coming up this evening, with Kamala Harris, the presumptive Vice President, speaking. She is an historic pick, a black-American, Asian-American and the first woman of color on an American Presidential ticket. Exciting things are in store!

"A More Perfect Union"

August 20, 2020

The third night of the Democratic National Convention was historic on many levels, and breathtakingly impressive. Historically, it was the 100th anniversary of the 19th Amendment to the Constitution, giving women the vote. However, it's important to know that black women didn't actually get the vote until the Voting Rights Act of 1965, signed by President Lyndon Johnson.

In light of that history, the nomination of Vice President Kamala Harris on the Democratic ticket was historic, a famous first. She is the first black-American and Asian American to be on a national ticket. The daughter of immigrants, born in Oakland, California, graduate of Howard University, a lawyer who became a district Attorney, then Attorney General of California, then Senator, she is eminently qualified for the office. Senator Harris gave a warm and revelatory speech, introducing us to her family and friends, her impressive history, and the values she holds of decency and justice for all.

Kamala Harris was the last speaker of the evening. It was a night filled with extraordinary political speakers, mainly women on both sides of the aisle and with their own points of view, each of which validated Kamala Harris' nomination.

Democrats revealed their values and policies through the real stories of women. One of the most inspiring was when former Rep. Gabby Giffords, a gun violence survivor who was shot as she was having a constituent event, spoke. She said, "I struggle to speak, but I have not lost my voice." She has worked for years with her husband, Mark Kelly, to regain her speech, and last night was a true personal victory for her.

Many diverse women were the highlight of the evening. Senator Elizabeth Warren is one of the most powerful speakers in the Democratic party. She is mesmerizing, and she weaved her biography into her strong call for universal child care. She spoke from a child care center, which accented the seriousness of her original struggle as a young mother, and the challenges that the cost of child care put in her way. Most important, the three things that she and Bernie Sanders have been espousing-subsidized child care, universal health care, and paid parental leave, once thought to be on the fringe-have become mainstream policies in many quarters.

Hillary Clinton, who won more than three million votes than Trump, but lost the Electoral College, reminded us that citizens need to vote (many millions did not in 2016), and we don't want a "woulda, coulda, shoulda" moment again, because look what we got.. On the first night, Michelle Obama gave us the data that was shocking. In one state, just two votes in each precinct won the state for Trump. The point for each woman is that **every vote counts.** As citizens, it's our responsibility to vote. Hearing Hillary Clinton affirm her faith in America, about how great we truly are, especially after what happened in 2016, was genuinely moving.

There were other excellent and moving speeches, again by women. Speaker Nancy Pelosi, our most consequential political leader, reminded us of the ongoing fight waged daily on behalf of all citizens, especially now in light of the attack on the Post Office and our right to vote.

Dr. Jill Biden, who may become our next First Lady, spoke warmly of Joe Biden and the lessons they have learned in the midst of tragedy. Dr. Biden loves teaching, and even as the wife of the Vice President, she continued teaching her students, much to the surprise of everyone. She spoke from her classroom, which reminded all of us that because of the coronavirus, and Donald Trump's non-response, many schools are closed and our education system is in chaos.

The next to the last speaker was former President, Barack Obama. He was supposed to be last, but graciously changed his spot, so that Kamala Harris could be the final speaker on this most historic evening for her and for the country.

In Philadelphia, the birthplace of our democracy, former President Obama spoke from the Museum with a large blowup of the Constitution as his backdrop. This was a different Obama. Normally speaking with reason and a restrained passion, he revealed his emotions, saying that Donald Trump (he rarely calls his name), is a threat to our democracy. "No drama, Obama" has been known for his steadiness, so it was shocking to see how afraid and heartsick he is for our democracy. President Obama seemed to have tears in his eyes. This was the most emotional Barack Obama that we have seen, with the exception of the time of the Newtown shooting. He spoke about the cynicism and hopelessness of the Trump presidency, and literally begged us to vote and preserve the democracy that people lost their lives to attain.

It was a moment in time. Presidents normally don't criticize a sitting president, but Barack Obama felt that the country was in so much jeopardy that he came out and said that, "I did hope for the sake of our country, that Donald Trump might show some interest in taking the job seriously, that he might come to feel the weight of the office and discover some reverence for the democracy that had been placed in his care. But he never did." And Obama went on in a brilliant overview of the Trump presidency, and he exhorted citizens to vote Trump out of office. (If you don't see the speech, I hope that you watch it)

As this third night was progressing, there were other wonderful segments that were produced by the campaign. The video pieces were especially moving, particularly one featuring a little girl whose dad was a Marine, and whose mom was deported. Immigration is no longer being treated as an abstract policy issue. Now it is personal for the Democrats.

In the past, when a political party was presenting its campaign, the other party would remain mostly, silent, out of respect. However, this changed with the presence of Donald Trump, who cross-campaigned in 2016 and for these days in 2020. He planned visits to battleground states in the last three days, including to Scranton, Pa. for the last night, when Joe Biden would be giving his acceptance speech. One more norm would be destroyed. While the DNC convention was happening, Donald Trump was tweeting insults at the speakers, including Michelle Obama. As Barack Obama spoke, Trump rage-tweeted in all-caps. His behavior was very disturbing.

On the fourth and final night, Joe Biden gave one of the finest speeches of his life. He emphasized inclusiveness, and that he would be the president for all the people, not just those who voted for him. He indicated that we had serious challenges, but that working together we could overcome the virus, get back our economy and work on justice for all.

There has been entirely too much to adequately describe the wonderful talks given on the third and fourth nights. I strongly suggest going back and watching some of the talks and the videos.

Interestingly, the online mode actually made the speeches more intimate, more understandable and more inspiring. The lack of huge crowds screaming and shouting was calming, especially in such a serious pandemic and job loss. Words matter. Tone matters.

While the convention was unfolding, huge events were being reported. I will talk about them in my next blog, because I don't want to sully the fine Democratic convention with news of criminals. Just as a teaser, yesterday morning, Steve Bannon, one of Donald Trump's closest advisors, was arrested on a 29 million-dollar yacht, cruising in Connecticut. He was arrested on wire fraud and money-laundering charges, stemming from a border wall scam that raised twenty-five million dollars, and from which Bannon stole money. There are many emails and other evidence that could send Bannon to jail for many years. More to come.

"We the people" were put on full display for the last two nights. We can be proud.

"We the People," (continued)

August 20, 2020

Continuing the convention coverage, the fourth night had another stellar lineup, many of whom were Joe Biden's opponents in the primary. Cory Booker, Pete Buttigieg, Andrew Yang and Michael Bloomberg each represented his own particular interest, and in each man's speech,

Joe Biden was enthusiastically endorsed by what was being said. My Senator, Cory Booker, is a special friend of Kamala Harris, a Senate colleague who he has gotten to know well, and he is thrilled with Biden's choice of Kamala to be Vice President. Mike Bloomberg, who described Trump's litany of business failures, wanted to know, "why the hell would you want to give this guy another four years?"

Joe Biden also included in the lineup of speakers two women who he had considered for Vice President. Keisha Lance Bottoms, Mayor of Atlanta and Senator Tammy Duckworth, each spoke about their areas of interest and expertise. Senator Duckworth, in particular, spoke of Trump's lack of caring for veterans, as well as for the soldiers in the field. Trump has not called out Vladimir Putin for paying bounties to the Taliban in order to murder American soldiers. That alone should be enough for another impeachment, but Trump has said nothing and neither have the Republican Senators.

One other beautiful and moving part of the evening was with a young boy-Brayden Harrington, from New Hampshire, who was a stutterer. When Joe Biden met him on a trip to his state, he told Braden that they were "members of the same club," of stutterers. Biden became friends with young Brayden, and gave him some tips about how he worked on his own speech, which is that he read poetry aloud and other writings. Brayden Harrington did a beautiful tribute to Joe Biden, and it was breathtaking. You could almost hear the entire country hold its breath as the young man struggled to speak. Brayden Harrington's story showed the humanity of the candidate for President, and the effect that Biden's reaching out had on this young man. I watched it in tears, and I heard that other people cried as well.

There is another extraordinary moment that I don't want to overlook. Jon Meacham, historian and writer of many wonderful books, took the opportunity to speak about our country as he endorsed Joe Biden. A native of Tennessee, Jon Meacham has never let us in on his personal political preferences until now. He spoke beautifully in the same way that he writes, and it was a wonderful opportunity to get a glimpse into Meacham's soul.

The Democrats let us know that "we the people" includes everyone, and the big tent will be welcoming and inclusive.

The four- day convention was creative and brought its message home. At the end of Joe Biden's speech, there was a marvelous celebration-in the parking lot of the venue-with fireworks! Cars were parked socially distant with headlights on and red, white and blue lights flashing. Considering that there are restraints on gathering, the last event was done in a marvelous way that allowed everyone to smile and relish the joy of a job well done.

When the President resembles a mob boss

Week of August 17th – 22, 2020

Not wanting to sully the fine people who spoke for four days at the Democratic Convention, here is a rundown of the latest example of Trump's excellent record for picking the "best people" for his administration.

Steve Bannon– Trump's campaign manager in 2016, and his chief strategist in the White House, was arrested the morning of the 18th, by a cohort of postal police and others on the Connecticut waters in a 29 million-dollar yacht. He is charged with wire fraud and money-laundering, based on promises that he was collecting money to build Trump's border wall. Instead, he and three others used the money for luxury items: lawyer bills, plastic surgery, and more. This case was pursued by the Southern District of New York, and apparently there are emails and much evidence that could conceivably send Bannon to jail for years. Since it is a state case, there are no pardons available from the federal jurisdiction, namely Trump.

Roger Stone -Trump's longtime friend and political advisor, who was convicted of lying under oath to Congress. He was also convicted of tampering with a witness during the investigation into Russian interference in the 2016 election. He sent signals to Trump that he would be loyal, kept his mouth shut, and Trump commuted his sentence.

Paul Manafort –Trump's former campaign chairman, who was deeply in debt, yet worked for free on the campaign. This should have raised alarm bells. He was convicted of bank fraud and tax fraud, and then he pled guilty to conspiracy charges related to money laundering, lobbying violations and witness tampering. He received millions of dollars from some pro-Russian Ukrainian politicians. He is presently in jail, but has kept his mouth shut on much of this. Trump has sent signals that he is planning to pardon him, again because his crimes are related to Russia.

Michael Cohen – Trump's former personal lawyer and "fixer." He pleaded guilty to paying "hush money," in order to keep two women quiet who said that Trump cheated with them on Melania. Cohen lied to Congress about a proposed Trump Tower in Moscow. When he testified before Congress, he implicated Trump, angered Trump, and so will never get a pardon. He also wrote a book, despite the fact that Trump and AG Barr tried to stop him from publishing it. Cohen's lawyers successfully got him out of jail, based on the fact that he had been put there improperly.

Michael Flynn – When Trump took office, Barack Obama told him NOT to bring Mike Flynn back into the White House, since he had previously fired Flynn. Trump ignored that good advice, and made Flynn National Security Advisor, which allowed him to avoid Senate approval. Flynn served for less than a month, since he was already on the take with a foreign power, Turkey. He pleaded guilty-twice-to lying to the FBI about his interactions with Russia's ambassador to the US. Flynn was compromised, and Sally Yates, United States Deputy Attorney General, actually came to the White House to tell Trump that Flynn was dangerous to our national security. Trump fired her, then he fired Flynn, because he lied to the FBI and to VP Pence. The chaos in the first days of Trump's presidency was shocking and deeply disturbing, to say the least, but the chaos was merely a precursor of what was to come.

Flynn was going to cooperate, and got some leeway from the feds, then he got a new lawyer and claimed that the FBI had entrapped him. At that point, Trump reversed and said that Flynn had been treated badly, whereas AG Barr dropped all charges. Emmet Sullivan, the judge in the case, was so furious that he refused to drop the charges, and he called for a hearing by all nine judges on the federal bench. Judge Sullivan, when he pronounced his sentence, told Flynn, "you sold out your country." Flynn may yet be pardoned, because he hasn't said anything bad about Trump.

Rick Gates – was the deputy chairman of Trump's 2016 presidential campaign, and Manafort's assistant. He pleaded guilty to conspiring against the United States, and lying to investigators. Gates cooperated with Robert Mueller and testified against Manafort and Stone. He served 45 days in jail for his cooperation.

George Papadopoulos – Trump's 2016 campaign advisor. He pleaded guilty to lying to the FBI about his contacts with Russian officials, as well as someone who promised him "dirt" on Hillary Clinton. He served 14 days.

There are so many more, including Russians who the intelligence agency named, but could not extradite from Russia. The list is long.

Most important, this week the Senate Intelligence report on connections between the 2016 Russian intelligence officer who received sensitive internal polling data from the campaign. The report goes on to say that Constantin Kilimnik may have been directly involved in hacking of Democratic National Committee emails and handing the stolen files to Wikileaks. The report also established that Trump often discussed the Wikileaks document dump with Roger Stone, then lied about those discussions with investigators. That single fact alone would seem to be enough for impeachment, for a second time. The level of criminality around this president is astounding and unparalleled.

The Washington Post columnist, Jennifer Rubin, published an article entitled, "As it turns out, there really was collusion between the Trump campaign and Russia." This is the fifth and final report by the Republican-led committee, and it is damning.

House Speaker, Nancy Pelosi, focused on the 2020 election, and said, "America's intelligence and law enforcement communities have made clear that the Russian Government is continuing to wage an assertive intervention campaign to benefit the President, warning of a '365-days-a- year threat' to compromise the 2020 elections and undermine our democracy.

Of course, we have our own internal threat, in the person of the president, who appointed a new Postmaster General. Louis DeJoy put changes in place that now threaten our voting and mail-in ballots. Moreover, since the new guy has no idea of the range of the Post Office, he didn't realize that denying the mail can often be a matter of life and death. Veterans get their meds in the mail, and everyone gets checks and other crucial business papers. The loss of overtime, sorters and blue boxes has caused such an outcry that DeJoy has been forced to appear before a Senate committee today, and before the House this coming week.

Also, this week news from Russia indicates that another opposition leader has been poisoned. Aleksei Navalny drank a cup of tea and got violently ill on an airplane. He was removed and taken to a hospital, where he was in intensive care, and breathing on a ventilator. There has been no word from either Trump or the State Department, that usually would lodge a serious complaint. America has been side-lined by its own actions, or inactions, in the last four years. The greatest country in the world has become irrelevant and a laughingstock.

We have our own mob boss planning his RNC convention, beginning Monday. No one knows much about it, but we will see soon enough. An unbelievable number of advisors have wound up in Jail or in trouble. I suspect there will be more.

Trump to Putin: "I'm a big fan of yours."

In the ongoing saga of Donald Trump's taxes, the latest is that the court denied the attempt by Trump to avoid showing his taxes. The United States Supreme Court made it clear that the President is not above the law. More on this as it unfolds. It is entirely possible that the case will go to the grand jury, and more time will be wasted. In that regard, Trump has lost in the courts, but he has managed to delay and delay, and in that way, he has won, at least for a while.

Imagine how different life would be if Donald Trump had spent this time working to defeat the virus in March.

The Trump Show

August 24-26th, 2020

The Republican party convention opened Monday morning, in Charlotte, North Carolina. The roll call vote nominated Donald Trump for a second term. Actually, the convention opened and closed with that meeting in Charlotte. Roll call is the only legal reason for the delegates to meet. The rest is like reality TV-the Trump Show.

Historically, the president does not appear until the fourth night when he gives his acceptance speech. However, Monday Trump appeared after the roll call and spoke for fifty minutes in a disorganized, unscripted rant. Then he appeared two more times on the first day, putting himself squarely in front of the public watching in person and on television. It was another norm-busting day.

Donald Trump is clearly determined to be reelected. He actually filed for reelection in January of 2017, as he was being inaugurated. This seemed like a strange thing to do at the time, jumping the gun, one might say. We have to wonder-WHY?

With Donald Trump the smart thing to do is follow the money. In fact, campaign money can be used to pay for lawyers in certain situations. Of course, the other reason would be to follow his legal jeopardy. Sure enough, as of May, the campaign spent more than $16 million on legal services. I have no way of knowing if these were legitimate campaign expenses, or not. In the past, Trump often blurred those lines and used the Trump Foundation to pay for personal legal fees and other expenses. Prior presidents-Obama ($5.5million), Bush ($8.8 million), who were in office for eight years, used considerably less campaign money.

For Donald Trump, finances and legal considerations intersect in a big way. For one thing, if Trump is reelected, the Department of Justice maintains that a sitting president cannot be indicted. It is not a law, merely a tradition based on a letter that could be easily reversed. Considering the dangers to Trump-from the Attorney General of New York and the Southern District in Manhattan, he could be indicted as a private citizen on both civil and criminal grounds if he loses the election.

Simultaneous with the RNC convention, this past week the Attorney General of New York, Letitia James, filed a lawsuit to compel the Trump Organization to comply with subpoenas related to an investigation into whether President Trump and his company improperly inflated the value of its assets on financial statements. This investigation was launched after the president's former personal attorney, Michael Cohen, testified in Congress that Trump inflated and deflated his net worth at various times, in order to obtain tax benefits and more favorable terms for loans.

The big picture is that the Attorney General's investigation is one of several probes that Trump and his company are facing, as he seeks reelection. Earlier on Monday, Manhattan District Attorney, Cyrus Vance, said he would hold off on a subpoena for Trump's financial records until an appeals court weighed in on that case.

Attorney General James said, "I took action to force the Trump Organization, and specifically Eric Trump, to comply with my office's ongoing investigation into its financial dealings. For months, the Trump Organization has failed to fully comply with our subpoenas in this investigation."

This is a civil fraud case, and it is very serious. Eric Trump and the Trump organization are accused of hiding income of at least 100 million dollars. Eric Trump refused to testify, and indicated that he was concerned that this case might be conjoined with the criminal case that the New York District Attorney, Cyrus Vance, was pursuing.

In this same week (and it's only Wednesday!), on Tuesday, New York Attorney General James accused Postmaster General Louis DeJoy and President Trump of turning the US Postal Service into "a political football to undermine a federal election," in a lawsuit seeking to block changes in postal policies.

I watched the House investigation of DeJoy on Monday, and it was very apparent that he has no idea what the postal system does, or even how much it costs to send a postcard or one of those square envelopes. He was belligerent, obviously annoyed, and when asked if he would return the sorters, he unequivocally said "no." Interestingly, DeJoy indicated that he didn't actually know who gave the orders to make all the changes. It's entirely possible that Secretary Mnuchin or someone familiar with the USPS actually implemented the changes. This is pure speculation.

The Post Office lawsuit is important, because more Americans than ever are expected to vote by mail during the coronavirus pandemic. Trump has spread the idea that increased mail-in voting will lead to widespread voter fraud. There is absolutely no evidence of this, even in the nine or so states that have had mail-in voting for years. Trump is trying to discourage people from voting, relying on the concept that the fewer people who vote, the better it is for him. However, in the past many Republicans have voted by mail, quite successfully, so it's not clear how or why Trump is talking about fraud. The House of Representatives passed a bill to provide funding for the USPS, but Trump has indicated he would block all funding for mail-in voting. He said in public statements that his denial is connected to the election. It's important to point out that interfering with the mail in an election is a crime.

The Trump organization and the Trump family by definition, have been mired in legal problems for many years. The prior Attorney General, Eric Schneiderman, brought a fraud suit against Trump University, which defrauded people who paid tuition and received nothing. Donald Trump, who was about to become president, settled the case, paid $25 million and that was the end of it. As a regular citizen, he most likely would have been in jail.

I've been working up to a discussion of The Trump Show, none of which was legally necessary after the initial roll call on Monday morning in Charlotte. Donald Trump, against all norms, has been using the White House as a backdrop for his campaign. He planned the next four nights as political validation of himself in order to influence voters.

The Hatch Act, passed in 1939, does not allow public property to be used for partisan politics, with the exception of the president and VP. Trump has been using the Marines, which is illegal. Through various surrogates who spoke on Monday and Tuesday, the message about the pandemic is that Donald Trump saved thousands of lives. The surrogates make it sound as if the coronavirus is a thing of the past. That message is a shameful lie. In fact, Trump ignored the virus, so that it wouldn't hinder his economic message and his reelection. Similarly, Larry Kudlow, talked about the economy in terms that indicate all is well, rather than acknowledge the fact that the pandemic has caused 28 million people to lose their jobs, and thousands of businesses are ruined.

We are definitely hearing about an alternative universe in the Trump show. The problem is that Americans have been used to believing our presidents. Unfortunately, Donald Trump traffics in misinformation, disinformation and outright lies. Thousands of people believe what he says, and that is going to be more of a problem in the next few months.

It was difficult to listen to the speeches. Donald Trump, Jr., said the Democrats stand for "rioting, looting and vandalism." South Carolina Governor, Nikki Hailey, said that race relations aren't bad in America after all. These statements were spoken in light of the killing of George Floyd and just yesterday, the shooting of Jacob Blake, shot in the back seven times and now paralyzed. One thousand black men have been killed in the last year. In comparison, only three people have been killed in Great Britain, where there are very few guns. In the year of "magical thinking," we are now at 180,000 dead, and still Trump has no plan for the federal government to fight the virus. I am very frustrated and angry. People are dying and nothing is being done by the president, who claims the virus is a "hoax" and "no big deal.". Unfortunately, millions of Americans believe him.

There was one notable exception to all the speakers in two days. Melania Trump offered her sincere condolences to all those who have lost loved ones. She called it Covid-19, rather than the China virus, and she spoke of parenting as well, a breath of fresh air in an otherwise squalid evening.

The Hatch Act was ignored. There were military men in the White House opening doors as if for a potentate. Trump was flanked by servicemen in the White House, naturalized five immigrants, pardoned a man, and generally defied all propriety and norms.

It's difficult to choose which was the most alarming and most hypocritical event. I would have to choose the "Naturalization" ceremony for five immigrants. There are thousands of immigrants seeking legal asylum and forced to wait on the border, many separated from their children, in one of the most inhumane acts in our history. Children have been put in cages, which is savage cruelty, and there will be serious damage to them emotionally. It is easily the most callous program of the Trump administration, promulgated by Steven Miller, the devil in charge of all bad things Trump.

Taking those five immigrants and using them as props really was horrible. The program was meant to show that Donald Trump honored immigration, when we know quite the opposite. The ceremony was conducted by Chad Wolf, who is not in his job legally. In addition, the Trump administration has acted to eliminate the process of proper asylum seeking from many of the people from Honduras, Guatemala and all Central American countries. The hypocrisy of the Trump Show in the last two days has been stunning, and was done to show that Trump is not anti-immigrant.

The other event that ties for hypocrisy (and illegality) was the speech from Jerusalem of Mike Pompeo, Secretary of State, who endorsed Trump's policies. No one in the State Department is allowed to attend a political convention or be partisan in any way. There was a memo sent around by Pompeo himself. He was in Israel on a state visit, but said it was personal. If that is true, then he should have flown United or Delta and paid for it himself. Even so, it was improper for Pompeo to speak supporting Trump, and an investigation has begun.

Melania Trump spoke from the Rose Garden to an in-person group, mostly not wearing masks. For some unfathomable reason, she decided to redo all of Jackie Kennedy's garden, from the 1960s, where she planned beautiful flowering trees and colorful flowers. The pictures of the replacement garden show it to be rather rigid and not colorful.

During the evening, Rachel Maddow, Nicolle Wallace and Joy Reid served as commentators and fact-checkers, since these two nights have strayed far from the truth. Their knowledge and ability to quickly present reality was important, and it will continue for the next few nights.

We have two more nights to go, but other history is being made in the wake of Jacob Blake's shooting. As I go to press, there is so much to cover and important things are happening. The NBA has cancelled all of its games, with the players indicating that they are not going to play until its members can feel safe in their cars. This is a breathtaking support of the black community, and a powerful one, since the basketball players are mostly black, and huge role models for millions of Americans of all ages. This is a game-changer. Let's see who else comes forward with support. I'm predicting baseball and football will make a statement.

I hope that you are safe and healthy, and will find some joy as well as some humor in the next few days, despite the tragic nature of what is happening around us.

Fifty-seven years ago, Martin Luther King had "a dream ..."

August 29, 2020

As a break from the lavishness and lawlessness of the last night of the RNC, I want to write today about historic events that are relevant to racial justice and our communities today.

The March on Washington for Jobs and Freedom was held on Wednesday, August 28th, 1963. It was held in Washington, D.C., and the purpose was to advocate for civil and economic rights for African-Americans. It was organized by the "big six" of the civil rights movement-A. Philip Randolph Whitney Young, Martin Luther King, James Farmer and John Lewis, the youngest by far. Bayard Rustin was the chief organizer, and he built an alliance of civil rights, labor and religious organizations that came together under the banner of "jobs and freedom." About 250,000 people came from all over the country to peacefully advocate for change. At the time, it was one of the largest political rallies for human rights in United States history. The pictures of the March at the Lincoln Memorial are iconic, and I remember the day well.

For one thing, the entertainment was awesome. Among many committed entertainers were Joan Baez, Bobby Darin, Odetta, Bob Dylan, Lena Horne and Peter, Paul and Mary. There were other celebrities as well, including Marlon Brando, Harry Belafonte, Paul Newman, Sammy Davis, Jr., James Baldwin, Jackie Robinson and many others. Wheesh! Just recalling that collection of artists makes my heart skip many beats. I was about to enter my junior year in college, and I honestly thought that something would be done for jobs and the civil rights of African-Americans. College students are often naive, and I was no exception.

In 1963, the "March" was celebrating the 1863 signing of the Emancipation Proclamation by President Abraham Lincoln. Martin Luther King, Jr. delivered his amazing "I have a dream" speech, which has inspired children and adults alike.

At the end of the day the leaders of the March met with President John F. Kennedy at the White House. Interestingly, the one man who represented the entire Jewish community at that meeting was Rabbi Joachim Prinz of Temple B'nai Abraham in Livingston, NJ. He was a close friend of Reverend King and someone who often marched with him.

On August 28th, 2013, the 50th anniversary of the March, one of the 1963 organizers, John Lewis, then a Congressman (D-GA) and U.S. Presidents Barack Obama, Bill Clinton and Jimmy Carter addressed a crowd on the steps of the Lincoln Memorial. Celebrities, such as Oprah Winfrey, also participated.

It is very disappointing to see that fifty-seven years later, civil rights and jobs for African-Americans are still serious challenges. While many gains have been made, there is much to do in the area of legislation and equal rights. Yesterday, in honor of the prior marches and organized by the National Action Network, the march was calling for racial justice and police reform. There have been 1,000 black men killed this year, including George Floyd, whose death was recorded on a video taken by a seventeen-year-old, and seen by millions. That video of the horrific eight minutes, literally changed the equation, and sparked thousands of protests in our country and around the world. Most recently, the shooting of Jacob Blake, seven times in the back by one police officer, sparked further outrage in both the black and white communities. Jacob Blake is paralyzed in a hospital.

The march yesterday has a legislative goal:1-a ban on chokeholds 2-serious police reform and ongoing training. and 3-renewing the voting rights act, naming it the John Lewis Voting Rights Act. Hopefully, these events will be taken up locally and in Congress, and there will finally be the change that was needed hundreds of years ago.

On August 29th, 1955, Emmett Till, a 14 -year old African-American boy was lynched, when he was accused of offending (flirting with her) a white woman in her family's grocery store. His lynching was a racist act that shocked the nation, and provided a catalyst for the emerging civil rights movement.

Because of social media, events that happen in real time are often recorded, and the fight for civil rights is moving more quickly than previously. One problem that has emerged is that equating the violence in the cities with the "black lives matter" movement, which has been mostly peaceful. In fact, white supremacists have committed many crimes this year, and white supremacy and antisemitism has risen exponentially during the presidency of Donald Trump.

We are living in dangerous times.

A Panoply of Disinformation-the fourth night of the Republicans

August 31, 2020

If you were searching for truth, the fourth night of the RNC convention yielded only a gaudy and excessive alternate reality- a shameless revision of what we are actually experiencing in life. In the Trump post-truth world, the president claims he has conquered the pandemic, produced a booming economy and healed racial strife. My head was spinning; fifteen hundred unmasked supporters were cheering, standing next to one another, apparently oblivious to the unfolding truth on earth. Do they really believe all that disinformation? Has no one in their orbit died of Covid-19, lost a job, or watched the protestors and the recent killing of Jacob Blake (who was never mentioned)? Is it FOX News all day, all the time?

Let's review. Trump did not acknowledge the serious nature of the virus for the most crucial six to eight weeks. Then he refused to invoke the Defense Production Act, which would have organized a universal testing program, supplied critical medical supplies and distributed them to the states. Instead, he told the states that they were on their own, and he took no responsibility for the outcome. One of the many shameless quotes of the evening came from Mike Pence, Trump's ever obsequious lackey, when he said, "President Trump marshaled the full resources of our federal government from the outset." (He did not) Pence continued, "He directed us to forge a seamless partnership with governors across America in both political parties." In fact, Trump played what he considered to be "red states" versus "blue states," and he distinguished between those who voted for him and those who did not. The truth is that we are all Americans, and Trump owed it to the American citizens in all states to work to protect us, which is what the oath of office promises.

Everything in Trumpland was upside down and backwards. In fact, it was surreal. I could barely squelch an impulse to start yelling at the television screen ("Don't you realize how phony and totally false this is?") Considering how far down in the polls Trump was, the desperation was palpable, and the desperate measures were understandable on some "fake news" level for a losing campaign.

However, lying is unforgivable, because Trump's lies and lack of action allowed the coronavirus to take hold and spread. To date, 180,000 citizens have died-fathers and mothers, sisters and brothers, friends and children. The country is grieving and Donald Trump is celebrating himself and his "victory." That is shameless.

Trump-full of bluff and bluster and patently insecure, began in Charlotte by accusing the Democrats of rigging the election (but only if he lost) because of mail-in voting, which has been historically secure. Trump, however, said it was "the greatest scam in the history of politics," which is false hyperbole. Didn't we hear that same thing in 2016, when he was sure he would lose? Only a small and petty, poor loser, spreads so much disinformation in order to create doubt about the election. Patriotic norms -a peaceful passing from one to another-have clearly gone into the dustbin. For me, it smacked of sixth grade elections for class officers, and the one kid who couldn't bear to lose who was a poor sport.

The decision to have the convention at the White House was improper, despite the fact that the Hatch Act exempted the president and VP. The Hatch Act forbids public property to be used for political purposes. What the Trump campaign put on was a slick, over the top, made for television set, with an overabundance of flags. Most inappropriate, huge campaign signs of TRUMP/PENCE were displayed all over the South Lawn of the White House. They turned the White House, "the peoples' house" (who he once said was a dump), into a huge campaign stage set.

The false accusations flew fast and furiously-that Joe Biden was in favor of defunding the police (he is not), the pandemic is in the past (it is not), that Donald Trump is not a racist (he is a bigot), and much more.

Possibly the most outrageous event of the fourth night was a "naturalization ceremony," staged in the White House, and meant to erase all the heinous treatment of immigrants on our borders and separated from their children. For years, immigrants coming to America could avail themselves of legal asylum proceedings. Donald Trump has totally eliminated that opportunity. As it turned out, two of the women who were filmed as they were becoming citizens, were never informed that the video would be used. At least one of them is not even a Trump supporter. They spoke out publicly afterwards, because it was a dishonest surprise.

Indeed, all of the people that night were used as props. The immigrants, the man who was pardoned, the McCloskeys, and even the US Marines, were used by Donald Trump to show that he is working to keep people safe, antithetical to his actual persona.

There were so many false accusations in one evening that created anxiety, confusion and agitation. Fortunately, MSNBC had a panel of fact-checkers in real time: Rachel Maddow, Nicolle Wallace, and Joy Reid, came on with the truth as some of the phony statements were spoken.

Speaker after speaker` another painted an America under Joe Biden- the carnage that would result if he is elected. Indeed, the irony is that the "American carnage" is exactly that of Trump's inauguration speech. One important thing to remember is that this IS Trump's America right now-the Trump who decries "lawlessness" on the streets is the most lawless president in our history. He breaks laws with impunity, stokes fears, disorients and demoralizes those who are listening. The confusion that he creates is very disturbing, and it is purposeful.

Earlier in the summer, the FBI issued an intelligence bulletin put out by the Department of Homeland Security and the National Counterterrorism Center, warning that "anarchist extremists continue to pose the most significant threat of targeted assaults against police." This is very important, and the FBI mentioned violent extremists, such as the "boogaloo" anarchist movement. The police officer who was killed in Oakland, California, was supposedly killed by a boogaloo supporter, not by protestors. It's important to make these distinctions.

Most recently, there was the alleged murder of two people in Kenosha, Wisconsin by Kyle Rittenhouse, a 17-year-old white teenager, who attended one of Trump's rallies, then crossed state borders. He had an illegal gun, and said he was there to protect a used car dealership, was bizarre. Trump seemed to have no interest in decrying that young man, or in quelling the unrest and violence in the cities.

In fact, one of Trump's advisors, Kellyanne Conway, indicated that the violence helps their campaign, a frightening admission.

Finally, somewhere around midnight on the fourth day, the convention concluded. While conventions often raise a man or woman to the height of peoples' perceptions, these four days were outrageous because of the lying and misinformation spread to the country. Trump has clearly learned that if you say something often enough, no matter how false, people start to believe it, or at least question their prior assumptions.

I think it was Michelle Obama who famously observed that the" Presidency doesn't make the man, it reveals who he is." We had enough fake revelation for a lifetime last week.

Continue to wear your masks, stay safe and keep healthy.

Is Another Four Years "Survivable" under Trump?

August 31, 2020

Last week, the weather report for the impending hurricane, "Laura", described the storm as "unsurvivable." That word (if it is a word) jumped out at me. In my seventy-six years, no other weather report had ever used such a shocking and definitive word. The powers that be clearly wanted everyone to leave, period.

Yes, I am a healthy senior, living in northern New Jersey and basically confined to my home since March, for my own safety. The first few months were spent watching the horrific news of thousands dying, freezer trucks being brought in for use as morgues, and neighbors dying without being able to see their loved ones. I worried that I might not survive. My children and grandchildren live in Brooklyn, and thankfully we communicate on Zoom. However, I am yearning for a hug!

The word "unsurvivable" has been haunting me. What is survivable and what is not? Watching the Democratic and Republican conventions was both illuminating and confusing. Is the bad news survivable, or is no truthful news unsurvivable? I learned what I needed to know from watching Governor Andrew Cuomo every day at 11:30am, giving us the bad news along with the possibilities, if we followed a few simple rules. Cuomo was inspiring and honest. As a result, we did what he said, and it succeeded. We learned that, while only 19 million people live in New York, an amazing 59 million people tuned in to listen when Governor Cuomo spoke. His news was authentic.

The four nights of the RNC presented an alternative universe to all the actual news. We have 180,000 people dead from the coronavirus, but that fact was never mentioned. Thirty million people lost their jobs in March and April, and a million people are still filing unemployment claims each week. That was never mentioned at the RNC convention. The Republican party seems to have gone on vacation, leaving unemployed millions with no help. This is not the America that I have known in the past, and it is deeply disappointing. In the Great Depression, FDR started programs under the New Deal, and they put people back to work in many areas. Donald Trump still has no unified plan to conquer the virus, to put people back to work, send our kids and grandkids to school safely, and establish calm and reestablish our norms. We are stuck in a nightmare of stagnancy and alternative reality.

Moreover, the use of the White House for a political rally -in violation of the Hatch Act, was gaudy and disdainful of the guidelines, which said that masks and social distancing were required, for safety.

The president railed against his opponent, Joe Biden, strangely saying that to elect him would bring chaos and many other ills to our country. He characterized Biden as being a" crazy, left-wing fanatic," which seemed nuts to me. Over forty years of watching Joe Biden in politics, I have only experienced him being a moderate. Stopping a moment and asking myself- "who is in charge of the country?" Ah, this is already Donald Trump's America, with all of these massive problems, and not a word about them. Where is the leadership?

My question of what is survivable began to take shape. I cannot survive when there is no truthful news, no reality.

Life during coronavirus is lived on a split screen, no, a triple screen. While people are dying, unemployed and hungry, a number of unarmed black males have been shot or physically killed by the police. Earlier, peaceful protestors, both black and white, joined together and brought "black lives matter" to the fore, yet no substantive actions have been taken. I began to despair that we would still have the status quo, with no actual progress.

But no! We may have reached an inflection point yesterday. The shooting of Jacob Blake, seven times in the back, was too much for everyone, especially the Wisconsin basketball team that refused to play its game, in protest. Other teams joined the Bucks, and the play-offs were cancelled. It was a very moving display of solidarity for social justice, a first for athletic teams and sports, and the result was very powerful.

The athletes found their voices. What a moment! Athletes appeal to all of us-young and old, black and white, and they were saying, "Enough." Athletes can influence everyone, and the message began to resonate throughout the country. I am hopeful that this leadership from the athletes will result in resounding change in our culture.

So much news in twenty-four hours. I must go with the people who tell the truth and take responsibility for solving our problems. Only with truth will I and the country survive.

Another four years will not be survivable in Donald Trump's America.

Crisis and Chaos: "losers and suckers"

September 3, 2020

We are in the middle of a number of serious crises. Let's review.

During the RNC convention, a black man was shot in Kenosha, Wisconsin, seven times in the back by a lone policeman. As a result, Jacob Black is paralyzed from the waist down. That event was not mentioned during the convention.

Why do we have these simultaneous crises?

The President is a science denier. He pushed the expert scientists to the shadows. I believe he is jealous of Dr. Fauci, who has served many presidents before Trump, with marvelous relationships.

Donald Trump is a climate denier, despite the fact that this past summer has been our hottest ever. He refuses to acknowledge that we need a national effort to save our environment and the planet.

Donald Trump is a racist. He refuses to say that there is systemic racism in our police departments and elsewhere.

In fact, none of our crises were acknowledged at the Republican convention: the pandemic (and resulting 187,000 deaths) was treated as if it was in the past. The systemic racism that exists in the police departments was ignored. The climate change crisis was never mentioned, even though we had the hottest summer on record. The wage gap and racial disparity in this country were not addressed, especially with the very wealthy, mostly white guests sitting on the South Lawn of the White House for the RNC, mostly without masks

The Friday after the RNC convention ended, Joe Biden was interviewed on MSNBC by Andrea Mitchell. He signaled his intention to be out and about and running an active campaign, while not endangering citizens. He then gave a powerful speech in Philadelphia, when he spoke of unity and discouraged the divisiveness that Donald Trump has sown. The Vice- Presidential candidate, Kamala Harris, gave a wonderful speech and she will prove to be an excellent asset on the campaign trail.

Returning to the protestors, who were characterized as looters, etc., rather than peaceful protestors of George Floyd's murder and those of other black citizens, the lies continued. However, there was a change in the atmosphere on the streets. "Black Lives Matter" joined white and black citizens marching together. Donald Trump knows that there has been more violence in our cities, but studies show that violence has been heightened by his rhetoric. Similarly, antisemitism has increased, and white supremacists have ramped up their activities, often coming into towns and creating violence.

The president went to Kenosha, Wisconsin against the wishes of both the governor and the mayor. Ostensibly, he went to express his sympathy, but it was clear that he used it as a campaign trip to change the conversation from the virus. It was transparent, because he insisted on making the trip, despite the fact that he was asked not to come. Trump clearly doesn't care about what the family needs. He wanted a campaign photo op, and met only with law enforcement.

Joe Biden went to Kenosha on Thursday, and met privately with Jacob Blake's family and spoke with Jacob Blake in the hospital. Joe Biden talked about the underlying causes-systemic racism-and met with community leaders. There was an important difference between the approaches of each man.

I will return to the events of the past week in detail, but now must take time to discuss an incredible, disturbing and stunning article by Jeffrey Goldberg, editor of *The Atlantic*, who wrote about Donald Trump's disdain for the military and his attitude about service. Just when I think things cannot get worse, Donald Trump fools me. In Trump's world, there is no bottom to what he can say and/or do.

Goldberg found that Trump has a real contempt for the troops, and considers them "losers" and "suckers, "especially if they are wounded in battle, or die.

Beginning in 2015, Goldberg was interested in the rather unusual attitude by Donald Trump towards John McCain, who was captured and held as a prisoner of war for five years. McCain's plane was shot down in 1967, by the North Vietnamese, and he was tortured. Trump was very fixated on John McCain, and in one interview, said "He's not a war hero." He then went on, "I like people who weren't captured." I remember that was a dreadful comment, and I thought for sure that would be the end of Donald Trump's career. Sadly, it wasn't. In contrast, Donald Trump never served in the military; he received five deferments for "bone spurs" in his feet.

Donald Trump has been so disrespectful of the troops, and especially of the wounded warriors. I remember when there were plans for a parade, Trump gave an order to not include soldiers who were wounded, because "no one wants to see that." As far as Trump is concerned, people who volunteer to serve in the military are "losers and suckers." There is no monetary gain in military service to one's country.

On June 6th, when America was paying tribute to D Day, Operation Overlord and the Normandy invasion, when the contingent was to honor fallen soldiers of Belleau Wood, Trump decided not to go. It was an outrageously insensitive and rude decision. Trump's excuse was that it was raining and the helicopter couldn't travel. The real truth is that Trump didn't want the rain to ruin his hair, and he had no idea why Belleau Wood was so historic. He said that the eighteen hundred Marines who died there were "losers" and "suckers." It is really difficult to write this piece, because so many of us know people who served and who lost family in war. We honor our dead, and we thank them for the sacrifices they made, so that we could be free.

Trump has no idea of our history, and even asked why America would go across the ocean to join the Allies. So ignorant. Very embarrassing that the Commander-in-Chief doesn't know anything. Goldberg's article is gut-wrenching. He tells a story of going to Arlington National Cemetery on Memorial Day in 2017, with John Kelly, who was then the Director of Homeland Security. Kelly's son, Robert, was a first lieutenant in the Marine Corps, and he was killed in Afghanistan in 2010. They went to the section where Kelly's son is buried, and Trump turned to Kelly and said, "I don't get it. What was in it for them?"

When he heard about the article, Donald Trump denied that he ever said those things, although many are on Twitter and were verified by numerous witnesses over the years. He continued to trash Jeffrey Goldberg and *The Atlantic* magazine (which he said he doesn't read). Trump said that the article was a "disgrace" and the people who spoke to Goldberg, "lowlifes."

I highly recommend that you read this article. In the midst of all the challenges and chaos, we still can be grateful that our journalism is free and Jeffrey Goldberg was able to write his article without retribution.

https://theatlantic.com/politics/archive/2020/09/trump-americans-who-died-at-war-are-losers-and suckers/615999/

Character Counts

September 5, 2020

Since Jeffrey Goldberg's story in *The Atlantic* described Donald Trump's bizarre and unpatriotic feelings towards the American military, the pushback on all sides has been furious. Trump denied he ever said it, but the horse is out of the barn, because too many things are out in the open. Joe Biden, the father of one who served, gave an impassioned speech about his disgust at Trump's statements.

I spent the last twenty-four hours listening to men and women who lost loved ones over the last century. Their tributes and their poignant responses had me weeping, because the feelings run so deep. Donald Trump's words besmirched the honor of their loved ones' loyalty to our country and their sacrifices.

My first shock at Donald Trump's attitude came in 2015, when he was being interviewed and indicated that he didn't consider John McCain a hero. That brought me up short. No one had ever said anything so crass before. "He's not a war hero. I like people who weren't captured." The impunity of Trump's statement, the rudeness of his anti-American comment, convinced me that would be the end of Donald Trump's presidency. I was wrong. Just as in the *Access Hollywood* "grabbing the pussy" statement, nothing seems to touch Donald Trump.

I have spent the last four years wondering why nothing touches him. Is it that he says things that other people wish they said, but didn't? Is it the absolute impunity and crassness of who he is? Is it the fact that he will never apologize and says so? I am still "gobsmacked" by the concept that millions of people don't care that he is an ignorant, crass, moron, and has made no effort to do the work required of a sitting president. It's clear that he knows no history and has never heard anything patriotic in his household, only money, money, money.

I always thought that character counted, and I am hoping that it will begin to count now. Have people who voted for Trump lost any loved ones or friends? One hundred thousand eighty-eight people are dead, because of the stubborn self-interest of one man, who refused to acknowledge the virus. Will those 40 million people who lost jobs, because of the virus shutdown, realize that Trump ("I am not responsible") caused this?

Will Donald Trump admit there is systemic racism? Probably not ever. It made me sad to hear the reality of Donald Trump's words. I wonder if he has ever really lived in America and on this planet. Nothing seems to have penetrated-not science, not climate change, not the Constitution.

Joe Biden provides the contrast. His heart, and his understanding of loss, provides us with the insight of a man who cares and wants to help people. In addition, his resilience in the face of overwhelming loss has helped him show his character. In thinking about what makes a leader months later than I first mentioned it, Biden is willing to take responsibility for our almost insurmountable problems. He shows quiet strength and humility in the face of harsh adversaries. He has known failure, and learned from it.

In the year 2021, we will need to have healing words and the motivation to unify as a country in order to successfully defeat the virus. Only then can we work to get our economy back, and respond to the racial divisiveness that has truly defeated our country. We are the laughingstock of the world, and people have actually pitied us, not a word ever heard before.

I hope that the military families know that we are behind them, and if Joe Biden is president, the United States will always have their backs. The election is November 3rd, and we have an opportunity to let the world know that we want change.

Sandra Day O'Connor, the former Supreme Court Justice, said that America has suffered greatly because we don't teach civics anymore. I totally agree. She started a foundation for the teaching of civics, so that kids will know what it really means to be an American, what the Constitution says, and why we pledge allegiance to it, not to one person.

Yes, character counts: leadership, resilience, honesty, humility, dignity, and hard work all make up the men and women who should be leading our country. Let's make sure that happens on November 3rd, so we can start looking forward.

Authoritarianism Rising/democracy declining

September 7, 2020

There is so much happening on a daily basis! It is impossible to discuss everything. Today I want to focus on the Post Office and Education.

During the Congressional questioning of Postmaster Louis DeJoy, Congressman Cooper, Democrat from Tennessee, asked DeJoy what seemed to be a very strange question. The Congressman wanted to know if DeJoy pressured his workers to donate to the GOP. DeJoy, taken by surprise, was outraged by such a seemingly impudent question, and said so. Cooper kept his cool and said, "I'm just asking a question." DeJoy gave a resounding, "NO, "and that is where things stood … until now.

The Wa*shington Post* did some fine investigative reporting, and found that DeJoy pressured people in his company to donate to the Republicans. DeJoy then gave those people large bonuses that covered the size of the donations plus taxes. The retired head of HR supplied all the details and paperwork of the five men who came forward. They had never donated to a political party beforehand, and they haven't donated since.

Reimbursing campaign contributions is illegal. The laws are based on the concept that the American people need to know who actually donated to a candidate. It is both a federal and a state offense. The statute of limitations may have run out for a federal offense (2014), but DeJoy's business, New Breed Logistics, is based in North Carolina, and the state Attorney General is looking into the crimes.

DeJoy seems to have committed other crimes. The morning of Congressman Cooper's question, DeJoy apparently lied to Congress, and could go to jail for it. In his testimony to Congress, it was clear that DeJoy knew precious little about the workings of USPS. So, how did he get the job? There was a list of 53 potential people with Post Office experience. His name was not on it.

Here is where the authority of the President comes into play. Trump appointed all the members of the Board of the USPS, and they "chose" the Postmaster. Trump cannot fire the Postmaster; only the chairman of the Board can do that, and everyone on the Board is a Trump appointed Republican.

Being able to choose a new Postmaster, who would do his bidding, has helped Trump in his goal to undermine the election. He met with DeJoy in the Oval office, one on one. That was very clever, because one on one meetings are not subject to being made public. DeJoy was asked if the President told him what he wanted him to do (slow down the mail, remove the sorters, abolish overtime, etc.) and DeJoy said he did not. However, shortly after that meeting in the Oval Office, the new Postmaster General began systematically handicapping the Postal Service's capacity to deliver the mail on time, ahead of the 2020 election. It is entirely possible that DeJoy lied once again to Congress.

Authoritarian governments are led by one person, with no desire to listen to the will of the people. Our country has been led by Donald Trump, who has even managed to bend the Republican party to his will. This is damaging to our democracy, which is supposed to have three branches of government. Americans should be alarmed and take notice. At the Democratic convention, former President Barack Obama said, "Don't let them take our democracy," and he meant it in the most serious way. Only one branch government-the Judicial- is actually working at this time. Voting is our right, and we should exercise it in November in order to put the three branches of government back in a working relationship.

Donald Trump has been sowing confusion and doubt about the legitimacy of our elections. This is unprecedented in American history. In fact, we are trying to make sure that more minorities vote this year, despite voter suppression on the part of the Republicans. The way that laws are put in place in certain states works to preclude voting by certain groups, mostly black Americans. Many polling places have already been closed in states run by Republicans.

One of the most recent of Trump's comments indicated that people should vote again if they are not sure about their first vote. Voting twice is illegal! It is a felony. Trump also told citizens they should come to the polling place to check on their vote. The election officials responded, and absolutely told citizens NOT to come to the polling place-it would cause chaos and slow the process. It's honestly difficult to know whether Donald Trump actually doesn't know the laws, or he is just talking nonsense.

More worrisome, Donald Trump has inserted himself into every area of our lives, often with disastrous results. He has ordered our children to go back to school in person, in order for life to look as if things were going back to normal, despite the pandemic. That is the single most callous and desperate thing that he has done. The virus has not been defeated, and our children should not be going to school in person, with minimal exceptions at this stage. If we had twice the space and twice the teachers there might be an opportunity. Again, there is no federal plan to bring children safely back to school. Notably, there was no federal money given to the 15,000 school districts that have had teachers and administrators scrambling since April to figure out how that might happen. Donald Trump likes to order people, but he never does the work to facilitate a reasonable program and allocate the money to implement it.

In a stunning contrast, millions of Chinese children returned to school in Wuhan, China. The video of their return showed a perfect plan, well-organized for gradual return, cleanliness, distancing and an infra-red system through which the children pass to monitor their temperatures. America is nowhere near being able to have children return to school, and I fear that we have lost another school year.

As if that wasn't enough, Donald Trump has started to mandate what schools should and shouldn't teach. For a racist ignoramus, nothing could be worse. The other day he said that the Department of Education will investigate states using curriculum based on the 1619 Project, (which came from the *New York Times). If they are using the program, chances are the school system will not receive funding.*

Government interference in our education programs smacks of a dictatorship. The 1619 Project bases our history on the premise that it should really start with the arrival of the first enslaved Africans to the shores of the Chesapeake. As I understand it, California is using a curriculum based on that program.

Authoritarian dictators control every aspect of a country's life, and Donald Trump has come dangerously close to succeeding in the life of the United States. Barack Obama, who has watched the arc of the Trump administration, warned us with good reason. We are at an inflection point, and the choice about which kind of America we want is at hand.

September 10, 2020

"It's all about the tapes"/1972 and 2020

September 9-10, 2020

Early in the morning of June 17, 1972, several burglars were arrested in the office of the Democratic National Committee, at the Watergate complex of buildings. The headline at the bottom of page one of the *Washington Post* on June 18, 1972 read, "Five Held in Plot to Bug Democratic Offices Here." That event marked the beginning of the Watergate scandal, a chain of events that convulsed Washington for two years, and led to Richard Nixon's resignation, the first ever of a president.

The story intrigued two young reporters on the Post's staff-Carl Bernstein and Bob Woodward, who were called in by Ben Bradlee, the Editor of the Post, to work the story. As Woodward's notes show, he learned from police sources that the burglars came from Miami, wore surgical gloves and carried thousands of dollars in cash. It was "a professional type operation."

To give some context, the origins of the break-in lay in the hostile political climate of the time. By 1972, when President Nixon was running for reelection, the United States was embroiled in the Vietnam War, and the country was deeply divided. A forceful presidential campaign seemed essential to the president and some of his key advisors. Their tactics turned out to be illegal espionage. In May, members of Nixon's Committee to Re-Elect the President (known derisively as CREEP) broke into the Watergate headquarters, stole copies of top -secret documents and bugged the office's phones.

The wiretaps failed to work properly, and on June 17th a group of five burglars returned to the Watergate building. As the prowlers were preparing to break into the office with a new microphone, a security guard noticed someone had taped over several of the building's door locks. The guard called the police, and they arrived just in time to arrest them.

It was not immediately known that the burglars were connected to Nixon, until detectives found copies of the reelection committee's White House phone number among the burglars' belongings.

In August, Nixon gave a speech during which he swore that the White House staff was not involved in the break-in. Most voters believed him, and in November 1972, the president was reelected in a landslide victory.

During the investigation, it became clear that Nixon was lying. A few days after the break-in, he arranged for thousands of dollars in "hush money" to be paid to the burglars.

Then Nixon and his closest aides formed a plan to order the CIA (Central Intelligence Agency) to block the FBI's investigation of the crime. This was obstruction of justice and abuse of presidential power, more serious than the break-in, and two crimes of impeachment.

As Woodward and Bernstein were investigating, there was now a trial judge and members of a Senate investigating committee, as well as a suspicion that there was a much larger scheme involved. An anonymous whistleblower presented himself, and was known as "Deep Throat," (taken from the name of a porn movie), who provided key information to Woodward and Bernstein over a number of years.

A handful of Nixon's aides, including White House counsel, John Dean, testified before a grand jury about the president's crimes. They also testified that Nixon had secretly taped every conversation that took place in the Oval Office! A shocking revelation, and one which revealed Nixon's narcissism. If prosecutors could get their hands on the tapes, they would have the smoking gun of his guilt in his own words.

Is this starting to sound familiar? There is actually much more. It is the most exciting and titillating investigative reporting in the history of our country. I highly recommend that you read *All the President's* Men, Woodward and Bernstein's detailed account of the two years that led to Nixon's resignation, for which they won a Pulitzer prize. For continued Covid-19 entertainment, see the movie, in which Woodward is played by Robert Redford and Dustin Hoffman plays Carl Bernstein.

There are stunning similarities between Nixon and Trump, and it all comes out in both men's tapes. Racism, insecurity, a desperation to get reelected and a sense that anything, no matter how illegal, was worth getting reelected, are obvious in the men's own words.

Bob Woodward became the premier investigative reporter who has written nineteen books about our presidents. He is a master interviewer and gets information from his subjects. In fact, Bob Woodward wrote a book about Donald Trump that was critical. He had not interviewed Trump, and that led the president to want to speak with Woodward. It was folly on Trump's part to think that he could impress Bob Woodward, but that is proof of his own paranoia. Having never read any of Woodward's books, Trump thought he could charm Woodward, and he was honored that Woodward wanted to talk with him. Donald Trump fell into his own narcissistic trap, and talked to Bob Woodward eighteen times. Having no filter, Donald Trump talked and talked and gave Woodward the kind of evidence that the Watergate tapes gave to Congress in 1973. The biggest difference is that the Republicans in 1974 held the wellbeing of the country first, and told Nixon it was time to go. He was not impeached, but in the Senate, he would be convicted.

Sadly, the Republicans in the Senate today, with the exception of Mitt Romney, were silent. They will most probably remain that way, but this debacle for Trump is not going away anytime soon, and we will be talking about it for the next weeks and years. The similarities of personality and ruthlessness between the two men are stunning, and the intrigue of Woodward and Bernstein's reporting is gripping.

9/11 honoring the 3,000 lost nineteen years ago

September 11, 2020

It's 8:45am on 9/11, nineteen years after the terrorist attack on the World Trade Center, exactly the time when the first plane hit. The firemen and policemen are bringing forward the somewhat damaged American flag rescued from the rubble, and the ceremony begins. The bell rings.

This is a sacred day. We are honoring those 3,000 people we lost, as we have every year since their deaths. But it is a different year. Because people cannot gather, the names were pre-recorded by their loved ones, and the names are resounding through the park with beautiful music in the background. Scottish bagpipers are playing. It is a crisp and clear day.

Everyone is wearing a mask.

There are similar ceremonies honoring this day in Shanksville, Pa., where four brave young men overcame the terrorists and forced the plane to crash land, rather than destroy the Capitol in Washington, DC. They became aware of the situation because loved ones on the ground alerted them to the attack in New York. The bravery and patriotism of those four men on that day was breathtaking. There is a beautiful memorial in Shanksville, Pa., commemorating the men and the day.

9:37 am-The reading stops for a moment to pay tribute. A fourth plane took off on that fateful morning, and it hit into the Pentagon in Washington, DC. at 9:37 am. The people on the plane all died, and many people in the Pentagon were killed as well. A great deal of damage was done to the Pentagon and it took months to repair. This morning a huge American flag is being lowered over the part of the Pentagon that was damaged and is now repaired.

As in past years, important leaders are here to pay tribute. Joe and Jill Biden are standing together, as the 3,000 names are being read. Governor Andrew Cuomo and Mayor de Blasio are here. It is a moving scene, with the beautiful water flowing, the names etched into the marble surrounds, and a white rose by each name.

This day has been ingrained in our DNA-the stories, the cell phone calls to loved ones, the bravery. The heroes-the 343 firemen and 23 policemen who rushed into buildings, not knowing if they would ever return, all lost, are etched in our memory.

After 9/11, people came from all over the country to work on "the pile" commonly referred to as "Ground Zero," to search for loved ones' belongings and connect with one another as Americans. We were not a divided nation on that day, and for a long time afterward.

However, there were serious problems as it became clear who the perpetrators were, mostly from Saudi Arabia. As a result, Muslims in our country were vilified, even though many had become citizens and their neighborhoods were well integrated into America. When President Bush heard about the victimization of our Muslim communities, he went to a mosque and met with the community. It was an important show of support and a symbolic message that the President of the United States understood how dangerous the situation was for them.

Sadly, the air quality at Ground Zero has killed more people than the 3,000 who died on 9/11. Those people are still dying of cancer, and many other diseases. There is a victim's fund, and it will be used for decades to come. Congress didn't want to extend it, but John Stewart, the brilliant comedian (the Daily Show) and activist, came and spoke so eloquently, that he won the day.

Shortly after 9/11, my daughter, Amanda Wiss, called one morning to say that a wonderful firehouse across the street from where she lives in Brooklyn, lost nine firefighters. Could we do something? Of course, we could. They protected her and everyone else on Middagh Street, and now we had an opportunity to show our gratitude. Since the holidays were coming, Amanda had an idea that we could do something for their families, and she was absolutely right. We connected with one of the firefighters, and spent time talking at the firehouse. Normally, we had a Hanukah party in December. This time, all gifts would be for the firehouse families and everything would be for Christmas. We got the names, sizes and gift wishes of the children and moms. A letter went out, and each of our friends adopted one of the families. When everyone arrived that night, they had done wonderful and generous things. Stuffed animals, tech, everything in red and green, and beautifully wrapped. We lit our lights, and each person told how good it felt to have something to do that would help the grieving families. Amanda's idea helped all of us. She gave us a project and something to do, as well as an opportunity to give of ourselves. When we brought the gifts, the firemen were overwhelmed and delighted. We unpacked our cars and talked with the firemen, who invited us to their party. We thanked them, but said it was truly their singular time-the first Christmas without a dad or a husband. "Tikun olam"-repair the world was very evident at our Hanukkah that year, and I was so grateful to Amanda for suggesting that we could help. That has always been who she is, and she helped each of us get through a very painful fall.

We received a heartfelt thank you card with a picture of all the remaining firemen. I often drive by the firehouse on Middagh Street and wonder how everyone is doing.

Watching on television, I recall that day and spend the morning listening to the names. They are mesmerizing. One can't help but think of all the people they left behind who are grieving, and will be grieving for the rest of their lives.

We need to be able to come together once again in this terrible time that has taken 195,000 of our people.

Simple Pleasures: more joy, more song, more friends, more life.

September 12, 2020

Always, more life.

As I watched the 9/11 memorial yesterday, so many feelings came to the surface-even nineteen years later.

I was teaching at the Horace Mann School in the Bronx, New York, on 9/11, and it was an horrific day, as it was for everyone. Amazingly, we did not lose a parent that day, primarily because many parents were bringing their children for the first day of kindergarten, and they were late to work, which saved their lives.

Horace Mann called in psychologists to help the faculty deal with our own shock and be able to help our students. We had many meetings over those next few weeks.

Teachers were not allowed to hug students, or touch them, actually. On 9/11 all bets were off. Kids were panicked and I gave hugs to anyone who wanted one. However, my seventh graders were going to need more than a one-off. I brought in a Gund stuffed bear that was wearing an American flag sweater. I explained that "Bear" wanted to come to school and be with me and the kids, and he would need many hugs during the day. My students put "Bear" on one of the chairs off to the side. Anyone who wanted Bear on his lap could come and get him for a while, then put him back. Interestingly, more boys than girls went to hug and touch our new friend, probably because boys don't get hugged nearly as much as girls. The other interesting thing was that seventh graders, who are supposed to be "grown up", accepted "Bear" immediately, and didn't think for a moment that hugging a stuffed animal was beneath them.

As for myself, I found that the only way to get to sleep after watching the news of the workers on "the pile," and hearing so many gut-wrenching stories, was to have a soothing glass of wine. The other thing that became a habit was to buy flowers with my groceries. Something live and blooming in my home was essential.

The conversations in my class that year were very open and revealing. Never planned, they might begin with a simple open-ended question from me- "How is everyone doing?" One boy shared that his mother insisted that their family sit down to dinner as a family, despite sports games and music lessons and schedules that had them scattered. A number of other students said that their mothers did the same thing. In addition, kids and parents didn't leave in the morning without a hug and "I love you." Everyone learned a lot about what was really important-family, and telling those we love how much they mean to us.

Another boy said that while he always liked to go to his friends' house, now he liked to have his friends at his house, and he appreciated his friends more.

Trying to provide a Horace Mann security plan, we now had drills to leave school in an emergency, telling us where we would go. There was also a "shooter in the school" plan (1999 was Columbine). However, our newly built middle school was totally glass, and there was nowhere to hide. I put a black piece of paper over the window of my door, and worried about how to protect my kids every day.

How were we actually doing? Months later, as I taught a class, there was a student looking past me and her head was moving. I asked her what she was looking at. "I'm tracking that plane which is flying very close to school." Clearly, everyone was still afraid and on guard.

A number of those students are friends of mine even now. They are in their thirties, successful and wonderfully interesting adults, and we have kept in touch all these years. One of the boys invited me out to lunch in the city. His very first question was- "what was going on (for me) that day and how did I deal with it personally?" I was initially surprised by his question, but when he explained that was the single most monumental event in his life, I understood. It was critical for me as well, but I had already been battle-tested when John F. Kennedy was assassinated. I still cry when I see those images, as well as the picture of the planes hitting the World Trade Center.

Which brings me back to our present predicament. Because of the pandemic, we are in a situation where we cannot necessarily see our loved ones and our friends in person. We are not supposed to hug one another. How are we staying sane and grounded? Many of us are reading more. We watch Netflix, Master Class and we do projects that we have wanted to tackle. I enjoy writing this blog, because it keeps me focused. In addition, we rely on Zoom, on phone calls and even cards and letters. Many of us are afraid. Living alone, I fear getting the virus and dying alone in the hospital where my babies were born.

As with everyone after 9/11, families are becoming closer. Children call more often, grandchildren connect on Zoom. Friends of mine, and a generation of children in their forties, have asked their parents to move closer to them, and that is exactly what is happening. They tell one another how much they mean to each other and that they want to live close. It is heartwarming that in this terrible crisis, loved ones once again realize how important it is to tell one another how much they mean to each other.

Despite physical distance, we can have more joy, more singing, more friends, more life and yes, more love, to the best of our creative and empathic ability.

Apocalypse in California, Oregon and Washington state

September 15, 2020

If you ever wondered why elections matter, wrap your mind around this: our president is a climate denier and a science denier. Did that ever come up in the debates? Shouldn't we know things like that in advance of voting? And other important things as well? Has the president read the Constitution, and is he fully conversant with the workings of the three branches of government and how checks and balances interact? Americans are in the unfortunate circumstance of having a president who is both a climate denier and a science denier in charge of protecting three hundred million citizens who are faced with a pandemic and an environmental Armageddon.

So far, thirty-five people have reportedly died in the fires, but the reality is that there will be many more. Many of the towns have been burned to the ground and, as a result it will be impossible to find out who is dead within their houses and other buildings.

While the fires have been raging, and entire towns incinerated, thousands of homes have been destroyed and people evacuated. The president largely ignored the devastation, possibly because it was in three "blue" states. Trump finally visited California and sat down with Governor Gavin Newsom and Wade Crowfoot, the California Secretary for Natural Resources. Watching the exchange was depressing and shocking. As Crowfoot was explaining the necessity of accepting and fighting climate change, the president answered, "It will get cooler," an ignorant and slick comment. Crowfoot replied, "science knows," To which Trump said, "I don't think science knows, actually." Gavin Newsom disagreed, "The hots are getting hotter." It's clear that Donald Trump doesn't know the difference between climate and weather. Most important, fifty-seven percent of California land is actually federal property.

Presidential candidate Joe Biden gave a speech yesterday, calling out Donald Trump's response to the virus, and to the raging fires in the west. He went further and discussed floods in the midwest and hurricanes in the east and south. He decried Trumps' nonresponse in all these areas.

When Joe Biden was in the Obama administration, they made a detailed plan to battle a pandemic, and established an office in the White House that could execute it. Trump eliminated the office and deep-sixed the plan. The same is true of the climate challenge. President Obama called together a task force to study the threat of climate in this country and around the world. They concluded that there is serious danger to the ice melting in the Antarctic, and actually formed a group with Great Britain to save the glaciers. As an example, ice melting would flood many of the cities in America and put many countries underwater, such as Bangladesh. Six feet of water would put Washington DC underwater since it is already a swamp. Biden said that when Trump thinks about climate change, he thinks "hoax." Biden said he thinks about jobs.

The world is burning and drowning, and we have to be proactive in saving our cities and our planet. The wildfires and the hurricanes have put the climate crisis into focus. Donald Trump continues to ignore the threat. For the last four hundred years America has excelled in civilization because we had good government- stable, legal, fair and a consistent passing of power. In the last four years, America has failed the good government test. With all of this destruction, Donald Trump showed no empathy for all the people who have lost their homes, their towns and their lives.

To be clear, our institutions have been corrupted, hollowed out and maligned. The State Department, Justice, Defense, Homeland Security and Health and Human Services, have all been taken over by Donald Trump and subverted. The amount of people who have died from the virus has been hidden, and the CDC has been forced to change guidelines. In fact, political appointees at the department of Health and Human Services have been altering the weekly reports on the numbers, which are issued by the CDC. These reports are relied upon, world-wide as the gold standard. When science is politicized we are in serious trouble, because we don't actually know the reality of what is happening. When the truth is hidden, we can't make decisions based on true numbers.

As I've said before, elections matter. Who we vote into office makes a difference regarding whether the president will lead, will unify the country for a consistent response, and use the powerful resources of America to defeat the problem, whether it be a virus or a climate crisis.

The Trump chaos is difficult to navigate. We have lived with a fact-based society all these years, until now. The idea that the president is spreading lies, untruths, disinformation and more, is very destabilizing personally and emotionally. Not being able to trust the leader of our country in a pandemic is particularly disorienting, especially when he goes against the norms of science and climate and politicizes them.

In the western part of the U.S., one million acres have been destroyed in just one week, more than in a year. The devastation is both horrifying and tragic. The air quality is dangerous for everyone, especially those with asthma, heart conditions and other underlying issues. The pictures show red air, thick with smoke and difficult to breathe. It seems as if we live on a different planet, possibly Mars.

In Oregon, six towns have been totally wiped off the map, and it looks like a war zone. So far, the perfect storm of losing your home in a pandemic has created massive dangers for all citizens.

As I write, hurricane Sally is waiting in the wings.

I hope that we don't continue to have a disinformation pandemic. We need some hopeful signs and some truth, since the last six months have been a disaster for our country in so many ways, and unsettling for me, personally.

Vote, vote, vote!

Constitution Day-September 17ᵗʰ: "blue states, red states?" No. The United States of America.

September 17ᵗʰ, 2020

Barack Obama said it best in a convention speech, when he said, "We are the United States of America." It has been clear that Donald Trump has divided us into the states that voted for him and those that did not. He rejects unity, and continues to play favorites. However, the coronavirus knows no politics. It doesn't respect borders. The virus is an "equal opportunity virus." Still, there is no federal plan to fight the virus, and people continue to die in alarming numbers.

There is so much news in the last three days, I can hardly breathe. Here are a few of the most important things to know.

Olivia Troye, lifelong Republican and a top staffer of Mike Pence, who was on the coronavirus task force and in every meeting, resigned. She made a video explaining her disgust with the Trump approach to the virus, that it endangered the health of American citizens, and she said that her vote will be for Joe Biden in November.

In a similar move, Joe Venable, the Chief of Staff of Betsy deVos, the so-called Education Secretary, resigned, along with other staff members. Remember that deVos cared nothing about public education or urban schools, etc. Her elite approach was unacceptable for dedicated people who wanted to make a difference for children, especially those who were underserved.

JUSTICE LIVES! Since it is Constitution Day, late last night a positive decision came down from a federal judge in the state of Washington. When Louis DeJoy, Trump's appointee who knew nothing about the Post Office, put in his program that slowed the mail, fourteen states filed a lawsuit against those changes. The lawsuit alleged that the changes were politically motivated, interfered with providing a clean election during a pandemic, and slowed important mail for all citizens of the country.

Yesterday, the judge delivered his decision-a bench warrant, a nationwide injunction, stating that everything has to be returned to the way that it was before all the changes. It is a stunning decision, and well worth reading (NYT and WAPO). One of the important things is that the judge ordered all mail ballots to be treated as First Class mail, no matter how they were sent. Sorters need to be returned, and if there is a problem, the various post offices should come to the judge directly. This is an amazing example of state governments using the justice system to protect its citizens, when the federal government tried to disrupt those services.

One Senator, Gary Peters of Michigan, took this problem on and followed it through. He found that 350 million pieces of mail were delayed in the first five weeks of DeJoy's changes. Some of that mail involved medication, checks for seniors and veterans and more, and not just in Michigan. Upon further review, Senator Peters found that mail was delayed in specific areas-battleground states like Ohio, Pennsylvania and his own state of Michigan. The report that his group filed laid out all of the findings, and they were damning.

More instances of subverting our institutions have come front and center. By investigative reporting by the NYT, it came to light that the CDC has been forced to change the newsletter that it sends weekly to the medical community throughout the world. The CDC is the penultimate leader in healthcare education for the entire world, and now the news is suspect. Science has been politicized with dire results. White House staffers have been rewriting the newsletter and changing it to downplay what doctors and others need to know. The scientists are frustrated and angry that they have been subverted. Recently, Robert Redfield, head of the CDC, testified in Congress and indicated that if 95% of Americans would wear masks for a number of weeks, the virus would be essentially defeated. That, and social distancing and avoiding crowds would successfully fight the virus. In other disturbing news, it came to light that the White House interfered with a plan to mail millions of masks to every household in the country, and it was cancelled by Donald Trump. Imagine how different our lives would be if everyone wore a mask starting in April.

One of the most important failings of the federal government has been the fact that our school-children have not been able to return to school safely. This situation NEVER had to be this way if the federal government followed the science guidelines last March, telling us how to battle the pandemic. It is outrageous and tragic that our school children must stay at home and attend school online. That fact has affected parents, teachers, and remains the single most awful result of Donald Trump's callous approach to our children's health. He wanted all children to go back to school for his own election optics. The CDC found that children can get the virus and they can infect others in their families, adults who are even more vulnerable. The White House denigrated the CDC, so the Republican administration has an historic disagreement with the CDC, the most respected organization in the world.

Returning to the divisive "blue states, red states" comment. New York, New Jersey, Connecticut, Massachusetts and California actually had huge challenges and overcame them. California and New York were the points of entry for millions of people. The Governors of those states took up the leadership that the federal government dropped, and the states succeeded.

Another very important thing. Those five states send the most money to Washington, and get precious little in return. The five states that take the most money Trump describes as "red states, including Kentucky, Mitch McConnell's state. Perhaps the "blue states" should withhold the money and use it to pay the huge debt that the pandemic forced them to incur? The president is supposed to be the leader of the country, not a partisan politician doling out help according to whether the state voted for him or not. That attitude is childish, partisan and petty, but unfortunately that is a description of the man in charge. It's apparent that within those states, lots of different Americans voted for each person running, so Trump's categorizing states in the middle of a pandemic, is bizarre.

There is another stunning example of patriotism. Yesterday, Chris Wray, head of the FBI, testified and said that Russia has been actively working to undermine the election, and besmirch Joe Biden, so Donald Trump will be elected. Wray was clear about the danger, and he told the truth, knowing that Trump would be angry. Indeed, the next hours found the president tweeting and saying that China was the culprit, and enough of Russia, Russia, Russia. Wray heads a crucial organization of men and women who are fighting 24/7 to keep Americans safe. They are dedicated and smart, and Chris Wray knows what is really happening. He did not back down. He also said that one of the dangers is the weakening of confidence of the people in the legitimacy of the election. He was very eloquent on that subject.

The school controversy continued throughout the day and at night, and there is more to report.

Fortunately, teachers, administrators and parents realized the danger of Trump's callous and bizarre approach. They pushed back against the order. New York is still struggling with its decision, and looking carefully at the metrics. It is very unsettling for parents and children alike.

Another good example came from the huge city of Des Moines, Iowa. The Superintendent of Schools, Thomas Aheart, looked at the metrics and decided, along with the teachers, that they were going to defy an order that all children be attending school in person. They are in defiance of the Governor. When he was interviewed, Superintendent Aheart indicated that the health of the people of Des Moines is his chief consideration.

As you can see by the news, brave people in all quarters are realizing that they need to step up and tell the truth. It is clear that the president and the people are on different tracks

As we approach the weekend, many people are preparing to celebrate the Jewish New year, Rosh Hashanah, albeit online. May it be a sweet year filled with joy, good health, closeness with family and a new occupant in the Oval Office.

L'shana tova!

Our sad September surprise: Ruth Bader Ginsburg dies at 87

September 18, 2020/ "Erev" Rosh Hashanah

At the stroke of 7:30, just as I was clicking to online services for the Jewish New Year, the news that Ruth Bader Ginsburg died flashed across my screen. Oh, my God. Not now. Not her. Deep breath. Unfortunately, it was true. RBG succumbed to pancreatic cancer after bravely fighting and continuing to work, despite her illness.

The year has been so devastating: children in cages, the rhetoric of the presidency creating antisemitism, and a pandemic with 200,000 people dead. What more could happen? When I thought about the worst that could happen, it was that RBG would lose her fight with cancer, and that it would happen before the election.

It's impossible to do Ruth Bader Ginsburg justice. She was larger than life-a diminutive woman with a big intellect, a principled woman with a passionate love of equality for all.

Born in Brooklyn in 1933, she went to public school, then got a full scholarship and met the love of her life at Cornell. Martin Ginsburg was another brilliant lawyer who appreciated how smart Ruth was. When they went to Oklahoma to follow his army service, despite the fact that she scored high on the civil service exam, RBG could only find work as a typist. Moreover, when she got pregnant with her daughter, Jane, she even lost her job.

Being fired was the first in a series of realizations for RBG that she began life as a woman with a limited horizon. According to Ruth, she had three strikes against her-that she was a woman, that she was a mother, and that she was Jewish.

Returning north from Oklahoma, Marty started at Harvard Law School, and Ruth followed the next year. She was one of only nine women, and the dean famously asked her why she was "taking the place of a man." Despite the insulting comment, or perhaps because of it, she performed brilliantly, and was the first woman on the Harvard Law Review.

Marty contracted cancer, and RBG gave birth, cared for her husband, and maintained her own studies. It was a superhuman effort for a year. After he graduated, Marty got a job in New York and Ruth then transferred to Columbia Law School, where she was at the top of her class. Nonetheless, in 1959 law firms weren't hiring women, and there were no jobs for law clerks who were women. Professor Gerald Gunther, who was a mentor, forced a judge to give Ruth a clerkship. This seems unbelievable in the 1960's, but women had just gotten the vote in 1920. Ruth served the clerkship, and went for two years to Sweden, where laws about gender equality were more lenient.

Ruth was a woman of faith. In fact, if someone dies on the eve of Rosh Hashanah, it is said that person is "blessed." So, it was ironic that on the eve of the Jewish New Year 5781, which is supposed to be a new beginning, there was such a sad death. Ruth Bader Ginsburg would like us to think of it as a beginning for women to feel empowered by her death, and everything for which she stood Ginsberg became one of America's first female law professors, and still it was difficult for her to get a job. Rutgers University hired her, and it was at that point that I first heard the name. My former husband completed his Army duty and returned to Rutgers Law as a student in 1969. While Ron did not have RBG as a professor, many friends did, and she was already a legend. Her students were in awe of her "mind like a steel trap," and they would never consider going to class without spending hours to prepare.

At Rutgers, she started trying cases that would level the playing field for men and women. She made the case that "equal protection under the law" included women. Knowing that she would always appear before male judges, she purposely chose male plaintiffs. RBG was a perfectionist in her writing, and her gift was in framing an argument in terms that a layman could understand. Basically, she was trying to educate the public about the unfairness and inequality of society. That approach was to continue throughout her career.

In 1972, Ruth founded the Women's Rights Project at the American Civil Liberties Union (the ACLU). Between 1973 and 1976, she argued six gender discrimination cases before the Supreme Court. She won five. Her opinions are masterpieces of wordsmithing, and worth reading.

In 1980, President Jimmy Carter nominated Ruth to the DC Court of Appeals. The DC Court is where she met Antonin Scalia, and they became fast friends, despite the fact that they did not agree politically or legally on much. They loved opera and each had a wicked sense of humor. That friendship with Scalia continued, when Bill Clinton nominated Ruth to the Supreme Court, where she was confirmed by a vote of 96 to 3. The woman, who was born with a limited horizon, had reached the pinnacle of the judicial hierarchy.

As the court changed, RBG became known for her blistering dissents. She had a marvelous collection of collars that she wore on different occasions. When she was dissenting, she wore a sequined collar. On occasion, when she felt particularly passionate about a case, she would read her dissent aloud, in the hopes that it might change some minds in the future.

In 2013, she famously dissented in Shelby County v. Holder, a case that gutted the Voting Rights Act. She wrote, "Throwing out a portion of Shelby, when it has worked and is continuing to work to stop discriminatory changes, is like throwing away your umbrella in a rainstorm because you are not getting wet."

Her dissents made her a cultural icon. One of her clerks gave her the name of "Notorious RBG" after the pop star, Notorious B.I.G She is the subject of a wonderful documentary movie that was Oscar-nominated. Her fitness program became a subject of pride and influenced many women who followed her. There are t-shirts, bobble-head dolls, mugs and more. All of this adoration in the last decades of her life amazed her, but also delighted her.

Mainly, Ruth Bader Ginsburg influenced young women and the next generation of young girls, who saw in her the opportunity to fight for women's rights and equality. Huge numbers of women went to law school. RBG saw in her life a movement to more justice, to a more level playing field and the promise of more inclusion, not only for women, but for Black Lives Matter. Her idea of more humanity and dignity for all human beings was greatly expanded to others, and she will be sorely missed. Ruth Bader Ginsburg was one of a kind, a unique individual, and we are unlikely to see another person of her talent, brains and passion anytime soon.

After our Rosh Hashanah services, I put on the television. Thousands of people had gathered in front of the Supreme Court with flowers, tears, and ultimately, song. I heard "Imagine," and others as the crowd continued to grow. People gathered in Brooklyn to honor a native daughter. That night, motivated by the concept of a Trump appointee to the Supreme Court, citizens raised more than 12.5 million dollars to democratic coffers. This is just the beginning of a major historic fight, and we are just 46 days away from the 2020 election.

The Arc of History and American Resilience

September 21, 2020

If you are worried about the situation in the country, concerned about the election, and despondent that Ruth Bader Ginsburg just died, take a moment to consider other historic times in our country when events seemed desperate.

Looking back at the beginning of the country, remember that the Founding Fathers broke their ties with the mother country, and had absolutely no idea if their bold gamble would succeed. Often, the life of the new country was in doubt. There were thirteen diverse colonies with many individual needs and fears. One such fear was whether the new government would have a king or not. The Constitution solved that problem by creating the three branches of government. When the people were afraid there were no personal rights guaranteed to them, the Founding Fathers added the Bill of Rights and the Constitution passed.

Fast forward to the 1860s and the division over slavery, completely splitting the country in half and leading to the bitter Civil War. It wasn't clear that the country would ever survive a subject that even divided families. Somehow, we did survive, and the country was brought together under Abraham Lincoln, even though many southerners hated the Emancipation Proclamation and did not want to grant rights to freed slaves.

The next century brought the First World War (1914-1918) involving many millions of people fighting in Europe. As an aftermath, the Spanish flu pandemic emerged in military personnel who spread it in the spring of 1918. We were fighting a war and a pandemic simultaneously, not unlike what we are facing now.

Thinking more about the twentieth century, we should recall the Great Depression of 1929. The stock market crashed, wiping out peoples' money, homes and all their belongings. Citizens were starving. Soup kitchens were opened by the government, and funded by generous people to feed others. Twenty-five percent of the population was unemployed. It wasn't clear what would become of the country and all the people living here. It was a period of overwhelming sadness and constant worry, but the country survived and started to move forward. Americans are amazingly resilient and adaptive, and that has helped us in the midst of our many crises.

In the 1940s, with the rise of Hitler, the Second World War began. America, under Franklin Roosevelt, tried to avoid joining the war, while quietly helping the British with lend-lease. The attack by the Japanese on Pearl Harbor made the matter moot, and we entered the war, fighting on both fronts. Again, Americans rose to the occasion, mobilized our manufacturing with the Defense Production Act, and were turning out airplanes daily.

With all of those challenges, there have been many difficult times for the Supreme Court as well. There were bitter fights, a presidency determined by one vote in the Supreme Court in 2000, and much more. Reading a history of the court may bring solace to you in our present situation. It is not unusual, but it is very troubling because so much is at stake: Roe v. Wade, voting rights, women's rights, the whole list of things that Ruth Bader Ginsburg won in the last few decades in the name of "equal justice."

I've taken a break today to discuss the arc of history, because eventually it bends toward justice. While events may seem hopeless, they are not all lost, as long as we as Americans work hard to keep our democracy. I hope that each of us will fight hard to maintain justice and equal rights. The life of our country and its democracy depends on it.

Honoring RBG and Mourning 201,000 American citizens dead from Covid-19

September 23, 2020

In the place where "Equal Justice Under Law" is carved on the stone lintel, the casket of Ruth Bader Ginsburg is lying in state under the portico of the Supreme Court of the United States. It is such a small casket, draped with the American flag. People are lining up and waiting to pay their respects. Mothers brought their teenage children, many daughters, who are being interviewed, and so articulate as they express how much they admired the Justice. Many people, including myself, are wiping tears from their eyes, as we watch this simple yet beautiful scene. RBG will lie in state today and tomorrow, and on Friday she will lie in state in Statuary Hall at the Capitol, an honor that no other Supreme Court Justice has ever been accorded.

Former President Bill Clinton, who appointed RBG twenty-seven years ago, is standing with former First Lady Hillary Clinton, waiting to pay their respects. Actually, it was Hillary Clinton who brought the name of Ruth Bader Ginsburg to Bill Clinton's attention. Hillary knew of RBG from her work with the ACLU, and with women's rights' groups generally. When Bill Clinton met with RBG, they got along famously, and he was incredibly impressed. Bill Clinton taught Constitutional Law earlier in his career, so he was very "sympatico" with RBG.

Bill Clinton sent the name of RBG to the Senate, and she was confirmed by a vote of 96 to 3. Interestingly, Joe Biden was the Chairman of the Judiciary Committee that oversaw the hearings on RBG's nomination.

Today, inside the Supreme Court, in a private ceremony of family, close friends like Nina Totenberg, (legal affairs correspondent for NPR), and members of the Court, there are two speakers. Chief Justice John Roberts spoke of RBG's love of family and said that the Court was also her family and her home. The only other speaker was Rabbi Lauren Holtzbaugh, who spoke beautifully of her deep knowledge of Ruth Bader Ginsburg.

As a counterpoint to this scene, we have 200,000 citizens dead from Covid-19 and no national mourning. In fact, the president has never mentioned any of the citizens who have died. When questioned, he either ignores the question or gives himself an A+, indicating that millions might have died, so 200,000 means he did a good job. That is all callous nonsense.

Wonderful journalists, who Trump mocked for years, beginning with his campaign, calling them "fake news," and other insulting appellations, have taken up the beautiful practice of talking about "lives well lived." At the end of her program on MSNBC, at 6PM, Nicolle Wallace describes a number of people who caught the virus and are lost to their families and the country. They were mothers, sisters, daughters, fathers and sons, all ages, races and religions. These were people who contributed to the life of their community, and they are gone. For each person lost, there are at least nine people around them who are grieving, perhaps more. So, we have thousands of citizens mourning 201,000 loved ones and we are a deeply saddened nation.

In addition to Nicolle Wallace, David Muir, who is the news anchor on channel 7 at 6:30, pays tribute to "Lives Lost." These are very moving tributes, often with pictures, and I find myself tearing up, as we contemplate how this never had to happen. I'm sure that there are many news-casters doing the same thing, but these are the ones I watch. If you have others you particularly follow, please share them. It is very awesome that the journalists have taken it upon themselves to honor some of our citizens, rich and poor alike, when the president has not uttered a word of remorse about their untimely deaths.

I also saw that the *New York Times* began to print biographies of many citizens lost to the virus, and I imagine that other newspapers and more newscasters will follow suit. The tributes are very special.

It is very nourishing to know that journalists are showing the humanity that has been missing from our president. Rest in peace, Ruth Bader Ginsburg, knowing that you have inspired an entire generation of young women as well as the next generation of young girls and boys. They will pick up your torch as you hoped they would, and go on to great things in the name of social justice. The promise of the Declaration, that "all men are created equal," was expanded to include women and people of color, and the "Notorious RBG" inspired a nation to become all it can be.

Five Alarm Fire!

September 24th, 2020

What has always made our country greater than all others is the peaceful transfer of power. This process is honored by losing presidential candidates, most notably Al Gore in 2000, John Kerry in 2004, John McCain in 2008, Mitt Romney in 2012 and Hillary Clinton in 2016.

Until now. A reporter this afternoon asked Donald Trump if he would commit to a peaceful transfer of power if he loses the election. Trump replied, "Well, we're going to have to see what happens. You know that I have been complaining very strongly about the ballots and the ballots are a disaster." Trump continued, "Get rid of the ballots and you'll have a very—we'll have a very peaceful—there won't be a transfer frankly, there will be a continuation."

Adam Schiff (D-CA) chair of the House intelligence Committee tweeted a message, "This is how democracy dies." Only one Republican, Mitt Romney (R-UT), condemned Trump's comments as "both unthinkable and unacceptable."

Most disturbing, an article in *The Atlantic,* which detailed the methods by which the Trump campaign is planning to steal the 2020 election, appeared yesterday. Barton Gellman wrote the piece, and he explains that Trump will never accept losing the 2020 election. If he cannot win it, Trump plans to cheat and steal it. It has been obvious that he is trying to suppress the vote, and the recently picked Postmaster General is working to slow the delivery of mail-in ballots. In his rallies, Trump has consistently spread disinformation and disdained mail-in voting, indicating that if he loses the election, it is because of phony ballots.

There are important things at work here. In national polling, Joe Biden leads Trump by 50 to 40%, so Trump is desperate to discourage voters from using mail-in ballots, which the majority of democrats employ. Moreover, Trump will use any methods possible to win this election, knowing that if he loses, the Attorney General of the State of New York is waiting for him with numerous indictments for fraud and other crimes, and he may well go to jail. That alone is motivation to intimidate and cheat in order to win, as far as Donald Trump is concerned.

Trump is pulling out all the stops. His team is recruiting 50,000 volunteers in 15 states (battleground) to challenge voters at polling places, which might also keep people from showing up at the polls.

There is more. Donald Trump plans to insist on calling a winner on the night of the election. Since mail-in ballots will still be counted days after November 3rd, he will challenge them, saying they are not valid or even fraudulent. These methods will create chaos at the very least, and put the outcome of the election into serious doubt in everyone's minds. Trump is a master at creating chaos, anxiety and uncertainty … and distraction, especially away from his handling of the coronavirus.

Author Barton Gellman, American journalist, also warns that the Trump team is exploring a way to work around the actual vote count in battleground states. This is complicated, because it involves each state's electors. As an example, Democratic electors who were chosen by the voters could be pushed aside by Republican legislatures and replaced by their slate of electors.

The scenarios in the article are very nuanced, and somewhat complicated for me to explain in this article, so I encourage you to read Barton Gellman's, *The Election that could Break America.* in *The Atlantic.* The article is incredibly scary, because there would be so much confusion. The double slate would then go to Congress, which would decide the winning slate, and ultimately, the case would go to the Supreme Court. That leads us to why Donald Trump is so set on seating his third Justice. He would have a solid majority that could rule in his favor on the election results.

There has been a lot of pushback to Trump's words. First, he is defying all the norms of our democracy. Appointing a judge whose name is taken from the Federalist Society list, insures a rightwing jurist, who will be the exact opposite of Ruth Bader Ginsburg. That rightwing jurist will put in jeopardy -Roe v. Wade, healthcare rights (Medicare and Medicaid exchanges), preexisting protection, and so much more. Voting rights will also be on the table, as well as the right to form unions, and so many issues connected to women's rights. Everything that was accomplished over the last many decades, could be reversed.

Some very knowledgeable and experienced journalists responded to Trump's words. Dan Rather wrote of living through the Depression, World War Two, the Cuban Missile Crisis, the assassinations of John F. Kennedy, Martin Luther King, Jr. and Robert Kennedy, Watergate and 9/11, and he said "This is a moment of reckoning unlike any I have seen in my lifetime. What Donald Trump said today are the words of a dictator. To telegraph that he would consider becoming the first president in American history not to accept the peaceful transfer of power is not a throwaway line. It's not a joke. He doesn't joke. And it is not prospective. The words are already seeding a threat of violence and illegitimacy into our electoral process."

Only Mitt Romney came out and said Trump's words were "unthinkable," and the peaceful transfer of power is "fundamental." No other Senators came out with a statement.

Trump was clearly trying to grab the headlines with his statements, and he succeeded. The numbers are not good in his favor. Fifty-eight percent of Americans do not approve of the way he handled the coronavirus. In polling, Joe Biden is seen as caring, more honest, intelligent, and a better leader.

At the same time, Joe Biden released a detailed plan for his administration going forward. Beating the virus is number #1. He focused on four other main areas: rebuilding jobs in manufacturing and technology, investing in infrastructure and clean energy, returning critical supply chains to America, and supporting the caregiving sector of the country. Too long ignored, caregivers need to be supported by increasing training and pay. For those workers who care for children, elderly Americans, and people with disabilities, much needs to be done.

In evaluating the effect of this give and take, Trump's statements are meant to intimidate, to cast doubt on the election and possibly frighten voters from going to the polls. That is why we have mail-in ballots-for health and safety. In addition, the head of the FBI, Christopher Wray, testified that Russia is very actively working to destroy our election process. The FBI published a very important warning, asking citizens not to pay attention to disinformation during the election. We cannot allow Russia to succeed in its goal. Putin wants to convince Americans that our democracy doesn't work. If we allow him to succeed, then Russia has won, despite the fact that the majority of Americans prefer Biden over Trump.

Be alert. The price of liberty is eternal vigilance.

This is our five-alarm fire!

Country, not party

September 25, 2020

Senator Bernie Sanders, Independent, argued in an impassioned speech Thursday that President Trump's refusal to commit to a peaceful transfer of power is a threat to American democracy.

It's been six months since Bernie withdrew his candidacy for president in favor of Joe Biden, and yesterday was the first time he spoke. It was a gracious withdrawal then, and today's speech was an incredibly passionate defense of our country's values and laws.

Because Bernie's words are better than I could ever describe, I quote:

"What I am going to talk about is something that, in my wildest dreams, I never thought I would be discussing. And that is the need to make certain that the president of the United States. if he loses the election, will abide by the will of the voters and leave office peacefully."

He continued: "This is not just an election between Donald Trump and Joe Biden. This is an election between Donald Trump and democracy-and democracy **must** win."

Bernie also referred to Trump as a "pathological liar," with "strong authoritarian tendencies,." and accused him of being "prepared to undermine American democracy in order to stay in power."

On two occasions in the last two days, Donald Trump declined to commit to a peaceful transition of power if Biden wins the election in November. On a number of occasions, Trump said, "the only way they can take this election away from us is if this is a rigged election." That is Trump's way of spreading doubt in our elections, and it is shameful.

Sanders continued: "I think it is terribly important that we actually listen to, and take seriously, what Donald Trump is saying. There is nothing in our Constitution or in our laws that gives Donald Trump the privilege of deciding whether or not he will step aside if he loses. **In the United States, the president does not determine who can or cannot vote and what ballots will be counted.**

Bernie Sanders went on to criticize Trump for continuing "to be obsessed with the belief that there is massive voter fraud in this country," even though instances of voter fraud are extremely rare, as the FBI Director testified this week.

Bernie then said, "Trump's strategy to delegitimize this election and to stay in office if he loses is not complicated. Finding himself behind in many polls, he is attempting massive voter suppression. He and his Republican colleagues are doing everything they can to make it harder and harder for people to vote. In addition, he is sowing the seeds of chaos, confusion and conspiracy theories by casting doubt on the integrity of this election and, if he loses, justifying why he should remain in office."

Bernie called on Majority Leader Mitch McConnell to hold more hearings on election security, and urged his Republican colleagues in the Senate to "stop the hypocrisy." Bernie Sanders has always been a straight talker, and a passionate man. He loves his country and he is clearly sounding the alarm.

Sanders also said that, "it is absolutely imperative that we have, by far, the largest voter turnout in American history and that people vote as early as possible."

The passion continued.

"As someone who is strongly supporting Joe Biden, let's be clear: A landslide victory for Biden will make it virtually impossible for Trump to deny the results and is our best means for defending democracy."

Bernie also called on states to begin counting mail-in votes ahead of Election Day., and to hold hearings, "to explain to the public how the Election Day process and the days that follow will be handled."

"The American people, no matter what their political persuasion, must make it clear that American democracy will not be destroyed," and "Regardless of what Donald Trump wants, the American people will preserve democracy in our country."

"Sorry, too many people fought and died to defend democracy to allow him to destroy it."

It is a powerful statement, and if you can see it delivered by Bernie live, you would see the passion, his anger at Trump, and his commitment to American democracy.

So many Republicans, who love country over party, have come to the fore and declared that they are supporting Joe Biden. One of the most extraordinary people is Cindy McCain, Arizona Senator John McCain's widow, endorsed Biden and said, "My husband John lived by a code: country first. We are Republicans, yes, but Americans foremost. There's only one candidate in this race who stands up for our values as a nation, and that is Joe Biden. She continued, "Joe is a good and honest man. He will lead us with dignity. He will be a commander in chief that the finest fighting force in the history of the world can depend on, because he knows what it is like to send a child off to fight."

Cindy McCain then reached out to housewives in the country and asked them to join her in crossing the aisle to support Joe Biden, based on love of country. In effect, she was giving Republican women cover to make the switch this year, and it might be incredibly effective.

These are two of the most inspiring people who came forward to express their love of country over party this week, and I wanted to bring them to you. There are more, and I will bring them to you in the next days and weeks. They are breathtaking in their commitment to American democracy, which is the foundation on which we have depended since the birth of the country, something we should never forget.

Rest in peace, Ruth Bader Ginsburg/Three days of honoring an icon of the law

September 25, 2020

The lines started gathering early at the Supreme Court on Wednesday, so that people could pay tribute to a woman who had changed the lives of so many of us. Ruth Bader Ginsburg died last Friday night, on the eve of Rosh Hashanah, as Jews everywhere were celebrating the New Year. As I mentioned, It is believed that if a person dies on that day, she is "blessed," indeed, "righteous," and Ruth Bader Ginsburg was certainly a righteous person in life as in death.

Standing on the steps leading to the Supreme Court were 120 of RBG's law clerks from the 27 years that she served on the Court, and some from her earlier District Court days. The clerks stood on the steps in silent honor, ready to protect her last journey and stand guard on the casket through the night. She treated her clerks like family, and the family was here to pay tribute.

The crowd was forming, and it was a sight to behold. Mothers with daughters wearing the kind of collar on their Justice robes that Ruth wore when she was dissenting. Signs everywhere, saying, "I dissent." Other signs saying, "thank you." Hundreds of mourners came to pay their respects, and they kept coming all day long, into the thousands. Many people were crying, and it was clear that at least three generations were deeply affected by her life, and now, her death. There was a marvelous young child in a Superwoman costume. Justice Ginsburg meant so much to all of us, as she forged groundbreaking decisions that gave men as well as women new opportunities to live their lives more equitably.

Because of the pandemic, everyone had a mask on, and there was social distancing. Similarly, the casket was brought outside to avoid crowds of people who would have been in close quarters inside. At the private ceremony in the Supreme Court, RBG's rabbi, spoke about Ruth's devotion to family, to equal justice and to the law. "She was our prophet, our North Star."

Since the marble inscription above the door on the Supreme Court reads, "Equal Justice under Law," Chief Justice John Roberts spoke beautifully about Ruth, the marvelous marriage with her life partner, Marty, about her children and closeness with grandchildren. Then he explained that the Supreme Court "was her home, too." Her relationship with Justice Antonin Scalia, with whom she disagreed on just about everything legal, blossomed over opera, about which they were both passionate. In addition, they made one another laugh, and they traveled to India together. Chief Justice Roberts pointed out that being able to have a wonderful friendship with someone with whom you disagreed so profoundly, is a role model for all of us.

The crowd swelled to thousands by 10pm on that first day, and people kept coming. The clerks stood guard overnight at her casket. On the second day, Donald and Melania Trump came, wearing masks, and when the people saw them, two chants arose, "keep her wish," and then, "Vote him out."

After two days, and thousands more visitors, Ruth Bader Ginsburg's flag-draped casket was moved to the Capitol building, where she would be the first woman to lie in state. She would also be the first Jewish American so honored. At the Capitol all of the women of Congress in both parties were lining the steps as Ruth's casket was brought up the steps, to be placed in Statuary Hall. The Congresswomen stood with their hands over their hearts, and it was breathtaking to see how women of all ages and persuasions were so moved by what she had done for them, and now she was gone.

There was a beautiful service in Statuary Hall, again with Rabbi Holtzblatt speaking. Nancy Pelosi, Speaker of the House, and Senate Minority Leader Schumer were in attendance, but Mitch McConnell and Kevin McCarthy, Senate majority leaders, did not attend, an unusual slight, since funerals historically bring together both parties.

After the three days honoring RBG were concluded, Ruth was buried next to her husband, Marty, in Arlington National Cemetery, in a private ceremony for family and closest friends. There is a hole in our hearts today, knowing that the world is a darker place, without Ruth guarding our rights.

On Friday evening, September 18, when it was announced that RBG had died, politics immediately entered the conversation. Within an hour, Mitch McConnell announced that President Trump would be proposing a name and the Republicans would be voting on her replacement. It was a crass and callous maneuver with so little time left to the election. Never before has a name been pushed through with only a few weeks left to November 3rd. In fact, when Antonin Scalia died, and Barack Obama proposed Merrick Garland, a moderate, to join the bench, Mitch McConnell and the Republicans kept that seat open for ten months, never giving Merrick Garland the courtesy of meeting with him, holding a hearing or a vote. It was the height of hypocrisy and rudeness, and the first time it had ever been done.

The 2016 election between Hillary Clinton and Trump resulted in three million more votes for Clinton, but Trump won the Electoral College and therefore the presidency. There was clear evidence that Russia interfered in our 2016 election with the intent of helping Trump, and the FBI Director, Wray, testified just last week, that Russia is very actively trying to interfere in the 2020 election once again.

While Ruth Bader Ginsburg was lying in state at the Supreme Court and the Capitol, Donald Trump proposed Amy Coney Barrett to fill the seat. Barrett is a right-wing conservative whose name was taken from the list of the Federalist Society. The members of both the Federalist and the Heritage Society are right-wing judges, who are pledged to overturn Roe v. Wade, thereby denying women a legal and safe abortion choice. In other words, seating Barrett would put the polar opposite to Ruth Bader Ginsburg in that seat, giving the conservative court a 6 to 3 advantage. That would likely overturn Obamacare and all of the gains made by Ruth Bader Ginsburg for the rights of men and women alike. We are at a serious moment in American history, and our democracy hangs in the balance.

The split screen of honoring an American icon was sadly politicized by the Republican party that couldn't wait to nominate a replacement. Polling in the country found that 67% of Americans feel that the winner of the election should nominate the new Justice. However, Donald Trump, who is behind in the polls, feels that he can create enough chaos to put the election into the Court, and wants a ninth member now. He said twice that he will not accede to a peaceful transfer of power, the first president to ever indicate he would not comply with that key tradition which singles-out America as unique in the world. Peaceful transfer of power is a model to all countries, and an example of the stability of our Constitution.

Unfortunately, in the middle of a serious health crisis with more than 200,000 dead, Donald Trump has injected more chaos and anxiety into the conversation. The reality of a nightmare election fight is upon us, and once again, our democracy is at stake.

Debate Night!

September 29, 2020

I took two days from writing for the Jewish holidays. No one can take two days off in this election year! So much happened in two days that my head is spinning this morning. Here are some serious things to know, in brief.

Donald Trump nominated Amy Coney Barrett for Ruth Bader Ginsburg's seat on the Supreme Court, before Justice Ginsburg had even been buried. Barrett is a right -wing judge, the polar opposite of RBG, who would vote to defeat Obamacare, thereby putting millions of people without health insurance. The seating of a new justice would put citizens in great financial danger during the pandemic and beyond. Voting rights and women's rights are equally in jeopardy. The Republicans have the votes to jam this through before the election, even though a majority of citizens polled said they would prefer to let the winner of the election choose the next Justice.

On Sunday, as I was online at services, The **New York Times** investigative reporters got Trump's tax returns and put out a detailed story that Donald Trump only paid $750 in federal income taxes the year he was elected, and the following year. More shocking, for ten of the prior fifteen years, he paid zero in taxes. Most important and serious for the country, he is four hundred million dollars in debt, and the papers show that he is a failed businessman. He squandered hundreds of millions, including the Republican campaign war chest, leaving him with little and no ability to run ads at the end.

The takeaway? Anyone with that level of debt is a serious security risk, would NEVER get a job in government. Hence, Trump himself would never get clearance, but he is sitting in the Oval office with access to all of our most top- secret information. Remember, his campaign chairman, Paul Manafort, was in close touch with a Russian operative and was sharing election polling that helped Trump defeat Hillary Clinton. Manafort went to jail for his numerous crimes.

Donald Trump paid no attention to the vetting process. Jared and Ivanka never got security clearances from the FBI, because they found disturbing information in their histories. Trump put them in the White House nonetheless.

Yesterday, The *New York Times* reported that the White House was pressuring the CDC and the FDA to change the numbers so that they looked good enough to send children back to school. That is criminally callous. We are not in a good place to send our children to school, especially with flu season approaching. It was reported that Dr. Scott Atlas, now Trump's favorite on science, has been feeding Trump false information. Dr. Redfield, head of the CDC, is very concerned about the misinformation, because it is hurting those who are listening.

That is a brief, very brief, overview of the last two days.

The debate:

Chris Wallace of Fox News will be the moderator. He has fact-checked Donald Trump in interviews, and should be a fair interviewer.

Some topics: Covid-19, the economy, race and violence in the cities.

Joe Biden is 10 points ahead of Donald Trump in a general election matchup. He is also ahead in many of the states. 86% of people watching have already decided for whom they are going to vote. A huge number of women have been driving the election numbers for Joe Biden, except for non-college educated women, many of whom are in battleground states.

Interestingly, the numbers of women supporting Joe Biden have risen after Trump's nomination of Amy Coney Barrett, who is in favor of overturning Roe v. Wade and the Affordable Care Act. Trump's nomination may have back-fired, even though evangelicals were cheering.

The debates begin at 9, and they will be for 90 minutes. Settle in with a coffee, a glass of wine and some good snacks and "we'll talk on the other side," as Brian Williams always says.

Debate: Deficit of Decency

September 30, 2020

Last night was disastrous for democracy. America was on display, and it was embarrassing for ourselves, our children and for the world to see. From the beginning, Chris Wallace of FOX news, set out the rules, mutually agreed upon. Donald Trump ignored the rules, constantly interrupted, talked over Joe Biden who was trying to answer a question. Trump was insulting, told lies and was generally obnoxious.

Chris Wallace lost control of the debate a few minutes into the evening. Trump talked over Wallace, insulted him, made faces while Biden was talking, and generally disrupted a debate that is an institution of American democracy. Debates go back to Lincoln-Douglas. In 1960, the first televised debate between Kennedy and Nixon was very historic.

Fifteen minutes into the debate, I had a massive headache. Ninety minutes were scheduled for this debacle, and I couldn't imagine watching the rest of the mess, but I did.

This was not a normal presidential debate, where the candidates honor the rules. Many children who were watching for the first time with their parents, wondered what was happening. Granted, it was a troubling, confusing train wreck, and kids everywhere were baffled. Parents had a lot of explaining to do!

Joe Biden tried not to take Trump's bait, mostly ignored Donald Trump, looked into the screen and spoke to the voters on any number of issues. He reminded the people that Trump had no plan to defeat the virus, no healthcare plan, although he has promised one is coming for the last four years. He also has no idea that the suburbs are diverse. In the absence of knowing anything, he blew up the entire event.

Bill Kristol, the conservative pundit, described it as "a spectacle … an embarrassment … a disgrace … because of the behavior of one man, Donald Trump. The interrupting and the bullying, the absence of both decency and dignity—those were Donald Trump's contributions to the evening, and they gave the affair the rare and sickening character of a national humiliation." Bill Kristol is scheduled to be the first speaker at our temple, Sharey Tefilo, on October 23rd, for our Scholar Series.

Donald Trump came out to solidify his base and encourage them to disrupt the election. That way, he can contest the results until the solution goes to the Supreme Court, where he feels a majority will give him the presidency. It was all there tonight. He did speak about the grievances and lies that his supporters have come to believe, although they are bogus. He totally ignored the 207,000 dead citizens of Covid-19, and insisted that he was the victim of Democrats' lies about the disease.

He did not speak well of Dr. Fauci and the scientists of the CDC and the FDA, that he has been demeaning. He has actively been influencing them to change the data, so he will look better.

The most extraordinary moment came when Chris Wallace asked, "Are you willing, tonight, to condemn white supremacists and militia groups and to say that they need to stand down?" Trump pretended he didn't know which groups, until Wallace and Biden named the Proud Boys, the hate group that helped to organize the riot in Charlottesville, Virginia. Trump hedged and didn't answer. Upon urging from Wallace, Trump finally answered. "Proud Boys, stand back and stand by. But I'll tell you what, somebody's got to do something about antifa and the left."

Trump immediately pivoted from the right to the left, which was a false narrative. The FBI has investigated and announced that white supremacist crimes are the major problem in America domestically, and it has grown dramatically under Trump's administration. The numbers are staggering.

The head of the Proud Boys said, "that's my president," and the Proud Boys posted on the one place that will host them. Twitter and Facebook have eliminated them from being able to post. Within an hour the group had new shoulder patches which said, "Stand Back and Stand By."

There is more. Trump asked his supporters to act as poll watchers to prevent a fraudulent vote. I was a poll watcher in Newark when Ken Gibson was running for mayor against Hugh Addonizio. Each candidate had one poll watcher, and no one else except the present voters were allowed in the room. I imagine that is the case now, because you can't have any signs or buttons supporting a candidate within a certain number of yards from the election. Advertisers need to stay outside. While it's been awhile since I did this, my guess is that Donald Trump has no idea what the rules and regulations are on Election Day inside the voting area.

Once again, Trump refused to commit to accepting a Biden victory, saying he could not agree to fraudulent results. Knowing that he is losing, he cast doubt on the integrity of the election, something that no other president in the history of our country, has ever done. Donald Trump is a sore loser, and unfortunately, he has the power of the presidency to make the next few weeks and months a nightmare.

As with all bullying, whether in middle school or with adults, it is a sign of weakness, of someone afraid he will lose and is making excuses.

Joe Biden, amidst all this noise and confusion, stayed calm and did well. He was able to say that Trump was responsible for the failure of his administration, that 205,000 Americans have died on Trump's watch. As a result, the economy is very bad, despite the stock market resilience. Very few people in middle America own stocks. Trump has shown no remorse over the dead Americans, the broken families and the sadness that has resulted. Joe Biden said that, under Donald Trump, "America has become weaker, sicker, poorer, more divided and more violent."

Biden also had his best moment when talking about Trump's description of the soldiers as "suckers and losers." Biden mentioned his son, Beau, who served in Iraq, and died of cancer. Not one word from Trump, when it would have been easy to acknowledge Biden's loss. Instead, Trump immediately brought up Hunter, Biden's other son. Biden looked directly at Trump and said that Hunter had a drug addiction he is managing, and Biden is proud of him. It was a moment. Biden spoke as a father defending his son, and that message will resonate to millions of Americans who are fighting addiction in their families. It was very authentic.

Biden often spoke to the American people, and that was very effective. He said that if we all worked together we can accomplish anything. He asked people to "Vote, vote vote." in whatever way is best for them. Biden then said, "he (Trump) will not be able to stop you from determining the outcome of this election.:

At the end, Biden refused to be cowed by Trump's threats not to honor the election results. Biden said, "I will accept it, and he will too. You know why? Because once the winner is declared once all the ballots are counted, that'll be the end of it."

And this is the end of my report today, thank goodness. It was unpleasant having to write about an American travesty.

Stay calm, and help a friend vote-either by mail or taking a friend to a polling place. We need to stick together for the sake of our democracy, and our dignity.

E Pluribus Unum …

The Reckoning

October 2, 2020

I awoke at 1:30 am to the news that the President of the United States and his wife had tested positive for the coronavirus. With all the rallies, thousands of people, not wearing masks, and sitting close together, it was only a matter of time that they would catch the virus.

One of Trump's closest advisors, Hope Hicks, tested positive for the virus on Wednesday, but it was kept quiet. Yesterday, the White House Press Secretary came out to a press conference and never told the press or the American public. Only this morning at 1:30am, did Donald Trump send a tweet with the information that he and the First Lady had tested positive.

Thinking he was invincible by holding massive rallies, Donald Trump was putting on his own reality tv show. The public would think all was well, and it wasn't necessary to wear a mask or to socially distance. Thursday the president went to a fundraiser in Bedminster, NJ, and told his supporters that the virus was turning a corner and would soon be gone. He was quite wrong.

Now that Trump has the. coronavirus, everyone around him has to quarantine and be tested. Presumably, there will be no more debates, and no campaigning. Joe Biden had been campaigning very carefully, in order to not endanger the supporters with whom he met. At the moment, Joe Biden is in the midst of a very successful train tour through the Midwest. On Tuesday night, during the debate, Donald Trump was yelling and spitting at the former Vice President. Those are the very conditions under which people catch the virus. Both men are in their seventies, and Donald Trump is overweight.

At the debate, four of Donald Trump's older children, along with Hope Hicks and Jim Jordan, were seated together, without masks, despite the fact that they were mandated to do so. It is apparent that rules to not apply to them, even if masks would keep others safe.

So, this is our "October Surprise." It certainly is a distraction on some level, but it reminds us how Donald Trump utterly failed fighting the virus for the American people. At this date, 210,000 citizens have died, and still no remorse from the president. Yesterday, on October 1st, the *New York Times* reported the unflattering news that in a study of 38 million articles about the pandemic, between January 1st and May 26th, Donald Trump was "likely the largest driver of Covid-19 misinformation." The Cornell University study showed that 38% of the misinformation mentioned Donald Trump.

Trump is the third world leader to contract the virus. Boris Johnson, from Britain, got quite sick and wound up in the ICU. He almost died. Interestingly, he was cared for by immigrant healthcare workers and the British healthcare system saved him. He changed his attitude after his near-death experience.

Looking back in history, Woodrow Wilson was very sick during the 1918 pandemic, and it was kept from the public.

There are thirty days before the election. All of these events are unfolding in a very difficult time for the country. As I am writing this, the news that Vice-President and Mrs. Pence tested negative for the virus was just reported. That is good news, because if Trump cannot do his duties, it would be the Vice President who would step in. The process is all laid out in the 25th Amendment, which was passed in the 60s, after John Kennedy was assassinated.

This could be a silver lining for the country. If Donald Trump's supporters see that even the president contracted the virus, then perhaps people would adopt the safety measures that have been put out by the CDC. It is a reckoning and a message to take this virus seriously, because it is a killer.

Stay safe, wear a mask and keep healthy!

October 4, 2020

The "hoax" arrived at the White House

October 3, 2020

The shock in the month of September came the night of Rosh Hashanah, September 18th, when Ruth Bader Ginsburg died. Within an hour of that news. Republican Majority Leader, Mitch McConnell, announced that they would be introducing her replacement that same week. It was a crude and graceless announcement that the nominee would be named before Justice Ginsburg would be honored and buried, and within a few weeks of the election. Barack Obama had been denied his one choice, Merrick Garland, on the premise that they wouldn't dream of accepting a nomination so close to the election, which was eight months away. The hypocrisy is obvious. Since the Republicans have the majority, they seem to have the votes, albeit a slim 4 Senator lead. Two Senators have already said they would like the nominee to be named by the winner of the election.

Last Saturday, September 26th, Donald Trump introduced his nominee for Ruth Bader Ginsburg's seat on the Supreme Court. In an outdoor event attended by a few hundred Republicans, Trump proudly introduced Judge Amy Coney Barrett, a Catholic, whose name came from a list given to him by the Federalist Society, a right-wing group dedicated to conservative courts. Based on her prior writings and rulings, Donald Trump understood that his choice was opposed to abortion, would vote to overturn Roe v. Wade and Obamacare, and all the other advances that women have made in the RBG court. Also, Barrett apparently belongs to a group that believes that men are in charge in the household, and women should be subservient. That should set us back seventy years.

Sitting close together in the Rose Garden, without masks, a number of attendees contracted coronavirus, including Father John Jenkins, President of Notre Dame, and two Senators, Thom Tillis (R-NC) and Mike Lee (R-UT). The Chair of the Republican National Committee. Ronna McDaniel, and three journalists also tested positive.

The debate was on Tuesday evening in Cleveland. A doctor from the Cleveland Clinic came to check the audience, and could not convince the Trump family to keep on masks. The debate was the nastiest, most disturbing debate in history, since the Kennedy/Nixon debate of 1960, the first time that debates were televised. Joe Biden's numbers increased after the country saw the contrast between the two men. During that debate, Donald Trump mocked Joe Biden for wearing a mask and following the science guidelines, among a lot of other bizarre comments. Trump refused to say he was not in favor of the white supremacists, rather, he pretended not to know who they were. Then he said, "stand back and stand by" when the name, Proud Boys, was mentioned by Biden. It set the conversation in the country on fire. Chris Wallace, moderator and journalist from the Fox News Channel, tried to contain Donald Trump, but it was useless. Trump was rude and insulting, and talked over Joe Biden. Wallace said that he was very disappointed in the debate, because it was an opportunity for the country to hear the policies of each candidate.

On Wednesday, the president started on a series of rallies, and attended two fundraisers, with no social distancing and no masks. Hope Hicks, a close advisor, was not feeling well, and subsequently tested positive for the virus. That news was not immediately shared. Despite the fact that he knew about Hope Hicks, who traveled to all these places with him, Donald Trump, flew to Bernardsville, Nj, for a fundraiser, where he met with hundreds of people, and exposed all of them to the virus. He was not feeling well at the time, and fell asleep on the plane. At 1:30am on Friday morning, Trump sent a tweet that he and Melania tested positive for the virus.

His tweet sent shockwaves through the country, and through the thousands of people he encountered at the rallies and fundraisers in close quarters. All the people at the New Jersey event are now being tested and subjected to contact tracing. Many of them are very angry, because they paid $250,000 for the privilege of rubbing elbows with Trump, but he showed no consideration for possibly infecting them.

Many more people have tested positive for the virus. Chris Christie, former Governor of New Jersey, was one high profile person. He spent four days at the White House helping Trump prep for the debate. Kellyanne Conway, also tested positive. Former Governor Christie is now in Morristown Hospital. Essentially, none of these people took the kind of precautions that would have kept them safe, because the president has denied masks and all other safety behaviors.

One of the most stunning news stories dropped in the same week. The New York Times received years' worth of Trump's taxes, and they are shocking. To briefly encapsulate, Trump paid zero taxes in eleven of eighteen years. During the first two years of his presidency, he paid only $750. Moreover, the returns show that he is at least four hundred million dollars in debt. Now we know why he didn't want to make his returns public-they are embarrassing and make him a serious security risk. To whom does he owe hundreds of millions of dollars? We need to know, especially if it is Russia or any other foreign entity. The Times did a marvelous job of reporting and analyzing. The money that Trump owes will become due in the next three years, when he might lose the second term. That explains why he is desperate not to lose. If he loses and is a citizen, the Attorney General of New York is waiting to indict him for tax fraud, bank fraud and other crimes. George Conway, Kellyanne's husband, indicated that Trump will be bankrupt and possibly have to go to jail. Since he has been using the country as his own personal ATM machine, the tax returns explain why he went to so many fundraisers and has the events at all his properties, many of which are losing money. The takeaway is that Donald Trump is a terrible businessman, and only made money when he was the star of "The Apprentice," which gave millions of people the false idea that he was a wealthy and successful businessman. Those people became the base of his supporters, and nothing has been able to sway them.

President Trump spent much of Friday in the White House, but it became clear that he needed to go to Walter Reed Medical Center for the most sophisticated care possible. At 4pm, Marine 1 helicopter arrived at the White House and took the president to the hospital. His chief of staff, Mark Meadows, unmasked, traveled with him. The Presidential Suite is fully equipped to accommodate everything that the president needs to continue to conduct business, even a secure room for top secret conversations and a very fancy dining room.

There have been different versions of Trump's timeline: when he knew he was positive, why he went to rallies, and a fundraiser on Thursday, etc. In addition, there is disagreement about his condition, whether he needed oxygen or not, and what his situation is. Trump is in his seventies, overweight, and a serious health risk for this virus. The doctors administered remdesivir, a cocktail that is given to people who are hospitalized. Apparently, the doctors gave him some supplemental oxygen at the White House.

The doctors at Walter Reed came out to discuss Trump's health. He is fever free at the moment, but not out of the woods. In fact, the virus often turns deadly in the second week. So, there is an abundance of caution at this time. Joe Biden came out and wished everyone well and a good recovery. He also stressed that the virus should not be turned politically. Biden took down his negative ads in respect for Trump being in the hospital. Biden went on to say that the country needs to come together, wear a mask and follow guidelines. More deaths are occurring daily, almost 1,000 people a day are dying, and there still is no federal plan. Donald Trump has to quarantine and the campaign is essentially over for him. Gratefully, the debates seem to be ended, except that Vice-Presidential candidate, Kamala Harris will debate VP Mike Pence. That should be very interesting.

The "hoax," the virus that didn't exist, that was going to "magically disappear," came to the White House and spread and spread throughout the Republican party and its supporters. The results of that foolish, callous and uncaring event in New Jersey are still resounding throughout the country, and it leaves the election results up in the air.

I VOTED! Please make sure to vote ASAP or make plans for how you are going to vote. New Jersey is one of NINE states that sends ballots automatically to every registered voter. Make sure that you have yours. Each town has a drop-box, generally by the fire/police stations, with 24-hour camera surveillance.

Stay safe and keep healthy …

Continuing chaos and confusion

October 5th, 2020

There are mixed messages coming from the White House, from the doctors and from the president himself. Two briefings from the head doctor at Walter Reed initially painted a rosy picture. Then, Mark Meadows, the Chief of Staff, gave an entirely different message-that the president was on serious medicine, had two instances where he had to be put on oxygen, had a high fever, and it was a dangerous situation that could deteriorate at any time. Reporters and journalists were skeptical of both messages, and felt that there was no transparency from any source. Meanwhile, three hundred million people don't actually know what the situation is, and that is very concerning.

Neither does the rest of the world know what is happening. The chaos that Donald Trump has created leaves the United States vulnerable. The Executive branch is basically not functioning, and neither is the Senate, because members have also caught the virus. Mike Pence, the Vice President has tested negative, and is going to debate Senator Kamala Harris, who also tested negative and is the Vice -Presidential candidate. Interestingly, Mike Pence was at the Rose Garden event, and could have easily become infected. According to the Twenty-Fifth Amendment, should the President and Vice President not be able to serve, the Speaker of the House, in this case Nancy Pelosi, would run the country, since the House represents the people more broadly.

Trump appeared inside his suite, and made two videos to put out to the public, each edited, where he said he was doing well. In line with the seriousness of the Covid-19, Trump was put on a steroid, also put on dexamethasone, which can induce delirium, and rendesavir, an elite IV cocktail administered in a hospital, not at the White House.

Trump saw that his supporters gathered outside. He decided to have a drive by photo op around the hospital, waving to all the people on the street who were holding flags and signs. Two secret service agents were in the front seat, wearing masks, but the windows were tight shut, and those agents will now have to quarantine, since they were put in danger of catching the virus. Secret Service agents in general are frustrated by Donald Trump's actions, which often put them in danger. They said, "he doesn't care about us." No love lost there.

It would be safe to say that much is in flux-the Supreme Court nomination, the remaining two debates, the health of the President, whether children can attend school safely and more. The United States is at one of the most dangerous times in our history. A bad global actor could decide to do something, and it is not clear that we could respond. This is very unsettling around the country. Corona cases are rising in many states, and almost one thousand citizens are dying daily. The total this morning is 210,000 dead, with seven million people testing positive for the virus.

On a sad note, the Supreme Court opens its session as it always does-on the first Monday in October, without Ruth Bader Ginsburg for the first time in twenty-seven years. Her chair is draped in black, and it will no doubt be a very difficult opening. RBG is gone, and the country is still grieving for her. Where is Ruth Bader Ginsburg when we need her? Who will step up to carry the flag for peoples' rights? My Senator, Cory Booker, has been passionately speaking out on the subject, as he has for decades. I hope that he and others in the Senate will wake up and do their jobs for the American people.

Be sure to **VOTE**! Wear a mask, practice social distancing, wash your hands, and stay safe.

Kamala Harris makes History

October 7, 2020

Tonight, the Vice-Presidential debate was held, with Democratic Vice-Presidential candidate, Senator Kamala Harris (D-CA), taking the stage against Vice-President Mike Pence. Senator Harris, with black and Indian ancestors, made history as the first black woman on a national ticket. She has an impressive list of accomplishments, including her role as Attorney General of California before she was elected Senator.

The debate was against the backdrop of tanking poll numbers showing that the president will lose the election to Joe Biden, who is up in each of the battleground states. It was also against the fact that the President of the United States, who downplayed the virus, is home from Walter Reed Hospital, having caught the virus, which he characterized as a "hoax." Moreover, Trump returned to a very empty White House, since his behavior and super-spreader in the Rose Garden, exposed thirty-four of his staff, who tested positive for Covid-19, and are home. In addition, the high command of the military was exposed at a White House meeting, and they are all in quarantine. The head of Security for the White House has Covid-19 and is very sick. What a nightmare.

The election is just in four weeks. The debate probably should not have been in person. Kamala Harris insisted that there be plexiglass protective screens and everyone had to wear a mask. If they refused, they would be escorted out of the hall.

Senator Harris is a skillful debater, and was able to show that she is conversant with each of the nine previously unannounced topics by the moderator, Susan Page, the Washington Bureau Chief for USA Today. Surprisingly, Susan Page seemed unprepared for Pence to disregard the rules and bully her and Senator Harris. Pence consistently talked beyond his time, interrupted Senator Harris, and refused to answer questions. Susan Page lost control of the debate early, because she couldn't stop him with her, "Thank you, Mr. President," which he ignored repeatedly. Knowing what happened with Donald Trump, it was inconceivable to me that Susan Page didn't mute the microphone, or stop him to reiterate that he needed to follow the rules of the timing. It was very frustrating to hear Pence continue talking. To her credit, Senator Harris did stop Pence a few times to indicate he was interrupting her, and she did it firmly and with a smile. It was classic.

Personally, I think that it was a very bad idea for Mike Pence to continue talking beyond his legitimate time. If the goal was to win over many of the women lost to the Trump-Pence ticket, Pence reminded every woman who has ever been in a meeting with men, how they often interrupt with impunity. Last night, women hated Mike Pence.

Kamala Harris was able to introduce herself to the country, by talking about her life and experiences as an Attorney General and as Senator. She showed herself to be commanding if something should happen to Joe Biden.

Pence was smooth and answered in his soft, measured, monotone voice. He looked tired, and he had a pesky fly on his hair. The one notable moment in his answers was when he refused to commit to a peaceful transfer of power if he and Trump lost the election. That was stunning, and also scary.

Another worrisome moment was the discussion of the Affordable Care Act, and the provisions of which Americans approve-the pre-existing conditions and also child protection on parents' insurance until age twenty-six. Trump has been saying he has a plan, which has never been produced in four years. Last night, Pence said that his administration has a plan to replace the ACA. When asked about it, he obfuscated and talked about the Supreme Court. Kamala Harris reminded the American people that Donald Trump is trying to overturn the ACA and it is in the Supreme Court right now. She had a strong moment, when she turned to the camera and talked to the Americans. If you value your pre-existing conditions and the ACA, "they are coming for you," referring to the Trump-Pence ticket. Kamala Harris also referenced the fact that Donald Trump has spent four years reversing everything that President Barack Obama accomplished-for climate, for clean air and water, and so much more. Wanting to take down the Affordable Care Act with absolutely no plan in sight, will take away protections from millions of citizens. It is a travesty, and a petty project on the part of Donald Trump.

Meanwhile, the White House is in chaos. The White House has become the most dangerous virus hotspot in the country, which is ironic. The people who work there are scared, because they were bullied into not wearing masks, and they may well get sick. Mike Pence was the head of the Coronavirus Task Force, which actually did nothing to protect American citizens, side-lined the science experts and watched as more people died. As of this writing, 213,109 citizens have died, and there is no end in sight, since 32 states have rising numbers and their hospitals are at maximum capacity.

The country is tired, healthcare workers are exhausted and their numbers depleted, since many have died, and parents are tired of having to home school their children rather than going back to work. None of this had to happen if Donald Trump had honestly admitted in February that we have a virus and we need to be mobilizing as if we are at war. The American people know how to come together to wage a war, as long as the leader is telling the truth and modeling the appropriate responses. From the beginning we should have been wearing masks, practicing social distancing, staying home and washing hands. If Trump had sent out that message to the entire country, we would be out of this morass by now.

The answer is to VOTE! Millions have already voted, and ballots are up more than 600% in the last two weeks. This is a referendum on what we want our country to become.

The week that was-October 2-10

October 2-10, 2020

With the president admitting that he had the virus, he was unexpectedly flown by helicopter to Walter Reed Hospital for the most sophisticated care. At the first briefing by his doctors, the White House doctor did not answer the journalists' questions directly, citing HIPAA (privacy for patients). However, the President of the United States owes the country more information. He is being treated in a hospital paid for by the American citizens who pay our taxes. Everything else that was used to treat him is paid for by taxes, which he either didn't pay for eleven years, or he paid $750 for the first two years of his presidency. He had access to elite and expensive medicines that no ordinary citizen would have.

While he was in the hospital, staff members reported that they tested positive for the virus. Many had to leave and isolate, quarantine or go to a hospital, as former Governor Chris Christie did. The White House is practically empty.

Trump saw his numbers going lower, was bored, and itching to get out and campaign. In a callous move, he had the two Secret Service agents drive him around Walter Reed so he could wave at supporters. It was an inconsiderate use of the Secret Service, who could easily become ill.

Then he insisted on returning to the White House, in what seemed like a triumphal return, which he scripted and directed. As he got to the top of the stairs, he dramatically took off his mask, then walked into the White House where he would expose the photographer, and many others who work there, to the virus. His breathing was labored, and despite his saying he was "cured," it seemed clear that he was still sick. He falsely claimed that he had "learned a lot about this virus," as if learning eight months later was something to admire. He should have listened to the scientists, learned everything possible about how to defeat the virus, and saved the country.

Trump made two videos that were rambling and incoherent, very disturbing. Not once did he indicate that the virus is dangerous, people need to wear a mask and be careful. In fact, he said just the opposite, forgetting that 45,000 would contract the virus that day in our country.

Donald Trump has been lashing out at everyone-Bill Barr because the Durham case will not be ready before the election, if ever. A key lawyer quit, because she said there was pressure on her from the Justice Department. Trump lashed out at Mike Pompeo, and of course, Chris Wray, who testified to the lack of fraud in our elections, and made a video speaking to the American people to have faith in the election, and vote. Most bizarre, Trump asked Bill Barr to arrest Joe Biden and Barack Obama for "crimes," as well as Hillary Clinton. He seems to be ranting and raving against everyone. Of course, asking the Attorney General to arrest your opponent is the most bizarre, and shows how he has gone off the deep end. There has been talk of the 25th Amendment, in Congress and in the country.

Talking about the 25th Amendment is not as outrageous as it may seem. Many things happened this week that showed Donald Trump to be incapable of making rational decisions, and that is the most worrisome of all. First, the committee that makes the rules for the debates, announced that the October 15th debate would be virtual, in order to protect all concerned. Considering the thirty-five people who tested positive after the Rose Garden event, caution seemed reasonable. Donald Trump was outraged, said that he wouldn't participate in a virtual event and would have a rally instead. Joe Biden said that he would stick to the schedule that was agreed upon, and would have an event on his own if Trump wasn't' coming.

There are some interesting problems here. One is that the president has yet to say when he had his last negative coronavirus test. No one knows, but he did admit that he was not tested daily, as he led us to believe. It's unclear if Trump is still contagious, since the time period was supposed to be twenty days after he showed symptoms, which was on October 1st, the night of the Bedminster event. Because no one is talking, the timeline is very difficult to nail down, and I apologize for that.

Donald Trump's staff tried to convince him to change his mind and attend the debate. Conversation went back and forth. Trump tried to have the dates changed to weeks later, but Biden stood firm.

In the midst of all this chaos, citizens began voting, and Trump tweeted in order to make Americans nervous about the validity of the vote. He has been acting manic, and his behavior shows that the possibility that he may lose the election is front and center in his mind. He clearly doesn't care how much damage he does to America's faith in its vote.

One reason for the bizarre behavior is that the doctors put the president on a very strong cocktail of drugs, a cocktail that indicated he was quite sick. One of the prescriptions was for steroids, which can make a person manic. Meanwhile, the country was getting more and more nervous about the president's behavior, and his numbers went even lower.

Is your head spinning? This is just a portion of all the crazy things that happened this week. For one thing, Donald Trump completely shut down talks on the stimulus bill, which millions of Americans desperately need. That was shocking. He had not conferred with any staff, so it was another example of making rash and unreasoned decisions. Within another twenty-four hours, Trump changed his mind again, and said he actually did want the stimulus bill, and he wanted more than the original amount.

As all this was unfolding, the FBI and law enforcement in Michigan uncovered a plot on the part of white nationalists. They planned to kidnap Governor Gretchen Whitmer, put her on trial and ultimately kill her. These are the right;;;-wing groups that Donald Trump refused to acknowledge exist. What he doesn't realize is that these groups are anti-government, all government. Trump doesn't know what they are about. Despite the horror of the plot, Trump took that opportunity to tweet terrible things about Governor Whitmer, indicating that she did a terrible job, even though she was trying to keep Michiganders safe in lockdown and wearing masks. The President's lack of support for one of his Governors was not only un-American, it was inhumane, disgusting and very dangerous. Trump's disdain made Gretchen Whitmer less secure and extremely vulnerable.

The Vice -Presidential debate took place on Wednesday evening, with Kamala Harris facing Mike Pence. It was Senator Harris's opportunity to introduce herself to the country, and she did a very good job, despite the fact that Pence kept interrupting her, and told outrageous lies. That said, Donald Trump called Kamala Harris a "monster," which was insulting and crass. Words matter, and Donald Trump has known how to use them to create a negative and lasting image. He continues to characterize people in order to denigrate them, so he can seem powerful. I'm sad to say that it has worked all these years, but Kamala Harris is strong enough to fight this in a firm way. I feel that she will overcome his jeers. The next day reviews of the debate indicated that Kamala Harris had done a credible job, and Pence had little to defend, since he was the head of the Task Force that failed to fight the virus.

I don't know about you, but I am exhausted, and also very tired of the chaos that one insecure bully can conjure. I'm sure that I have forgotten other things.

At this moment, Trump is having an event at the White House, talking about the "China" virus, which I prefer to call the "Trump virus," and lying about how soon we would have a vaccine.

Just to be clear, it is a violation of the Hatch Act to have a partisan event at the "People's House." No partisan events are to be held there, so another norm was broken. Trump had the Republican Convention at the White House, which violated the Hatch Act, because it had all the trappings of a totally partisan event, and many people were very angry.

No one knows when Trump was last tested for the virus, and what the results might be. He is saying nothing, except that they will be hearing about the results "soon." It sounds a lot like his taxes, something Trump wanted to hide for good reason, and maybe he wants to hide the fact that he is still sick as well. I imagine we will hear about how many people got sick as a result of this "super-spreader." It's two weeks to the day that the first event was held in the Rose Garden, where thirty-five staff and friends were exposed, making the White House a major hot spot in Washington. Even Mitch McConnell said that he wouldn't come to the White House, and hasn't been there since August 6th. He is no fool, recognizing irresponsible behavior when he sees it. Attendees at the event were not tested, were not required to wear masks, and were spoken to by an infected Donald Trump. A pretty extraordinary nine months, fantasizing about the virus, saying it would go away. Now he is having super-spreader events, talking from the balcony, far away from all the people standing together and clapping. This could have been a moment where Donald Trump pivoted and said he was wrong and people should take the virus seriously, but he did not.

VOTE, VOTE, VOTE. Please wear a mask and take care of yourselves.

Hypocrisy unlimited

October 12, 2020

This morning is Day 1 of the Senate hearings on the nomination of Judge Amy Coney Barrett for Ruth Bader Ginsburg's seat on the Supreme Court. At the very least, it is an emotional and difficult morning. There is so much at stake: the ACA, LGBT rights, women's rights, ad infinitum.

By now, everyone knows the story of Mitch McConnell in 2016, indicating that a nominee should not be floated in the last year before an election. Barack Obama nominated Merrick Garland, a well-known moderate, for the seat vacated when Antonin Scalia unexpectedly died. No president had ever been denied a hearing on his nominee, but McConnell engineered his Senate so that no hearing was held and no vote was taken. It was an insult to a president and a brilliant judge. In prior years, the Senate voted across party lines to confirm Justice Ginsburg (96-3) and (98-2) for Antonin Scalia, recognizing that each judge had different views, but each would bring honor to the court.

1. This is not the Senate of past years. In 2020 it is partisan, totally political and cares only for a win, not for ethics, or the danger to the American people. Judge Barrett has been nominated by a president who will likely lose the election on November 3rd, so he is pushing her through. The polling of the American people indicates 70% prefer to have the elected president choose the nominee. Polling also indicates that 75% don't want Roe v. Wade to be overturned. The numbers are clear. This nomination by Donald Trump, flies in the face of the will of the American people, and the hypocrisy is galling. He has stuck his finger in our eye.

Moreover, on November 10th, the Supreme Court will hear a case brought by the Court to completely declare the Affordable Care Act unconstitutional. The effort by Trump to eliminate the ACA failed 71 times in Congress, so the case has been brought by states to the Supreme Court. Donald Trump wants to overturn everything that Barack Obama did in his presidency, and he has succeeded on many levels-clean air, water and much more. Millions of citizens will lose their healthcare protection, in the middle of a pandemic that has killed 216,000, but Trump shows no remorse. Even more bizarre, Donald Trump and the Republicans have not drafted a plan to replace the ACA. Trump has been saying for four years that a plan is coming, but nothing has been produced. There will be no reasonable replacement for taking healthcare away from millions of Americans. This is spiteful and vindictive.

Hypocrisy continues. You probably saw Donald Trump returning from the hospital and raving about his medicines, especially Regeneron. He called it a "cure," and said that he wants all Americans to have it.

Is Donald Trump as totally clueless as he seems? First of all, the medicine that he was given is still in trials. It is not accessible to just anyone, except on an emergency basis for the President of the United States. That is how the doctors at Walter Reed were able to administer it to him. If Regeneron was accessible, it could cost thousands of dollars at this stage of development.

Moreover, and probably something of which Donald Trump is unaware, the medicines that he received were made possible by research from lines of cells that were derived from fetal tissue. The Trump administration, in June 2019, banned the use of fetal tissue derived from abortions, and defunded all such research. What Donald Trump did not realize is that important scientific research has relied on using these lines. Fetal tissue from abortions has been crucial to developing the exact medicines that Trump was touting as a "cure."

Does Donald Trump really care about babies and children? Compare the concern for aborted fetuses with the thousands of children who have been separated from their families at our southern border. In a criminally inhumane policy, the administration called for children to be taken from their parents, put in cages, and treated like animals. They came here seeking asylum from dangerous lives, thinking that the United States would welcome them, and they got exactly the opposite treatment. Attorney General Jeff Sessions, Donald Trump and Steven Miller, felt that this inhumane treatment would discourage others from coming here.

It is a travesty. To date, we know of fifty-four hundred children who have been separated. Some children were flown to other cities, like New York, without telling the mayor. deBlasio complained bitterly. There was never a plan to reunite these children with their parents, many of whom were deported back to their countries. There is no database, because no one cared about keeping track of the children. Of all the horrific things that the Trump administration has done, I suggest to you that this is criminal and the most inhumane. A child separated from a parent for a few hours can have a traumatic experience. These children will be damaged for the rest of their lives, and the administration passed it off as "immigration policy." So, these people, who don't want legal abortions, are happy to be separating families, with no thought to the long-term consequences.

Many people have gone down to the border to survey the situation, and they report that it is horrific. Jacob Soboroff has written a book, *Separated,* which I highly recommend. He has spent years on the border, talking to families, children, etc., and he is incredibly knowledgeable and sensitive. This is NOT who we are as Americans. We welcomed asylum seekers, and had a process to help them gain admission to our country. That process was eliminated by the Trump administration. The hypocrisy of defunding research of abortion fetal tissue and criminalizing asylum seekers is emblematic of the people in charge of our country right now. I don't recognize my country anymore, and I want to take it back.

Please VOTE and wear a mask.

Dueling realities

October 16, 2020

Last night was supposed to be the second debate between President Donald Trump and Democratic Presidential nominee, Joe Biden. Originally, the meeting was to be in person, but after Trump contracted the coronavirus and was hospitalized, the organizers of the debates decided that the second debate would be virtual. Trump was outraged at that decision, and said that he would not participate. At that point, Joe Biden arranged a Town Hall meeting for an hour and a half of his own, on ABC. That Town Hall would give him an opportunity to present himself after the train wreck of the first evening, when Trump kept interrupting him. George Stephanopoulos would be the host.

Trump's advisors were not consulted when he decided to withdraw from the virtual meeting. He is behind in the polling, and giving up an opportunity to be seen by millions of people was foolish, to say the least. Since his illness, and having been given steroids, Trump had been acting irrationally, changing his mind on many issues, including the stimulus bill, which Americans need. Upon rethinking his rash response, Trump was able to arrange an hour-long Town Hall on NBC. There was an outcry at Trump's ability to get time after he withdrew from the original plan. NBC responded to the criticism by naming Savannah Guthrie as moderator. She is a skilled journalist who has a J.D. from Georgetown Law School and was a litigator before becoming a television personality. The result for all of us watchers, was that we would have dueling candidates.

I had two screens, and was watching carefully in the first half hour. Even the environment of each candidate was strikingly different. NBC had masked women who were nodding when the president spoke, so it seemed very partisan. Savannah Guthrie really pressed Trump on all his answers, which were vague and evasive. He also did his talking, talking, talking thing-if I am talking you are not getting in a word edgewise. But Savannah persisted, and she was excellent. She "unmasked" (forgive the pun) his shallow excuses that were not rooted in fact, and he became increasingly frustrated. The temperature in the debate kept rising, and it was very uncomfortable. Clearly, Trump lives in his own alternative reality. He refused to say when his last negative test was, or if he had been tested the day of the first debate. He refused to distance himself from QAnon, which traffics in weird conspiracy theories. He said that he did owe 400 million dollars, but it was a small percentage of his actual wealth, which is bizarre. He has not produced his taxes, which Savannah Guthrie noted, to visible anger on Trump's part. When Guthrie pressed Trump on the fact that the administration is in court trying to eliminate the Affordable Care Act in the middle of a pandemic, he insisted that he has a plan to replace it. She indicated that in four years that "plan" has not emerged and he could not describe it, other than it would be "better" and "cheaper." Meanwhile, millions of citizens are going to lose their protection of pre-existing conditions, and being protected on their parents' insurance until age 26. At the end, when Savannah lobbed Trump a softball, he merely said he "did a good job." As usual, the conversation was all about Trump, all the time, not about the people who died from the virus, or lost their jobs, or were hungry and worried that they might lose their homes. It was an X-ray into the soul of a callous man, and having the Town Hall expose him for who he is: unempathetic, shallow and self-absorbed.

Even before the event. Trump was disdainful, which seemed foolish, since NBC didn't have to offer him a platform. "They asked me if I'd do it. I figured, "What the hell? We get a free hour on television." I was surprised that NBC didn't withdraw its offer after that response, and I wish it had.

Joe Biden, on the other hand, had a successful, calm and informative Town Hall. There were citizens sitting far apart in the balcony who had questions, and Biden came prepared to answer them. He showed himself to be knowledgeable, and came prepared with statistics and history, and provided details about what he would do to solve the nation's myriad problems, many caused by Trump's inaction. The questions were wide-ranging-from foreign affairs, to racial inequality, to taxes, and what he would have done when we knew there was a virus in February. George was a knowledgeable host, and interjected with important comments. Biden came with a card so that he could answer with specific numbers and explain how his plans would impact voters. Joe Biden was an enthusiastic candidate, showed himself eager to win the presidency and get his programs underway. He certainly put to rest all of Trump's insults about his age and ability, and senility. In fact, it was Trump who came across as unable to mention anything substantive. When Savannah gave him a softball at the end, Trump merely said that he "did a good job." With millions sick, others dead, the economy devastated and people without jobs or food, that is hard to explain. In a classic comment, Savannah asked Trump about hiw outrageous tweets, and said, "it isn't as if you are someone's crazy uncle," indicating he was president and should act responsibly. It was a marvelous moment that really pulled Trump up short. Savannah was brilliant and bold, and Trump managed to humiliate himself by his rambling answers that were nonesense.

In a similar moment, George asked Biden, "If you lose, what will that say to you about where America is today?" Showing responsibility, which we have not seen in four years of the Trump presidency, Joe Biden said, "It could say that I'm a lousy candidate and I didn't do a good job, he answered the question. He continued, "But I hope that it doesn't say that we are as racially, ethnically and religiously at odds with one another as it appears the president wants us to be … Because we have the greatest opportunity than any country in the world to own the 21st century and we can't do it divided."

After the debates, fact-checkers (Rachel Maddow in particular) talked about the obvious-Trump lied and obfuscated. Biden had stayed very close to the facts, getting a few details wrong (like troop levels).

Biden's demeanor and preparedness, humility and decency were a relief. It was a reminder of what a president should be doing-talking about the citizens and the issues that concern them. Trump, on the other hand, talked only about himself.

After the Biden Town Hall ended, Joe Biden stayed for half an hour and talked to anyone who had another question. It was a lovely thing to do, and frankly the behavior of a politician who is actually interested in what people are thinking.

We clearly had very opposite views of two men, polar opposites, in fact.

While this was happening, it was impossible to overlook the fact that eight million Americans have contracted the virus, and as of today, 118,981 citizens have died. None of this had to happen if we had a leader who took control of the federal resources, and used them when he knew in January that a pandemic was on its way.

Elections have consequences. Please VOTE and defend our democracy.

Decency

October 16, 2020 (Friday night, Saturday morning)

Being saturated with unpleasant news cycles, I took a welcome break, and want to share it with you.

Friday night reminded me that there was decency in the world, in years gone by and in the White House. On MSNBC at 10pm, Pete Souza narrated an inspiring documentary ("As I See It") about his years as the photographer to Presidents Ronald Reagan and Barack Obama. Souza is a master of capturing the moment. The genius of his photography was that he could make himself quietly invisible in a room and be there at the perfect instant. Souza captured the feelings, the humor and the seriousness of history that was being recorded during the Obama administration. Nothing was staged. Most of all, the decency of each man shone through in the pictures and the dialogue of Souza, who obviously admired both men.

Pete Souza was never a political man. He worked for a Republican and a Democrat and made it clear in his documentary that he admired the humanity in each man.

Why did he do this documentary? Originally, he never planned to be the center of the spotlight for his work. However, Souza saw in the last four years the denigrating of the office of the President, and it disgusted him. He felt driven to make a statement, and he did it with his photographs and comments. In the wonderful pictures, Pete Souza showed how citizens were welcomed to the "peoples' house" with warmth, with joy and with respect. The pictures of each president with his wife-Michelle Obama and Nancy Reagan-show affectionate and deeply supportive and loving marriages.

In his photographs, Pete Souza showed a contrast that is gut-wrenching on the one hand, yet positively delightful, as we view his remarkable experiences. Souza is saying that the last four years are not who we are, that we can remember prior days of respect, intelligence, truth and humor and hopefully regain them. There are some beautiful books of Souza's photographs available on Amazon, and I recommend them to you.

Having seen the photographic documentary, I decided that I had to find solace in other, similar programs where I could take refuge from hostility, grievances and disinformation that was being spread.

The perfect bookmark to Friday night is Aaron Sorkin's extraordinary series, "The West Wing." Written in 2005, Sorkin is a genius who is intimate with the nuances of politics, of people and the aspirations we have for ourselves and our country. The seven-season series is brilliant, as it captures the essence of the people who work in the White House, and those on the other side who want to be there.

In 2005, Sorkin wrote episodes on climate change, immigrants, the fight for a Supreme Court nominee and so much more. In fact, the series is so prescient on current problems, that it relates to problems of NOW if you didn't know the date was 2005. The difference is that the people living in Sorkin's White House are truly dedicated to country and patriotism. Aaron Sorkin wrote episodes about the violence of white-supremacists against a black aid to "President Bartlett," about the dangers facing the military, as well as fights over Medicare and Social Security. His dialogue is true to history, and actually educates anyone not initially conversant with the issues. The acting is brilliant, and the characters are finely drawn. We are immediately pulled into their lives.

It is a wonderful alternative to right now, and I highly recommend it. I decided to take this break in reporting hostilities because we all need to remember those days that came before, those who were dedicated to service and from whom we can take inspiration.

If you have not already voted, please make sure that you VOTE,

Biden and Trump ... the final meeting ... gratefully

October 22, 2020 (Thursday night)

Well, it's over. Scowl versus smile, anger versus empathy. Ninety minutes of watching a lying man defending himself against a good man who was outraged by the truth-on Covid, on immigration, on "black lives matter," on a vision for the future, and more.

No longer an outsider, Donald Trump has much to answer for, with 224,000 citizens dead and millions infected. The man who said, "I alone can fix it," did nothing. Worse, he denied it, tried to sweep it under the rug of reality, and the virus, that knows no country boundaries, came here from Europe and started wreaking havoc.

The Trump administration cancelled the millions of masks that were supposed to be sent to every American household at the outbreak. Cancelled them. Even though the science Task Force said unequivocally that we needed nationwide testing, Donald Trump refused to put that in place. He assumed, incorrectly, that testing would create more cases, rather than identify where the cases are and who had them. Donald Trump does not understand the science, and spent no time learning about it. Why should he? This is a man who doesn't read and hates experts who know more than he does, which is just about everybody.

Even though Donald Trump contracted the virus, he clearly has no idea about it, how it travels and where it goes as we approach the fall. The daily death toll is 1,000 per day, and Trump said it "will go away." He did not activate the Defense Production Act, as Franklin Roosevelt did in World War Two. That would have provided all the materials needed to fight the virus.

Trump refuses to say that Americans should all wear masks and practice social distancing. Instead, he continues to hold "super spreader events," while many other people are working from home. Trump also calls for our children to "go back to school." Educators have decided to keep children working at home, as Boston did the other day, for everyone's safety. Donald Trump, calling for everything to open, shows a decided lack of caring for citizens who could contract the virus, become ill and even die. Leaders have been making decisions based on the data, but Trump pays no attention to the important numbers of where each state is. He is only concerned about the optics. Forty states now have surging cases.

The president mocked Dr. Anthony Fauci, and sidelined him from speaking to the public. When a pandemic is rocking the country, it is hard to be successful when the elected leader is a science denier. Trump refuses to learn the science of the virus, and has given no good information to the public at large. Presidents are supposed to be role models, give a consistent message and encourage the public in hard times. Donald Trump has done exactly the opposite, putting our country in even more danger as the flu season approaches. The possibilities are frightening, Yesterday, as Donald Trump was saying "the virus will disappear," and "we are turning the curve," we had 77,640 daily cases, a record for the country, and 224,280 people have died. Trump's comment, "We're learning to live with it," to which Biden responded, "we're dying with it." was stunning. Joe Biden indicated that there is no Trump government strategy, and that has resulted in thousands of people dying needlessly.

Trump also took a few swipes at Governor Cuomo and New York (that he loves?), because he is jealous of him. Trump's, "I alone can fix it," resulted in pitting governors against one another, competing for masks and materials and having to handle the business of getting hospitals up to speed. Trump did nothing to facilitate helping the healthcare workers. Doing nothing left the states in crushing debt, with no help in sight, especially the "blue states," which Trump and Jared Kushner decided not to help, which is madness. Not wanting to help "the blue states" was the ultimate fact that led to their decision to do nothing. Of interest, those states-New York, Connecticut, NJ, California, and Massachusetts, send more money to Washington than any others. Yet, Congress did not send help, which well may result in those states having to fire police, firefighters and teachers, when they are needed the most.

Moreover, as a result of doing nothing, businesses had to close, forty million people lost their jobs and the economy is in tatters. Some of those jobs have returned, but many will never be able to reopen. Donald Trump referenced the Stock Market, but Joe Biden said that is not what the average American faces at the breakfast table. Trying to figure out what is affordable, much of which is not, affects citizens who lost their jobs and lost their healthcare. The biggest hit has been on women, which is why they are leaving Trump.

Most damaging, the Trump administration has brought a case against the Affordable Care Act, looking to overturn it, and having NO plan to replace it. The case will be heard in the Supreme Court, the week after the election. There seems to be no rhyme or reason for Trump to want to eliminate Obamacare, except jealous spite. While Trump has been promising to replace ACA with a new and better plan, no such plan has emerged in four years. More citizens will be at risk than ever before.

Last night, it was difficult to listen to the lies. Immigration was the single most painful situation about which the president lied. In the Trump administration five hundred thirty-five children were separated from their parents, and there was no plan to reunite them. HHS, Homeland Security and IT all said that this would result in terrible lifelong damage for children, who have no idea where their parents are. Trump and Steven Miller devised this callous plan, meant to discourage others from coming to our country. Initially, 4,000 families were separated. Moreover, the legal means by which families could apply for asylum was eliminated. The lawyers at the border indicated that they needed more lawyers to help the families. Instead, the entire program was trashed.

Donald Trump, showing absolutely no empathy, said that the children were living in clean circumstances. It was a stunning lie, disproved by all who went to the border and saw the tragic circumstances of the children's' lives. As I mentioned, Jacob Soboroff's book, *Separated,"* written with Julia Ainsley, uncovers Trump's lie in detail. Joe Biden pointed out that this was a terrible "moral failure" of our country. It is, "not who we are." Social justice organizations have described it as "government sanctioned "child abuse," and more.

We have community members, professionals, who have visited the border numerous times. One friend, Susan Siegultuch, has written beautifully about the tragic circumstances and the probable psychological outcomes for these children. We will explore much more on this in the next few weeks. It is crucial for us to know how brutal this program has been. America has lost so much of our reputation. The world thinks about us as callous, where we used to welcome immigrants. How could we have done such a terrible thing?

Ninety minutes of this back and forth were exhausting, and frustrating to hear lies that we know are blatant. Kristen Welker did a credible job as moderator, although Donald Trump interrupted often. During the entire time, Donald Trump did not smile once. He also never spoke directly to the people, as Joe Biden did when he turned to the cameras and addressed us. The differences were stark.

Forty-five million people have already voted. It is not clear that this evening made a difference in the minds of Americans. We are getting Covid-19, and there is no national plan. That is incredibly disturbing, as we look toward the fall and winter, easily the most dangerous seasons where the coronavirus thrives. We need to be careful, wear our masks, practice social distancing and stay healthy.

Please VOTE!

October 26, 2020

The Unraveling … things are right side up and upside down … ten days to the election

There is too much happening every day, and it's difficult to make sense of events.

Donald Trump is raging and angry … probably the result of looking at the poll numbers, which show that he is trailing Joe Biden by a considerable number. As he begins his day, Trump is railing against Joe Biden, rather than talking about why he wants to be reelected for another term. It is a bad scene. He has no plan. The Republicans made no new platform, only what Trump wanted the first time. He is playing all his power cards to get elected, knowing that if he loses the Attorney General of New York is waiting to indict him on bank fraud and tax fraud, for openers.

The rhetoric has gotten louder and nastier, and is riddled with false accusations. For his part, Joe Biden has quite a detailed plan if he is elected-on the Coronavirus, the economy, racial justice and more. Trump has made so much noise that Biden's plan has by and large been in the background. He has given some excellent speeches in recent weeks, and Trump has thrown everything at him, but nothing seems to have stuck.

Having contracted the virus and been treated with the best care, Trump has never pivoted and told the American public to wear masks and practice social distancing. He was extraordinarily lucky, having been given trial medicines, to which no regular American has access. All of that care paid by the American taxpayer, which doesn't include Donald Trump.

Meanwhile, the virus surges. Forty states have larger cases than ever before, and have not made efforts to control it. President Trump continues to hold super-spreader rallies, mostly with no masks or social distancing. It is a terrible model for the country. The latest news is that six staffers of Vice- President Pence have tested positive for the virus. Pence is still negative, but he is continuing to campaign and travel, even though others will be endangered.

In his anger, Donald Trump is talking about withholding millions of dollars of much needed monies from Democratic-led cities-New York, Portland, Oregon, Washington, D.C and Seattle Washington. In his continuing war with "blue states," (those that he feels didn't vote for him), he calls the cities "anarchist jurisdictions." This attitude goes against the grain of the concept that we are "The United States of America." Wanting to slash money from those cities is vindictive, and will result in serious firing of civil service workers and others.

Most important, Donald Trump nominated a far-right conservative judge to take the seat of Ruth Bader Ginsburg. Amy Coney Barrett clerked for Antonin Scalia, and Congress held hearings on her nomination for three days last week. I will discuss those hearings in my next blog, and the ramifications for our democracy.

Returning to the week in general, the night before the third debate, former President, Barack Obama, came out and gave a powerful speech in favor of Joe Biden's candidacy. Obama is planning to make other appearances, some online, and some at a drive-through rally, to talk to young voters and other groups with whom he has clout. Strangely, Donald Trump has called for William Barr to bring charges against Joe Biden, who he says is a criminal. In the history of the country, no candidate has ever called for his opponent to be charged and jailed. That is just one example of how crazy life has gotten. In fact, Trump is so out of control that he called Jeff Mason, a respected journalist from Reuters, a criminal, because he asked a particular question. It's not the first time. Things are going off the rails for Trump and to some degree for the Republican Party, with members coming forward and denouncing Donald Trump.

The next nine days should be chaotic in the extreme. Millions of people have already voted. However, there is a dark cloud of possible violence hanging over the election, due to Donald Trump asking people to come to the polls and see whether they were honest. In some states, they could come with guns. Someone already came and videotaped citizens who were voting in Philadelphia. After it was reported, the police came and shut that down. The virus keeps surging and the citizens are nervous. I would say that the country is at a serious inflection point right now.

Breaking Norms

October 27, 2020

Yesterday, Amy Coney Barrett was confirmed 52-48, in the Senate as the ninth justice. The vote was along party lines, with only Susan Collins (R-Maine) voting against. Many norms were broken yesterday of which you should be aware. It is the first time that a Justice was named without one single vote from the other party. In fact, they boycotted the final day, to protest the rush to confirm her just days away from the election. This, despite statements to the contrary from Republicans, when Barack Obama nominated Merrick Garland, a moderate, and he did not receive the courtesy of hearings or a vote. It was a total partisan disgrace. Obama chose Garland because he was a moderate, and he felt that Senators on both sides could vote for him, based on his credentials.

When President Barack Obama named two Justices to the Court, Sonia Sotomayor and Elena Kagan, they were sworn in at the Court, underlining the important separation of the three branches of government and particularly the independence of the Judiciary. That is not what happened yesterday. Donald Trump arranged what looked like a swearing-in ceremony at the White House. In many ways it was a sham, because Barrett doesn't actually become the 115th Justice until she is sworn in at the Supreme Court by Chief Justice Roberts.

It's unfortunate that Barrett didn't insist on following the precedent of a quiet ceremony at the Supreme Court. Instead, she allowed Donald Trump to give her a gathering in the Rose Garden, not unlike the super-spreader of a few weeks earlier, when she was introduced. For the phony swearing-in, she chose Justice Clarence Thomas to do the event.

There is more than a little irony to her choice of Thomas. He is the most conservative Justice on the Court. Moreover, the hearings on his nomination were extremely contentious, when in 1991 Anita Hill, a lawyer, came before Congress to say that Thomas had sexually harassed her. It was a moment, and in my humble opinion, it took a great deal of courage on her part to come forward at all.

In the first place, many people who were watching the hearings had no idea that sexual harassment was actionable, that they could file complaints if it happened to them. Times have definitely changed, and we have come a long way since 1991. The change is due in large part to that seminal moment of Anita Hill saying that Thomas should not be allowed to join the bench. She testified in front of the all-male white Judiciary Committee and said that Thomas harassed her when she was working as his aide at the Equal Employment Opportunity Commission.

It was a seemingly shocking allegation, and many people believed that she had lied. Moreover, more than 70% of the citizens felt that Thomas should be confirmed. Ironically, Joe Biden was the Chairman of the Judiciary Committee, and he did not do himself proud. He was disdainful, and it is a time in his history that I'm sure he would like to forget. Most recently, he called Anita Hill to apologize, but she said that, "I'm sorry" is not enough. How could it be?

Anita Hill was vilified and embarrassed for many years afterward. However, as a graduate of Yale Law school she was an academic, and is now a professor of social policy, law, and women's studies at Brandeis University. In 2014, there was a documentary made of that time in history, and it is well worth watching.

For his part, Clarence Thomas joined the Supreme Court, and rarely if ever speaks from the bench. Disappointingly, he occupies the seat of Thurgood Marshall, the highly respected and only other black member of the Court. Even more, Thomas has spoken out against affirmative action, which is ironic, because he benefited from that program, when he gained acceptance to Yale Law. He is the most conservative member of the bench, even more so than Scalia, for whom Amy Coney Barrett clerked. All three of them consider themselves "originalists," which is a strict reading of the law, with no room for interpretation or attention to the social situation of the time.

After the "swearing-in," in another total breaking of norms, Barrett and Donald Trump appeared together on the balcony of the White House to wave and have pictures. That coming together violated the concept of three separate branches. Moreover, being at the White House makes it seem as if she owes Trump her undying loyalty in all the cases that will now come before the Court. It is inappropriate and wreaks of influence from which the Supreme Court has gone out of its way to distance itself. Many important cases, plus the election, are now coming before the Court, and it appears that Donald Trump has Amy Coney Barrett in his hip pocket.

The actual, legitimate swearing-in is taking place today.

There is much more on this subject ... to be continued ...

VOTE! Please ...

America Strong! Joy to the Polls!

October 27th, 2020

In the midst of a pandemic, a bitter election, purposefully slower mail, long lines at the polls and voter suppression, Americans always find a way to rise above the fray and add some joy, music and humor into a terrible situation.

Today I want to pay tribute to all the amazing impromptu groups that have arisen to entertain and cheer for the people who are waiting hours in many towns and cities to cast their vote. Voting has gotten incredibly important. There is a palpable seriousness in the people standing the line- a dedication, dogged persistence, and a patriotism in the face of voter suppression. We will not be cowed.

Citizens are waiting in the rain, in the heat, bringing chairs, loaning chairs, bringing water. helping one another-our neighbors. Fabulously creative people have created entertainment.

There is a group known as **ELECTION DEFENDERS**, a non-partisan coalition of people who got together, decorated a flatbed truck with a huge sign that reads:

JOY TO THE POLLS!!!!

And that's not all. In Brooklyn, there was the UNITED MARCHING BAND AND DRUMLINE, easily 25 people playing and drumming to the delight of those waiting to do their patriotic duty.

In other towns, high school bands arrived to play for those waiting in the long lines. Everyone joined together to applaud and enjoy the spirit.

On many lines, people delivered pizzas to those who were stubbornly standing, grateful for the pizza.

One amazing group danced the "cha, cha, slide," socially distancing, of course.

Recalling our history, in 1965, a young John Lewis walked on the Edmund Pettus Bridge, and was badly beaten in his quest to guarantee the vote for all.

President Lyndon Johnson was horrified by that violent sight, and he admired the passion of Lewis and other black Americans. In 1965, Johnson signed the Voting Rights Act, as part of the Civil Rights Act. In 1966, in the south especially, black women and men were finally able to vote. More importantly, Johnson put the protection of the federal government behind that bill. Federal marshals oversaw the polls and people were safe to vote for the first time in their lives. There are amazing pictures of the lines they formed in order to avail themselves of their right to vote, which had long been denied, especially in Alabama and then in Arkansas, the home of Governor George Wallace, a virulent racist.

Fast forward to 2020. Citizens are making a statement in the face of voter suppression by the government. 70 million people have already cast their votes. It is a time of coming together, of making a statement, and finally understanding that people died for the right to vote. It should not be taken lightly, or casually. It requires civility, civic duty, kindness to one another and yes, empathy. We have been divided for the last four years by crass rhetoric, and we need to understand that differing opinions should not end in violent speech or actions.

Six days to the election.

Naked power grabs and minority rule

October 30, 2020

For a look back in history, both of the last two Republican presidents-Bush and Trump-lost the popular vote and were still able to nominate two Supreme Court justices who were confirmed by the votes of senators who represented a minority of the American people. That reality is more than troubling, and points to the electoral system that we have. It is flawed at best.

As I mentioned, in 2016, President Barack Obama nominated a moderate, Merrick Garland, to take the seat of Antonin Scalia, who died suddenly. Mitch McConnell, Majority Leader, said that it was within a year of the next election and improper to fill the seat at that time. The Senate kept the seat open, denying Merrick Garland a hearing, Donald Trump won the election and the honor of nominating his own choice for Justice. He chose Neil Gorsuch. That is one reason why elections matter, and people who stayed home influenced the future in more ways than anyone realized.

There is more, and it relates to the manipulation of Trump and McConnell and moving the Court far to the right. Justice Anthony Kennedy was considering retirement, but had not announced. Referred to as the "swing" justice, Kennedy was not swayed by ideological dogma. He voted based on his case by case deliberations, he became known as a proponent of individual rights, as when he co-authored the majority opinion in Planned Parenthood v. Casey. A study of his cases and how he voted is fascinating. The latest case was Obergefell v. Hodges, which guarantees the right to same-sex marriage. It was never clear how Kennedy would vote, and that made him something of a problem for Donald Trump and the right-wing conservatives.

Since Kennedy was considering retirement, Mitch McConnell and Donald Trump put a lot of pressure on him to announce while Trump was in office. They basically pushed Kennedy out, and that is how Donald Trump got Brett Kavanaugh, straight from the list of the Federalist Society and a definite problem from the beginning. Nonetheless, despite accusations of sexual misconduct, Kavanaugh won the nomination and now sits on the Supreme Court. Two decades before, he was on the legal team that helped elect George Bush President, even though Al Gore had won more votes. Two others on the Bush legal team were (now)Justice John Roberts and Amy Coney Barrett, whose law firm was representing Bush at the time. It is a very tight group. When Bush became president, he nominated Roberts to the bench.

Kavanaugh recently came out with a political statement and an error about mail-in voting in Vermont and was forced to fix it. The statement was wrong, highly improper, and the leaders in Vermont were very angry.

More importantly, Donald Trump made it clear that he thinks the election may wind up in the Supreme Court, and that explains his reason for wanting Amy Barrett rushed through with only days until the election. It is shameless, especially in light of the Republican reasons for refusing to hold hearings on President Barack Obama's nominee.

All of this by way of saying that through hypocrisy, double-dealing, influence-peddling and outright cheating, Donald Trump was able to get three judges on the Supreme Court, and they could change the laws of the land for decades.

What is at stake? The hearing on the Affordable Care Act is one week away. Donald Trump has no replacement for the ACA, which gives citizens protections for pre-existing conditions, and keeps children on their parents' insurance until age 26, among other things. Out of jealousy and spite, Trump has tried to eliminate the Healthcare Act 71 times, and it failed in Congress, because citizens like the law. Feeling frustrated, he decided to send it to the Supreme Court. In four years, Donald Trump has not produced a replacement bill, although he keeps saying that it exists. Most recently, in an interview, Lesley Stahl, the distinguished journalist, asked him about his healthcare bill, and wondered where it was if it existed. Trump, caught in his lies, walked out of the interview, since she did not allow him to get away with any other disinformation. Stahl has since been threatened, and now requires security. Life in these United States has gotten very dangerous and rough. This is not the country that I have known all these years.

Now we have Amy Coney Barrett, who was also culled from the Federalist Society list. As you know from the hearings, she is actually to the right of Antonin Scalia, which is scary. She will have no problem voting down the Affordable Care Act, Roe V. Wade, or any of the bills that protect same sex marriage and the LGBT community. We are about to return to the 1950's when using contraception in Connecticut was illegal. Griswold v. Connecticut was a landmark decision in which the Court ruled that the Constitution of the US protects the liberty of married couples to buy and use contraceptives without government restriction.

Every citizen is in for a wild ride, especially if the election is close and Trump decides to contest it to the point where it has to be heard in the Supreme Court. With three justices on the Court who were on the Bush legal team in 2000, the outcome could be catastrophic, even if Biden wins by millions of votes.

Please VOTE in person if you haven't already voted. Our democracy and the future of the country is at stake.

Democracy is not a Spectator Sport

October 31, 2020

We are almost at the end of the 2020 election season. Thank goodness! Many of us are exhausted and tired of the chaos of the last five years. The rhetoric, the name- calling, disinformation and outright cheating, has been upsetting and discouraging. Many of us are angry and scared. In the middle of a pandemic, with thousands dying, we have been called on to make decisions for ourselves and our country, while some people have sown distrust and dismay.

We have experienced a slowdown of the mail meant to intimidate and discourage voting. Loud Republican calls that mail-in balloting is fraudulent, combined with legal challenges meant to suppress the vote, would have been enough to keep us home.

But it didn't. Our democracy seems to be alive and well in the darkness of disinformation and thugs wanting to cheat their way to victory. As my Senator, Cory Booker, (D-NJ) often says, "Democracy is not a spectator sport." We have long lines at polling places, and millions are voting.

After years of voter apathy, America has awakened. Democracy is on the ballot. People died for the privilege of voting, yet far too few citizens actually vote. Teaching history for many years, I always told my students that they had to vote when they were old enough. The numbers were never good.

But now, I see a future where more citizens will see the country as their personal responsibility. Each person has to participate, voice an opinion, learn the issues. Don't believe everything you hear.

The *Washington Post* had it right-"*Democracy dies in darkness.*"

I have no idea what the outcome will be, but there has been a new awareness. "Black Lives Matter," and the horror of watching George Floyd killed, brought black, white and brown people of all religions marching together, realizing that we can do more together. We have much to do to overcome systemic racism, but it is a beginning.

We have a lot on our plate. First, we must control the Covid-19 virus and fix our healthcare system for all Americans, not just the wealthy. We must address the immediate challenge of climate change. We are out of time as others are denying. We must reinstate the scientists to their rightful place of respect. They are worldwide champions and they have been battered. We have to offer education for all children on a level playing field, including internet access. We cannot afford to lose another generation of impoverished and poorly educated children who are often hungry.

We have to take back our country from the ignorant influence of thugs and white supremacists, from name-calling and threatening. Many of us are tired, and are not taken in by shiny objects that are dangled in front of our eyes.

If we are successful on Tuesday, or not, we must still begin working to move into the next century on all of these issues. It will take everyone working together to achieve progress in what may seem insurmountable.

It is not insurmountable if we work together. Democracy is worth the fight. I have faith that coming together, listening, and committing to the cause of freedom for all, will achieve great things. We have done it before-notably in World War 2, and we can do it again.

I firmly believe that we can get America back on track to be the great country that it was in the past, and can be in the future. Keep the faith.

Election Day-November 3, 2020

November 2, 2020

One day that will change our lives forever. Come on America, you can do it, when you know the truth. What is the "truth?"

If you have been wondering these last months-how it is that Donald Trump is holding "super-spreader" rallies where people are not wearing masks and are close together, and here is the reason.

The Pew Foundation conducted a survey of attitudes concerning Donald Trump and Joe Biden toward the virus. The findings were extraordinary, and account for the division in this country.

Pew found that 84% of Biden supporters believe that the virus is real and can be fatal. They wear masks and practice social distancing, to protect themselves and others. Pew found that **only 24% of Trump supporters believe that the virus exists, and all the others believe that it is a "hoax" and nothing to worry about.** Hence, Trump is conducting the rallies with relatively unconcerned supporters. It would be important to recognize that in every location that Trump held these rallies, cases spiked a week or two afterwards, flooding the local hospitals.

Therein lies a very dangerous divide-for health and for politics. The Trump supporters get their news from Fox, whereas Biden's followers read the New York Times, Washington Post and the local papers in their states across the country, as well as legitimate news programs. Where we each get our information determines our fate and our attitudes.

In 2016, Donald Trump was a candidate who keyed in to white grievances and he spoke of "American carnage." This campaign in 2020, is about Trump's own grievances, attacking everyone from Dr. Fauci to LeBron James, Lady Gaga and calling Kamala Harris a "monster." It is a sad state of affairs. Bullies are immature, and rely on name-calling to make themselves feel strong and paint the victim as weak. One hopes that an immature bully is not the President of the United State, but it seems that's what we have.

Moreover, Trump is engaging in voter intimidation and declaring the election fraudulent if he loses. That's an arrogant approach to a contest! He is demeaning mail-in ballots in the middle of a pandemic. An interesting approach, showing no concern for the health of our citizens.

Meanwhile, millions of us have already voted. I put my ballot in the South Orange dropbox and just received a card from the Essex County Clerk, thanking me for my ballot and indicating it is counted. One way Trump is trying to besmirch the vote is to appoint a new Postmaster General – a big Republican donor, with clear directions to slow the mail. He is also trying to win the election by many lawsuits in states where he wants the votes to be discarded. So far, he has lost those suits. Josh Shapiro, Attorney General of Pennsylvania, has won six of six Trump lawsuits and is ready for anything else that is thrown at him.

Trump has also said that the winner must be declared on Election Day. He has indicated that he will declare himself the winner if the "red mirage" of same day voters shows he is doing well, although the ballots still need to be counted in the days following. Donald Trump clearly does not understand the Constitution, which I think we know he has never read or studied. Voting is all about the states. The election is not over until each state has counted the votes and CERTIFIED the numbers. A candidate, not even the President, cannot declare a winner. So, if you hear Trump saying disturbing things on that subject, ignore it, because he has no credibility to declare the winner. He is trying to game the system.

Meanwhile, 97 million people have already voted. In 2016, 139 million people voted. Long lines everywhere show the enthusiasm of citizens refusing to be cowed, or not allowed to exercise their rights. With triple the number of voters, everyone needs to be patient, because we may not know the victor until days later.

Another concern is "open carry," guns allowed at the polls. Trump has also threatened to send in people to "observe" to see if everything is being done properly. There are rules and laws in each state about who is allowed in polling places. One important law is that voter intimidation is a state and a federal felony. Law enforcement is watching carefully and will act promptly if anyone complains or is troubled by the presence of unlawful people in a polling place.

Trump's efforts at intimidation have escalated, as his supporters have arrived at places where Joe Biden is scheduled to speak. Two days ago in Texas, a caravan of Trump trucks and cars flying Trump flags surrounded a Biden-Harris bus, forcing it to slow to 20 miles an hour and then forcing it to cancel the rest of the planned events, for safety concerns. One of the Biden staffer's cars was hit by a Trump truck.

Worse still, but not surprising, Donald Trump cheered on the perpetrators, showing the video of the vehicles swarming around the bus with the words, "I LOVE TEXAS!" He recounted this event at a rally the following night, indicating how popular he is. It is a very bad time when the president is encouraging violence against his opponent. Remember that he asked William Barr to arrest Joe Biden. There are no grounds on which to arrest Biden for anything. The FBI is investigating the incident.

In fact, Joe Biden has run a very calm and stable campaign-no vitriol and no name calling. While Trump has been angry and raging against everyone, Joe Biden's message has been one of unity, coming together to solve the nation's problems. It is a stark contrast.

And still, the country is voting by the millions.

While there are many disturbing stories of violence and threats, one stands out among the rest. In Graham, North Carolina, sheriff's deputies and city police officers pepper-sprayed a small crowd of about 200 who were marching peacefully to the polls. The crowd included disabled people and children. What will no doubt become a major problem for the officers in court, is that it included political pundit David Frum's children, who filmed the event. It should be noted that the County Sheriff has such a toxic record of racism and intimidation that the Department of Justice sent election monitors to the county in 2004, 2008 and 2012. The FBI is also investigating this event.

The Trump supporters continued their activities. They disrupted the northbound traffic on the Garden State Parkway and the Mario Cuomo Bridge over the Hudson River. I can't imagine what they thought they were accomplishing, since nothing is more aggravating than huge traffic delays in each of those places.

Meanwhile, thousands of election workers are busy today, as they have been months in advance, preparing for a safe and fair election. It is a monumental job with election officials, state law enforcement officers, and neighbors who volunteer to work. The most important idea is that our elections are open to all and it is a fundamental principle that everyone has a say in our local, state and national elections.

Meanwhile, millions of citizens are standing in line to cast their votes. It is a beautiful and inspiring sight, most likely the calm before the storm.

Stand tall and dignified, America.

November 4, 2020 … Still counting the votes

November 4th, 2020

It is 4am and I am very tired. However, there are a few things you must know.

Let's be clear … The election is not over until all fifty states have counted all of its votes, and CERTIFIED the numbers. It could take a long time. Patience is important, so that every vote is counted.

Only then, is there a winner.

President Trump cannot declare himself a winner and call for counting to stop. That Is NOT the process. It may take a few days for each state to count and certify the numbers, and Donald Trump should know this. He came out at about 2am and declared himself the winner.

Coming out and speaking as he did, besides being rude and incorrect, spread doubt as to the legitimacy of the outcome, no matter who wins. It is a very dark day for our country and for our democracy.

No candidate has ever come out in the middle of the process and declared victory. Moreover, no candidate has ever disregarded the norms and held a campaign event at the White House, even if he was president for the first term. Speaking from the East Room of the White House was improper. He should have secured an election venue and had his followers there. It is illegal, and it flies in the face of the Hatch Act-the White House is not to be used for political activities. There is supposed to be a clear line between the business of the country and the business of politics.

Moreover, when Trump held the Republican National Convention at the White House that also violated the Hatch Act. He had blown through the billion-dollar campaign fund and used the country's resources for his own political benefit. That is illegal.

If you think about it, when Donald Trump was jetting around the countryside for rallies and his reelection, he used taxpayer money for Air Force One to facilitate his campaign. He also had a huge head start on his brand being known as a sitting candidate for reelection.

All of those rallies are about reelection.

The Governor of Pennsylvania told the country to be calm and wait for the final results. The Attorney General of Pennsylvania, Josh Shapiro, has already appeared in court in response to six Republican lawsuits, and he has beaten Trump in all six. From the beginning, Donald Trump has tried to suppress the vote and sow the seeds of doubt if he loses. No one has been able to prove that there is fraud in our state elections.

November 5, 2020

Counting, waiting and protecting the vote

Nothing has been decided, because everything is too close in battleground states:

Here are the battlegrounds and their electoral numbers:

ARIZONA- 11 electoral votes

GEORGIA – 16 electoral votes

MICHIGAN – 16 electoral votes

NORTH CAROLINA– 15 electoral votes

NEVADA – 6 electoral votes

PENNSYLVANIA – 20 electoral votes

Joe Biden has 224 votes, and Donald Trump has 213. Neither man has 270, which is needed to win.

This afternoon, Wisconsin was called for Biden, and so was Michigan, and those numbers will be added to his totals.

The Trump campaign has sued to stop counting the votes in Arizona, Michigan and Pennsylvania. However, all ballots will be counted. Hundreds of thousands of votes are coming in from Maricopa County in Arizona. As the counting continues, the numbers are changing. Mark Kelly won the Senate seat, and this is the late John McCain's state. Cindy McCain has come out and said that she is supporting Joe Biden.

Stay tuned …

The Case of the Missing 300,523 ballots

November 5, 2020

As of Election Day morning. 300,523 ballots nationwide had received incoming scans but no exit scans, meaning they could be "trapped in the mail system." Typically, the post office is expected to process the mail 97 percent, an excellent rate. But in the past five days, the rate dropped to 89.6. "In 17 postal districts that cover 151 electoral votes, Monday's on-time processing rate was even lower: 81.1 percent," according to the post office.

To address this situation, Federal Judge, Emmett Sullivan, issued an order for officials from the Postal Inspection Service, the agency's law enforcement arm, and the Postal Service Office of the Inspector General, its independent watchdog, to inspect all processing facilities in the districts of Central Pennsylvania, Philadelphia and 30 other districts in states such as Vermont, South Carolina, Florida, Wisconsin, and Arizona, by 3pm.

However, in a filing sent to the court just before 5pm, DOJ attorneys representing the Postal Service, said the agency would not abide by the order, saying that it would find the ballots through other means between 4 and 8pm.

Judge Emmet Sullivan (the judge also in Michael Flynn's case), was less than impressed, with this non-response to his order, and has put the officials on notice to "be prepared to discuss the apparent lack of compliance with his order." He has threatened to call Trump's Postmaster General, Louis DeJoy, into court to personally answer for this defiance of the order.

The case was brought to court by the NAACP Legal Defense Fund, a crucial arm for social justice in our country. Sherrilyn Ifill, the President and General Director of the NAACP Legal Defense Fund, has been a critical leader in holding the DOJ's feet to the fire. I had the pleasure of meeting her when she was honored by the New Jersey Institute for Social Justice in Newark. She gave an extraordinary speech, brilliant and inspiring. I was lucky to be the guest of my good friend, Doug Eakeley, Chairman of the NJISJ board. Since then, I have seen Ms. Ifill speaking on television and particularly now, to safeguard the rights of black citizens.

Judge Sullivan was initially appointed to the federal bench by Ronald Reagan, and promoted by George H.W.Bush. The judge has been aggressive in his oversight. On Monday, he lambasted the patchwork of voting rules and regulations, and compared it to the uniform federal tax deadline.

In the same way that Judge Sullivan had no patience for Michael Flynn, telling him he "sold out his country," the udge has no patience for the damage done to the Post Office by Louis DeJoy, and its effect on the election.

Meanwhile, the counting continues. As of this writing, Joe Biden has 253 electoral votes and Donald Trump has 214. Keep your eye on Pennsylvania. With 20 votes, it could be the key to a new president.

Again, it isn't over until it's over, and all the votes are certified.

The Center Holds, as Ballots are still being Counted

November 6th, 2020

The ballot counting continues.

It's the fourth day and the presidency is still unresolved.

Ballots are being counted by thousands of volunteers and civil workers throughout the country. In addition, there are cameras in the counting places and in some states, we can livestream the counting. In addition, there are watchers from each political party that have permission to be present.

Thinking he would lose the popular vote, Donald Trump accused mail-in ballots of being fraudulent. There is no evidence of that. Moreover, the message is a dangerous one, because millions of people might believe it, and that delegitimizes the results of the election. Trump indicated that he wanted the election results to be over by the end of the day.

With that plan, Donald Trump was a victim of our democracy. All ballots need to be counted, especially in a pandemic. Trump is having a meltdown, sending tweets in caps, "STOP THE COUNT!" and "STOP THE FRAUD." Twitter took down a number of his tweets and sent a message explaining the proper election process.

Trump planned to challenge the counting in the courts, but the lawsuits have all been tossed as being "frivolous." Then, he tried to indicate that the election was being "stolen" from him.

In addition to his embarrassing and improper claim at 2:30 am on Wednesday morning, that he had already won the election, Donald Trump decided to have yet another press conference last night. It was from the White House with the seal of the President, and he lied about the situation. Within minutes, Brian Williams shut it down and came on to tell people that the president was "lying." The boldness of the statement was shocking, but the journalists have clearly had four years of Donald Trump's dishonesty and making his own reality, and they are now blunt in their responses. They let him get away with a lot in the beginning, and realized that was a serious error.

Joe Biden is ahead in the popular vote by about 4 million votes. If we didn't have this ridiculous Electoral College system, he would already be the victor. The goal is 270, and Biden has 253 to Trump's 213. There is a lot of tension.

Trump's calculation was based on a number of strategies. First, he wanted to keep voters from the polls in states like Texas and Florida. Initially, the strategy seemed to be working. On Tuesday night, he won Florida, 29 electoral votes. The win was certainly helped by the disenfranchisement of 1.5 ex-felons, even though Floridians had voted to restore their voting rights in 2018. They had to pay fines, and even Mike Bloomberg pledged money so they could satisfy the fines. Things were looking good for Trump, and he was planning to declare victory, even though many states were still counting millions of ballots. His plan was to claim victory early on Tuesday, then any other mail-in numbers would make it look as if the election was "stolen" from him.

As all this maneuvering was going on, Joe Biden came on to say to the American public that they were watching the numbers, felt good about what they saw and that everyone should remain calm. The contrast between the two candidates was stark.

By Thursday, things got crazier. Rudy Giuliani and other supporters were attacking the election process. Somewhat humorously, the lawsuits indicated that in states where Trump was ahead they should keep counting, and in states where he was behind, no more counting should be allowed. What Trump didn't realize is that in states where Biden was ahead, if he was successful in stopping the counting, it would be a win for Biden.

We saw a very pathetic and desperate man flailing in the face of possible defeat. One of the most graphic descriptions came from CNN's Anderson Cooper. "It was sad and pathetic … that is the most powerful person in the world, and we see him like an obese turtle on his back, flailing in the hot sun, realizing his time is over. But he just hasn't accepted it, and he wants to take everybody down with him, including this country."

A number of Republicans, including Mitch McConnell, came out and said that all ballots must be counted. Mitt Romney (R-UT) and Ben Sasse (R-Neb), made similar statements.

As I write, Joe Biden is sequestered with his family and friends, watching the results as they come in. He made another statement, indicating that politics can be messy, but all of us should be patient and keep calm. It is a relief to hear such a presidential message to the people. This has been a tough slog and a chaotic one. I, for one, hope to welcome the decency and stability of a man rooted in truth and community.

Numbers are starting to come in from Philadelphia, and now Joe Biden is ahead. By my next blog, we should have final numbers, and hopefully, a new president.

This is an election for the history books!

If you are looking for a great book to read, try *The Making of the President 1960* by Theodore White. It is the fascinating story of John F. Kennedy's rise to the presidency as he defeated Richard Nixon.

Long Day's Journey into Night/Fifth Day

November 7, 2020

And the counting continues.

Nothing about this election was expected, except that Donald Trump would not go peacefully or gracefully, as he indicated.

For myself, I expected Joe Biden to win with big numbers, and I was wrong. The election is very close, razor thin in about six states. 74 million votes were cast for Joe Biden, a record, and 70 million were cast for Trump, also a record.

More surprising, I expected the country to repudiate President Trump, and I was wrong.

That's the piece that is a head-scratcher. I keep thinking about this over and over. Who are those people who voted for a man who ignored a dangerous virus, who showed no empathy for 230,000 dead citizens, who crashed the economy with 40 million people losing their jobs, who doesn't like blacks, Muslims or immigrants, doesn't believe in science or climate change and owes 400 million dollars to various creditors? Beyond the crass language, the callous separating of children from their parents, of dividing the country into red states and blue, of embracing white supremacists, of bullying and calling people insulting names, who is this man and why do they like him?

I am personally baffled by this reality. I need to learn more, and try to understand why anyone would want him to represent us in times of terrible trouble, much of which he created or ignored, making matters worse.

Meanwhile, the world is watching. Maybe the citizens of the world are wondering the same things that are confounding me. After all, I only mentioned a few of the domestic problems. The global behavior has been equally bizarre and unattractive, breaking all norms. Siding with dictators, insulting NATO, removing us from the Paris climate accord and so much more. We are the laughingstock of the world, although many have expressed pity for our situation and are praying for this election to change things.

But the election has brought out the worst of Trump. Fearing a loss, he has threatened voter fraud, putting that idea in peoples' minds, even though there is no evidence of fraud in our elections.

As a matter of fact, this election has been the most organized and excellent of the last hundred years. Trump has also indicated that he would not participate in a peaceful transfer of power, a norm on which our country has been built, and which is the envy of the world. The concept of a concession is also beyond Donald Trump. Some of the finest speeches from presidential candidates are among the proud historic memories of our country: George H.W. Bush when he lost to Bill Clinton, Al Gore when he conceded to George Bush, Jimmy Carter when he lost to Ronald Reagan, and John McCain when he conceded to Barack Obama. These men were eloquent and showed their personal patriotism on which America depends in times of tension. They each spoke of the importance of unity at a time when we needed to come together as a nation.

According to those around Donald Trump, there is no hope of any such speech. Moreover, he has indicated over and over that many of the mail-in ballots are illegal, even in a pandemic, when people legitimately chose not to come in person.

Joe Biden has been measured in his messaging to the American public. He prepared last night for a victory speech, but since the states have not been called, he spoke instead of unity and cautioned patience.

Nonetheless, Trump protestors have arrived at the counting venues with huge Trump flags, signs that indicate the election may be "stolen," and guns, which are allowed in Arizona and Nevada. That sight is very unnerving for me, and the poll counters had to be escorted to their cars when they finished late at night. We have never had anything like this in our country.

Interestingly, the states of Georgia and Arizona are likely to be a win for Biden. This is due to changing demographics in each state. In the case of Georgia, it is a tribute to Stacey Abrams, who lost her race for Governor, and immediately spent the next years organizing Georgians as voters and active participants. She is amazing, and a woman to watch in the new government.

Legal challenges have been sent by a hodgepodge of Trump lawyers, and each challenge has been rejected. There is no evidence of fraud to show in any of the lawsuits brought by the Trump lawyers.

The states that are still counting are Nevada, Pennsylvania, Arizona, Georgia, North Carolina. A win in Pennsylvania would give Joe Biden 20 votes and the presidency. For the other states to reach 270 would require two states combined.

And we continue to wait while the counting continues.

Joe Biden has been elected the 46th President of the United States!

November 7th, 2020

Philadelphia spoke in 1787, when we got a new country, and now in 2020 with the election of the Biden-Harris ticket. In another historic moment, Kamala Harris is the first elected woman, and black and Asian woman, elected Vice- President. It's a triple first!

The country needs to begin the business of healing.

November 8, 2020

IT'S A NEW DAY IN AMERICA ... HOPEFULLY.

November 7th, 8th 2020

On November 7th, at around noon, Joe Biden, former Vice-President, was named the President-elect of the United States by the media. Senator Kamala Harris, Biden's running mate, is the first woman Vice-President elect. She is also a black woman of an Indian mother, so incredibly diverse and talented, and historic in this accomplishment.

There was an immediate sigh of relief and joy in the streets of New York, with dancing and singing and a sense of a new day for American possibilities. Interestingly, we have been through a health-care war-Covid-19, and we are losing that war, because Donald Trump refused to acknowledge the virus and told the country it was a "hoax" and that it would "magically disappear." That disastrous rejection of the science has so far resulted in 230,000 citizens dead, and millions who caught the virus. The loss of wonderful people is tragic, and has never been acknowledged or even mentioned by Donald Trump. We are a nation grieving and struggling.

Because Americans traditionally believe our presidents, many of Trump's supporters believed him, almost half the country, while the rest of us realized that he had politicized the virus and that the scientists had it right. That deep divide is going to make it difficult to bring the country together under Joe Biden, who has been talking about unity.

The election process is not actually completed. Each of the fifty states has to certify its numbers, although some states are still counting provisional and military ballots. Once the numbers are certified, then the electors from each state must vote in December to finalize the outcome.

Donald Trump has not accepted Joe Biden's win. He is still filing lawsuits, insisting that the election was "rigged." However, each court has asked for evidence of wrongdoing, and the Trump administration has not been able to provide any substantive proof of illegitimate ballots.

Last night, Joe Biden and Kamala Harris had a victory celebration, a car rally at night with lights and fireworks and each of their families. In an inspiring speech, Kamala Harris spoke first, indicating how important it is for women of all ethnicities to realize the "possibility" that each of them can become elected leaders in America. She gave credit to all of her supporters for marching, calling, running for office, writing letters, and using our democracy to insure our democracy. We can be the masters of our fate.

It was a great moment in time. Joe Biden then spoke, thanked the citizens for the millions of votes that put him in office, even in a pandemic. He appealed to the country to be the "United States of America," not blue states and red states. He pointed out that, while we may be "adversaries," we shouldn't be enemies. It was a speech filled with hope for the future, and outlining many things he wants to do on the first day of his Presidency, much of which he mentioned in the campaign. He will fight to defeat the virus, and keep a number of other promises. Biden wants to undo much of Trump's right wing and dangerous actions. America will rejoin WHO, protect the "Dreamers", eliminate the Muslim ban, join the Paris Climate Accord, and work to reunite the 545 children separated at the border, Trump's most callous and despicable program.

Clearly, there is a lot of joy and relief in Biden's and Harris' election, but there is a lot of work to be done, and it will not be easy. Seventy million people voted for Trump, showing the divide in the country. In Biden's speeches and plans, I hear hope, the most important ingredient in effecting change, but I am not optimistic. Much will depend on who holds the Senate, and that is not yet clear. Two Georgia Senate seats are up for election. If the Democrats win those seats, then the equation will change for Joe Biden and his plans for the country. If not, then Mitch McConnell is still the majority leader, and he loves nothing more than to stymie progress for the country.

That said, it is definitely a new day in America, and we are free to greet it with hope in our hearts and in our actions.

Decency and Democracy

November 10, 2020

If we thought that things would calm down once the election results were clear, that was a fantasy. Life in these United States has gotten more chaotic and more disturbing, since some of the things Donald Trump is doing have a wide-ranging impact on the safety and security of the country, including his own followers.

For one thing, Donald Trump refuses to concede, breaking another norm that is shocking and disturbing. It shows that, beyond being a poor loser, he has no sense of how important it is for the country -for the loser to ask for unity among all citizens. That is never going to happen With Donald Trump, which is very upsetting. Many Republicans are actually backing Trump's resistance to concede. I am very surprised and disappointed at this turn of events. Moreover, AG Barr authorized prosecutors to investigate voter fraud, even though there is none. The head of Elections resigned as a result.

No one has heard Donald Trump speak since last Thursday, when he spent the weekend playing golf. He sent many twitter messages, insisting that he won the election and the mail-in ballots are a fraud. He continues to sow discord and division across the country. His legal team and lawyers from private law firms (Jones Day), were forced to file seven lawsuits, but they have each been thrown out, based on the lack of evidence for anything they are asserting. Some of the lawyers, who were embarrassed by these efforts, have resigned. None of this would appreciably change the outcome of the election, yet Trump and his followers are continuing to create unrest and doubt, rather than acceptance. In a court filing yesterday, the goal was to eliminate all the mail-in ballots in Pennsylvania. A Republican member of the election commission came out and publicly said that the election was clean, and that it was improper to suggest otherwise. It was also demeaning to the thousands of workers who were putting in hours of time to make sure that each ballot was recorded properly. Many of them had to be escorted to their cars at the end of the day because they felt unsafe. That reality is very disturbing, and it is a first.

While the new team of Biden-Harris does not depend on a Trump concession speech, it does depend upon the General Services Administration issuing an "ascertainment" of the new President and Vice-President winning the election. Generally, it is done within a day. However, the Trump administration appointee, Emily Murphy, is refusing to sign off on the paperwork that is needed for the transition to begin in earnest. Trump has not agreed that the election is in order. In every swing state the rules were made by the legislatures with Republican majorities, and the rules need to be followed.

Make no mistake, the "ascertainment" is crucial, and denying it is vindictive. The transition gives the new administration classified PDB's (presidential daily briefs) access to office space and equipment, to process the disclosure and conflict of interest forms, and learn about ongoing government programs. Literally, hundreds of people who need to be vetted for the White House staff, are involved, and later for Cabinet appointees. The "ascertainment" also opens up access to $9.9 million dollars for the purpose of the new administration setting up its program. The Biden administration may have to sue the GSA, if Emily Murphy remains intransigent and refuses. This has never happened before in the history of our country.

Meanwhile, Mitch McConnell opened the session of the Senate after adjourning for weeks. He never congratulated Joe Biden on the election victory, although he served with Biden for many years in the Senate. Except for Mitt Romney and former President George Bush, no other Republicans have reached out to congratulate Joe Biden. Notably, there are TWO Senate seats in Georgia that will have a runoff. If the Democrats can prevail and win the two seats, that will change the equation in the Senate, and allow the Biden team to win some important victories in Congress.

While all of this rhetoric and accusation of fraud were being hurled into the atmosphere, the coronavirus was spiking with huge numbers – 240,162 people have died, 10 million people have been infected, and many have residual problems after they survive the virus.

During this period, the Trump administration has not been engaged with fighting the pandemic. The U.S. recorded more than 130,000 daily cases for the first time. On the other side of the coin, with orders from the president, the health organizations have been told not to share the numbers with hospitals and doctors who would benefit from the knowledge. This is very dangerous in the middle of a huge virus spike.

On another front, Pfizer came out with an announcement that the vaccine it has been working on has almost 90% success rate. This is very early data, and needs to have more statistics from a second thirty- day trial. In addition, storing the vaccine requires refrigeration of minus 94 degrees. We don't have that kind of ability, and would have to make it available. The question of how it would be given out remains to be seen. VP Pence tried to politicize this news, but Pfizer came out and clarified that it took no money from the government, purposely, so that it would be independent from politics.

Just in case you thought the transition period would be peaceful, President Trump fired Mark Esper yesterday, leaving the Secretary of Defense embarrassed on Twitter and the country without an important military leader. He will be replaced by Chris Miller, who worked on counter-terrorism issues, but not a military man. Why is Trump doing this now? Apparently, Secretary Esper was not sufficiently loyal to Trump. I smell a rat. Trump has something up his sleeve.

Trump also has indicated that he intends to fire Chris Wray, the FBI head and Gina Haspel, head of the CIA. These firings are very dangerous for our country, because the world is watching and it is clear that America is in chaos, and unprotected from outside actors. These firings are also unbelievably destructive to our country. Frighteningly, the Republicans are scared of Donald Trump, of his tweets and the damage he can do to their careers. This is very dangerous, because Trump has influenced 71 million people who believe whatever he says. We have the fifth Secretary of Defense and our fourth National Security Advisor. This is looking very bad in China and Russia, who see disorganization and chaos in America.

Just when we thought we could take a deep breath; the opposite is true. Trump is on a vindictive rampage, denying transition, and filing lawsuits that are delaying certifying the vote and creating chaos everywhere. Fortunately, the people on the Biden team have had long years of experience, had a warning, and are able to move forward despite everything that has been thrown at them. Two Republican Senators, Marco Rubio and Mitt Romney, have called for the GSA to certify for national security.

Meanwhile, Joe Biden formed a Coronavirus Task Force filled with eminent scientists, and it met yesterday. Afterwards, President-elect Biden gave a report and a speech. He indicated that we all need to come together in order to defeat this terrible virus. Biden said that he will be the president of everyone, whether they voted for him or not, and he urged people to "give him a chance," as well as follow the guidance of wearing masks to protect all Americans. It was a speech that carried through Biden's original messages from the campaign- that it was important to unify the government so that everyone is together on what will keep us all safe.

There are entirely too many things to mention this morning. The single most important thing is that the Biden-Harris team must get the proper paperwork, so it can facilitate the transition.

It's going to be a wild ride until January 20th, Inauguration Day. Fasten your seatbelts and hold on tight. Biden-Harris will be pursuing decency for our democracy. Listen for that in all the noise.

The decency that we used to rely on, has disappeared under the Trump administration.

Two different worlds, two different realities ... chaos versus calm and competent

November 11, 2020 Veterans Day

Despite winning in the Electoral College and millions more in the popular vote, Donald Trump continues to insist that the election of Joe Biden was fraudulent and that he won. There is absolutely no evidence to suggest this, and yet Trump refuses to concede.

Crazily, right- wing media has called for a new election, and for rallies that would produce a new vote count. The numbers are in the tens of thousands, and a recount would not yield a different outcome. In truth, no one expected Donald Trump to go quietly in the night when he lost. But I never expected this to continue ad infinitum. He has been raging, tweeting and firing people, including the Secretary of Defense, but no one has heard him speak. What Trump is doing is sad, petty and vindictive, and now it is dangerous on many levels.

Joe Biden, on the other hand, has been a Senator since he was elected at age 29. He knows his way around Washington and the highest levels of government, serving as Vice-President with Barack Obama for eight years.

That said, the Biden transition team needs to receive the President's Daily Brief, which keeps the president up to date on situations in the country and around the world. Gathered from the seventeen intelligence agencies, it is detailed and crucial for an incoming administration. According to the White House leaders, Donald Trump never read his PDB's. In fact, he never read anything. Occasionally, he would ask to have a card with three key points put on it before a meeting.

On Monday, Joe Biden and Kamala Harris began their transition with a meeting on Covid-19. The committee consists of 12 of the most brilliant scientists. Then President-elect Biden gave a speech on healthcare, assuring the nation that his administration would fight for healthcare for all citizens. Vice President Harris also spoke on issues facing the country, and the overall messages were of strength, commitment, intelligence and calm, in the midst of the Trump chaos. Joe Biden had a press conference after the speeches. When asked how he felt about President Trump's refusing to concede, Joe Biden said he thought it was "embarrassing," and "wouldn't help Trump's legacy." He also indicated that they had the resources and the organization to move forward without Trump's help. They have already recruited approximately five hundred people to work in different agencies.

Donald Trump never worked on a transition when he entered the White House. Rather than appoint people to positions, he chose his family to fill jobs, left hundreds of positions empty and went on victory rallies instead. Thousands of jobs at State, Defense, Justice, etc. were left empty. There was "no one home" at State.

The Biden administration has to fill approximately one hundred positions that will staff the White House, and four hundred-fifty major positions for the Inaugural and in important agencies. Then, there are four thousand jobs to fill in every agency in the country and around the globe. Biden needs to name his Chief of Staff, and it is reported to be Ron Klain, who is presently serving in that role. Klain also served as Chief of Staff to Al Gore years ago. The reality of the new administration being competent and creative is hopeful. There will be a serious vetting process, and that is why they need the appropriate forms and procedures. Remember that Joe Biden has not been in the White House in four years.

The last time that a transition was delayed with serious consequences was in 2000. In the 9/11 Commission Report, the commission found that the unavoidable delay in Bush v. Gore was most likely responsible for the 9/11 attack, since the vulnerability of the U.S. was clear to Osama Bin Laden and those around him. Because of that, George and Laura Bush went out of their way to facilitate a good transition when Barack Obama was elected in 2008. It was fortunate, because the country was in the middle of a desperate financial calamity that could have sent America into a Depression. As it turned out, both George Bush and Barack Obama worked together to avoid the country falling off a cliff.

In that vein, Trump's firing Secretary of Defense Esper is seen as taking a risk with the safety of the United States. Trump has put in some of his cronies in the DOD, and it is curious that he would do this now. It is worrisome, since they will be his yes-men. I'm concerned that he intends to call out the National Guard or declare martial law to stay in the White House. Those changes arc very troubling to me, mainly because only the Secretary of Defense can all out the National Guard, with the approval of the president. That is the chain of command in Washington, DC. The Mayor cannot call out the Guard, because DC is not a state.

And the counting continues, along with accusations of fraud. The rhetoric has had monumental influence on the opinions in the country. In a survey of Republicans, seven out of ten felt that the election was "stolen" from Donald Trump, and that the election was not fair. On the other side of the coin, *the New York Times* called forty-six states, and each one reported that there was no fraud. Moreover, an International group that was invited by the Trump administration to oversee the election, reported that it was excellent, with no evidence of any irregularities. And that is very important, because thousands of volunteers across the country were counting the ballots, committed to excellence. On *CBS News' 60 Minutes,* Philadelphia City Commissioner Al Schmidt, a Republican, said the people counting ballots in the city received death threats. That is another result of the rhetoric and violent tone of the last four years.

As the Biden team moves forward, leaders from all around the world have called to congratulate Joe Biden and Kamala Harris: Angela Merkel of Germany, Macron of France, and even Erdowan of Turkey, as well as Boris Johnson of the UK. China and Russia have yet to call.

Meanwhile, there is a callous disregard of all the people working for Trump. They will be out of a job on January 20th, but were told if they were caught applying for jobs they would be immediately fired. All the hundreds of people coming to Washington need to plan to move, find a home, and arrange for schools for their children. This delay has affected everyone.

On a hopeful note, the Supreme Court met yesterday to hear oral arguments on the Affordable Care Act. While I only heard parts of the back and forth, it seems that Justice Roberts and Justice Kavanaugh, both conservative, may rule in favor of keeping the Act. If this happens, they would join the three liberal justices and a 5 to 4 majority would preserve the Healthcare Act. This would be the best news in the last months, because losing the protections of the ACA, especially in the middle of a raging virus, would be catastrophic for the country. In the midst of the Trump chaos and vitriol, keeping healthcare will be a blessing and very positive.

In addition to that good news, we heard from Pfizer that its vaccine trials are showing a 90% rate. I need to read and research more in order to report on this, but one result was that the stock market went wild. As you can see, the news in the country created a roller coaster of good and bad news happening simultaneously. How do we handle all of this? It's hard to say. Much of it, especially the election, will work itself out. Joe Biden seems calm and in control.

Similarly, it seems as if the Supreme Court has also operated with a calm approach to interpreting the law, and has not succumbed to politics, as many people feared it might. As for the potential vaccine, there are any number of companies that are getting close, both here and in the UK. We may know more as the news unfolds.

Meanwhile, the coronavirus is surging, and we are about to experience the worst of it. Please be careful in this environment, avoid group gatherings, think strategically about where you decide to go, wear a mask and wash your hands.

The two realities are challenging, the yin and yang of our lives. Keep your eye on the new administration and the hope that it brings to so many people.

WHY TRANSITIONS MATTER

November 13, 2020

It's been a week since the Biden-Harris ticket was declared the winner by a large margin-four million more people and 273 to 214 electoral votes, but no one has heard from Donald Trump. He has not conceded. In fact, Trump keeps tweeting that the election was "stolen" from him.

Ever the obstructionist, President Trump is actively denying Joe Biden the President's Daily Brief that an incoming president needs to get up to speed. Biden is taking calls from world leaders and acquainting himself with the full nature of the intelligence activities around the globe. Trump has put a lock on the General Services Administration, so that the necessary paper-the "ascertainment" has not been signed.

Under normal circumstances the newly elected President would be having these conversations on a secured line with the proper translators. That has not been provided to Joe Biden. In fact, the Trump administration and all the agencies have been told not to communicate with the incoming President-elect and his team. This has serious implications for the country, especially since our virus numbers are spiking, and something needs to be done countrywide to manage the response.

Every new president is tested by our adversaries. North Korea launched a nuclear test in Trump's first year, and all presidents have been tested in one way or another by China, Russia, North Korea. Those countries want to know what they can get away with, while chaos reigns in America.

Let me take you back to the election of 2000, Bush v. Gore and the state of Florida. George Bush and Al Gore were separated by 537 votes. Florida's ballot was terribly designed, so that people thought they voted for Gore, but they actually hadn't. Indeed, there were numerous third-party candidates, including Ralph Nader, whose candidacy may have made the difference for Gore if Nader hadn't run.

The ballots needed to be checked by hand. Hundreds of people were examining them and everything was a mess (remember "hanging chads?"). This went on for days and the Florida State Supreme Court was involved. In a highly unusual move, the federal Supreme Court decided to take the issue out of the hands of the state and make the final decision. When Sandra Day O'Connor voted for George Bush, he became the president, literally having won by a single vote. It's something that we never want to see happen again, although Donald Trump would have been happy to have SCOTUS make the decision, because the Republicans hold the majority on the Court.

All this by way of saying that weeks went by until George Bush was declared President on December 13th of 2000. The uncertainty and chaos caused a great deal of anxiety in the country, and it had another unfortunate consequence. George Bush had very little time to get acclimated to the job, and do the hard work that it required until he was inaugurated on January 20th.

In the meantime, there were warnings. Richard Clarke wrote a book, *Against All Enemies,* indicating that Osama Bin Laden and his followers were planning to destroy America. Clarke was a government official who was National Coordinator for Security, Infrastructure Protections and Counter Terrorism for the United States between 1998 and 2003. Clarke spoke with George Bush in August of 2001 and warned him of the possibility. However, Bush was struggling with a much-delayed transition, and he ignored Clarke. Similarly, Peter Bergen, American journalist, had been following Osama bin Laden for years and wrote a book, *Holy War, Inc, Inside the Secret World of Osama bin Laden*, which I highly recommend. Peter Bergen was prescient. He produced the first television interview with bin Laden in 1997. Bergen had one of the few trusted connections with the terrorist, yet to my knowledge, no one from the administration spoke at length with Peter Bergen.

As a result of all these mixed messages and the delay, when Barack Obama was elected President, George Bush and his entire administration conducted what has been considered the ultimate thorough and important transition. Obama has mentioned it numerous times, and indicated how grateful he was for the Bush welcome and help in navigating the world's most challenging job. In fact, as the story goes, George Bush met with President-elect Obama in a secured room in Chicago and showed him the Intelligence Briefing. Obama was shocked at the contents of the briefing and the dangerous situations around the world. As described, it was ———(expletive) WOW!

In the 2016 election, with Hillary Clinton winning the popular vote by three million, she nonetheless lost the Electoral College. Hillary Clinton conceded and gave a gracious speech the next day to the country, indicating that unity was important and so was the peaceful transfer of power. Barack Obama had Donald Trump to the White House two days later and made available everything that Trump would need for the transition. He also warned Trump that there were two things he needed to know. President Obama told Donald Trump that his one big problem would be North Korea. In that meeting Barack Obama told Donald Trump not to bring Michael Flynn into the White. Obama had just recently fired Flynn, based on very good information from the intelligence agencies.

Donald Trump disdained the transition that Obama and his entire administration offered. The outgoing administration even did tabletop role playing of possible situations. They also told Trump of the organization that was setup in the White House to manage a possible pandemic, which they feared could be coming. (They had just fought the "Ebola" crisis successfully).

Trump never engaged in the PDB (never reads them at all), brought Michael Flynn into the White House as his National Security Advisor (circumventing Senate approval), and fooled himself into making "friends" with Kim Jong Un of North Korea. Then, Donald Trump eliminated the science group that was organized in the White House, and discarded the detailed plan that was left for a potential healthcare crisis. He totally rejected any help that Barack Obama offered. Considering the "birther" controversy that Trump began, it was actually quite gracious of Obama to welcome him to the White House. For Barack Obama, country and the traditions of the election mattered more than any personal animosity, as it has been for all participating presidential candidates, winners and losers.

Until now. Donald Trump has been acting like a petulant child, and a vengeful one. He lost the election, by the popular vote and the Electoral College. The safety, security and stability of America is at stake, and the world is watching, including our adversaries. The Biden-Harris administration needs to populate the White House, plan the Inauguration and fill the four thousand jobs in all of our agencies that need to be up and running on January 20th, 2021.

We have a serious health crisis and the President is absent, except for holding maskless rallies, which often have tragic results with people testing positive for the virus. In fact, much of Trump's White House staff is side-lined, because they attended all the events without masks or social distancing.

This transition period is crucial to implement ordering masks, PPE, and everything that is needed to survive the worst of the virus. President Trump is not interested in leading, except for taking victory-lap rallies. The country is essentially leaderless, as it was in March when Trump needed to fight the coronavirus war with all the resources of the federal government.

We have transitions for a very important reason, for good leadership and continuity. Absent those two things, we are once again in a state of chaos, experiencing anxiety and wondering what to do with the holidays approaching.

Good leadership is the key to good transitions and a calmer country.

OUR HEALTH CRISIS:

Coronavirus numbers" 161,651 new cases in the last 24 hours. Numbers are rising.

BE KIND TO ONE ANOTHER!!

States are begging people to stay home and not travel for Thanksgiving, if they have the choice.

Nurses are begging people to care about one another, wear masks and practice social distancing.

We need to care about one another and our country.

Inflection Point/ The President is MIA

November 14, 2020

We are in the middle of two crises, which are intersecting: Covid-19 healthcare crisis, and a political crisis for the newly elected President Joe Biden. These two serious situations have one thing in common. President Trump is "missing in action." He wants nothing to do with either situation. Unfortunately, federal action is required to solve both crises.

The immediate problem is the surge in viruses. Yesterday, there were 184,000 coronavirus cases. Many of our hospitals are filled to overflowing, and there are no more beds. Some hospitals have been forced to go to "rationing" care, which is very problematic. The healthcare workers are exhausted, and there are none to replace them. Many nurses have been the only person holding the hand of someone who is dying. The emotional toll is devastating. One nurse said that she had been with twenty-three patients in one day, and held their hands as they each died. Breathtakingly sad.

Moreover, there are now long lines and delays at testing sites. In March, we needed President Trump to organize a universal testing program. He took no responsibility for that, saying mistakenly that testing would create more cases. He never really grasped any of the science and the import of testing. Now we are in a worse situation than nine months ago. For example, the man in charge of the Trump administration's effort to produce a coronavirus vaccine, wants to brief Biden, but has been forbidden to do so. More than 150 former national security officials, from both parties, warned that Trump's refusing to facilitate the transition is a "serious risk to national security."

In fact, Donald Trump has never mentioned the citizens who have died-he has shown no sorrow, no remorse and no empathy. Perhaps he knows that they are dying, because he totally failed to lead a federal response to the virus. Millions of people know that he is responsible for this tragedy, and that is a major reason why they voted against him.

Apparently, Donald Trump and Jared Kushner are responsible for the decision not to help New York, New Jersey, and Connecticut- the "so-called blue states." On its face, that decision seemed blatantly political, but it may be more personally protective than we know. In an interview with Chris Cuomo of CNN, Andrew McCabe, former deputy director of the FBI, intimated that Trump may have more serious reasons for not wanting to give the Biden team access to confidential information and decision-making. McCabe may have felt that it would show "the president in a very negative light." That would certainly include Trump's reluctance to reveal actions regarding the Russia investigation. Josh Marshall, of *Talking Points Memo,* picked up on the McCabe comment and opined that Trump's unwillingness to let Biden see intelligence reports goes beyond just being a poor sport. Likely, there is damaging information in those reports that would implicate Trump and others in malfeasance and other crimes.

Nonetheless, the immediate result is that Biden-Harris has been kept out of the loop by the GSA. Fortunately, Joe Biden is the single most experienced person becoming president, having spent eight years in the Obama orbit. He is able to reach out to people he knows in the various agencies, even though Trump has forbidden people to talk to the new president. While this behavior is petty and childish, it does have serious consequences.

Joe Biden met with his Covid-19 Advisory Committee and made an important statement. He said that the government has to be responsive to citizens. "This crisis demands a robust and immediately federal response." Biden continued, "which has been woefully lacking. I am the President-elect, but I will not be president until next year. The crisis does not respect dates on the calendar, it is accelerating right now. Urgent action is needed today, by the current administration." Biden called for more badly needed supplies, more PPE's for the healthcare workers, testing and masks, and science- based guidelines for controlling the pandemic. He also asked Americans to "step up and do your part on social distancing, hand washing and mask wearing to protect yourselves and to protect others."

It is highly unlikely that Trump will do anything of the sort. For one thing, he is still claiming that he won the election, which is nonsense. The numbers tell the tale. Trump has lawsuits in the various states, and so far, all of them have lost or been thrown out, because they are so frivolous.

Lawyers don't like being asked to file nonsense lawsuits. In court, a lawyer can face fines or lose his license for unfounded allegations. When the lawyers have appeared in court, they have been asked for evidence to support their claims, and there is none. Very embarrassing.

Respectable law firms are refusing to represent him, just as they did years ago when he didn't pay them, and they denied him representation. Two reputable law firms, have asked to be removed from the cases. This is serious, because requests like that put a bad light on the client. However, it seems that the judges will allow these firms to remove themselves. Donald Trump has now put Rudy Giuliani in charge of his legal business.

Despite all this proof of chicanery, lying and stonewalling, Trump supporters still believe that Trump won the election, since that is what he tells them. This blind following of the "cult of Trump" is very dangerous to our democracy. In point of fact, sixteen US attorneys who were assigned to monitor the elections for any signs of cheating, told AG Barr that they found no evidence of fraud.

A very dangerous notion is being promulgated on social media. There is a "Stop the Steal" campaign, which pushes the idea that the election was stolen from Trump. He has done nothing to dissuade his followers, and is encouraging them. There is a "Stop the Steal" rally today in Washington, D.C., a week after Joe Biden was declared president. He is trying to move forward in planning the new administration.

The campaign is the work of Roger Stone, Trump's old friend, who has been a "dirty trickster." Stone has been a political operative for years. He was convicted of seven felonies, and as he was about to go to prison, Trump commuted his sentence, thereby shutting up Stone, who is forever in his debt. Stone started the "Stop the Steal" website in 2016, raising money on the claim that the Democrats were going to steal the election. Of course, the opposite was true, with the Russians helping Trump squeak by with 77,000 votes in three swing states that gave him the presidency. Now, Stone is back at it. It's important to know that the rally is well-organized groups, not just followers, but right-wing groups. More on this tomorrow.

Donald Trump is not just a sore loser. He is a dangerous loser who has influenced a lot of citizens to believe his lies and they are willing to follow him off a cliff. Rather than calling for unity, he continues to divide, and that is reprehensible. We have a health tragedy, a new administration trying to solve the Covid crisis and establish a working government, but President Trump is missing in action, on purpose.

For the Good of Country

November 18, 2020

When I was teaching history, Horace Mann School had a beautiful new building, and we decided to institute a Student Council. As the advisor, I taught hundreds of middle schoolers how to hold an election. We learned how to respectfully debate, to run a campaign, give speeches, make rules for good sportsmanship and hold a secret ballot. My students were passionate and competitive, enthusiastic and creative sign-makers, intelligent and persuasive speakers. After weeks of prep, the day of the vote arrived. There were winners and losers for each class and ultimately for the Middle School Council that would be the organizers for all of the projects we planned for the year.

Having spent weeks on this activity, it was heartening to see the losers, while disappointed, congratulate the classmate who won, (we practiced this), and the winners did not gloat (a very important part of the lesson). I'm happy to report that no one tried to buy anyone else's vote with candy, or accuse a classmate of cheating. There were no efforts to stuff the ballot box, and the counting of ballots was done in the open. The results were accepted graciously and not challenged.

The lessons of that year were twofold-learning how to be good winners and losers, and most important-coming together as a school and working together on all the community service projects that we planned to accomplish. No right-wing fringe group was formed that refused to participate.

Disappointments were put aside as we made sandwiches for Midnight Run to feed the homeless, donated coats for the fall Coat Drive, brought our books for those who had none. Students brought suitcases for foster children, so they didn't have to bring their belongings to a new home in garbage bags. That year was a wonderful opportunity for everyone to come together and feel proud about the good things they were doing together to help people in the community.

A lot of leadership skills were developed by those wonderful students who ran for office in 6th, 7th and 8th grades. They went on to become high schoolers, go to college, attend law school, become doctors, innovative entrepreneurs, and business and community leaders. The seeds of giving back to make all peoples' lives better were born in that petri dish of running for office and using the power of being president, VP or Secretary for the greater good. The kids had elected their leaders and given them their trust. Yes, it was really about trust. No one abused his new-found title, as new projects were proposed and voted. In the years afterward, it is a pleasure to read about my former students and the contributions they are making to the community. Clearly, those intelligent human beings are making a difference.

As I watch the Election of 2020, it is sad to see the behavior of the grownup who lost. Even in the first debate, he was rude and disrespectful. Now he exhibits poor sportsmanship, unwillingness to accept the results of the election, no polite concession, no handshake, accusations of cheating and a "rigged" activity. No honor has been given to the rules and regulations of the Constitution, and the states themselves. What is being promulgated is doubt in the system, and no sense that coming together as a country is more important than party.

There are dire consequences for not coming together as a country at this moment. The country is in the midst of a grave threat, and life and death are at stake. Seventy-five thousand people are hospitalized, and our hospitals are at capacity. We need to stop politicizing the guidelines for health and safety in this pandemic. We must all wear masks, stay home if possible, make smart decisions about travel, quarantine, and work for the greater good.

Shockingly, Chris Krebs, the CISA Director, who oversaw the United States election security, was fired last night by Donald Trump. The president, the sorest loser this country has ever seen, hated the great job that Krebs did protecting our country. and fired him in a rude tweet. This is not the way to treat anyone who works for our country's well-being. Recently, Krebs said that our 2020 election was the "most secure in the history of America." Some people on the president's side of the aisle are grateful for the job Krebs did, and they have come out with statements about Krebs and what he did to protect the American vote in the cyber- community. Being fired for serving the country is a very sad occurrence in this administration, and it happens all too often.

As of this morning, we have 249,820 deaths in our country, and the president has nothing on his schedule. We have a major leadership vacuum. The president is spending his days issuing angry tweets, playing golf and firing people with whom he disagrees.

Our country is in a place that we have never witnessed in our history. It is dangerous, deeply disturbing and essentially lawless, as we watch the staggering coronavirus numbers rise and the federal government do nothing.

For the good of the country, everyone needs to come together to keep one another well-informed and safe. We need to regain our trust in America as one people. Only then will we be able to defeat the virus, make a viable economy, return to work and school and live our lives.

United States Total Deaths: 253,633 citizens have died as of today, November 20, 2020

As we began the year, we are ending the year with Covid-19.

193,000 Covid-19 new daily cases were confirmed yesterday.

There is NO NATIONAL STRATEGY.

Early in 2020, Donald Trump was warned by the CDC, Dr. Fauci, and many other scientists, that the virus would be really bad in the fall, which is flu season.

The Trump Administration has totally blocked the incoming Biden-Harris people from having access to information, so that they can plan their response on January 20ᵗʰ, day 1 of the Biden administration. Meanwhile, Biden has been meeting with a Task Force made of eminent scientists and is thoroughly conversant with the virus. However, Donald Trump has denied him access to Warp Speed and what has already been done.

The CDC has asked all citizens not to travel for Thanksgiving.

There Is no national invocation of the Defense Production Act.

There are shortages for testing materials, because the government made no effort to replenish our supplies, indicating that the virus is like a flu and would, "magically disappear."

This is willful negligence. Early in 2020 while taping with Bob Woodward, Donald Trump told Woodward how dangerous this virus is, that it can travel through the air and kill people.

One shocking reality is that ICU nurses are reporting that patients they are treating didn't believe there was a virus. This is what happens when disinformation is spread by the leader of the free world. Millions of people actually believed Donald Trump, and took no precautions-no mask wearing, no social distancing, and now they are in the hospital very sick and many will die.

This is what happens when a person gets to be president by a fluke. A man ran for office on a lark, had no campaign organization, and with the help of Russia, won. Donald Trump has been spreading dangerous information and the Republicans, except for Mitt Romney, are enabling this nonsense

Donald Trump's government stepped aside and let this virus wreak havoc on the country.

Meanwhile, it's embarrassing to see a grown man have a childish tantrum because he lost an election. He has responded with vindictive lawsuits that have no basis in fact, and they are preventing the duly-elected Biden-Harris ticket to organize the government in a timely way.

Trump insists that the vote was fraudulent, and that he actually won reelection.

Trump's lawyers filed thirty-three lawsuits and they all either failed or were withdrawn. There is NO evidence of fraud to present to the judges. Most important, lying to a judge in court puts the lawyer in serious jeopardy of legal consequences for himself.

More on Trump's efforts to subvert the VOTE and the TRUTH tomorrow.

Trump campaign continues as he tries to steal the election in a clown show

November 22, 2020

November 22 has always been one of the most excruciatingly sad days in my memory. John F. Kennedy was killed in Dallas on November 22nd. Vice President Lyndon Baines Johnson, who was in Dallas that day, was sworn in as President, seamlessly, with the transfer of power that the Constitution provides. At a time when other countries might devolve into chaos, The United States relied on faith in our laws and trust in the process. It has been like this until the election of 2020, because of Donald Trump's refusal to accept the outcome of Joe Biden and Kamala Harris being duly elected. It was "the single most secure election in American history," according to Chris Krebs the Chief of Cybersecurity, who Trump fired after Krebs made that statement.

The country needs to move on, so that Joe Biden and Kamala Harris can have access to important intelligence briefings, and begin to set up their new government. Trump has created more chaos with angry tweets proclaiming that he won the election.

As I watch Donald Trump trying to turn the election in his favor, what he is doing is horrifying, as he spreads various conspiracy theories. Wild theories are found in third world countries! Meanwhile, Mitch McConnell has remained silent.

Chris Christie, former Governor of New Jersey, a loyal Republican, and former Attorney General, came out over the weekend and said that the lawsuits are a "national embarrassment," and that Donald Trump should drop them. Christie also said that it is obvious that there is no evidence for Trump's claims. "If evidence existed, then it would have been presented in court." Larry Hogan, Republican Governor of Maryland, called for Donald Trump to "stop golfing and concede." He also called the shameless actions of Trump trying to overturn a legitimate election, "a national embarrassment."

Christie and Hogan are just a few Republicans who were willing to come out publicly. Senators Mitt Romney, Lisa Murkowski, Susan Collins and Pat Toomey are the other Senators who have congratulated Joe Biden and acknowledged his electoral win. The Republican Party has been silent, and we watch Donald Trump continue to shred Constitutional norms.

Ed Luce, Editor of the *Financial Times*, wrote, "Do Not Exhale Yet America." He pointed out that Trump's firing of the Secretary of Defense and putting many Trump loyalists in the Defense positions, is dangerous. He indicated that Trump, having failed in the courts, is now trying to turn the state electors to vote for him, even if the states, like Michigan and Pennsylvania, voted for Joe Biden. In a move that was designed to influence electors, Trump invited them to the White House. It's important to remember that tampering with the mail is a federal offense, and trying to influence the results of an election is a state and federal crime. The ACLU has brought a lawsuit against Donald Trump for his actions in trying to change the outcome of the vote. Vote tampering is outrageous and shameless, as well as illegal. The soul of our country is that we stand for free and fair elections.

Senator Marco Rubio (R-Florida), also wrote in September that the biggest achievement of foreign election interference would be to influence half of the country to distrust the system. That is what Trump has been doing with his relentless messages, and he seems to be succeeding. This is very damaging to our country. Donald Trump is trying to steal an election in the middle of a pandemic.

Importantly, this weekend a Pennsylvania judge, Matthew Brann, dismissed a Trump federal lawsuit with a scathing opinion. Judge Brann is a former Republican Party official, and a member of the conservative Federalist Society. He was appointed to the bench by President Barack Obama. He ruled that the Trump campaign lacked standing to make a claim that helping voters "cure" flawed ballots of minor problems violated the equal protection clause of the Constitution. Judge Brann likened the argument to Frankenstein's monster which had been "haphazardly stitched together."

Another serious disruptor is Emily Murphy, who refuses to sign the ascertainment paper, which gives the new government access to money, office space and resources to set up the new government. We have never been in a situation where the loser in an election has ordered someone not to sign that paper. Congress has sent her a letter, indicating that she needs to come before them to explain why she has decided not to sign the paper, and what influenced her.

Most important, the Biden team needs access to "Warp Speed," the vaccine program, and information about what has already been done to distribute a vaccine. Making a vaccine available to three hundred million people is a massive organizational job. All of this information has been forbidden by Trump, and that is very dangerous. The virus numbers are spiking, and every day that Trump refuses information to the Biden team, "people will die." Joe Biden explained the urgency when asked why time was essential. The Biden team is continuing to work to frame out the Cabinet and the hundred people who need to work in the White House. In addition, there are four thousand jobs in our agencies that need to be filled.

In the midst of all this chaos, Joe Biden and Kamala Harris are meeting with potential civil workers and trying to set up their government. Fortunately, Joe Biden knows his way around Washington, and he has many connections to knowledgeable people who can serve.

I am eager to see the end of the "Trump show." His narcissistic and off the wall tweets have continued for five years. I yearn for a stable and calm administration. Hopefully, it will come soon, because most of the country is exhausted from the drama and the angst.

A New Day Dawning

November 23, 2020

Joe Biden is the apparent winner of the presidency, but the woman whose job it was to "ascertain" the election, refused to do so. After three weeks, Emily Murphy finally issued the much needed "ascertainment." Now President-elect Biden will have the money he needs to set up the new administration, as well as access to the all-important intelligence briefs. The delay has definitely made the transition more difficult.

Many of the Biden nominees are very experienced, and they have worked in government for a long time. They are career civil servants, and there are famous firsts! This afternoon, as Joe Biden introduced his team, each member spoke, and it was a breathtaking moment. Biden has named Anthony Blinken, his longtime aid, to be Secretary of State. Blinken spoke of the honor it will be to lead the State Department. President-elect Biden indicated that America is back in the business of diplomacy. Mr. Blinken's stepfather was the only one of nine hundred children who survived the Holocaust in a particular place, and the story brought tears to my eyes. If you can go and see these short talks, it is well worth hearing them in person. My description doesn't begin to do them justice.

Alejandro Mayorkas will head DHS, Department of Homeland Security, the first Cuban-American to have that job. His story is breathtaking as well. An immigrant, he certainly understands the emotions of those trying to come to the United States. Trying to straighten out the mess from the prior administration is a huge job. Importantly, we will be a welcoming country once again.

Joe Biden nominated John Kerry to be the "Climate Tsar." Former Secretary of State, he has connections all over the world, and he was the Democratic Senator from Massachusetts. Kerry will be" Special Presidential Envoy for Climate."

Avril Haines will be the CIA head, the first woman, and a true professional. She was former Deputy Director of CIA. 2013 – 2015. She spoke of always telling the truth, no matter how difficult it will sometimes be, and that she knows Joe Biden wants to hear it. What a breath of fresh air!

Jake Sullivan- has been nominated to serve as National Security Advisor. He was Deputy Chief of Staff to Secretary of State Hillary Clinton. He spoke of his roots in Minnesota, and his parents, who were educators. He has an exceptional understanding of the threats that America faces, and he is prepared for the challenge.

Linda Thomas-Greenfield was nominated to be United Nations Ambassador for the United States. Formerly Head of the Foreign Service, Assistant Secretary of State for African Affairs. Linda grew up in segregated Louisiana. She will have Cabinet status. A career diplomat, she was formerly Director General of the United States Foreign Service and Ambassador to Liberia. She spoke of

"Gumbo Diplomacy." "Life can be hard and cruel, but there is hope in the struggle. America is back." I was scrambling to take notes while each person was speaking.

Truthfully, it was inspiring to hear each story, but I was not able to take the usual notes. With apologies, watching and/or reading the speeches is well worth the time, because they lay out the Biden administration's goals and philosophy and set out its tone.

In a nutshell, no more "America First." America will be back, working with our allies, and following truth to power. We will be rejoining all the organizations that Trump took us out of which put us on the sidelines. The nominees are a wonderful team of professionals who will be following the data, the science and working to keep America safe. No more political do-nothings, no big-donor friends, no incompetent family. Everyone will be vetted with proper security clearances, something that never happened in the Trump administration.

Due to the prior administration, Biden/Harris and all these nominees have a huge mess to clean up. Millions of people have food insecurity, thousands are dying daily and the CARES ACT is going to end shortly. That situation will leave people struggling to pay their rent and their bills. Unemployment insurance will also be ending in December. The Senate did not pass the stimulus bill that the House passed in May, which was desperately needed. The Senate left town without doing its job. Worse, Joe Biden does not become president until January 20th, leaving Donald Trump to spread misinformation and attack our democracy for the next few weeks. We are in a vulnerable time period until the next administration takes office.

I breathed a sigh of relief when I heard all of the nominees. Brilliant, talented and committed, many of them have worked together in one or another capacity, and Joe Biden knows all of them well. It is a new day dawning.

BUILD BACK BETTER

Continuing President-elect Biden's exciting choices for Cabinet

November 25, 2020

President-elect Biden plans to nominate Janet Yellen as Treasury Secretary. She will be the first woman to hold this post, and she has deep prior experience. Yellen served as Chair of the Federal Reserve from 2014-2018, until Donald Trump unceremoniously replaced her with William Powell. She is respected on both sides of the aisle, so this nomination will be a welcome one. Janet Yellen is a brilliant economist, specializing in labor and monetary policy. Another reason that she is a perfect pick at this time is that she cares deeply about problems of inequality, and this is the moment. She also served as head of the White House Council of Economic Advisors under President Bill Clinton.

When she chaired the Federal Reserve, Yellen was respected equally by labor and Wall Street, an interesting range. During the Obama Presidency, the labor market was strong, and it continued until the coronavirus pandemic, when 40 million people lost their jobs. Janet Yellen is widely respected as a stable and steady force, who will promote an economy that works for everyone in these volatile and extremely difficult times.

Senator Elizabeth Warren, (D-Mass), a progressive, messaged that Yellen is "outstanding … She is smart, tough, and principled … She has stood up to Wall Street banks …" Joe Biden mentioned that while Bernic Sanders and Elizabeth Warren are popular choices for a role in the new government, they are needed in the Senate, since the margin is so tight. Both Sanders and Warren came out and supported Biden in full-throated comments. Some of their philosophy is very popular in Democratic circles, and may be incorporated in a Biden presidency.

The choices from yesterday exuded stability, expertise and a return to normalcy. The nomination of Janet Yellen carries that forward. President-elect Biden has a number of "firsts" in his choices. Janet Yellen is another example of the first time a woman will be Treasury Secretary. Joe Biden honors brilliance, competence, commitment and excellence, regardless of gender.

We are returning to the concept that Democrats believe in using government to help mainstream Americans. The Republicans left all citizens high and dry when faced with the pandemic. Government was not activated to solve the problem. In a Biden presidency, the resources of government will be used to help all Americans.

Monday the 23rd was a big day for Dow Jones. The announcement of possible vaccines with a high rate of viability was wonderful news, and the market reacted. Added to that was the certification of the Biden vote by Pennsylvania. The stock market responds to stability, and future stability going forward. Donald Trump was very erratic and made the markets nervous. Trump also criticized various businesses, based on whether they helped him or not. In fact, he played favorites, and so it was impossible to rely on what would happen to the Dow Jones. Donald Trump was so erratic that often he had markets roiling. Unable to accept his loss gracefully, Trump has been attacking our democratic system and undermining faith and confidence in our elections. I am very nervous as a result of his behavior.

The appointment of Janet Yellen is a master stroke on the part of President-elect Biden. It signals a return to calm and stability, and a steadiness that will be good for American business.

We are still waiting for more important nominations- for Attorney General, Justice, and Defense, to name a few. When we know, it will be my pleasure to talk about the outstanding men and women who will be joining the Biden-Harris administration.

HAPPY THANKSGIVING! There is much for which to be grateful, even in the midst of serious life and death events. Try to stay safe, make good decisions and enjoy your day, whatever you choose to do. I am having a ZOOM Thanksgiving with my family, complete with turkey, stuffing, cranberry sauce, and the works delivered to my apartment building by Eppes Essen in Livingston. It even arrived warm!

Grateful-in a time of the pandemic, food insecurity, and a bitter election

November 26, 2020

It's Thanksgiving, and we are living through the single most challenging and difficult time, including a bitter election. It's hard to be grateful when so many are suffering.

Many of us cannot celebrate with our families. There will be many empty chairs at our tables.

The virus is so dangerous and contagious that we have been advised NOT to travel anywhere. I will be celebrating by myself, and happy to see my family and close friends on Zoom. I am grateful to be healthy.

It's hard to feel grateful without feeling incredibly guilty. What is the situation?

270,000 citizens have died of the virus.

It's the beginning of the holiday season, and millions of people are food insecure. The lines of cars at our Food Banks are miles long. People are waiting for hours to get food to feed their families.

17 million children are hungry in America, the wealthiest country in the world. Local food banks are running out of the ability to feed everyone who is hungry.

The CARES ACT is about to end. The Senate left town without doing anything to alleviate the pain and suffering of people who lost their jobs, and were relying on the Stimulus Bill and the $600. The House of Representatives passed the Stimulus Bill in May, and it has been sitting on Mitch McConnell's Senate desk ever since. He does not care to take it up, and his Republican Senators disagree amongst themselves about whether to help citizens or not.

The unemployment program is about to end in December. Some people have been rehired, but we still have millions of people unemployed. For example, 90,000 airline workers are jobless. Many restaurants had to close because of the virus, and never were able to reopen. Stores are shuttered, because we cannot gather.

We are now in the third wave of the pandemic. Without a second stimulus, citizens will not be able to pay their rent or their bills. Many people will become homeless with no health protection. This is a nightmare for millions of people.

While the virus numbers are spiking, so are the deaths of our amazing healthcare workers. They have come to work, despite leaving their own families, and they often get sick. As a result, we have a tragic situation, and a shortage of workers for this virus. Ventilators require skillful people, and more than one person per patient. We are in the midst of a tragedy that is beyond our control.

That said, there is actually much for which to be grateful.

In a bitter and punishing election, **we saved our democracy.** On November 3rd, Joe Biden and Kamala Harris were elected President and Vice President by millions of votes, defeating Donald Trump, who refuses to concede and insists that the election was "stolen from him." It's the first time that a losing candidate has refused to concede or acknowledge the transition. A key tenet of American exceptionalism is the "peaceful transfer of power." Trump has trashed it.

He also pressured the GSA not to issue the ascertainment paper for three weeks, which slowed down the huge job of setting up a new administration. Joe Biden has to clean up a four-year mess from Donald Trump.

On a local level, my temple, Sharey-Tefilo-Israel, has a turkey drive and we bring the turkeys for dinner as well-cranberry sauce, stuffing, the works. Sharey -Tefilo is all about community and giving, and that is a wonderful tradition that carries through each season, and has gone on for years.

On a personal level, I am thankful for my family, the grownups and grandchildren, who are healthy, and for wonderful friends, both here and scattered. I have cousins, who meet weekly on Zoom. Since March, the clergy have made a superhuman effort to keep connected and meet with us every week. I truly feel that their caring and support have gotten us through the year to this point, and there is still much to do.

I give thanks to: the frontline workers, the healthcare workers, the essential workers, people who voted, all the poll workers, people who are wearing masks, the patriots who testified, and patriots in our hometowns, teachers, for SOMA, the Rescue Squad, our firemen, those people who donated dinners to hospitals, and so many more Americans who came out of the woodwork to get involved.

Thanks to President-elect Joe Biden, who gave a beautiful and inspiring Thanksgiving message yesterday, telling us to take heart, that we will get through this. He offered a plea for unity.

In addition, deciding to write these blogs has forced me to focus and made me feel substantive and worthwhile. I appreciate each of your comments as well as your thoughtful opinions.

To each and every one of you, a healthy Thanksgiving and a day as happy as possible.

In Concessions, Character Counts, for Country and Continuity

November 28, 2020

Losing a hard-fought campaign is difficult, painful really. What the loser says and does afterward tells us a great deal about that person's character.

There is actually nothing in the Constitution that calls for a concession speech on the part of a losing candidate. Watching the clips of all the wonderful presidential candidates who lost an election makes me proud, and also sad. Each concession speech is a window into the soul and the patriotism of the person conceding.

In 1860, Stephen Douglas congratulated Abraham Lincoln on his victory. Of course, the "victory" was going to presage the single most divisive event in our history. With the election of Lincoln, the southern states knew that he would abolish slavery. They seceded from the Union and formed the Confederacy. What followed was the Civil War, the most bitter and bloody war ever fought within our borders. For those citizens who think that we are divided beyond repair, remember the Civil War.

While there is no legal or constitutional requirement that the loser of a U.S. presidential election must concede, courtesy began as a simple gesture. After the election of 1896, William Jennings Bryan sent a telegram to his opponent, William McKinley, two days after the election. It read:

"Senator Jones has just informed me that the returns indicate your election, and I hasten to extend my congratulations. We have submitted the issue to the American people and their will is law."

Those two sentences are considered to be the first public concession in U.S. presidential politics. The tradition has continued in some form or another, in every election since. Until now.

Al Smith gave the first radio concession in 1928, after losing to Herbert Hoover. In 1940, moviegoers watched Wendell Willkie concede to Franklin D. Roosevelt in a newsreel. After losing in 1952, Adlai Stevenson gave his concession to Dwight Eisenhower.

Over the past 120 years, there have been 32 concession speeches. There's actually a roadmap, a template if you will, that candidates follow for the speech they hoped they'd never have to give.

The statement of defeat– although they never use the word "defeat." The candidate acknowledges the opponent's victory and congratulates the opponent.

The call to unite-in a show of bipartisanship, the candidate expresses support for the former opponent and calls for unity on all sides. In 1960, Richard Nixon sent this message to John F. Kennedy, the first Catholic president.

"I have great faith that our people, Republicans, Democrats alike, will unite behind our next president."

The celebration of democracy-The candidate reflects on the power of our democratic system. In 2016, Hillary Clinton said, "our constitutional democracy enshrines the peaceful transfer of power. We don't just respect that. We cherish it," when she conceded to Donald Trump, having received three million more votes, but not the prescribed amount in the Electoral College.

The vow to continue the fight-The loser speaks about the importance of the issues raised in the campaign and the policies .

The concession I know best is that of Hubert Humphrey. In 1968, I volunteered for Hubert in Washington, D.C., when he was running against Richard Nixon. My husband was drafted out of Rutgers Law School and sent to the Pentagon. I finished my teaching job in Summit, and moved to Alexandria, Virginia. 1968 was the most volatile year. I worked for a man named Ofield Dukes, Hubert's press man, and the only black member of his staff. There was serious division over the Vietnam War- a huge generational divide, and much more. It was a dangerous time to be alone in the city, and there was violence at the Chicago convention, which I did not attend. On election night my friends, Trish and George Vradenberg and I, stayed up all night watching the returns. In defeat, Humphrey sent Nixon a telegram:

"Please know that you have my support in leading this nation. This has been a difficult year for the American people. I am confident that constructive leaders from both parties will join together now, and we shall be able to go on to the business of building the America we all seek in the spirit of peace and harmony. The democratic process has worked its will. Now we need to get on with the business of uniting the country."

Of course, the rest is history. As we suspected, Nixon was a crook, and would stop at nothing to advance his cause. All the people around him went to jail, including his Attorney General and closest advisors. When the tapes that Nixon made were released, we all learned a great deal about his biases and his crass, competitive opinion of his competitors.

In that vein, language matters. Robert Dole, in his concession speech, indicated that the winner was his "opponent," not his "enemy," a very important distinction.

The most important concept is that once the decision is made, we unite behind the man who has been elected.

Partisan feeling must yield to patriotism.

One of the most gracious and moving concession speeches was given by Al Gore, who lost after 35 days of chaos, a recount, and one vote of the Supreme Court. it was generally accepted that he had received more votes than George W. Bush. Gore said, "This is America. We close ranks when the decision is made"

Another incredibly gracious concession speech was that of Senator John McCain. He acknowledged the historic nature of America electing its first African-American president. Then, he paid tribute to the campaign of Barack Obama, and to the people who raised him. McCain said that he loves America first, and that will always be the case.

Even though there are common threads throughout all of these concession speeches, it took me longer than I anticipated to write this blog. I listened to all the videos, and was so moved by each candidate's love of country, commitment to unity and the dignity with which each person spoke. I found myself feeling very emotional and wiping away tears, when I considered the depth of feeling of each person who lost.

Writing their phrases does no justice to the actual speeches. I strongly suggest that you google "concession speeches," and listen to the real thing. You are in for a treat. In this difficult and dystopian period, you will be inspired by the patriots who have served our country-whether they won or lost an election-over the last many years. Hopefully, we will be returning to those feelings in the new administration, which is filled with lifelong civil servants.

Similarly, in 1992, when George H.W. Bush lost after only one term, he said, "America must always come first. We will get behind this new president.

"Georgia on My Mind"

December 2, 2020

I hope you had a nice Thanksgiving, however weird it might have been without gatherings. The craziness of the last three days was happily interrupted for me, because I work with high school students on their college applications. The deadline was December 1st, so I was able to take a hiatus and work with wonderful teenagers, who are sane and tell the truth, and take a break from the many adults who are crazy and spread conspiracy theories.

Back to Georgia, one of six swing states. For the first time in decades, Georgia went for a Democrat. Georgia turning "blue" was due in part to the monumental efforts of Stacie Abrams, who registered more than 800,000 voters, many of them for the first time. There is a very consequential runoff for both of Georgia's Senate seats. With the count in the Senate being 48 Democrats and 50 Republicans, the democratic opportunity to win both of those seats and make the count 50/50 would be a game-changer for the Democrats. For the first time in years, Democrats would be able to move legislation. Since the Democrats will be in power, Kamala Harris, as Vice President, would be sitting in the Senate as President and have the tie-breaking vote.

Why is this important? When Barack Obama was elected President, the Democrats were in the majority in the Senate. As a result, all of Obama's nominees for Cabinet and other offices were easily confirmed. That is not the case in 2020. The Republicans have been in power, and Majority Leader Mitch McConnell has blocked everything: legislation, Supreme Court nominees and the stimulus bill. Needless to say, those two Senate seats are crucial.

Georgia's election administrators have been unduly pressured, threatened and been the subjects of scary tweets, because they said that the election was safe and fair. Brad Raffensberger, Georgia's Secretary of State, a Republican, has come under increasing pressure for standing by the election results. Donald Trump wants them overturned, and he doesn't care how. Thirty-seven lawsuits in all the states have failed in the courts, much to Trump's dismay. He has always used litigation to gain what he wants, or he didn't pay either his lawyers or building contractors. He railed against the fact that he cannot bring his case to the Supreme Court, saying, "How is it that the President of the United States cannot bring a case to the Supreme Court? What do they mean, I don't have standing?"

Of course, if Donald Trump ever read the Constitution and learned about the process, he would have discovered that the states are in charge of elections, and he doesn't have standing. There are three branches of government, and checks and balances.

Georgia has remained the focal point of pressure to change its vote, and the pressure has been brutal. Donald Trump has tweeted that "there is massive voter fraud in Georgia." He forced three separate recounts, and Joe Biden won Georgia by 12,000 votes. The other day, Gabe Sterling, one of the administrators of Georgia's election and a Republican, called out President Trump and the two sitting Senators. He said:

"This has to stop. You have to be responsible. You have to be responsible in your rhetoric. Mr. President, you have not condemned these actions or this language. Senators, you have not condemned this language or these actions. This has to stop. We need you to step up, and if you are going to take a position of leadership, show some. People have been driving in caravans past Brad Raffensberger's home, have come onto his property and have sent sexualized threats to his wife's cell phone. A twenty-year-old election worker, who just took a job, is receiving death threats."

Gabe Sterling is very angry, and he let it be known on the steps of Georgia's state capital. He and Brad Raffensberger now have police officers stationed outside their homes, and the Georgia Bureau of Investigation is investigating.

This has happened in every swing state, where Donald Trump has tried to reverse the vote by threats of violence, intimidation and firing. Chris Krebs, who was in charge of keeping hackers away from our election, came out and proclaimed 2020 the safest and most clean election we ever had. Donald Trump fired him in a nasty tweet.

Michigan has also been the target of Trump's ire. The Michigan Welfare Rights Organization (plaintiff) has filed a lawsuit against Donald Trump and Donald J. Trump for President, Inc. It reads in part:

"Since decisively losing the November 2020 presidential election, Defendants Donald J. Trump and his campaign committee Donald J. Trump for President, Inc. have engaged in a variety of tactics designed to overturn the result of that election. Having unsuccessfully filed numerous unsuccessful lawsuits, Defendants have now turned to a new strategy: pressure state and local officials not to certify election results in key states and then have state legislatures override the will of the voters by installing President Trump's slate of electors. They have actively pursued this strategy, compromising the integrity of the election process, and unlawfully interfering with the will of the voters."

The lawsuit continues, outlining various unlawful tactics. On one occasion, Trump had the electors to the White House. Remember that interfering with the result of an election is a federal crime, as well as a state crime. When Trump put in Postmaster DeJoy months ago, and told him to slow down the mail and tamper with it, that was a crime, punishable with years in jail.

Donald Trump has been melting down, insisting that he won the election, spreading the conspiracy theory that he is the rightful winner, that the election was "stolen" from him. The people around him are supporting this nonsense. Reporters who would question him were not allowed in the press room yesterday, as he stood in front of the White House lectern and spread baseless lies, in a forty-eight-minute diatribe. We have never seen anything like this in the history of our country.

Most disturbing, Trump has walked away from the death toll that keeps rising, with not a word mentioned about the American citizens who are dying. The daily deaths equal the 3,000 citizens who were killed on 9/11, but this is our daily toll. The next three months will be the darkest and most deadly. However, there is a light at the end of the tunnel. Both Pfizer and Moderna have announced their successful vaccines and filed for approval. As more details are known, I hope to bring them to you.

In the meantime, be especially careful, be sure to wear a mask, wash your hands, and contemplate decisions about where you go.

Stay healthy and we will get to the end of this tunnel.

Returning to Georgia, the runoff for the Senate seats is January 5th. All eyes are on Georgia, because the outcome will be important for the future of the Biden presidency and our country.

Our American Tragedy/split screen

December 4, 2020

We are in the middle of a tragic situation that is about to go off a cliff. As of this date, 276,874 people have died of the coronavirus, and the number continues to spike. Yesterday, 2802 citizens died, the highest ever, and the same amount that died on 9/11. Months ago, Dr. Fauci warned America that December, January and February would be the dark days of winter, and we are approaching the peak, but we are not there yet.

Worse still, thousands of skilled healthcare workers have already died. It is nearly impossible to replace them. The remaining skilled workers are exhausted for many reasons. In Covid cases, it takes 4 or 5 nurses and doctors to operate the many machines that are hooked up to each patient, and also for "proning." We have ventilators, but we don't have enough skilled people to operate them. Things are worse in the rural areas, where the hospitals don't have enough masks and PPE gowns that need to be changed after each patient. Moreover, because families are not allowed to see their loved ones, nurses or doctors are the only people able to hold a dying patient's hand in her last moments. Often, two or three people die like that and the nurse or doctor is physically and emotionally drained. The news programs have been able to interview some of these brave healthcare workers, and it is gut-wrenching to hear what they have to say, through their tears. One nurse said that 23 people died on one day when she was holding their hands. The healthcare workers are not only physically exhausted, they are emotionally drained and they need help.

This is the tragedy of America. Our healthcare system, once the envy of the world, has been stretched to its limit and is about to snap. We don't even have enough ambulances, because hospitals in forty-eight of fifty states (except for Maine and Hawaii), are full, ICUs are full, and often people have to be taken elsewhere. Ambulance drivers are exhausted. Refrigerator trucks have been brought in, because morgues don't have enough space to receive bodies when someone dies. Funeral homes are in similar circumstances, and in many cases only a few people can come to a cemetery service because of Covid restrictions.

That is SCREEN #1. It scares me and it breaks my heart.

SCREEN #2 is the American President-Donald Trump, who, when informed of the deadly virus, decided to do nothing about it. He and Jared Kushner decided that the virus was in the "blue states," and they were not going to help the people in states that had not voted for Trump. Donald Trump has never mentioned anything about the citizens who have died. He refuses to wear a mask, and has told everyone that the virus is a "hoax." As a result of politicizing a deadly virus, hundreds of thousands of people have died, and there will be more.

Donald Trump lost the election for the presidency, based on the fact that he refused to do anything to fight the virus. Since he lost, he is in a deep funk, and has spent time trying to overturn the outcome, committing crimes as he tried to influence electors.

The virus has ruined our economy. Millions of people lost their jobs and their businesses. No one has used the word, but I think that we are in a Depression. Trump has little on his schedule, despite the raging pandemic. Instead, he has a few mediocre lawyers filing lawsuits-37 in all- that have been thrown out, because there is no evidence that the election was "rigged" or flawed, or that fraud existed. Trump keeps spreading that message, and some people actually believe it, or are starting to doubt the efficacy of our election. Some election administrators, Republicans, have been threatened with violence when they reported a Biden victory. That violates the very core of our election system, which has always been the gold standard of the United States democracy.

Unlike all the other presidential years, Trump refuses to concede. He is a very sore loser, and has also indicated that he will not be welcoming the incoming President and First Lady to the White House, as every other president has done. That is very disappointing, and it violates the tradition of transfer of power. In fact, Trump has indicated that he might have a rally on Inauguration Day, and will declare his candidacy for 2024. Very vindictive.

Donald Trump has done many things to make Joe Biden's life difficult. As our citizens are suffering and dying, the Trumps have planned twenty holiday parties for the next three weeks- in the White House- for hundreds of people. The contrast is stark, isn't it? For Trump, there is no sense that the country is grieving. He has no time to devote to fighting the virus, and will not mention it. Many states have had to institute more restrictions.

The split screen? Hundreds of people will be gathering at festive parties while others will be fighting for their lives.

I am frightened for my country, and angry that one man could have done so much damage with selfish and cowardly enablers. The next six weeks will be essential, and we will have a new President who is willing to fight this war, because it is a war. President Biden cannot get here fast enough.

Split screen/The Vote/The Virus

December 8, 2020

Today is "Safe Harbor Day.". You've never heard of it? That's not surprising. It is the deadline when Congress, since 1887, has to recognize the certified votes of each state. It is an insurance policy that states have to lock in their numbers, then send them to Congress to be locked in before the Electoral College meets. The election is over, but Donald Trump has continued to spread his lies that he won and the election was "rigged" and "stolen" from him. In a rally Saturday night, he told thousands of supporters "you are victims."

Trump has learned that if you say something often enough and loud enough, even if it is a total lie, people begin to question and ultimately to believe it. Repetition is the key, and Trump is a master, especially since he is President of the United States and has a huge bully pulpit.

A "safe harbor" is crucial, because there has been serious pressure on the swing states-Pennsylvania, Georgia, Florida, Michigan- to literally overturn the votes for President-Elect Joe Biden, making Donald Trump president again. Interfering in an election and changing the vote is a federal offense, punishable with jail time. It is also a state offense, because the Constitution provides for the individual states to run our elections.

Donald Trump is out of time. Thirty-seven plus lawsuits have been thrown out for" lack of evidence" by many judges who were scathing in their opinions of the sloppy lawsuits. One judge said, "elections are decided by voters, not lawyers."

Our peaceful democracy is in danger, as we veer towards fascism under Donald Trump. Here are a few examples:

The state election administrators have come under fire publicly for certifying the vote, and their personal safety has been threatened. This is the behavior of people living in a fascist state. Trump is the closest thing to an authoritarian dictator, a mob boss if you will, encouraging violence on his behalf.

In Michigan, scores of armed Trump supporters arrived at the home of the Michigan Secretary of State Jocelyn Benson, who was watching a Christmas movie with her son. The Trump supporters chanted about the "stolen" vote.

In Pennsylvania, Donald Trump called the Pennsylvania Speaker of the House Bryan Cutler, and asked him to "fix" what he said were "issues" in Pennsylvania. That request is another criminal offense, despite the fact that the votes had already been certified.

In Georgia, Brad Raffensberger, the Republican Secretary of State, announced that the third count, ordered and paid for by Trump, yielded another Biden win. Raffensberger said that disinformation was damaging, and that "truth matters." As I mentioned, Gabe Sterling, an election official, angrily spoke about the tactics being used for Georgia to change its vote. "This has to stop." Sterling indicated that "someone might get killed.."

The nightmare of Trump exerting pressure on officials has gone on since he lost the election and refused to concede. Many of the state administrators have been heroes, profiles in courage, and many are Republicans. Country over party, state over party. Integrity, truth, personal responsibility matter to these officials who spoke up defending the sacredness of our elections, despite the cost.

Democracy is not a spectator sport.

Now for the SPLIT SCREEN-VACCINE

On the good news front, both Pfizer and Moderna have developed vaccines which have an unusually high rate of protection (in the 90s). They have each applied for fast track acceptance from the FDA.

Donald Trump, who wants to take credit for these vaccines, even though he did nothing to prevent the virus, has called a VACCINE SUMMIT, celebrating "Warp Speed," the name given to the government sponsored program. Although invited, neither Pfizer nor Moderna will be attending. There is a potential conflict of interest with one of the other attendees, the FDA official who will be deciding on the fast-track applications. Both companies came under intense pressure from the White House to deliver a vaccine before the election, thus politicizing the vaccines, and creating doubt in their efficacy. Unfortunately, the result of that pressure is that many people will refuse to take the vaccines that are effective. Many citizens were aware that Trump was seeking to rush the science for his own reelection. Despite extreme pressure, Pfizer did not accept any government money for the development of its vaccine. However, Pfizer did arrange to make 100 million doses (two doses per person) available for purchase by the United States.

Yesterday, the *New York Times* broke the story that Pfizer offered more vaccine units to the administration, and the administration passed on it. Apparently, the government had invested in Moderna and other vaccine companies that accepted government money. Once rebuffed, Pfizer then turned to the European Union and it quickly ordered the units. The result? The EU has twice the Pfizer vaccine than the U.S. does. This is more incredibly stupid decision on the part of the Trump administration. Pfizer says it will not have more vaccines available for purchase until the summer. Donald Trump signed an Executive Order prioritizing America to receive the vaccine over other countries. It's probably impossible to tell the independent companies what they will do regarding their vaccines, so this is all nonsense. White House officials deny the offer and the opportunity from Pfizer. Clearly, the administration was hedging its bets.

As with the rest of the transition, there was a serious delay in the Trump administration getting information about the "vaccine plan" to the Biden team. What finally arrived is very complicated and expensive, with equipment having to be moved to about 50,000 sites around the county. My informal guess is that the plan will be replaced by the Biden team. It may have been thrown together at the last moment, once Biden won the election. Remember that Donald Trump kept saying that a healthcare plan to replace Obamacare would be coming "in a few weeks" over a period of four years. The "plan" was never produced.

The split screen involves the Biden administration introducing its health team, and it is filled with capable and experienced people. An unusual choice to head HHS is Javier Becerra, a former member of Congress and Attorney General of California. We will be hearing more about each member of the health team as Biden introduces them today.

On television this morning I saw a feed from Cardiff, Wales, as the first person in the EU was administered the Pfizer vaccine. The woman was 90 years old, and delighted to be receiving this protection.

In his program to exclude Joe Biden, Donald Trump has not invited the incoming administration, although the new leaders will be responsible for developing the program that will vaccinate 300 million citizens. I'm sure that the split screen of CNN will shed considerable light in the two different administrations-one calm and moving forward, the other in chaos and disorganized.

America is hungry, sick, and on the edge of falling off a financial cliff, but help is on the way ...

December 11, 2020

Things are crazy in our country.

Yesterday, the daily toll of deaths in America topped 3,000. The total deaths are 293, 360. The numbers surpass heart disease and cancer. 107,000 are in hospitals, which are overcrowded to the maximum they can hold. People are sick, and need life-saving care. Saving people in the ICU requires human resources to operate the machines. This is Donald Trump's virus. He is responsible for all the misinformation he spewed to the American people. He was more interested in his political future than keeping Americans safe. On some level that makes him a traitor. If he betrays his own government, does that constitute treason?

The deaths in the United States have surpassed the people who died in Pearl Harbor (2403) September 11 (2977), WW2 (291,557), the Civil War (214, 938), and all other wars.

More shocking, 106 House Republicans back a Texas lawsuit to overturn our election results. Without 'standing,' the case was sent to the Supreme Court. Elections are state run. Unless there is some "harm" done by one state to another, this lawsuit is without merit. Joe Biden won the election by 7 million votes, and 306 to 232 in the Electoral College. Each state has just certified its numbers and Biden's victory was decisive. There was no evidence of fraud, and there are no irregularities that need investigation. Nonetheless, under the pressure from Donald Trump and his insistence that he won the election, many people are on his bandwagon. There is a definite split in opinion, because of where people get their news. We have never had this happen in America, and it endangers our democracy and the tradition of "peaceful transfer of power."

Jobless claims rose 853,000 yesterday, the highest level since September, but lower than in April, when it was 7 million. Mitch McConnell has just signaled that there will be no relief bill, which is devastating. There is no agreement in the Republican led Senate about two important issues. One issue is state and local funding, which the democrats support, because the states had to spend so much money during the coronavirus. If they don't get the help, the states will be in debt. Unlike the federal government, states have to balance their budgets. Firefighters, teachers and other workers need to be paid, and if state and local towns don't get help from the federal government, they will have to fire very essential workers.

The "Profiles in Courage" of John F. Kennedy, would be a small pamphlet these days. Senator Mitt Romney issued a statement. "It's just simply madness … The idea of supplanting the vote of the people with partisan legislators is so completely out of our national character that it's simply mad." The four states named in the suit have indicated they are standing up for democracy. Some of the other administrators of elections stood up for their work, but heroes are in short supply.

The craziness extends to the fact that Ken Paxton, who leads the suit, is under indictment for various crimes. This morning the FBI knocked on his door with a subpoena. It seems that Paxton has put himself in the limelight in a bid for one of Trump's pardons, party favors as he exits the White House. On a more humorous side, whoever wrote the brief spelled Louisiana wrong and had the wrong number of electors. The last case that was sent to SCOTUS was denied in one brief sentence. The same thing may happen in this instance; the court has no patience for frivolous lawsuits, and it may send that message as well.

There is more. Unemployment benefits expire the day before Christmas. People don't know if they can buy gifts for their children, or anything. Sadly, individuals have been caught stealing food, and when asked, they said they were hungry. Congress has shown no desire to help any of these tragic and serious situations.

While our hospitals and ICUs are overrun with just under 3,000 Americans dying yesterday, Donald Trump spent his time trying to overturn Joe Biden's win for President. The number dead to date is 290,616, and not one word from Donald Trump. We have the highest number of deaths and the highest number of infections in the world. While more people are dying, Donald Trump has not mentioned it once. He was only worried about getting re-elected, and overturning Joe Biden's win. Trump's lack of empathy, and his lack of accepting personal responsibility for this disaster, is stunning. Meanwhile, he is giving 20 parties at the White House this week and next for the holidays and on our nickel.

That said, there is VERY GOOD NEWS on the vaccines. Yesterday, the FDA approved emergency use of the Pfizer vaccine, and the system is in place to start getting it to all parts of the country. The main distribution centers are in Michigan and Wisconsin. FedEx is delivering to the western part of the country, and UPS to the east. It is a monumental job to distribute, train and also educate people about the safety of this vaccine.

Moreover, the United States is #32 in available vaccines, and we will not have enough vaccines for all Americans. The Trump administration passed on an offer from Pfizer to get millions more doses, when the company saw that its vaccine was going to be successful. Pfizer will not have more doses available until the summer. Moderna is second, right behind Pfizer for emergency use, and hopes to be passed by the FDA in a week.

Meanwhile, Richard Engel lives in the UK, and he showed us pictures of men and women in their eighties and nineties happily receiving the Pfizer vaccine, and encouraging others to follow suit. The first woman, age 90, was wearing a colorful Christmas shirt, and enjoyed a "cuppa tea" with those who administered the "jab." It was a marvelously optimistic sight for all to see.

One caveat-Two healthcare workers who received the vaccine had allergic reactions. They each have a history of allergies, carry epi-pens, and were treated successfully immediately. As a result, a warning to all people who have serious allergies to either food or drugs, was issued immediately.

The news of this week has been too much to process. Most important is to stay safe and make good decisions. The main directive is- NO TRAVELING. I know that is hard, but we need to take the long view in order to see everyone next year. If we all wear our masks we can save thousands of lives in the next few months.

While our numbers are soaring, and people are suffering, Congress has not yet passed any relief bills. More than ten programs are due to expire right now. Those programs include rent and eviction relief, small business relief, unemployment relief, and so much more. The fact that people could become homeless is especially worrisome, because the next three are the worst months for the dangerous virus. The virus, politics and the economy are tragic intersections. In addition, millions of Americans are waiting in line to get food. There is monumental food insecurity in this country, and millions of children are hungry, in addition to adults.

Unfortunately, we have to wait until January 20th for the new administration to take the reins of government. Until then, thousands will die, unless we institute safe precautions-masks, safe distancing, washing hands and not gathering.

Despite this chaos, the Biden-Harris ticket has moved ahead, appointing marvelous teams of experts to handle each of these overwhelming problems. TIME magazine came out this morning, and Joe Biden and Kamala Harris are on the cover, having been chosen PEOPLE OF THE YEAR. I am eager to get my copy.

Once again, the news of this week has been too much to process. Most important is to stay safe and make good decisions. The main directive is- NO TRAVELING. I know that is hard, but we need to take the long view in order to see everyone next year.

HAPPY HANUKKAH to all who celebrate! We can use some light in the darkness of winter.

December 13, 2020

American Exceptionalism!

December 12, 2020

Pfizer did it! Yesterday, after an intense public hearing, the FDA passed the Pfizer vaccine on an emergency basis. Now the CDC, led by Dr. Robert Redfield, has to give the final OK. The data is really amazing. According to all tests, the vaccine has a 95% protection rate. The flu vaccine that we all take each year only has 65% protection.

I watched as MSNBC broadcast all weekend from the Houston Medical Center, the largest and one of the most prestigious in the world. Needless to say, the mood was one of elation. Many doctors were interviewed, and they were both relieved and happy about the extraordinary achievement-the possibility that millions of citizens can now be vaccinated and protected. While watching, I was very proud and emotional that it was American scientists who brought the vaccine to fruition, although neither CEO was born in this country. The doctors' relief was clear, since science has been mocked by none other than the American president for months, putting a huge burden on our science community. The extraordinary success of vaccines in a short space of time is historic. It has been a rough situation for science and also for journalists in this country, who were insulted on a daily basis.

Being able to deliver millions of doses of vaccine is a logistical challenge. The process of delivery is something that has never been done in the history of our country, and maybe anywhere. The Pfizer vaccine can only survive for five days in 90 degrees below zero temperature. In order to get it to rural US, dry ice companies are scrambling to have enough dry ice to put into containers in order to send it. This is also true for the over 600 locations throughout the country that will be receiving deliveries on Tuesday. The country has been divided in half-FEDEX will be delivering to the western half of America, and UPS will be taking the precious cargo to the eastern half. The FAA has also been put on notice to be prepared to fly some of the vaccine to specific locations.

Shipments are beginning this weekend, and there are many moving parts, overseen by the Army and Warp Speed. Very sensitive technology is programmed to follow the vaccine during every inch of its travel and arrival. Using GPS tracking, with military escorts, the monitors will know exactly where each shipment is at every minute of the trip. More precise, the team will know the temperature in each of the huge refrigerator boxes, bought in advance, so that the Pfizer vaccine could be sent immediately in dry ice and delivered to storage units. Planning has been in the works for months.

Pfizer's largest facility is in Kalamazoo, Michigan, centrally located so there can be a major movement in both directions. While developing the vaccine is a huge scientific moment, the delivery challenge is equally monumental. One of the delivery centers is in Chicago, and the crews have been practicing for months so that getting it to citizens is effective and seamless. The level of planning reminded me of Normandy invasion stories.

The CEO of Pfizer gave a statement yesterday. Albert Bourla was born in Thessaloniki, Greece of Jewish parents. He has a fascinating biography, earning his doctorate in the biotechnology of reproduction at Aristotle University of Thessolaniki Veterinary School. Considering his background, the partnership with BioNTech in Europe is no surprise. Pfizer is the only company that refused government money, and therefore remained free of government control. There were reports that CEO Bourla was very offended by extreme pressure from the White House, and it seems he made a good choice. Donald Trump's government invested in eight other companies, hedging its bets, but it was Pfizer that was successful first. There were also reports that Bourla was less than impressed by the president in the first debate. It is noteworthy that Bourla released Pfizer's positive numbers after the election. In addition, there was an offer of millions more Pfizer doses last summer, on which the administration passed. Pfizer then offered the vaccine outside the U.S. The EU bought millions of doses, and began vaccinating its citizens before the United States. Needless to say, when citizens found out that the vaccine was made available and it wasn't accepted, citizens were furious.

Who will be receiving the vaccine? There are approximately 20 million healthcare workers in the country, and they will be first, followed by the elderly in nursing homes. As for the rest, I am not aware of a hard and fast plan, since the vaccine is being sent to so many locations-hospitals, etc., and states that will devise a system based on need. The vaccine needs to be given in two doses, about three weeks apart, so people need to come back for the second jab. In the UK, it became clear that people with serious allergies should not take this particular protocol. There is a good alternative. Moderna is the only other company that has passed the trials, and a public hearing is scheduled for next week. With the prospect of a vaccine, thoughts are turning to businesses reopening, but we need to be extremely careful. All the guidance-masks, etc., needs to be followed until millions of citizens are vaccinated. We can't let down our guard.

Oh yes, there was another monumental news event. On Friday night, in a brief statement, the Supreme Court denied the Texas lawsuit on which Donald Trump was relying to make him president.

Food

December 16, 2020

Monday was actually a triple screen- vaccine joy and relief, Electoral College final count, and the millions of Americans who are in dire need of food.

America is hungry. In every state the line of cars to get food stretches for miles, and it is stunning.

I spent yesterday morning watching the vaccine arrive at University Hospital in Newark, NJ, which was often the epicenter of tragic loss in the early days of the pandemic. New Jersey and New York lost thousands of people, many of them black and brown, and their families are suffering, homeless and hungry.

Until recently, Newark was a food desert. There was no ability to get fresh fruit, green vegetables or any kind of grocery. Now there is a Whole Foods, which is special, but many people don't have the money to shop there, especially this last year. The need for food doubled when the pandemic forced people to lose their jobs.

The situation in the country has also affected the middle class. **Forty per cent** of the cars in those lines are there **for the first time.** They are embarrassed and desperate. Many of the stories are gut-wrenching. One woman who talked about her family and food, said that she puts her children to bed early, so they don't realize there will be no dinner.

The stories are hard to hear.

Many stories are of desperate people stealing food. Upon being caught, their only explanation is, "I was hungry." This is not the way life should be in the wealthiest country on earth.

However, we do have a history of being the most generous country, because citizens of all means step up to the plate (pardon the pun), and donate, thousands of individuals and companies have worked to fill the breach.

Broadcasting from Houston, many companies are delivering thousands of pounds of food. TARGET delivered 800,000 meals and planned to increase to one million.

In Connecticut, Pepsi has been delivering 70,000 pounds of food daily.

MEND, a wonderful consortium of nineteen food banks in New Jersey, has helped thousands of people. Our own Interfaith Food Pantry, a member of MEND, has been working tirelessly in the last months.

Food Banks everywhere are stretched to the limit. What I have described here is the outline of a major problem in our country that needs to be addressed, hopefully by the incoming administration.

If you are able, please consider donating to the local food bank in your town. Neighbors helping neighbors is so important. There are also large organizations that do wonderful work, such as MAZON.

The best Hanukkah gift I received this year was from a close friend of many years who lives in California. She sent a donation to MAZON (food in Hebrew) A Jewish Response to Hunger. The gift announcement came with a beautiful card and message, indicating the gift was in my honor. There is no better gift than love.

No matter what religion we are, this is the moment to reach into our hearts and our pockets, and help those who are struggling. That will allow neighbors to feed their families at the holidays and beyond.

Warmest hopes that each of you is staying safe and keeping healthy.

December 19, 2020

Defending Democracy in a Dangerous time

December 12, 2020

I waited to write about last Friday, because what happened was scary and dangerous to our democracy. To wit: 126 Republican members of the House joined the partisan lawsuit brought by the Texas Attorney General, Ken Paxton, asking the Supreme Court to throw out the presidential electors for Pennsylvania, Georgia, Michigan and Wisconsin, all of which Joe Biden won. In addition, seventeen Republican state Attorneys General signed onto the suit. Nothing like this has ever happened before. Strangely, the brief that the House Republicans filed, indicated that the general election-the one in which most of them had been re-elected, was "riddled with an unprecedented number of serious allegations of fraud and irregularities."

Not only is President Trump refusing to concede, which is a historic first for our country that values the peaceful transfer of power, but he is insisting that he won the election. He continues to spread the message that the election was "riddled with fraud," and "stolen." In his quest, Trump brought 60 cases to various courts to have the election results overturned. Fifty-nine of them have been thrown out, many by Republican judges, because there is "no evidence" of fraud.

Trump was banking on the Supreme Court to rule in his favor, especially since three justices were appointed by him, and now the conservative majority is 6/3. However, the Supreme Court refused to hear the case. Justices Alito and Thomas said they would have allowed the case to be heard, but they would have voted against it. So, basically it was a 9 to nothing decision. That decision was a stunning defeat for Trump, who also joined the lawsuit. Apparently, he was shocked. There was a big party Friday night at the White House, and he referenced the case earlier in the day, but after the decision was handed down, he never attended the party.

It's clear that Donald Trump has never read the Constitution. He has no idea about the separate roles of the three branches of government, checks and balances and the double tier of federal and state courts. A state can sue another state, but only under very special circumstances. A state cannot sue four other states with the goal of overturning its legitimate election results, and not only the ones that were in favor of his opponent. It was laughable in many ways, but it seems that no one has ever said "no" to Donald Trump before now.

Trump continues to break all norms. He is spreading the message that he actually won the election, that it was stolen from him. There is no credible evidence to back up his ridiculous claims. Unfortunately, many of his followers believe him, and that is a danger to our democracy, to the rule of law, and the peaceful transfer of power. Rather than the losing candidate conceding graciously and asking the country to unite behind the winner, Donald Trump has done the exact opposite. Within the Republican Party, there is a faction that is very dangerous. Remember that each of the Attorneys General and the members of Congress took oaths of office to uphold the Constitution, so we are looking at an insurrection, and possibly the makings of a civil war.

Looking back in history, when the southern democrats were unhappy that Republican Abraham Lincoln won the presidency in the election of 1860, the southern states seceded from the Union. They knew that Lincoln was against slavery, and they were about to lose the control they had as the wealthy, white, elite class of planters.

Ironically, the situation is somewhat similar today. Within the Republican Party there are two visions of democracy and freedom. Among the Trump followers there is antipathy towards government and democracy as we know it. The rebellious faction in the Republican Party would like to overthrow the winners of a legitimate election, and set up their own government. In the country, Trump plays to his base, never more than about 30%, and a number of them consider violence an option. Disturbingly, more than half of the House Republican delegation was in favor of stealing the election for Trump. These virulent factions have put the country in a hot mess. Because citizens are used to listening to the president, 77% of Republicans believe that the election was stolen, and that President-elect Biden is not legitimate. This will have serious consequences when the new administration takes office on January 20th, 2021, and asks citizens to join together in unity to defeat the virus.

Wondering at the motives, it seems that each person had a particular reason for joining the lawsuit. Ken Paxton is in legal trouble and has been indicted. His leadership of the lawsuit put him square into Donald Trump's orbit, and made him a candidate for one of Trump's pardons. Many others were afraid that Trump was watching, since it was clear that he was taking names to see who did and who didn't join the lawsuit. There was a lot of presidential pressure put on all of these men, and it was reported on the news and in the newspapers for many days. Many people were afraid of Trump's tweets, of being "primaried" and losing in the next election.

Meanwhile, the coronavirus numbers keep rising, and the situation is bittersweet. The Pfizer vaccine is set and ready to go on Monday morning, the 14th.

Politically, the Electoral College meets on Monday as well. There will be a lot happening in the upcoming week.

Hanukkah began on Thursday, the 10th, for eight days. It's certainly a fun distraction for children and adults alike. Enjoy a break from the routine!

December 20, 2020

Democracy at Risk /Vaccine Rollout

Week of December 14th to 20th

On December 14th the Electoral College was due to meet. Most of the time, Americans pay little attention to the Electoral College. We take it for granted that once the votes are counted and then certified, the Electoral College is a pro- forma event. As with everything else in 2020 and the age of Trump, nothing is normal.

The threat of violence has entered our election process for the first time. The state Capitol of Michigan and then Wisconsin had to be closed to the public out of safety concerns before the Electoral College delegates met. Trump loyalists came out with flags and guns (in open carry states), making what once was a benign civic duty into a frightening job that could be dangerous. We saw this earlier in many of the battleground states, when the poll workers had to be escorted to their cars, because Trump supporters had surrounded the building. In addition to Michigan and Wisconsin, the Arizona electors had to meet in an undisclosed location. Georgia had equally serious problems when an election worker was threatened with a noose, and Trump tweeted insults to the Georgia Republicans in charge of the election, and indicated they should be in jail. Georgia was forced to count its vote three times, and found legitimate numbers each time. There was no fraud, and no "stolen election." Due to threats of violence against them the Georgia Republicans in charge of elections now have security at their homes. In truth, Donald Trump has been motivating his followers to do anything possible to take back the election, which he claims he "won." This is a nightmare that I never thought would happen in America, and it continues every day. In the midst of people dying of a virus, Donald Trump has put the entire country on edge and created anxiety that no one needed, because he can't accept the results of the election.

Trump's repeated claims have actually made a difference in the beliefs and perceptions of his followers, and therein lies the danger. Despite the overwhelming victory of Joe Biden and Kamala Harris by seven million votes, 82% of Trump voters think that the Biden win is illegitimate. On one level this is astounding, but remember that everyone gets his news from different places. Trump voters listen to Fox News, which is filled with lies and disinformation. Unlike any other American voter in years past, Trump's voters think that he should not concede and do everything possible to stay in power. That point of view is totally against all of our American norms and understanding of the rule of law. In the past, we operated on trust. With this particular group of people, trust is out the window and violence is one way to attain their goal.

Meanwhile, Donald Trump is literally having a childish tantrum, unseemly and blatantly foolish, as the sixty lawsuits get thrown out by judges citing "no evidence of fraud." What is so astounding is the Republican tolerance of his behavior. Clearly, no one has come into the Oval Office and said that the vote was legal, as described by Chris Krebs, head of the Cyber Security Agency. No one in the Oval office has said that Trump was making a fool of himself in the eyes of the world, in addition to our country.

On the contrary, Trump continued on a daily basis, tweeting and talking and repeating his phony claims. I would not believe this if I didn't see it with my own eyes, but these lies raised upwards of 200 million dollars, supposedly for his legal battles, which were essentially over. He started discussing running for president in 2024, and threatening to disrupt the Inauguration by not leaving the White House on January 20th, where at 12:01, he will become a trespasser. Will the Secret Service have to remove him from the premises? That remains to be seen.

As the Electoral college drew to a close, President-elect Biden delivered an address to the nation. However, Donald Trump interrupted the news cycle by announcing that Attorney General William Barr was stepping down on December 23rd. It's not known whether he resigned or was pushed, but it does seem relatively peaceful. Barr wrote a letter praising Donald Trump to the skies, and he has certainly carried water for the president in some very questionable roles.

Barr actually politicized the Justice Department, first describing the report by Special Counsel Mueller as resulting in no finding of fault in the Russia investigation. He beat Robert Mueller to the punch, by characterizing it in that way. In fact, the report shows blatant abuses of power in connection with Russia. However, Mueller was going on the assumption that a sitting president cannot be indicted. That concept is not law; it goes back to the Nixon-Agnew administration which is detailed in Rachael Maddow's new book, *Bag Man*.

The politicizing of the Department of Justice is one of the most dangerous outcomes of the Trump administration. Many good people were fired, and other talented lawyers left in protest. Donald Trump had no business inserting himself to the running of Justice, and telling Barr who to investigate. Trump, having no idea how government is supposed to work, thinks that these agencies are his and he can tell them what to do. This is the danger of electing an ignorant moron who doesn't read. He does not comprehend that separation of powers is for good reason, and the Executive is just one branch.

After all this nonsense, one Congressman had enough. Paul Mitchell, Representative of Michigan, who was retiring, called out "political candidates," who "treat our election system as though we are a third-world country and incite distrust of something so basic as the sanctity of our vote." He resigned from the Republican Party, and announced that he would be an Independent.

Despite all of the chaotic noise and anxiety that Trump created, the Electoral College confirmed the votes as specified. That evening, President-elect Biden gave a strong speech, criticizing Donald Trump for the first time. Biden called for the nation to come together and heal, to unite in order to keep one another safe, and defeat the virus that has been killing thousands of us daily.

Monday morning, in the undercurrent of these challenges to our democracy, the exceptionalism of Pfizer-BioNTech Covid-19 vaccine was on display. We were treated to the first vaccine being given by Dr. Michelle Chester to Sandra Lindsay, a Covid-19 nurse at Long Island Jewish Medical Center. It was very emotional for everyone. Both women are African-American, and Ms. Lindsay spoke about how important it is for everyone to accept the vaccine. She said, "I have seen the alternative, and do not want it for you." The pandemic has hit Americans of color disproportionately hard, so it seemed appropriate that the vaccine was administered by a black doctor to a black nurse.

There is a bittersweet irony in the fact of 300,000 official deaths from Covid-10 and 16 million infections, while we see millions of doses being given to Americans. If the government had acted in February to fight the virus, activate the Defense Production Act and model proper behavior, many thousands of citizens would not have died. It is a terribly sad fact of a massive failure of leadership, malfeasance and malpractice.

There is also an issue with the distribution of the vaccine. The federal government invested in eight of the nine companies that were working on the development of the vaccines.

The problem should not surprise you. The federal government invested in the development of the vaccine, but it only provided funding to get the vaccine to the states. Getting millions of doses from the central point into peoples' arms is unfunded and unplanned. The CDC and the Department of Health and Human Services used some of their budgets to help the states plan, but there is at this time no money for states to distribute the vaccine. This is exacerbated by the financial crisis caused by the pandemic. As with all the other efforts to make life difficult for the incoming Biden administration, federal funding of vaccine delivery is set to end about February 1st, just in time for it to fall into Joe Biden's lap.

It's Monday the 14th and Congress has not passed the coronavirus relief package. With Christmas coming, this is terribly insensitive to the families who are desperate and may become homeless. There are no words to describe the lack of empathy of Mitch McConnell, since the House bill has been sitting on his desk since last May. The election has given the Republicans more leverage and less desire to come to the table. The amount has been reduced considerably to $749 billion. State and local help has been taken off the table, as has a liability protection for businesses who workers contract the Covid. The deadline is this Friday.

Politics, the vaccine and the relief bill all came together today to create a very busy news day, clearly overwhelming.

And it's only Monday.

December 22, 2020

State of Anxiety

Week of December 14 to 21st (continued)

Trump's attempted coup is failing, but it will have serious consequences. His antidemocratic stunts set a dangerous precedent. These maneuvers are becoming more outrageous, edging on insanity. Trump refuses to acknowledge that he lost the election.

Peter Wehner, conservative writer for *The Atlantic*, wrote, "This is where Trump's crippling psychological condition-has complete inability to face unpleasant facts, his toxic narcissism, and his utter lack of empathy-became lethal." Wehner served in three Republican administrations, often as a speech writer.

With the virus raging, the relief bill unsigned, and people desperate for food, Trump ignores all of that and continues to try and overturn the election. Trump's behavior is causing escalating anxiety in the country. On a very important level, his lack of involvement shows that he is unconcerned about what happens to Americans, only to himself. With his constant threats, angry tweets, and crazy conspiracy theories, Trump continues to create nervousness in the country every day.

One important story that became public this week is the extent to which the Trump administration inserted itself into the CDC and the Department of Health and Human Services. Science was politicized, and politics overrode the work of the career officials at the Center for Disease Control. Representative James Clyburn(D-SC), came in possession of revealing documents that showed the degree to which the political appointees advocated for "herd immunity," a dangerous strategy whereby the virus was deliberately allowed to spread. Herd immunity was diametrically opposed to the science and the concept of fighting the virus intelligently. Clyburn presented these papers to his Congress committee, and ultimately to the public, and the substance was shocking.

Paul Alexander was one of the political appointees put into HHS by Trump. There were emails back and forth, indicating that Alexander attacked Dr. Fauci for trying to protect Americans. Alexander also advocated spreading the infection to younger Americans, "So the bottom line is if it is more infectedness now the issue is who cares? If it is causing more cases in the young, my word is who cares?"

Frighteningly, Alexander wrote to another political appointee, "Infants, kids, teens, young people, young adults, middle-aged with no conditions, etc., have zero to little risk … so we use them to develop herd … and we want them infected."

Of course, we know this is dangerous talk, totally false, but it indicates the kind of thinking that was influencing our most important science organizations, known the world over for its excellence.

The CDC and HHS were infiltrated by Trump and his appointees, and they changed the strategy of science, to the detriment of the citizens of America.

The concept that young people are safe from getting the virus was wrong. The idea that kids should get infected, was clearly the reason Trump wanted schools and colleges to open. Administrators were watching the statistics and knew that they would have to be flexible as things unfolded. Similarly, teachers, school administrators and parents were watching the virus and the dangers, and changed their minds a number of times, keeping the health of the children as their foremost concern.

Other former members of the CDC spoke out as they watched science being ignored for political purposes. CDC guidelines changed and budgets were cut. Politics essentially took over the CDC, the most admired agency worldwide.

To prove the point, *Politifact*, the Pulitzer Prize winning fact-checking group from the Poynter Institute, named the downplaying, and even the denial of the seriousness of the coronavirus as the "Lie of the Year."

As if that wasn't enough, last Friday Reuters announced that there was a massive computer hack of the United States. It's the largest and worst in our history, and Russia seems to be the culprit. The hackers gained access to government computers and major US companies. It reaches into Treasury, State, DHS, Commerce and parts of the Pentagon, in addition to other targets. The hack was discovered when the cybersecurity company, FireEye, realized that it had been hacked and immediately alerted the FBI.

It seems that the campaign began last March, and was undetected for months. The United States has been hit hard. The hackers placed malware on commercial network management software upgrades, essentially coming in through the side door. The Russians are particularly good at this kind of hacking. The FBI, CISA and the Office of the Director of National Intelligence issued a joint statement indicating they are investigating the extent of the damage, and it will take months.

While all this was happening, Joe Biden has been organizing the new administration and introducing his nominees to the country, department by department. Happily, they are experts in their fields, dedicated civil servants many of whom know one another from long years of service. That expertise will be a welcome relief. We will not be having "government by tweet," President-elect Biden assured the country, and he will be respectful of the three branches of government and their Constitutional boundaries.

There was no statement from Donald Trump concerning the massive hack, and the conclusion that it was Russia behind the incursion. In fact, Trump has not rebuked Russia in the four years of his presidency, giving Vladimir Putin a free rein to do whatever he wants.

The *New York Times* called the hack "among the greatest intelligence failures of modern times." Senator Blumenthal (D-CT) was very upset that the extent of the damage was not made public to the American citizens. Congress only had a classified meeting. Similarly, in February, Senator Blumenthal recognized the danger of the coronavirus, as Joe Biden had in January. The public was not informed. Donald Trump wanted to keep the virus as unimportant as possible, because it interfered with his re-election plans. Senator Blumenthal tweeted that he was astonished at the lack of preparedness and prevention plans of the United States government.

As of midweek, the relief bill had not been passed. The deadline was Friday, but it was dubious that an agreement would be reached. On the other hand, it was impossible to imagine that Congress would have the nerve to leave on vacation without giving some help to suffering citizens, although it was long delayed. Senate Majority leader McConnell is now becoming nervous because two Georgia Senate seats are up for election on January 5th. If the Democrats win them, then the Senate will be 50/50 and the new Vice President, Kamala Harris, could break the tie. Needless to say, these two seats are crucial, and could be a game-changer. Presently, Kelly Loeffler and David Perdue, Republicans, hold the seats. They are running against Raphael Warnock, an African-American pastor, and Jon Ossoff, Jewish and 33 years old. If elected, he will be the youngest member of the Senate. Excitement for this election is high, donations are huge, and speculation is that it will be a very close election.

As bad as all this seems, some attitudes are changing. Former Governor Chris Christie, Republican, went to a super spreader, caught the virus and was quite sick for days in a hospital. Since he was released, Christie has come out strongly for wearing a mask and following the guidelines. He made a video describing to people how important wearing a mask is, and how horrible it is to catch the virus. His experience and the realization of the consequences, has put Christie on a different path, and that is to be admired.

In addition, many people are leaving the Republican Party, especially since they see Donald Trump and the craziness that he has been promulgating. Every day is another nutty comment or action. Meanwhile, Trump is basically hiding in the White House, concerned only with losing the election.

To be continued. As we work our way through "the week that was," anxiety has been rising in each of us on a daily basis.

The President is losing his mind

Week of December 14 to 21st(cont.)

The breadth and depth of the hack continued to unfold, and it was stunning. Donald Trump refused to acknowledge that it was Russia, which was how Trump's presidency began.

A year ago, on December 18ᵗʰ, the House of Representatives voted to impeach Donald Trump. The charges were "abuse of power" and "obstruction of justice.". Trump threatened the newly elected President of Ukraine with a quid pro quo. Trump would invite Ukrainian President Zelensky to the White House, and in return Zelensky would receive the money he needs to fight the Russians. Of course, that money had already been allocated by Congress, and Trump had no business withholding it. In fact, it was illegal, and that is why he was impeached.

Alexander Vindman, the former Director for European Affairs for the United States National Security Council was on the call, which was proper intelligence procedure. Colonel Vindman heard Trump make the threat- quid pro quo, and he reported it, which was protocol. The Democrats, and especially Adam Schiff (D-CA), the lead impeachment manager for the House, put on an extraordinary case against Trump. Schiff asked penetrating questions, such as "How much damage can Donald Trump do between now and the next election?" He also asked, "Can you have the least bit of confidence that Donald Trump will protect our national interest over his own personal interest?"

Adam Schiff hit the crux of everyone's concerns, but the Republicans were offended by the questions. They identified themselves as the people to whom Schiff was referring. they voted to acquit Trump, with the exception of Mitt Romney (R-UTAH), who voted him guilty.

Exactly a year later, Adam Schiff's question has been answered, in spades. We have a pandemic which Trump chose to ignore. As a result, 315,000 of us have died of the virus. Millions more have been infected, but survived with residual effects. In addition to the pandemic, and as a result of it, the economy is destroyed, with more than six million Americans applying for unemployment benefits. Initially, 40 million people lost their jobs. Restaurants and many other businesses had to close, and many will not be reopening. It is a tragic situation that didn't have to happen. If Donald Trump had decided to fight the virus using the resources of the country, activate the Defense Production Act, less people would be sick, jobs would be returned and kids would be in school.

Donald Trump, in a series of revenge acts, fired Alexander Vindman, Fiona Hill, and all the other dedicated career civil service men and women who testified at his impeachment. It was vindictive and horrible, because we lost a lot of extraordinary men and women who were committed to government service.

And still, President-elect Biden and Vice-President elect Harris are continuing to fill the ranks with wonderful nominees for the new administration. Because it took four weeks before Biden/Harris could begin the transition, which normally would have begun a day after the votes were counted, they have a lot of catching up to do. Originally, Trump told the heads of the agencies not to cooperate with the nominees for the same agencies they were about to join, making the transition very difficult. Fortunately, Biden chose very experienced people for these jobs, with excellent connections over the last many decades.

Gradually, communication started to loosen up. However, Donald Trump forbade giving the President's Daily Brief to Biden/Harris for weeks, which is very dangerous for national security. Donald Trump doesn't read the PDB at all, which is why we have such crazy and transactional foreign and domestic policies. Then, without warning, the Pentagon abruptly halted the transition briefings it had been providing, which are required by law, to the incoming team. A transition process has never been halted before, still another break with norms, and an unsettling one. Many different stories were floated, none of which are important enough to be described here. It all went back to Donald Trump being angry about perceived slights, and the fact that he lost the election. He is a dangerously sore loser.

All of this harked back to the overriding story of the monumental and dangerous hack, which cast a pall over the other stories. The Pfizer-BioNTech vaccine was being delivered to fifty states. A second vaccine was approved, and Moderna started delivering millions of doses to all fifty states. It is an extraordinary achievement to have two vaccines in such a short time. Unlike the Pfizer vaccine, Moderna does not have to be refrigerated at 95 degrees below, which makes it easier to distribute to smaller, local places. There are other vaccines in the pipeline, but only these two have been approved by the FDA for emergency use.

The Trump administration has tried everything to make the Biden people look bad. Trump has sabotaged everything conceivable to put Biden at a disadvantage. The Republicans tried to limit the ability of the Federal Reserve to borrow money and fight the recession. Ultimately, that stumbling block was resolved, but not without a fight. There has been absolutely no cooperation between Trump and the incoming administration, unlike many other transitions.

Every day Donald Trump is repeating that he won the election and that it was stolen from him. This is not true. The numbers have been certified by all fifty states and the Electoral College verified the Biden-Harris ticket.

Every day brings some new scheme that Donald Trump will employ to make himself the winner. Hold on to your hats, everyone. We are in for a wild ride in the next few weeks.

Donald Trump continues to ignore the virus and the pain of joblessness, homelessness, poverty and food insecurity. None of that matters to him. Overturning the vote is the only thing that matters, and he is considering crazy things-unthinkable things-in order to achieve that goal. I am personally worried, because I think that Donald Trump will stop at nothing to keep the presidency, even serious violence. I believe that he is seriously mentally ill.

Meanwhile, the wheels seem to have come off the country. We have weeks to go before January 20th-Inauguration Day, and Adam Schiff's question is haunting me. "How much damage can Donald Trump do between now (one year ago) and then? Quite a bit, apparently.

Pardon me?

December 23, 2020

Today is Attorney General Bill Barr's last day. Having carried water for Donald Trump in the most judicially destructive way, Barr had his last press conference on Sunday. His comments were sure to enrage Trump. First, Barr indicated that there was no evidence of fraud in the 2020 election. Secondly, he said that the investigation of Hunter Biden's taxes is best left to those already conducting it, and he would not be involved. Thirdly, he had no plan to appoint a special prosecutor. And with that, he was leaving the administration.

Barr also spoke about something extraordinary. Referring to the tragic plane crash #103 over Lockerbie, Scotland, thirty years ago, Barr said that the FBI had pinpointed the third bomber and would be asking Libya for his extradition. That crash is second only to 9/11 in devastating sabotage against America. Close to home, thirty-five students were on a Syracuse University study abroad trip, returning home for the holidays, and they all died. Many were from New Jersey, and grieving families took an active role in trying to bring the perpetrators to justice. I'm sure that we will hear from them this week. Barr gave credit to the FBI group that stuck with this horrific crime for thirty years.

In his statements, Barr distanced himself from Donald Trump. It may be that he has had a revelation that his reputation is on the line, in light of his actions during the Trump administration. Beginning with the Mueller report and going forward from there, it seems that Barr has purposely set his departure date so that he is not in office as Trump begins his pardons, which are bound to be very embarrassing.

Donald Trump is well aware that he has only a few weeks left of his presidency, and he is making the most of them. While there is nothing much on his schedule, he is spending his time tweeting about the election being "stolen" from him. His actions fall into two categories, pardons and destruction of the government to leave Joe Biden a weak hand.

Late last, night Trump released his first list of pardons, like party favors. Not surprisingly, many of those pardoned were involved in the Russia investigation, lied about their involvement, lied to Congress and to the FBI. They committed federal crimes, for which they were charged, tried and found guilty. Judge Amy Berman Jackson made it clear that thinking there was no guilt found in the Mueller report was because each and every one of those men lied. The lack of honesty corrupted the opportunity to have a clear picture of what really happened regarding Russia's role in our elections.

The pardon list includes three Congressmen, each of whom was found guilty of crimes, but were early Trump supporters. Most damning, Trump pardoned four Blackwater men who murdered seventeen Iraqi civilians for no reason, including two children. It was one of the most shameful acts on the part of Americans who were working in Iraq. Blackwater is a company that was founded by Eric Prince, the brother of Secretary of Education, Betsy DeVos, and the connection to Donald Trump is inescapable.

In fact, of the forty-five Trump pardons to date, forty of those have connections to Donald Trump in one way or another. This was not the purpose of pardons. The founding fathers gave the president plenary power, absolute power. It was on the assumption that the president would act in good faith. The pardons were supposed to be on the basis of "grace and mercy," where perhaps mistakes had been made in a court case, etc.

Barack Obama pardoned many people who were convicted on minimal drug charges. Notably, Richard Nixon did not use his pardon power for his closest advisors, who ultimately went to jail. Nixon thought it would be unseemly, since it involved an obvious crime, for which he was now leaving office. Gerald Ford became president, and pardoned Nixon on the grounds that he needed to clear the air. American citizens were so angry when Ford pardoned Nixon, that they voted him out of office.

This is just the first salvo in Trump's pardon party. The big fish are yet to come. Will it be Manafort? Trump's children? Himself? There is actually a pardon process and there are officials who oversee it. Donald Trump has not gone the route of following the process for just about everything. It will be interesting to see if he is forced to follow some of the rules and regulations. To date, the pardons Trump chose show a distinct debasement of the office of the presidency. Unfortunately, there will be more.

Stay tuned. Stay safe …

Showdown

December 24, 2020

Donald Trump left on vacation yesterday, having vetoed the Defense Bill, which funds our military and includes a 3% raise for those serving here and abroad. This bill has always been signed, until now. Congress will have to meet in order to override Trump's veto.

No one really knows what is in Trump's mind (have we ever?), except anger at McConnell and the Republicans who didn't get the presidency back for him. Not that they could have, but this shows how totally unhinged Trump is. He is making crazy and vindictive decisions that affect millions of people, including the military.

As if that wasn't enough. Donald Trump threatened to veto the Covid-19 Relief Bill, which millions of Americans are desperate to have signed. Among other things, the bill provides money ($600), and an unemployment insurance extension. After months of negotiation, in which Donald

Trump played no role whatsoever, he finally read the bill, and said he didn't like it and it had to be changed.

It is one day before Christmas, and Donald Trump has created financial chaos for millions, and anxiety for the entire country. He has yet to mention one death from Covid-19, shown no empathy or concern.

The death toll to this day is 327,173. For the last week, we have had the highest number of those dying, above 3,000 each day. Our hospitals are maxed out and have few if any ICU beds available, especially in California. Worse, the healthcare workers are exhausted, tired, and their ranks have been seriously depleted. They cannot be easily replaced, not even with graduating medical school doctors early. The skills required to navigate the many machines it takes to treat each Covid patient only come with years of experience. With the virus raging, we are reaching a serious inflection point, where hospitals are having to triage who to save, and who is beyond help. That is the tragic reality of where we are today. Donald Trump has never said a word about the virus or those who have died.

Knowing all this, I should tell you that I have been living alone in my apartment for the last nine months, incredibly isolated. My children and grandchildren all live in Brooklyn, and I have only seen them on a few brief occasions sitting outside with our masks on and social distancing. No hugging. Fortunately, there is ZOOM, my computer, Netflix, wonderful books and music, and the focus required to write this blog. I would be lying if I didn't tell you that I am deathly (pardon the pun), afraid of contracting the virus and am very careful.

We could have a government shutdown in addition to all of this. If the budget is not passed on Monday, the government will be unfunded and that would force a shut down. Trump has instigated this fight, and he is forcing Congress to be present for these votes while he is in sunny Florida playing golf. There is nothing on his schedule, and those who know report that he spends most of his time watching television.

In truth, Donald Trump has only worked hard on trying to overturn the 2020 election and on constructing his pardon list. This is bizarre, since we are in the middle of major crises-cyber, economic, and coronavirus, and he paid no attention to any of them.

He also has not mentioned that we are in the middle of the most serious attack on our country ever promulgated. Russia broke through our cyber defenses in the most important agencies, including Treasury and Homeland Security. It will take months to know the true depth of the attack, but it is very big according to experts. Donald Trump has said nothing about it.

The good news is that this week the United States has vaccinated 1 million people. The goal is one million per day, so we will have to ramp up the effort. The government, having been roundly criticized for passing on an offer by Pfizer, has announced that it will be receiving 100 million doses from Pfizer in the next few months. In addition, Moderna, which can provide doses at refrigerator temperature, is now delivering to all fifty states. A third vaccine may be coming soon from Johnson and Johnson.

A very sweet bit of news! Today is Dr. Anthony Fauci's 80th birthday. He lives in Washington, DC, and the mayor of DC has named it "Anthony Fauci Day." Dr. Fauci, unfairly maligned by Donald Trump, has now joined the Biden-Harris team to advise the effort to defeat the virus.

As all this is unfolding, the president issued another wave of pardons and many people are outraged. So far, 65 pardons have been given, of which 60 are connected to Trump, who is trying to eliminate the truth of the Mueller investigation. When the entire pardon party is complete, we need to look at what was done, and what can be done in the future when Joe Biden is President. There is an official office of pardons, where people apply for a pardon and have to write about why they think they deserve one. Donald Trump has totally ignored the office, and verbalized his own personal pardons. Yet another legal norm, ignored and debased.

Meanwhile, Merry Christmas to those who celebrate. May you have joy with your family, good health and peace.

Tracking Santa

December 24, 2020

Twenty-four hours a day, 365 days a year NORAD tracks everything that flies in and around North America in defense of our homeland. However, on December 24th, NORAD has a very special job of tracking Santa.

NORAD has been tracking Santa since 1955, when a young child accidentally dialed the unlisted phone number of the Continental Air defense Command (CONAD) Operations Center in Colorado Springs, Colorado, believing she was calling Santa Claus. She saw an ad in a newspaper and dialed the number, missing one.

Air Force Colonel Harry Shoup, the Commander on duty that night, was quick to realize a mistake had been made, and assured the youngster that CONAD would guarantee Santa a safe journey from the North Pole.

Thus, a tradition was born that rolled over to NORAD when it was formed in 1958. Each year since, NORAD has dutifully reported Santa's location on December 24th to millions across the globe.

Thanks to the services and resources generously provided by numerous corporate contributors and volunteers, NORAD Tracks Santa has persevered for more than 60 years.

Though the program began due to a misdialed number, NORAD Tracks Santa has flourished, and is recognized as one of the Department of Defense's largest community outreach programs.

Each year, the NORAD Tracks Santa Website receives nearly fifteen million unique visitors from more than 200 countries and territories around the world. Volunteers receive more than 130,000 calls to the NORAD Tracks Santa hotline from children around the globe.

This year, children and the young-at-heart are able to track Santa through Facebook, Twitter, YouTube and Instagram. NORAD is now the North American Aerospace Defense. http://www. noradsanta.org for more information."

"Yes, Virginia, there is a Santa Claus." It's special to know that people need to believe in Santa, and want children to hold on to their dreams.

Santa has loaded his sleigh and is preparing for the journey. Have fun Tracking Santa tonight. Leave him some milk and cookies.

"Merry Christmas to all and to all a Good Night."

December 25, 2020

Santa is safe from Covid-19

Christmas Day, 2020

On CNN's *Sesame Street*, Dr. Anthony Fauci made a video to assure thousands of concerned kids around the world that Santa was safe. Dr. Fauci told the kids that he paid a house call to the North Pole and gave Santa the vaccine himself. Many sighs of relief were heard throughout the globe, since concerned kids had been writing to Santa that they didn't want him to get the virus.

The coronavirus has affected kids of all ages who are aware of the dangers and the death around them.

Take some time to hug your kids and grandchildren. Assure them that they will be safe, now that the vaccine has arrived. There is a lot of anxiety in little kids (and big kids, too), that they cannot always verbalize.

Merry Christmas, peace, joy and love to each and every one of you. Be kind, wear your mask, wash hands and stay safe.

There are no words ...

December 27, 2020

Everything is so chaotic, unknown and unstable in Washington, that I want to wait and see how the next day unfolds.

Meanwhile, let's focus on the good news. The vaccine has arrived in New Jersey!

Specifically, Governor Murphy set up sites throughout the state. For Essex County, go onto EssexCOVID.org or call 973-877-8456.

The first priority group is paid and unpaid hospital workers, followed by those in healthcare, first responders, education, childcare, law enforcement, transportation and high-risk populations.

Appointments can be made on the county's COVID-19 information site.

Many of the Essex County towns, such as South Orange, Maplewood, Millburn, Livingston, parts of Newark, etc., will be going to the Livingston Mall, where the SEARS is empty, having gone out of business.

Governor Murphy indicated that the inoculations would begin in January, although we saw on television that some of the hospitals in Newark and elsewhere are already administering the vaccine to hospital frontline workers.

We were also told that New Jersey would be receiving the Moderna version of the vaccine, which can be easily stored in refrigerator temperatures.

In the midst of so much despair, there is hope. Stay strong, make good decisions and be careful.

A new year is coming on many levels.

December 28, 2020

A Day Late and a Dollar Short

December 27, 2020

*U.S. Total cases top 19.2 million/1 in every 1,000 Americans has died of Covid-19

Another split screen moment, which was gut-wrenching.

As Donald Trump was playing golf and tweeting his grievances against everyone, millions of Americans were lined up to get food for Christmas dinner and prepare to possibly be homeless. Late last night, the president finally decided to sign the Covid Relief bill that had been negotiated by both parties without any involvement of Trump. He was angry that the news media made it seem that he was on the sidelines, which he was.

The truth is that Donald Trump has no idea how Congress works. After four years in office, he never got down in the weeds of any legislation. He still has no idea that his interference will not yield a difference in the outcome. Trump never worked hard, never read any legislative bills, and never developed a working knowledge of how to navigate Congress. He governed by fear, threatening Senators to do his bidding, that he would primary or insult a Congressman on twitter. It seems to have worked, which is disappointing.

Trump created this present crisis, and now seems to be trying to solve it. He also doesn't know the difference between the Consolidated Appropriations Act and the National Defense Authorization Act. which sets policy, but does not fund the military. There are reasons why Trump vetoed the bill, but one very important one has never been mentioned.

The NDAA has always passed, since the 1960s. Inside the bill is something called the Corporate Transparency Act, which works to police shell companies and money laundering in America. It requires owners to file a report and name each person associated with the company, indicate who has 25% or more control of the company and give detailed information. That goes to the Financial Crimes Enforcement Network (FinCEN). The Act also increases penalties for money laundering, and it eases cooperation between foreign law enforcement and banks. America is the easiest place for shell companies to launder money, and this act seeks to put a stop to it.

The Trump family uses shell companies. We learned from Michael Cohen that Donald Trump used a shell company to pay Stormy Daniels. More recently, we learned that Jared Kushner approved a shell company that moved more than $600 million in campaign funds, which was spent. This provides a deep reason why Donald Trump doesn't like this bill. The Trump family would be culpable. Trump has not publicly mentioned the CTA, but the bill needs to be passed over the veto. It will be interesting to see the fate of CTA when the bill is passed.

The holiday was not a peaceful one on other grounds. In Nashville, Tenn. a bomb went off on Christmas morning in front of an AT&T building. The motive is still unclear, so I have little or nothing to report at this time.

We began the year with inaction on the part of President Trump, who refused to acknowledge the coronavirus. We are ending it in the same way-little or no concern about the health and welfare of the American people.

His delay meant the loss of unemployment benefits for 14 million Americans, one day late during Christmas week. Heartbreaking, really. Lots of families didn't have money for food or toys for children. Trump's delay was callous and cruel, words often used to describe his behavior since day one of his administration.

The New York Post, a Trump supporter, issued a blistering editorial, telling Trump to "Give it up, Mr. President-for your sake and the nations'. *The Post* is a Murdoch property, but Trump has not been focused on Covid Relief. Instead, he has spent every day trying to overturn the election, by any means possible, including an undemocratic coup, which *The Post* referenced.

Serious things about which to worry:

Jobless benefits in jeopardy,

Extended benefits for gig workers will run out tonight

900 BILLION Covid Relief package hangs in limbo

The eviction moratorium will expire tonight

Pandemic unemployment assistance expires tonight

Pelosi planning full floor vote Monday

Government may shut down on Monday if Trump does not fund the government

Nero Fiddled while Rome Burned

December 30, 2020

The coronavirus is surging, and in no more desperate place than Los Angeles, California. Cases are rising, healthcare workers are exhausted and there are no ICU beds left. The numbers are staggering. In some of the hospitals, healthcare workers are not able to accept ambulances. As in war, doctors have to evaluate which people can be saved and which cannot. Shockingly, they are forced to triage. Some patients have had to wait many hours before being seen. Out of space, patients are being put into the chapel, and even the gift shop. There is no room for all the sick citizens, and supplies are running low.

As we have seen throughout the year, there is a painful split screen. One side of the picture is President Trump playing golf every day, and saying nothing about the pandemic. He did insist that Congress change a bill already passed on a bipartisan basis, gumming up the works. We'll see what happens in Congress this week. Moreover, Vice-President Pence, Chairman of the Coronavirus Task Force, is skiing in Vail with his family. In the midst of a financial and health-care crisis, Treasury Secretary Mnuchin is vacationing in Mexico. There is no one home in the

American government to deal with the greatest crisis that has befallen our country. The silence is deafening. The Republicans are fiddling while the country is on fire.

Transitions of power are extremely important. During the time that it took to sort out the Bush v. Gore election – 35 days- the 9/11 Commission found that those days rendered America seriously weak, because it created a vacuum. Osama bin Laden and the Arabs were aware of the situation. and that an opportunity existed. George Bush became president, with little time to learn about the national security situation in the country and the world, although neither Bush nor Gore was at fault.

However, this past Monday President-elect Biden came out and said that his administration, "has encountered roadblocks, specifically from the Department of Defense. The DOD has purposely hidden national security information that is crucial. In the last month, Trump fired DOD Secretary Esper, and a number of people in the DOD and the OMB, and replaced them with his own loyalists, who are not being cooperative. Denying an incoming administration crucial national security information is dangerous for the country. None of that seems to matter to Donald Trump, who is trying to put Joe Biden at a disadvantage.

"It's nothing short of irresponsibility," President-elect Biden said.

There are tactical, operational and strategic problems that the new president needs to know. The new administration must be briefed on what was said between Trump and China, Trump and Russia, and those conversations were not shared, which is improper protocol. How and when do we push back? What is the situation with Taiwan? There are many other important issues to confront-Iran, for instance.

Biden continued. "Many of our agencies that are critical to our security-State, Justice, Defense and others- have incurred enormous damage. Many of them have been hollowed out in personnel, capacity and in morale." Biden also spoke about the massive cyberattack on U.S. federal agencies and companies, which is a grave risk to national security. Donald Trump has said nothing, perhaps because Secretary Pompeo indicated that the Russians are the bad actors.

Joe Biden praised career officials in certain government departments, and said that his team had received "exemplary cooperation" from some agencies.

From his comments, it is clear that Trump has left us in a seriously weakened position, domestically and around the globe. The president seems to have checked out, except where his own personal interests are concerned. If he spent as much time on the pandemic, joblessness and hunger in the country, he would have done his job. Having done nothing, it is clear that he likes the trappings of the presidency, but none of the hard work. He is playing golf, while people are dying and starving.

Deja Vu

December 31, 2020

As we began 2020, with Donald Trump indicating that "15 people had the virus, nothing to worry about, would be gone, we needn't be concerned, because the states could handle it," we are in that situation, only it isn't exactly what Trump described.

With millions infected and hundreds of thousands dying, we are in the most serious part of the pandemic. Both Pfizer and Moderna developed vaccines for the virus with amazing speed. The challenge will be to distribute and get it to all corners of the country, because there is no government plan. Having no plan is typical of Donald Trump, since there was no Covid plan and no healthcare plan either. Planning involves hard work and getting down into the details of a problem.

The Trump administration did not plan for the distribution of the virus. Nor did it fund the states that would need the money to set up the distribution systems. Trump said that Pfizer had not delivered the doses. Albert Bourla, CEO of Pfizer, said that the company has millions of doses on its shelves, "and is waiting for instructions from the government about where they should be sent." The Trump administration, either purposely or by total ineptitude, failed yet again. I watched one morning as the Pfizer vaccines were being packaged and sent in UPS and FEDEX trucks to all fifty states. The rollout from its headquarters was awesome. Pfizer had done its job magnificently.

President-elect Biden gave a speech on Tuesday. He said that the administration was slow-walking the distribution of the vaccines. Now it seems that Donald Trump is doing another "it's up to the states" message. States are forced to balance their budgets. Congress and Trump have not wanted to give the states money to complete the vaccine program. The states are basically broke, and have received little to reimburse them for all the millions spent when the pandemic hit. Many of the so-called "blue states," – New York, New Jersey, Connecticut, Massachusetts and California, were among the first. Since they did not vote for the president, Trump and his son-in-law decided to ignore the pandemic. They didn't want to help the "blue states."

This time, life (and death) is different. The coronavirus is in all fifty states. The government has still not made a systemic and effective plan that each state can put in place. In Colorado, the Governor organized his own plan and it is working. People are scheduled at certain times, based on which group they are in. Healthcare workers are first. In Florida, where the governor did not support mask wearing or anything except Donald Trump, they have no plan. Elderly citizens were showing up and standing in line (in the middle of a pandemic), in order to get the vaccine. Chaos ensued. Donald Trump ignored the whole situation, except to tweet that the states needed to "get going."

It goes without saying that Joe Biden is inheriting a mess, largely promulgated by Donald Trump's refusal to be helpful in any way. In fact, Trump has been destructive in telling his loyalists in agencies to be uncooperative. Because of obstruction, the crisis has been made worse for the country and the incoming administration.

Nothing like this has ever happened in the United States since its inception. The confluence of health, financial and political problems is stunning and disturbing. The country is on edge, and rightly so.

We welcome the New Year with hope that it will indeed bring a "new year," in months to come-with vaccine distribution, kids back in school, people gathering and our new government working for the American people.

Whatever you are able to do tonight, I hope you are healthy, can connect with friends and family online, decide to stay home and look forward to a change in the atmosphere and the way we talk to one another.

Happy 2021!

Welcome 2021-with Hope

January 1, 2021 New Year's Day

Another Year:

What will the New Year bring?

In this year of so much grief and sorrow, there is also much for which to be grateful. We are more connected than ever before, albeit online. We have a better appreciation for our essential workers, and our neighbors, who often came forward to help an older person with groceries or just walking. The scientific community has given us two vaccines, and the hope of defeating the coronavirus, if we follow the guidelines.

Millions came out to vote, and we saved our democracy, which was in doubt. Now it is up to us to help the new administration succeed. To quote Senator Cory Booker, (D-NJ) "Democracy is not a spectator sport."

Happy 2021! We have a lot of work to do, and we will succeed for ourselves and for the country if we pull together.

January 4, 2021

Shocking and Illegal

January 3, 2021

There are a lot of crazy things happening on the Republican side, with eleven Senators planning to object to some states' electoral votes that have already been certified. That "stunt" is highly irregular, and has not been done before. However, the absolutely most shocking event was the phone call between Donald Trump and Secretary of State, Brad Raffensberger, on Saturday.

The *Washington Post* released the call. In an hour- long rant, we hear Trump pressuring the Secretary of State of Georgia to overturn the election by "finding" the 11,780 plus votes that would give Georgia to Trump. The call clearly indicates a criminal act being promulgated, as Trump is tampering with the results of an election, in an effort to overturn it in his favor. If local officials were caught engaging in such pressure, they would be arrested. Some Trump attorneys and his Chief of Staff, Mark Meadows, were also on the call, which makes it even more bizarre. What could they have been thinking?

Trump cannot accept that he lost the election. All of his efforts have failed. The court cases-sixty of 61- have either lost, or been dismissed for lack of evidence. While Trump was accusing the election of fraud, and so were his followers, lawyers will not claim fraud when asked by a judge in court. If they have no evidence of fraud, indicating fraud in court leaves the lawyer open to serious consequences. No one was willing to insist on fraud in court. Two cases actually went to the Supreme Court, where three of Trump's appointees sit. The Court refused to hear the cases, indicating Trump had no standing to bring them. He was furious and insulted the Court in tweets. Trump continues to peddle conspiracy theories that his own FBI, and Attorney General Barr, have rejected.

The phone call has Donald Trump threatening the Georgia Secretary of State, and indicating that Raffensberger has to find those votes. It is undemocratic to say the least, immoral, illegal and dishonest, especially since the president is the chief law enforcement officer of the county. I suggest that you access the hour- long call, because it shows how unhinged Donald Trump has become over losing this election.

For his part, Raffensberger bravely reiterated that the Georgia numbers are correct, that they were certified, and that no other change will be made. Trump kept saying that the voters are angry, most likely his base and himself. He has also said that the election was rigged, confusing everyone, since many of the Republicans won in the down ballot races, but they did not vote for Trump at the top.

It is incredible that Trump is trying to overthrow an election, while the country is faced with serious crises. In the first place, the pandemic is raging, hospitals are full and healthcare workers are exhausted. Secondly, citizens are fighting hunger and there is no relief. The cyber-attack on our internet has been found to be deeper and more dangerous than initially thought. Donald Trump, the president of the United States, has not acknowledged any of these crises. He spent last week mostly playing golf and trying to turn the election. The Senate left Washington for the Christmas holiday, without bringing the relief bill to the table, thanks to Mitch McConnell, the Majority leader.

Add to that, the total lack of planning and funding of the vaccine rollout to the fifty states. Pfizer and Moderna have done their job, but the individual states received no federal plan and no money to facilitate getting the vaccine into the arms of citizens. Knowing that this was coming down the road, the administration needed to develop some continuity and send the plan to each state in advance. Having a system would avoid chaos. None of that was done. The convergence of all these crises, with a disconnected president, puts America in a very vulnerable position. The entire situation is chaotic, and it is difficult to know how the craziness will proceed from minute to minute.

Stay tuned this Tuesday for the Georgia runoff election that will decide the balance in the Senate, whether the Republicans stay in control, or not

Moreover, America is bracing for a post-holiday surge of the Covid virus, following Christmas holiday travel, and despite warnings to stay home.

As the week unfolds, let's remember that Joe Biden won the election by seven million votes, a large number. The governors of all fifty states certified the numbers. However, Trump and his acolytes have continued to spread the word that the election was rigged, that it was "stolen" from him and that there was fraud. Repeating those charges and the conspiracy theory has found its way into the minds of many citizens, putting doubt into the efficacy of the election. That is the true danger of what Donald Trump has wrought in the last years. Telling lies and spreading misinformation has damaged many peoples' trust in the American democratic system. It is going to take a long time to undo that damage.

With that said, I wish you and yours a happy 2021, filled with good health, the promise of a better time, joy with family and love.

January 4, 2021

"The future ain't what it used to be" (Yogi Berra)

January 4, 2021

Yes, it's hard to know what is going to happen this week. On Tuesday, the Georgia runoff for two Senate seats will determine whether the Senate will be in the hands of the Republicans or the Democrats. A lot depends on the outcome. If the Democrats win, it will make it easier for

President Biden to put through his program and get his nominees voted into office. If not, it will be a difficult road ahead.

On Wednesday, something that was nominally accepted as merely a ministerial event, where the President of the Senate reads the final numbers and declares who the President and Vice President are, is actually fraught with potential chaos. Congressional Republicans and eleven Senators are planning to object to the electors, based on a false narrative that there were irregularities and fraud in the vote. It is clearly a ploy to get on Donald Trump's good guy list for the future political ambitions of those on board. However, it's not clear, in light of the phone call where Trump broke the law in asking the Georgia Secretary of State to change the numbers, whether all of those sycophants will stick with Trump or not. As Yogi Berra so wisely said, "The future ain't what it used to be," when we could take certain things, such as the certification of voting numbers, for granted.

As Donald Trump ramped up his desperation, it became clear that there is nothing he won't do, no line that he wouldn't cross to hang on to the presidency. Why would anyone put themselves into serious jeopardy by breaking the law so blatantly in public? On January 20th, Trump loses the immunity that has protected him for the last four years. There are cases awaiting him in New York, where he will most certainly be indicted for bank fraud, tax fraud, and other crimes. In addition, he owes four hundred million dollars, some of it to foreign entities. Truthfully, he would not get a security clearance if the tax returns were known from the very beginning. That is a conversation for another time.

Meanwhile, as Trump spirals down into his own reality, a letter written by ten former Secretaries of Defense, sounded the alarm that Trump might try to involve the United States military in the political process. Initiated by all ten living former Secretaries of Defense, led by Republicans Dick Cheney, Donald Rumsfeld and joined by others, the letter expresses concern that Trump would try that move. In addition, Congresswoman Liz Cheney sent a twenty-one-page letter, describing why this is anti-democratic and against all of our American values and norms. Trump's behavior is seditious and traitorous. These are very dark times for the United States, brought about by a very demented man who doesn't care that people are dying because he ignored the coronavirus.

Both President-elect Biden and President Trump will be in Georgia tonight, in an effort to "get out the vote" the night before the consequential Georgia Senate vote. It will be interesting to see what they each say to the Georgians in the midst of all the confusion and chaos.

Quoting the wisdom of Yogi, "The future ain't what it used to be." Stay tuned

January 5, 2021

Can we Keep our Democracy?

January 5, 2021

There is too much craziness happening this week. Today is the Georgia runoff for the two Senate seats that will decide whether the Senate will remain majority Republican or change to 50/50, with Vice-President Harris being able to break the tie. A Democratic win would greatly improve Joe Biden's ability to move his program forward.

Wednesday is the day when the election numbers are read into the record and the President/Vice President are legally proclaimed the winners. The states have already certified their numbers, so historically this has been a non-event. Not so this year! Donald Trump has managed to influence many of his supporters in Congress to challenge the reading of the numbers. Nothing on this scale has ever happened before, and it seriously damages our democracy, especially since it will not actually change the outcome.

One can only conjecture that the support for this comes from the Senators and Congressmen who are considering their own political futures, and not the values of the country as a democracy. Speeches will take hours, and may not conclude until the next day, because everyone gets to talk. Mike Pence, as the President of the Senate, has only a ministerial job. He reads the numbers as they are given to him, period, despite Donald Trump pressuring him. This is a political show that could undercut the Constitution. There is the Electoral Count Act, enacted hundreds of years ago after the Civil War in a totally different historical situation, but it allows for members to speak.

In the midst of all this, Gabe Sterling, the Republican Georgia election official, felt that he had to hold yet another press conference. You will recall that he was the frustrated and angry election official who admonished Donald Trump weeks ago about how dangerous his rhetoric was, ("someone is going to get hurt"). As a result of that press conference, Sterling was threatened, and he now has security guarding his home. Still as frustrated as he was weeks ago, Mr. Sterling went point by point debunking the lies that have been floated about the Georgia election. His pride in the fact that the election was clean, not fraudulent and recounted many times, was clearly on display. The reason to "reexamine" the vote is because Donald Trump spread the idea that the election was "stolen" from him. People believed Trump's message, spread on social media and in many rallies that Trump held.

As mentioned before, last Saturday we heard the single most appalling conversation of a president trying to change the outcome of an election. After reaching out to him eighteen times, Trump finally connected with the Secretary of State, and was asking him to "recalculate," basically to commit a crime. We heard the hour-long tape of Donald Trump pressuring Raffensberger, begging him really, in a desperate voice, to "find" the 11,780 votes that would make him the winner of Georgia. Raffensberger, to his credit, calmly responded that the data that Trump had was wrong, that Georgia's numbers were correct and would not be changed. After hearing the conversation on the phone, two Representatives -Kathleen Rice (D-NY) and Ted Lieu (D-CA) wrote to the FBI Director, Christopher Wray, and asked him to "open an immediate criminal investigation into the President," for committing election crimes. In this case, it might be left to the Georgia AG to bring charges, although election law can be violated federally and statewide. As if this wasn't enough, the U.S Attorney in Atlanta, Byung Pak, suddenly resigned and left today. He cited "unforeseen circumstances." While I don't usually speculate, it's entirely possible that if charges were brought in Atlanta, it would be the U.S. Attorney who would be running the case, and Pak would suffer the same pressure that he heard on the phone call.

While Donald Trump was focused on overturning an election that he lost by seven million votes and 60 lawsuits, 354,313 American citizens have died. 20 million citizens have been infected by the virus, and many of them have residual physical effects.

Not one word has been mentioned by Donald Trump about these deaths or their residual illnesses. Similarly, we have two vaccines, but no provision has been made by Trump and the federal government to facilitate getting the doses into peoples' arms. The states need resources, and Trump is unconcerned. He spent last week playing golf and phoning his supporters to come to Washington on January 6th to support his "stolen" presidency. Two crucial reasons for supporting the incoming administration are that it is tasked with fighting the pandemic and restoring the economy. This is no time for partisan battling when the virus is killing thousands across the country. The peaceful transfer of power has already been delayed unnecessarily, and the results are dangerous for the country.

The challenge to the electoral votes has split the Republican Party between those who support Trump and those who want to maintain our democracy, which has been our greatest asset. We fought a war because we did not want a king. When we established our government, the Constitution gave equal weight to the states and the system of checks and balances to create boundaries for the President. The states were tasked with running our elections. Moreover, historically the Republican Party has been for small, limited government, and fiscal responsibility with our budgets. None of that has happened under President Trump, so it is baffling that Republicans have followed Trump mindlessly down a rabbit hole. What is even more troubling is that Josh Hawley (R-MO) went to Yale Law School and Ted Cruz (R-TX) went to Harvard Law School. They obviously have an intimate knowledge of the Constitution, and know that what they are planning is improper, illegal, and against the process that has been set out since after the Civil War.

There are many Republicans who recognize the Biden presidency, and they are disturbed by Trump and his supporters. Senators are coming out in support of the Biden ticket and providing support for democracy. Some of them are Mitt Romney (R-UT), Senator Pat Toomey (R-PA), Kevin Cramer R-ND), and many others. One of the most interesting Republicans supporting Biden's presidency is Tom Cotton (R-AR), an avid Trump supporter, who has political ambitions.

He may have decided that he doesn't want to throw in his lot with the Trump supporters, who are likely to be embarrassed at the end of the day. Cotton opposes the overturn of the election by congressional action, because he thinks that the power needs to reside with the states.

There is an Electoral Voter Law that allows lawmakers to speak, but not to change the votes, since the votes were certified on December 14th. The desire to put the votes of the states onto Congress is troubling. These lawmakers cannot change the outcome. Donald Trump is an autocrat, so it is puzzling that certain people have been cowed by his power rather than pushing back against it. We clearly need to ramp up our Civics courses for kids (and adults). Former Justice, Sandra Day O'Connor, felt that civics was sadly lacking, and she began a foundation to alleviate that situation. People need to know why we are Americans and how that uniquely distinguishes us from other countries.

Meanwhile, in Washington, the leader of the Proud Boys was arrested for destroying property during his last visit to DC, when he burned a "Black Lives Matter" banner that had been pulled down from the Asbury Methodist Church. After his arrest, law enforcement officers found two high-capacity firearms. He was ready to be "standing by."

As I indicated, it's going to be one of those weeks where there is too much happening, where it is hard to process so much that is troubling. It will all shake out with the passing of each day.

Meanwhile, stay safe, wear your mask, stay calm and observe social distancing. New Jersey, where I live, is the densest state in the union, so we need to be careful how we interact with everyone, keeping ourselves and our neighbors safe.

January 6, 2021

Yes, we can … America is still the land of opportunity!

January 6, 2021/10am

Last night was a historic moment in our history. Georgia elected Raphael Warnock, black minister and a Democrat, to the Georgia Senate. This is monumental. It shows that America is still the land of opportunity, where a poor child can get an education and go on to become Senator. There hasn't been a black Senator from Georgia, ever. Warnock joins two other black Senators-Cory Booker (D-NJ) and Tim Scott (R-SC), who are now serving. Vice-President elect, Kamala Harris, was the other black Senator, and she will still be in the Senate, but as the presiding President when there is a tie.

Warnock is the eleventh child in a family of twelve. He is the first sibling to attend college-Morehouse, courtesy of Pell Grants, which the government funds. He is the minister of Ebenezer Church, where Martin Luther King was the minister and John Lewis was a parishioner. The intersections are breathtaking.

The historic nature of the vote last night goes back even further. When we look at the original guarantee of equality, it only extended to a small group of white men who owned property. The democracy expanded to other men, then some immigrants, African-American men after the Civil War with the 13th, 14th and 15th Amendments, then to women with the 19th Amendment in 1920. They were followed by Asian immigrants, (Many from Vietnam), Latinos and native Americans. When each group arrived, it was often met with disdain, born of fear that jobs would be taken, and the latest group was put at the bottom rung of the status ladder. Gradually, many of the members of these groups went to college and worked their way through the American system, based on a new equality that rewarded hard work and creativity.

American democracy has never been perfect. In fact, far from it. It has ineluctably moved through each century since 1776, and improved the opportunities for many, but not all. Depending on the group, there are varying degrees of how they view democracy. Some have been hampered by gerrymandering, others by voter suppression and others by outright bigotry. The country has been lurching toward social justice, motivated by the death of George Floyd, which was recorded on video. It opened a wider acceptance of "Black Lives Matter," and the concept of police brutality needing to be changed through education and sensitivity training.

As America was leaning towards an autocratic leader, citizens came to their senses. The 2020 vote elected Joe Biden, a moderate and Kamala Harris, Senator from California, as President and Vice President. They have a lot of work to do, since Donald Trump is leaving them a mess to clean up in our agencies and whether elections are honest and fair. It's going to be a long, hard struggle to get this country together in order to fight Covid-19 and all the other problems looking over us.

Presently, we are waiting to see if Jon Ossoff wins the other Georgia Senate seat. That could be historic on many levels, and it will be a pleasure to discuss how and why when it happens.

Meanwhile, as I am watching and writing, hundreds of Trump followers are pouring into Washington, having been invited by the president. What do they think their presence will accomplish?

January 7, 2021

"A Day that will live in infamy"

January 6th, 2021

Our country was attacked by Japan on December 7th, 1941, when thousands died on ships in Pearl Harbor. On December 8th, 1941, Franklin Roosevelt spoke to a joint session of Congress, and spoke of "a day that will live in infamy." We entered World War 11 shortly afterward.

Shockingly, our country was attacked yesterday, by our own sitting President and the minions of followers who believe his lies that the election was "stolen" from him.

Yesterday, as I was writing about the amazing victory of two Democratic men in the Georgia run-off, which would change the game for the new Biden administration, something very disturbing crossed on my television screen. January 6th was supposed to be the final reading of the election numbers by Vice-President Pence in the Senate, and the confirmation of Joe Biden as President and Kamala Harris as Vice President.

Strangely, not far from the Capital was a large structure with a podium, flags and signs for Trump. This seemed to me to be a finger in the eye of the incoming administration, and I wondered why Donald Trump would be allowed to do that so close to where the Senate and the House would be meeting. Hundreds of people were gathering to hear Donald Trump speak at 11 o'clock.

The crowd grew bigger as I was watching on my television. They were wearing what looked like battle gear and carrying flags, poles, items that looked threatening. It was scary. I couldn't take my eyes off the screen.

Donald Trump's rhetoric was fiery in the last few weeks, telling his supporters the blatant lie that he had won the election "by a landslide." For the last few weeks Trump talked about January 6th and invited people to come to DC ("it will be wild!"). As the people were gathering- with huge Trump flags, red, white and blue outfits and firearms, an alarm went off in my head. I stopped to listen to Trump's speech (something I hate to do, because it is always lies and misinformation). What he said was very inflammatory. He was basically inciting this gathering, which now seemed in the thousands, to riot, to go down to the Capital and "take back our country."

The confirmation was supposed to begin around 1pm, and simultaneously thousands of angry rioters (not peaceful protestors, let's be clear) descended on the Capitol building and breached the building. Watching on television was horrifying. Where were the Metropolitan police? The National Guard? It didn't seem to me that there was a heavy presence to guard the building or the leaders of the free world.

The video of what happened is horrifying. The police were overwhelmed by the masses, who pushed into the building. Fortunately, the Vice President and Speaker of the House Pelosi were rushed to safety, along with others. The building was put into lockdown. The pro-Trump rioters. Insurrectionists really, took over the Senate and the House, destroyed property, broke windows and defaced statues. Rioters were breaking down the doors of the House. The pictures tell a thousand words. Members of the House were crouching down for their safety in fear that they would be killed. Insurrectionists were yelling "stop the steal." Congressman Jason Crow, a former Ranger, was comforting one of his colleagues. There was a scaffold and a noose, supposedly to "hang Mike Pence," who had tole trump that he could not change the numbers.

Donald Trump did not go down to the Capitol with the crowd, as he promised. Instead, he was hiding in the White House and watching television, happy and delighted at what he saw, according to those who saw him that day. Leaders called and begged Trump to do something, but he did nothing. Vice President Pence, from where he was put in a safe place, in conversation with the Dept. of Defense, ordered the National Guard to be called, and it came hours later. Trump was silent. Kevin McCarthy called Trump and told him the people out there were "his people," and he needed to call them off. Chris Christie called and begged him to put a stop to the rioting and violence. We have seen the videos and they are horrific.

The House and the Senate finally met and confirmed the Biden-Harris ticket at 3:31 am. I was watching. It normally takes half an hour. Mike Pence read the confirmation that Trump tried to bully him not to read.

Looking back to the summer when there was a violent group of police ready to kill "Black Lives Matter" people, who were marching peacefully, it is clear that white people have a license in this country that blacks do not.

The last time this happened was 1812, when the British stormed Washington, D.C., and burned it. In 2021, the violence was insurrection and sedition. We got the government we deserve by electing Trump, the destructor. Seven people died, and only 52 people were arrested, so far. Why weren't all these people arrested? It is a crime to breach the Capitol, breaking and entering, etc. These are felonies.

I don't understand how the security of the Capitol was breached, and I would like an answer. By all estimates, there were thousands of people, and it was very well-planned. People there were from QANON, Proud Boys and other conspiracy theory groups. They came prepared. Watching the beloved Capitol ransacked was horrible. I spent many happy times there when I lived in Washington.

There will be much more to write. Sixteen people in the White House resigned. I am writing this at 6:20 am, having been awake all day and night.

While this chaos was continuing, Jon Ossoff was named the new Senator from Georgia, joining Raphael Warnock. This was a stunning victory for Democrats and for the Biden administration. In addition, Biden spoke to the country and urged unity among citizens. He was articulate and strong. Still, Washington was reeling from all these thugs, yelling and invading the seat of our government. We we're all in shock. How did this happen? Why did it happen?

It was at this point that President-elect Biden named Judge Merrick Garland to be his next Attorney General. What goes around comes around. President Barack Obama nominated Garland to the Supreme Court, but McConnell and the Republicans never gave him the courtesy of a hearing or a vote. He held that seat open until the next president was elected. Donald Trump won and he got to nominate the Supreme Court Justice.

Twelve days until the Inauguration, but I worry how we are going to be safe with this maniac still in power.

January 8, 2021

Shock and awe, this is not who we are

January 8, 2021

Seeing the videos of the horror in the Capitol sends chills down my spine. The anger of the thugs, the fright of the unknown and the physical fear, is beyond imagination, except that we have videos to remind us.

Watching the thugs who wanted to do harm, one realizes it is a miracle that the members of the House and Senate weren't killed. This is not hyperbole. They were saved by a few fast-thinking Capitol police.

Seven people, including a member of the Capitol Police, are dead. The Capitol policeman was hit in the head with a fire extinguisher, and died in the hospital of his wounds. The entire event came within inches of being a complete tragedy-an insurrection facilitated by the President of the United States. Shocking, The reality is nonetheless hard to process when you see all the images, which are frightening and grotesque.

An act of sedition promulgated on the country from within the Oval Office is hard to believe, but ultimately believable, because the president is a sick man. He is a reality TV showman, who orchestrated something he thought would be terrific, and he engaged his son, Don, Jr and his daughter, Ivanka, who are now vulnerable to prosecution as well. Trump's people would stop the confirmation of Biden/Harris and turn the election to Trump, even though Mike Pence told him that he had no ability to change any of the numbers. Trump was furious, and told his minions that Pence wasn't loyal. As a result, the raucous mob went looking for Pence, in order to kill him. However, Mike Pence had been quickly spirited away by the Capitol Police to a safe location.

While the devastation was continuing, Trump was egging on his followers via Twitter, which finally had the wisdom to lock down his Twitter account for twelve hours. Ultimately, Twitter took down his account and banned him forever. Thank goodness. Twitter wrote that it has "permanently suspended his account," based on his "glorification of violence." Facebook and other accounts followed suit.

There is so much that happened that Wednesday, and it will be investigated by no less than three different groups. The country is in pain for many reasons. Our democracy was attacked. Our citizens are dying of the coronavirus in record numbers-4,000 daily.

I would like to turn from these painful and difficult realities to other, more inspiring ones.

It is exactly ten years ago that Congresswoman Gabby Giffords (D-AZ), was having a "meet and greet" for constituents outside at a shopping center. She was shot in the head and almost died. Her husband, astronaut Mark Kelly, stayed by her side and miraculously, she lived. Not only did she live, but as a result of ten years of intense work, Gabby now can walk and talk and communicate her sparkle. I saw this yesterday in a marvelous interview with Savannah Guthrie. Gabby Giffords is a testament to what a woman can do with faith, with love and the support of friends and family. She is a miracle of strength of character and the desire to overcome the worst challenges.

The people who I want to talk about today are similar, because they overcame many challenges to achieve their potential and manifest their goals.

Last Wednesday morning, I was writing about the two winners of the Georgia Senate election, when I had to stop to watch the DC debacle. However, Jon Ossoff and Reverend Raphael Warnock deserve to be honored, admired and congratulated for their achievement, against all odds. Jon Ossoff, the son of Jewish immigrants, will be the youngest U.S. Senator, at age 33. He ran a very impressive campaign, measured and bold, especially when he called David Perdue a "crook" to his face, in the middle of a debate. As a result, Perdue refused to debate Ossoff for the second time. It was stunning.

Raphael Warnock is a child of Georgia, raised in poverty, the eleventh child of twelve siblings, and the first to attend college. I told you about him in an earlier blog. What I didn't mention is that in s civil rights event, Warnock was arrested in the Capitol. Now he is returning as a Senator.

Both of these men have achieved something we might never have thought possible. A Democrat has not represented Georgia in decades. A Jewish man and a black man have never been Georgia Senators. We are in a new reality that is demographically changing and becoming more open and less bigoted, more willing to admire merit and reward it. The admission of Ossoff and Warnock to the Senate will make the numbers even-50/50, with Vice President Kamala Harris being able to cast the vote in the event of a tie.

And the new Vice President-elect is an Asian-American black woman whose election is historic. Kamala Harris, is the first woman and the first woman of color to become Vice President of the United States. A graduate of Howard University, a lawyer, she became Attorney General of California and is now one of two California Senators. The new administration is filled with exciting and talented people, like the three that I have mentioned. Their lives are a testament to hard work, to education, to motivation and a desire to serve their country.

As President-elect Biden introduces his administration, it is clear that this is the most diverse group of people with racial and ethnic backgrounds that we have ever seen before.

I am looking forward to detailing more of President-elect Biden's choices, as we are introduced to them. He has now chosen all of the people to fill the major positions in his administration, with the exception of Attorney General, and we can look forward to a new day in our country, even as we are grieving for the terrible acts of a deranged man. We need to leave the work of bringing the criminals to justice to the full extent of the law.

Take a deep breath, try to rid yourself of the malignant images and look forward to thinking about the possibility of our American democracy, now that we will have decent people representing us. America is still the land of opportunity, and fortunately we have a chance to take the toxic elements out of our government and look to working on the future of our country. Politics is about the mediation of problems, not constant war.

January 11, 2021

The President incited a terror attack against the government, an insurrection. People died and our democracy is in peril.

January 11, 2021

There is no one home in the federal government. Anyone who is there, listens to Donald Trump, mocking the concept of "separation of powers." How did this happen?

In the last four years Donald Trump systematically hollowed out our agencies: State, Justice, Defense, Homeland Security, and put his own loyalists into leadership. We saw this happen from the beginning of Trump's presidency, when the job openings at State were left unfilled, purposely, and the Secretary of State was told to "streamline" the agency. Many career diplomats left, and others were fired, and that was the opening salvo of the beginning of the end for our government's effectiveness. Four years of firing the Secretaries of each agency and replacing them with "active" Secretaries, cemented Trump's control over agency after agency. Thus, Donald Trump circumvented the appropriate process of Senate confirmation of each Secretary, which would have given that person the ability to act independently. "Acting" served at the pleasure of the president, and allowed Trump to control every aspect of government.

One such agency is the Department of Defense. A few short weeks before this event, Donald Trump fired Secretary Esper and put four of his own loyalists in office. Personally, I saw that as a red flag that Trump was thinking ahead to the week of January 6th. It would be difficult to get protection, and indeed it was. When the call went out for the National Guard, it took hours for police protection to arrive. The explanation was that, with D.C. not a state, the call for the National Guard and other protectors had to be walked up the chain of command to the Defense Department with the President at the head. The change in the DOD was purposely planned by President Trump, and no one in the Republican Senate even questioned it.

That said, we must fast forward to Wednesday. Donald Trump spent the weeks after he lost the election insisting that he won. After a fiery speech exhorting thousands of Trump supporters to "fight, fight, fight," they stormed the Capitol building, where Congress was in session in order to confirm Joe Biden, Democrat, as the President of the United States, and Kamala Harris as the Vice President. The numbers had already been independently certified by each state. Actually, this was just a pro forma meeting that has been done for centuries and would have changed nothing.

Nonetheless, Donald Trump wanted the numbers changed, so that the election would be given to him. Trump specifically pressured Mike Pence, his VP, to change the numbers. Pence informed Trump that the Constitution is clear, and that he could not do any such thing. Trump was furious at Pence, who had been the most loyal for four years, and he called Pence out to the angry mob. When they got to the Capitol, there were calls to "hang Mike Pence." Pence and some of the Senate had been quickly spirited to safety, just one minute before the angry mob breached the Senate chamber, where all the members of the Senate and Mike Pence had been meeting.

By the actions of a few quick -thinking people, total tragedy was averted. It's clear that the angry mob came to eliminate the entire leadership of the country. Fortunately, one Capitol Police officer, an African-American, purposely led a violent mob away from the Senate chamber House members and staff hid under their desks and remained silent for two and a half hours while the mob banged on the doors. One Senator recorded the chilling noise on his phone.

Donald Trump watched all of this from the White House, and by all accounts, "he was delighted." Ben Sasse (R-NE) said, "Trump wanted there to be division, and he was confused about why other people on his team weren't as happy as he was." Trump has not reached out to Pence since he asked him to change the numbers. Here we have a fascist who was walking around talking about "law and order." These are the actions and the words of a very sick man. Trump was urged to ask the mob to stop what it was doing, but he refused. He also would not lower the flag to half-staff in memory of Brian Sicknick, the Capitol policeman who died trying to protect the Congress and the Capitol. There are reports that two Capitol policemen committed suicide.

Four years of Donald Trump's rhetoric inflamed his followers at many rallies. Bret Stephens, Republican, brilliant journalist, conservative, referred to Trump's rallies as "training grounds for mob rule." The Republicans are enablers here, allowing Trump to insult journalists and Stephens says, "degrade our political culture, by normalizing his behavior." Stephen's essay in the NYT is worth reading, because it nails who Trump was from the very beginning. (it is from January 6th)

Yes, we were in the middle of a coup, motivated by Trump and his use of social media to spread his message. Trump is outraged that Twitter and other companies took down his accounts. It's disappointing that he Is "ballistic" about that, rather than the attack on the Capitol or the murder of a police officer. Again, it's all about him and his lack of empathy and character.

The videos that came out in the last four days are terrifying. Each one was worse than the one the day before. As I watched, the reality of the possibilities continued to sink in. After years of relying on our democracy, it became clear that our culture has been seriously damaged around the world and within our country. Many tears have been shed by all of us in the last four days.

Some Republicans are joining Democrats in responding to the horror of the Trump presidency, and what it has wrought. Finally. from *Forbes*, there is a "truth reckoning," which is a sense of "holding people accountable for those who lied for Trump." It will be a large group of people. Many of these people know they have been propagating his lies. They have buckled, because of fear-of retribution and more from Trump.

It's Monday morning and Speaker of the House Nancy Pelosi has given Trump an ultimatum. He should either resign, be removed by the 25th Amendment, or the House of Representatives will present an Article of Impeachment this morning.

There is so much happening, and events are moving fast. It is a struggle to process the threat to our democracy and how we will need to respond to it. We have the inauguration of a new administration scheduled for January 20th. We need to keep it safe. We also have 374, 996 deaths to date and 22 million citizens infected. We have terrible job numbers, losing 140,00 jobs this week. The jobs, the virus and the threat to the government are all interrelated. Donald Trump will now leave office with a negative loss of jobs, the first president ever. The administration has also badly botched the vaccine rollout. The scientists invented the vaccine, but Donald Trump spent no time or money planning how to get it into peoples' arms. Everything that Donald Trump was supposed to do was totally left to the states, similar to the coronavirus.

This week will be historic for our country in terms of what transpires, what individuals decide to do. Will there be heroes? John F. Kennedy's book, *Profiles in Courage*, is rather small.

The FBI and the NYPD warned the Capitol Police days before the violence on January 6th that plans were obvious for crowds of Trump supporters planning to come to DC. Moreover, the Anti-Defamation League, that monitors the internet for chatter between white supremacists, Nazi groups, Proud Boys, etc., called in similar threats, shared them with the Capitol Police. They were ignored, according to the CEO of the ADL. The FBI actually disrupted and dissuaded the worst organizers from going to Washington. More than a dozen extremists, who were confronted by the FBI, did not travel.

Domestic terrorism is actually not illegal in this country, but it is the number one problem in America. It has certainly come to the fore in the last four years, with the encouragement of Trump, along with discussions of fascism and intelligence monitoring. While Twitter has banned Donald Trump and Amazon just eliminated Parler, other sites, like Instagram and Facebook, have followed the lead.

The GOP is supposed to be the party of responsibility, but it has not taken any responsibility. Seven people are dead, including a dedicated Capitol Policeman, Brian Sicknick, age forty-two, who apparently was hit on the head and died in the hospital that evening. The flags are flying at half-staff in New Jersey today, the place of his birth. A motorcade wound its way through the streets of Washington to Arlington National Cemetery, where he is now buried.

Thanks to the pictures and selfies that were taken in the Capitol, more than one hundred of the perpetrators were arrested. All fifty-six offices of the FBI are combing through the videos, posting pictures on the media and asking people all over the county to identify the faces.

Since watching the horror of the Capitol being stormed, the potential of what might have happened that could have been much worse, washes over me, and I get chills. I hardly know how to deal with the reality. The entire country is anxious. It's hard to concentrate, to read a book, to write a paper or a blog, for that matter. Making sense of the unthinkable is beyond our human abilities.

The truth is that this might have been a tragedy of even more major proportions, and a few minutes and quick thinking on the part of some people prevented the members of the House and Senate from all being killed. All members of Congress, the Senate and the House, were in the building, along with Vice President Pence, who was presiding.

The Inauguration is ten days away. Was Wednesday just a dress rehearsal for what is to come? Make no mistake-this was an attempted coup. The goal was to stop the legal declaration of Joe Biden as President and Kamala Harris as Vice President. Every time I see another video of violence and Congressmen in gas masks, the United States flag torn down and replaced with the Trump flag and the Confederate flag, I cringe. It's almost impossible to process. Did that really happen? More daily videos showing the violence of the thugs prove the case. These were not followers of Joe Biden who came out to support a candidate. In many cases, the thugs that showed up had been trained to conduct warfare, and they came with the tools needed to fight.

High Anxiety

January 13, 2021

As details emerge of the damage done to the Capitol and the police, it is clear that one hundred forty were injured in different ways, and it is shocking. One man will lose an eye, others are seriously wounded, many have brain damage, having been hit with pipes and flag poles and five men died, two of them by suicide.

Until yesterday, Donald Trump had not acknowledged the violence, and he didn't yesterday either. On his way to Alamo, Texas, he said that his speech was "totally appropriate." He veered away from the question of the insurrection, and talked about the riots in Portland and Seattle, which bear no resemblance to last Wednesday. In his usual style, Trump said that it was all the Democrats who were attacking him unfairly. He is a very sick man.

This lack of reality and blaming everyone, but himself, may be responsible for a change in the atmosphere around Trump. Some Republicans are rethinking their behavior, Trump's lack of responsibility, and deciding they may vote to impeach Trump. It is interesting how this has come to pass. With each day, the details and the reality of what happened last Wednesday are sinking in for each member of Congress, and for the rest of us as well.

Trump's rhetoric may be his final undoing. He called the impeachment a "witch-hunt," and in a veiled threat indicated this could cause "tremendous danger to our country."

There is a definite split in the Republican Party, with the more radical members still believing that they are going to stay behind Donald Trump. The FBI announced that more than 160 cases have already been opened, and there would be hundreds more. There was chatter on the web that the extremists were going to launch a "war", coming again to Washington, DC. Equally disturbing, the extremists seem to be planning insurgencies in each capital city in the country. That threat has put each state on alert. Security has been ramped up in Washington, to assure the safety of the Inauguration, and in each state.

Some Republicans are starting to announce that they are backing impeachment. Liz Cheney, the third most powerful Congresswoman, gave a scathing rebuke to Donald Trump, and said that she would be voting to impeach. There may be as many as thirty Republicans ready to break rank and vote with the Democrats. Mitch McConnell, the Majority Leader of the Senate, said that he believed that Trump had committed "impeachable acts." The story was carried by the *New York Times* and reported that McConnell would not be opposed to having Trump forced out of the Republican party. He blames Trump for the loss in the Senate, and his loss of the leadership.

The US Attorney reported to the Congress, and indicated that they would be shocked by some of the things that were done inside the Capitol, and who was ultimately responsible. There was urine and feces on the floor, statues were defaced, offices were trashed, windows broken, doors ripped off and items stolen. The members of Congress were told that they could use their expense money to buy protective bullet-proof vests. Of great interest is the fact that the Department of Justice is considering filing sedition charges against some of the leaders. It's not inconceivable that would include Donald Trump, once he is out of office. The threat is real and chilling. The *New York Times* Editorial Board wrote a definitive piece saying that it was a "brazen crime," and deserves the highest form of accountability that the legislature can deliver."

Meanwhile, many corporations have withdrawn their support of the Republicans, and Trump in particular. Walmart, Citibank, JP Morgan, Amazon and twenty more have said that they will withdraw support of the lawmakers who did not support Biden's win, and continued to support the idea that Trump had won, when in fact he had not. The actions of those companies got McConnell's attention. He came out and gave his party members the cover to vote as they wish. It seems that McConnell figured out that it might be a good thing to get Trump out of the party

Last night, by a vote of 223-205 the House passed the Raskin resolution, urging the Vice President to invoke the 25th Amendment and remove the President from office. Pence is not going to do that, which leaves impeachment as the next process. To date, five House Republicans have announced that they will join the Democrats and support the measure. As the details of the riot start to sink in for each person, it is entirely possible that the impeachment will be a bipartisan moment.

Only one week to go, and meanwhile each state is ramping up its own security. Citizens and leaders are anxious, since no one really knows what will be coming. Everyone is experiencing high anxiety.

Mob Boss

January 15th, 2021

Yesterday, Donald Trump was impeached for the second time in just a little over a year. The single article of impeachment was that he had "incited an insurrection," that endangered the members of Congress, and was intended to stop the process of the government.

Seven people died, including three Capitol policemen. The vote was 232 Representatives (222 Democrats and 10 Republicans) to 197. The fact that 10 Republicans joined the Democrats is noteworthy, because that made it a bipartisan vote. The disappointing thing is that only ten people agreed with the Democrats, while 197 disagreed.

One year ago, Adam Schiff (D-CA) presented a brilliant case in favor of finding Trump guilty. However, the majority in the Senate was Republican, and only Mitt Romney (R-UT) voted to remove him from office. The case was left for everyone to ponder, to think about now, and many people are thinking back to Adam Schiff's prescient words and warning.

Schiff said, "you know you can't trust this President to do what's right for this country. You can trust he will do what's right for Donald Trump. He'll do it now. He's done it before. He'll do it for the next several months. He'll do it in the election if he's allowed to."

The events of the last year have shown that Adam Schiff knew exactly what would happen. When Chris Krebs, the head of cybersecurity, announced that the election had been the most secure in our history, Donald Trump unceremoniously fired him. Trump insisted that he won the election, a blatant lie, and nothing else would stand in his way. He used his considerable power to pressure election officials in many states. The Secretary of State of Georgia, Raffensberger, validated his numbers, and Trump used his Twitter account to mock and berate him. Moreover, disgusting emails were sent to his wife, and people came to his home to threaten him. As a result, Mr. Raffensberger needs security to protect him and his family.

Trump reached out to officials in five other swing states, where he wanted the numbers changed so that the election would be in his favor. There is nothing more lawless than trying to disenfranchise the votes of citizens, and threatening them. Another Georgia election official, Gabe Sterling, spoke publicly three times, addressing the President, and telling him he had to "stop this. Someone is going to get hurt." Mr. Sterling now has to have security to protect his family.

We have never had a mob boss for a president, until now. These stories are right out of "The Sopranos." Our American signature is the "peaceful transfer of power." Trump has given no concession, no peaceful transfer, only efforts to delay the transition by weeks, and hamstring the incoming president. Trump has done every conceivable thing to ruin Joe Biden's ability to start an effective administration, but Biden has continued to recruit talented and experienced men and women for the new government. He will also have to rid the agencies of all the loyalist chaff that Trump appointed.

The Republican Party is deeply divided between the Trump base, which is loyal to the concept that he won the election, and the other Republicans. Those Republicans operate by fear, warning that it is dangerous to try to hold Trump accountable, because it will anger his supporters. Underneath that concept lies a threat.

While the House was debating impeachment, the FBI hunted the individuals identified in the videos. Two hundred were arrested, and there will be hundreds more. The threat of violence is pervasive. Should they vote against Trump, Republicans are afraid of consequences to themselves and their families. They have been warned. That changes the equation of Americans having free and fair elections. If you are threatened by the mob boss, you actually have no choice. Donald Trump has traumatized Congressional voters who used to be able to vote their consciences. Now, they have to take into consideration what serious consequences might ensue, like losing their election.

While the FBI was hunting down insurgents, many companies withdrew their support from Republicans who supported the attacks on the election. The PGA cancelled its plans to hold its golf tournament at Trump's Bedminster course, infuriating Trump. New York City cancelled $17 million worth of contracts with the Trump administration. Deutsche Bank removed itself from doing business with Trump, and the list goes on for many other companies.

The Article of Impeachment is still with Nancy Pelosi. She is deciding when to send it to the Senate. When she does send it over, the trial has to start the next day, as I understand it. Interestingly, Majority Leader McConnell actually suggested that he supported impeachment, and he leaked that to the newspapers. Donald Trump was furious. While the Senate could have taken up the Article immediately, McConnell said he would not have the schedule changed until the 19th when the Senate is scheduled to return. It seemed that McConnell was hoping that the threat of impeachment might motivate Trump to resign. Failing that, McConnell has now changed his behavior, doing just the bare minimum as the leader of the party. He's keeping his decision close to the vest, so we don't know whether he will vote to impeach Trump or not. Many perks are at stake with an impeachment trial-pension, travel allowance and secret service protection, to name a few examples. There is also the possibility that a separate bill could be introduced to prevent Trump from ever holding office. To find him guilty, the Democrats would need 17 Republicans to join them in a bipartisan vote. That is a tall mountain to climb under these circumstances.

Congresswoman Mikie Sherrill (D-NJ), a former Navy helicopter pilot, noticed that on January 5th there were groups of people going on tours of the Capitol. Trained to watch for anything out of the ordinary, the groups immediately set off a red flag. The Capitol has been closed to visitors since March. Sherrill called the Sergeant at Arms, since it could only be a Congressman or staff member who led the tours. In light of the siege the next day, and the obvious knowledge of the layout of the Capitol by the mob, it seems that those tours were reconnaissance. Who were those people? How did they get the tours? That brings up the frightening possibility that it was an inside job, and now the FBI is investigating.

The briefings by the FBI Chief, Christopher Wray, and the acting U.S. Attorney for the District of Columbia, indicated that the unfolding story of what happened on January 6th will be shocking. It might involve people in government. Many House Democrats called attention to the tours the day before, especially in light of the restrictions brought on by the coronavirus. It is frightening to think that there are enemies inside Congress. People don't know who to trust. Did members of Congress collude with the mob? The FBI will have more of the story as it unfolds. Speaker Pelosi mentioned that members of Congress should wear bullet-proof vests and their business allowance will pay for it. That sent a chill, since it is based on the facts that the FBI have uncovered. The threat is great.

Nearly 20,000 National Guard soldiers have been deployed to Washington, for the week, in order to protect the city and the inauguration from The Mob. All fifty states are on "high alert" in their capital cities. Nine feet tall fences have been erected around the Capitol and the Supreme Court. The Mall has been closed to visitors. AirBNB cancelled all reservations.

The beautiful city of Washington, that I lived in and love, looks like a war zone. The rehearsal for the Inauguration had to be cancelled, because of security concerns. Joe Biden cannot take his beloved Amtrak train from Wilmington to D.C., because it's too dangerous. Donald Trump and his mob of thugs have injected fear into the administration and the entire country. America and Joe Biden deserved a celebratory Inauguration, but that doesn't seem to be possible.

Today, looking at those black fences and the thousands of soldiers, including soldiers sleeping in the halls of the Capitol, I am incredibly sad. It seems inconceivable that a sitting president invoked an insurrection against his own country and wreaked such havoc. It's true, and I despise him for it.

Remembering Martin Luther King provides a breath of fresh air in the middle of Trump days

January 18, 2021 Martin Luther King Day

It's hard to describe the feelings about this week. Today is the Martin Luther King Day of Service, something that motivates us to give to others. We have certainly had our share of darkness in the last five years, beginning with the first day of the Trump Inaugural and "American carnage." Five years of carnage, ending with the sacking of the Capitol, have been heartbreaking. We came within inches of losing our democracy during the 2020 election. This country would not survive four more years of Donald Trump and his scorched earth, negative and destructive presidency.

With 400,000 citizens dead of the coronavirus, that sobering number filters our reality. It's a staggering number. It is important to remember that Martin Luther King encouraged us to live together as loving neighbors. Now is the time with President Biden, to come together, to follow the guidelines in order to fight this virus and become a healthy population, so that businesses can return and children can attend school safely. We have been through a lot, more than anyone anticipated, and that is because the federal government did nothing to alleviate the situation. Now, we have a chance.

Brilliantly, Moderna and Pfizer came up with the vaccines to fight this scourge in ten months. In fairness, they each had developed platforms from which to work years ago. The urgency of the killer virus pushed them to succeed. Unfortunately, the doses that the Trump government indicated it was sending, do not exist, and neither does a plan to get it into peoples' arms. Yet one more total failure of the government. It will be left to the Biden government to figure out a workable and succesful system.

We need an inspiring leader, such as Martin Luther King, right now. He left us all too soon, at age 39, killed by an assassin's bullet. We need to protect our leaders and our children from crazy people with guns. I hope you had a good experience on this day of service. Next time, we will be together. I am hoping that Joe Biden will reach out and succeed in the first days of the presidency to establish some calm and a sense of stability. He has chosen extraordinary people with much experience.

January 20, 2021

Washington in Lockdown

January 19, 2021

Last night Joe Biden and Kamala Harris and their spouses paid tribute to the 400,000 citizens who have died from Covid-19. It's been ten months, with no prior acknowledgement of what we have lost, and how the nation is grieving. Four hundred lights lined the reflecting pool with Lincoln at one end overlooking the majesty of the moment.

The bells of the National Cathedral rang out in mourning those we've lost, plaintive in its beautiful starkness.

A stunning moment in its simplicity, offering the opportunity for family and friends to feel the empathy of Joe Biden embracing them in their loss. A nurse who worked in her hospital ICU ward sang "Amazing Grace," and someone else sang "Hallelujah." Gorgeous. President Biden gave meaningful remarks that reached out to all those who have lost loved ones. We are all Americans.

It was a wonderful move towards our healing.

As we look out onto the Mall where hundreds of flags are flying in the breeze, we see that the city is eerily empty, populated by the 25,000 National Guard, police and Secret Service, here to protect the Capitol and the Congress. It's incredibly sad and chilling that Washington is a fortress and a ghost town, in order to keep the new administration and citizens safe for the Inauguration. Where there would be thousands of people, there are empty streets, roads closed, no cars or tourists. It is a strange reality, but a soothing one, in light of the chaos of the last two weeks when white supremacists came to the Capitol to get the vote for Donald Trump, who lost the election by seven million votes.

I can't stop thinking back to that horror, and it sends chills up my spine. The morning began when I was writing about the success of two Democrats who won the Georgia Senate seats, and my joy quickly faded as I realized we were in an unfolding nightmare in real time. I couldn't believe my eyes. Thugs carrying Trump flags and weapons, and dressed in riot gear, were storming the Capitol and beating up the police, who were trying to defend it. All those MAGA hats. And all the members of Congress inside.

The results of that nightmare are evident in the 25,000 soldiers and the empty streets. It might have been different because of the Covid-19, if social distancing was required. There could have been thousands more people to come to celebrate the Inauguration in January, if it hadn't been for the violence and the security problems. It was a terrorist attack against Congress, and we were lucky to save our democracy and the members of Congress, who might have been killed if it hadn't been for the quick thinking and bravery of the Capitol and Metropolitan police. We might be having a very different day today, and the country is breathing a sigh of relief and gratitude this morning. We needed a moment of shared grief and Joe Biden has provided it. Now we have to move forward to try to defeat the virus.

There are a lot of emotions I feel on every Inauguration Day: pride, patriotism and the possibility that a new administration offers. It is a new day dawning, but it is bittersweet because of all the horror.

January 20, 2021 Inauguration Day

Inauguration Day

January 20, 2021

Three Wednesdays - the first, shocking, the second, historic, the third, the moment we decide who we are and what we want our country to be.

It has taken me days to process the last three weeks, and I may not fully understand all the threads for a long time- months, possibly years. All my assumptions about democracy were smashed in one afternoon of hatred, violence and destruction. Trying to achieve perspective on something three weeks old is not easy.

What is clear is that this anger, hatred and disconnect is much more widespread and more deep-seated than many of us knew. Those anti-democratic, white- supremacist ideas were gleaned from the internet. Feelings of "us" versus "them" were waiting to be acknowledged and encouraged, as they did on January 6th by the President of the United States, whose anger incited them to an insurrection and possibly a coup. This is a shocking first for the United States. The president orchestrated a violent overthrow of his own government. The Constitution doesn't cover this eventuality, since the founding fathers never dreamed that such a heinous individual would occupy the Oval office and dare to destroy our democracy in his own name. The reality is surreal. No concession, just revenge and violence.

The city is a fortress, kept safe by 25,000 troops. Even so, I and others are nervous about how the Inauguration is going to be secure. Last night was a good indication of calm and a certain serenity, as the country was invited to pay tribute to the more than 400,000 people who were lost to Covid. They were honored by President and Mrs. Biden and Vice President Kamala Harris and the Second Gentleman, Douglas Emhoff. The tribute, overlooking the Lincoln Memorial and the reflecting pool, was simple and elegant, and it went off without a hitch. Our country was beginning to breathe more easily.

Moreover, the fact that Twitter banned the former guy, forever, was a blessing. Our phones were quiet. We heard nothing from him, and calm was beginning to settle over us. Joe Biden and Kamala Harris wanted to bring stability to the country, and it was such a relief.

My first Inauguration was in 1960, when John F. Kennedy was sworn in as President of the United States. His soaring speech captivated me, and I was hooked forever. After that, I never missed an Inauguration, no matter who the president was going to be. The pomp and patriotism, the solemnity and celebration of the moment, seduced me forever. And that is the point of "peaceful transfer of power." I wanted Al Gore to be president, but when the election was decided for George W. Bush, he was now in charge of the country and the Constitution, and he became my president in the American tradition.

In 1968, I worked for Hubert Humphrey in Washington, and I was devastated when he lost. Getting behind Nixon was difficult, because I knew that he was not a good person, since our offices were bugged. Getting behind Trump was next to impossible, considering his crass campaign and that Hillary won by three million votes. Hillary's loss was truly a tragedy, and it became more so as the Trump years unfolded. Our lives and our country would have been so different with Hillary Clinton at the helm. No use crying over spilt milk now,

But the day is starting. Trump leaves and goes to Florida. No one knew that he committed one last hateful act by firing the Head Usher of the White House, so when President and Mrs. Biden were at the door, after the Inaugural parade, the Head Usher was not there to open it and welcome them.

President-elect Biden arrives and goes to church, having invited Republicans to join him. There is a nice bipartisan feeling about the day. Joe Biden was a son of the Senate for decades and Senators on both sides of the aisle are friends of his. (Out of respect for the occasion, I put on my pearls and a dress, something I haven't done in ten months.) It feels good!

Guests are arriving on the balcony where the event will take place. It is the exact place where just a few days ago, insurrection blood was shed and policemen died. Those pictures are inescapable and certainly on the minds of those who were threatened and survived. The blood stains had to be cleaned up for the Inauguration. The pictures of that January 6th afternoon are still ingrained in everyone's memory and the contrast is chilling. It is heartening to see the Obamas, the Clintons, and the Bushes arrive, and greet one another warmly. It's a relief that Donald Trump did not attend, but unfortunate that he couldn't extend a word and a hand to change the substance of his obvious loss. He needed to acknowledge that Joe Biden won in a fair election, and unfortunately, Trump, the sore loser, would never do that.

Everyone is sitting socially distant and wearing masks. There is a celebratory mood that is cautious but happy. Vice President Pence came, rather than going to see the outgoing president, who wanted him killed, leave.

The presenting of the colors always leaves me feeling proud. The dignity and majesty of the moment is beautiful, and the program begins. I can't help but wonder what everyone is thinking. After all, the Capitol is now scrubbed and gleaming, but just two weeks earlier there was blood in the same place that everyone is setting. The members of the House and the Senate must be running through the events of that day, and feeling grateful to be alive. They were just minutes away from being killed by that angry mob, incited by Trump.

The Capitol policeman who saved the Senate has been promoted, and he will be receiving the Congressional Medal. He is introduced, and he is in charge of Vice-President Harris and her husband, the Second Gentleman, Doug Emhoff.

The prayers are meaningful. Vice President Harris, the first woman, first black and first Asian, is sworn in by the first Latino Justice, Sonia Sotomayor. It is a wonderful day of so many firsts. I am crying with joy and relief. It's been a horrible five years.

Lady Gaga, gorgeous in a long, flowing red satin skirt, sings the National Anthem, and I am crying again because she sings it so beautifully. J Lo sings "This Land is your Land," and she is stunning in all-white. Still, more tears. Tim McGraw sings and asks the entire group of guests to sing the third verse with him, creating a wonderful feeling of togetherness.

Joe Biden is sworn in by Chief Justice John Roberts, an historical moment. President Biden gives a wonderful address. He is not a soaring speaker, but his speech is actually one of the best, because it is so honest. He acknowledges the moment, the horrific difficulty of January 6th, and asks for unity, many times. President Biden mentions white supremacy and all of our country's problems that must be overcome. It is very clear in his speech that Biden has major intersecting crises to handle, the first of which is defeating the Covid-19 virus.

The Inaugural Poet, Amanda Gorman, comes to the podium.. Only twenty-two years old, she is exquisite. Her delivery, combined with her graceful hand motions, is beautiful and powerful. She wrote the poem on the night of the insurrection, and it refers to our problems that can still be overcome, if we do it together. Her poetry, the cadence and the language of her poem, are breathtaking.

I came across Amanda when she was the Youth Poet, only sixteen years old, and I was deeply impressed at that time. Since then, she has been interviewed many times and read her poems to many groups who have been enthralled. Interestingly, Amanda Gorman had a speech impediment, and she overcame it by saying her poetry aloud, much as Joe Biden and the young man who Biden mentors does. Amanda was raised by a single mother, went to Harvard and has ambitions to one day be president. I have no doubt that she will succeed. Many of the guests at the Inauguration had never heard her, and by the looks on their faces, it is clear that they are spellbound. "The Hill we Climb" is a powerful poem, and she invokes many recent and personal memories. Amanda bows her head as she finishes, guests clap and Amanda takes her seat. It is clear that she has mesmerized the crowd. After another prayer, the colors are retired and the guests of honor leave the podium. In every way, this Inauguration has been extraordinary.

America has come back from a dreadful event, and Americans have shown that we value our democracy and the Constitution. Let's hope that we can keep the gift that the Founding Fathers gave us.

I am grateful for a beautiful day, and now Joe Biden will be getting to the work of running the country. I pray that he is successful.

God bless America!

Epilogue

Hoping that the Biden/Harris inauguration would preclude the necessity for an epilogue, I was naïve. Donald Trump is not going to let us alone and enjoy the peace that came from Twitter banning him from its site.

I prefer to acknowledge the amazing progress that President Biden has made in fighting the virus, by utilizing the Defense Production Act in getting the vaccine distributed to all fifty states. He exceeded his goal of hundreds of millions of doses, and announced that a large portion of Americans have been vaccinated. Unfortunately, a large portion of the country, mostly white Republican men, are refusing to be vaccinated. This is a sad state of affairs, and the government is promoting a vast "get a vaccine" program so that we can reach 80%, which would be herd immunity. Also, five million Americans are missing their second shot of Moderna and Pfizer, which are eminently safe. The second dose is critical to gaining full immunity.

Most important, under the aegis of the former president, there is a serious challenge to our democracy. Republicans are working to gain the majority in state legislatures in advance of the elections of 2022/2024. Their goal is to overturn voting rights, and take over the country by winning back the Senate and the House. The "Big Lie," that the election was stolen from the former president, is alive and well in Trump country, and it is extremely dangerous. I am deeply concerned about the future of America, because there is a major push for voter suppression by the Republicans.

There are two important voting bills – HR1 and the John Lewis Voting rights bill, that need to pass, and quickly. We need to be focused laser-like on getting that done.

Meanwhile, President Biden has upheld science, climate, racial justice and tackled poverty in the country. He has introduced an infrastructure bill that would build our crumbling roads and bridges, broadband and more, while providing jobs. The second bill would provide a human infrastructure, a safety net for Americans, but it is not clear that it will pass. President Biden has said that we can pay for these items by raising the taxes of corporations, many of which use a loophole and pay no taxes at all. Taxes under President Obama were 38% and Trump lowered them to 21%, putting a lot of money in the pockets of the richest Americans. President Biden is indicating that putting them at 25% would be a major move in paying for his plan. Republicans are against that moderate change, which is unfortunate.

Donald Trump's defeat last November did not close the book on his disastrous presidency. There have been countless attempts to overturn the results of the election, culminating in the attack on the Capitol on January 6th, a shocking attack on our democracy that came close to succeeding.

In addition, the recently arrived and contagious Delta virus has been ravaging the country. In the way that masks were politicized, vaccines have now become political. Tragically, only half of the country will take the vaccine, and the result is that thousands of people are dying, hospitals are overrun, and there is no end in sight. Worse still, these deaths were preventable. The vaccine would have protected the citizens who are now sick and dying.

This is where we are today-on a slim margin politically, and walking a tightrope that could upend our democracy. Overwhelmed by a raging virus in certain states that banned masks and made the vaccine political, the country is sick. School is starting to open, and into this chaos, parents, teachers and students have to make serious decisions that will affect their lives. Anxiety is high, and this is not where we wanted to be in August of 2021.

President Biden's plan to fix so many things that are broken in our country is imperiled. I pray that all of us will rally and support issues that are in our mutual best interest- voting and the virus, but it's going to be a very tough fight.

Warm regards,
Lois Larkey
July 30th, 2021

Photo credit:
Celestina Ando

Author Bio

Lois Larkey is a lifelong teacher, community activist and social justice advocate. A native of Newark, New Jersey, she has devoted her energies to helping Newark children, since she joined the board of the Newark Boys and Girls Club in 1975, the first woman. Lois graduated from Connecticut College with a Bachelor of Arts in History, and remains deeply committed to her college. Married and moving to South Orange, Lois taught English and history in both public and private schools for twenty-five years, the last at the Horace Mann School in the Bronx. In South Orange, she served as Chairman of the Community Relations Committee, and oversaw the initiation of many current traditions, such as the "Gaslight" newsletter. After classroom teaching, Lois fulfilled a lifelong dream of becoming an author. Her family memoir, *Looking Back, Moving Forward: The View from Beyond Seventy,* published in 2019. Lois is the proud mother of two married daughters and four wonderful grandchildren, all of whom live in Brooklyn.

Acknowledgements

Very much gratitude to Ryan Jacobsen, a great friend and tech guru, who worked with me for many hours, editing and getting my blogs ready to publish. To his wife, Ora, for your nourishing friendship and constant connectedness. Your concern and affection helped me survive fifteen months alone.

Warmest thanks to the Adult Education Committee, for your creativity and hard work that planned classes, scholar talks, art presentations and everything that kept us engaged and interested. Thank you especially to Tracy Horwitz, Program Director extraordinaire, who is the glue that pulled everything together, and made it all work with patience and humor. There is no one like you!

Deep gratitude to Jane Nadler, for your wonderful friendship and the wordsmithing that suggested the title of this book.

To Jason Nadler, for reading the submission form and suggesting things for me to consider, since I was a novice. Jason and Ryan, while on opposite coasts, provided tech help and their awesome expertise that got me over the hump, in addition to their caring concern.

Warmest thanks to authors Ben Reiter, Elizabeth Brundage, and Petie and Don Kladstrup, for your encouragement and special comments. Your friendship through the years has been very special and important for me.

Many thanks to my cousin, Susan Larkey Galatz who read my blogs and commented on particular topics that she found interesting. Thanks also to Susan for inviting me to present online to her JCC group about the unfolding history, and suggesting that I might speak to other groups. Her interest in my family memoir was very important and motivating.

Much gratitude to Fran Larkey, from the West Caldwell Public Library, who read my blogs and invited me to her Literary Café, to talk about writing my memoir. Her suggestion that I should make my writings available to a larger audience, encouraged me to publish these blogs. Most recently, it was a pleasure to be invited to speak during Women's History month, and talk about women who made a difference.

Thanks to my nephew, Jon Hirsch, on the west coast, for reading my blogs and writing thoughtful responses, which became great conversations between us.

Grateful thanks to Ted Li, editor extraordinaire.

Thanks to Max Weisenfeld for leading Sharey Tefilo and Beth Blackman for our finances in these challenging times.

Thanks go to treasured friends Hinda Simon, Jane Nadler, Susie Mandelbaum, Joanne Schroeder and Linda Palazzolo for connecting with me throughout this tragic and difficult time. To Barry Kornspan for an exciting new website, and to my BBNL business group, whose meetings were so motivating. Your thoughts and your encouragement were very important.

Grateful thanks to Archway Publishing, especially Bob DeGroff, and the editors who patiently walked me through a process about which I knew very little, and helped me achieve this goal.

Many thanks to all those who read my blogs and had such thoughtful comments during this difficult time..

Lois Ann Larkey
July 27th, 2021
South Orange, New Jersey

Printed in the United States
by Baker & Taylor Publisher Services